I0815453

LOUISIANA
CULTURE FROM THE COLONIAL ERA TO KATRINA

SOUTHERN LITERARY STUDIES

Fred Hobson, Series Editor

LOUISIANA CULTURE FROM THE COLONIAL ERA TO KATRINA

Edited by JOHN LOWE

LOUISIANA STATE UNIVERSITY PRESS  BATON ROUGE

Published by Louisiana State University Press

Manufactured in the United States of America
First printing

Designer: Laura Roubique Gleason
Typeface: Minion Pro
Typesetter: J. Jarrett Engineering, Inc.
Printer and binder: Thomson-Shore, Inc.

Library of Congress Cataloging-in-Publication Data

Louisiana culture from the colonial era to Katrina / edited by John Lowe.
p. cm. — (Southern literary studies)
Includes bibliographical references and index.
ISBN 978-0-8071-3337-8 (cloth : alk. paper) 1. Louisiana—Civilization. 2. Louisiana—Ethnic relations. 3. Louisiana—Intellectual life. 4. American literature—Louisiana—History and criticism. 5. Louisiana—Social life and customs. I. Lowe, John, 1945–
F369.L884 2008
305.8009763—dc22

2008003546

Margaret Bauer's essay "Ellen Gilchrist's False Eden: The New Orleans Stories of *In the Land of Dreamy Dreams*" originally appeared in the Spring 1996 issue of *Xavier Review* and is reprinted here with permission of the editors. Brenda Marie Osbey's "I Want to Die in New Orleans" originally appeared in *American Voice* no. 38, Tenth Anniversary Issue (1995); her "One More Last Chance: Ritual and the Jazz Funeral" originally appeared in *Georgia Review* 50, no. 1 (Spring 1996). Both are reprinted with permission of the author.

The paper in this book meets the guidelines for permanence and durability of the Committee on Production Guidelines for Book Longevity of the Council on Library Resources. ♾

We dedicate this collection to the memory of our fellow citizens who lost their lives in the hurricanes of 2005, to those who are still displaced from their homes, and to all those who continue to work to restore our land and our culture.

CONTENTS

PART 3 LOUISIANA LITERATURE: THE TRADITION AND THREE CONTEMPORARY WRITERS

PART 4 LOUISIANA MYTHOLOGIES, FROM THE KINGFISH TO THE PECULIAR FASCINATION WITH THE DEAD

PART 5 MUSIC THAT SOOTHES THE SOUL

ACKNOWLEDGMENTS

This collection took shape over a number of years, and many people had a hand in its making. My late colleague, Professor Lewis P. Simpson, took an early interest in this book and offered valued advice as it took shape. Michael Sartisky, Executive Director of the Louisiana Endowment for the Humanities, has provided a sterling example of how to display Louisiana culture in his estimable journal *Cultural Vistas.* Colleagues at Louisiana State University who gave me pointers and encouragement include Carl Freedman, Malcolm Richardson, Katherine Henninger, Brannon Costello, William Boelhower, James Olney, Carolyn Ware, Solimar Otero, Paul Hoffman, Gaines Foster, Sylvie Du Bois, and Femi Euba. At LSU Press, I thank MaryKatherine Callaway and John Easterly for their dedication to this project, and for their patience. My gratitude also extends beyond LSU to Barbara Eckstein, Richard Megraw, Maida Owen, Fred Hobson, Susan Donaldson, Barbara Ladd, Suzanne Jones, Deborah E. McDowell, Joseph Skerrett Jr., James Robert Payne, Thadious Davis, Seetha Srinavasan, Werner Sollors, Keith Cartwright, Eric Anderson, Annette Trefzer, and the late Lorenzo Thomas. I would also like to thank the staff and fellows for spring 2007 of the Virginia Foundation for the Humanities, where the final work for the volume took place, especially Roberta Culbertson, Ann Spencer, Pablo Davis, Chip Turner, Lawrie Balfour, Wayne Durrill, and Bill Freehling. Finally, as always, my debt to my wife, June Conaway Lowe, is incalculable.

LOUISIANA
CULTURE FROM THE COLONIAL ERA TO KATRINA

INTRODUCTION

Creole Cultures and National Identity after Katrina

JOHN LOWE

> It is by knowing where you stand that you grow able to judge where you are. Place absorbs our earliest notice and attention, it bestows upon us our original awareness; and our critical powers spring up from the study of it and the growth experiences inside it. . . . One place comprehended can make us understand other places better. Sense of place gives us equilibrium; extended, it is sense of direction too.
>
> EUDORA WELTY

> I don't want to live anywhere where they have
> tried to kill us even if it was once a place
> I called home. . . .
>
> KALAMU YA SALAAM

The study of place has traditionally been a special concern for southerners in general, and Louisianans in particular. In the past, however, this activity all too often focused on rather narrow definitions of Louisianan or southern society. Fortunately, the last twenty years have witnessed an explosion of new work that has brought forward new concepts of place, self, and region, perhaps nowhere more dramatically than in Louisiana, whose rich multicultural society we now see as part of the South, yes, but also as a hub of a vast Caribbean wheel, where Cajuns, Creoles, Cubans, Haitians, Jamaicans, and others are part of a New World configuration, the components of which prosper from the contributions of the African, Jewish, Asian, French, and Hispanic diasporas. New Orleans emerges from this new concept as a transnational city. The year 2003 proved to be a perfect moment in which to reconnect the people of Louisiana, its friends, and its scholars with the state's fabled history and culture, as it marked the bicentennial of one of the most momentous events in American history, the acquisition of the vast territory known as the Louisiana Purchase. Today what we know as Louisiana is only a small portion of that mass, yet this diminutive state has arguably produced the most unique culture in the nation. As an amalgam of African, Caribbean, and European cultures, it echoes others in other states, but in no other place has the particular confluence of influences existed for so long a time and against such a dramatic backdrop. For the flora and fauna of South Louisiana, the dramatic location of New Orleans, and the steamy tropical wetlands of the lower Mississippi Delta—a great nursery for seafood but also conducive to labor-intensive crops such as sugarcane, rice, and cotton, and more recently, the source of rich deposits in oil and natural gas—have had much to do with the development of the state's famous Creole and Cajun cultures. Louisiana has had a fabled political history as well, which extends backward in time to epochs well before the purchase. The contact era featured interactions between unique Native American cultures such as the Natchez, the Houma, the Chitimacha, and the Coushatta and the bands of Frenchmen and Spaniards who began to navigate up and down the Father of Waters and the surrounding bayous and swamps.

Another great whirling wheel, Hurricane Katrina, changed the calculus for this vast region forever in late August 2005. Eighty percent of the city of New Orleans was destroyed, and the parishes south of the city were similarly devastated, as were towns and cities along the Gulf Coast of Mississippi and Alabama, which share the same culture and topography. Just days later, another fierce storm named Rita wiped out whole towns on the eastern Texas/southwestern Louisiana border, ravaging homes, businesses, schools, hospitals, and the region's swamps, wetlands, forests, and wildlife. Since these catastrophes, a whole new literature has grown up dealing with the storms and their aftermath; the continuing, frustrating story of efforts to rebuild continues to dominate regional newspapers, and hosts of volunteers from around the nation have pitched in to do their share. The massive failure of state, regional, and national institutions to deal adequately with the crisis has raised issues far beyond the storms themselves and has cast the phrase "homeland security" into a new register. Mayor Ray Nagin, Governor Kathleen Babineaux Blanco, and President George Bush were all held accountable, as was the U.S. Army Corps of Engineers, whose failure to adequately maintain the city's ancient levees and their "Mr. Go" channel to the gulf led directly to the flooding of the city in the aftermath of the storm. Whereas Mayor Nagin was recently returned to office by the voters, Governor Blanco has decided not to seek reelection, and the president's low polls are regularly traced, at least in part, to his perceived failure to respond properly to this national emergency. The various recovery programs fashioned by FEMA and the state of Louisiana have brought a new wrinkle into the always contentious discussion of the state's political system and its relationship to the federal government.

One of the principle effects of the catastrophe has been the diaspora of coastal Americans away from the homeland they love. In New Orleans, the entire city had to be evacuated for weeks, and many poor citizens were put on buses, trains, and planes without knowing where they would wind up. Families were separated, and many people remained unaccounted for, for some time. Some of them eventually appeared on the lists of the dead—more than thirteen hundred in Louisiana alone. But many other families were fragmented by the diaspora, and most of them have been unable to return to the city, where virtually all the poor neighborhoods were destroyed or damaged.[1]

The question of exile, Edward Said has remarked, "is strangely compelling to think about but terrible to experience. It is the unhealable rift forced between a human being and a native place, between the self and its true home: its essential sadness can never be surmounted. . . . The achievements of exile are permanently undermined by the loss of something left behind forever" (173). Said of course is mainly thinking of political exiles, and many would say that displaced New Orleaneans can return if they wish. However, two years have passed since the storms, and very little has been done to create new housing and hospitals or to rebuild schools, community centers, or vital businesses in the affected areas. Further, in light of the highly political nature of the impasses that persist between contending political and institutional forces, it would be wrong to declare this diaspora apolitical. Certainly the fact that many of the voters who are now gone were primarily Democrats has something to do with the disinterest in bringing them back to Louisiana. But most of these displaced persons *want* to return; even though many of them have made new lives in new cities, "home" will always mean Louisiana and its cultural gumbo. The classic Louis Armstrong anthem "Do You Know What It Means to Miss New Orleans" has acquired a contemporary and deeply ironic meaning because of the diaspora and takes us back to the meaning of Said's term "the true home," which is redolent of the cultural heritage of one of the world's most distinctive locales, and to Kalamu ya Salaam's haunting question, "What is life without a home?" (Rowell 1347).

Home, clearly, must be supported not only in terms of cultural tradition but also by the local economy. Agriculture and industries vital to the state's economy were severely damaged by the storms, including petroleum, petrochemical, and shipping businesses. Prosperous gambling boats were destroyed, and most casinos that survived had to shut down indefinitely for repairs. The tourist industry suffered months of inactivity, even though most New Orleans hotels were either not affected or were salvageable. Restaurants, however, had no clientele, and many could not marshal an adequate staff after the massive loss of housing. Fishing industries especially suffered, not only because the boats were destroyed but also because the processing plants and the icehouses were devastated. The fisheries were almost wiped out, and many different species of fish were devastated. In addition, one estimate is that a quarter of the state's alligators were killed; the harvesting of these animals have in the past provided significant income for farmers and trappers in terms of meat and hides. On the other hand, nutrias, the notorious pest animals, were also decimated, a good thing, as their burrowings have helped destroy levees.

The greatest tragedy, however, was the loss of human life. The most moving and extensive collection of stories and events drawn from the first terrible week after the storm is found in Douglas Brinkley's *Great Deluge,* which provides the first mapping of the tragic events that followed the breaks in the levees, including the deaths in the nursing homes and the projects, the chaos at the Superdome and the Convention Center, and the massive casualties in St. Bernard and Plaquemines Parishes to the south.

Katrina had a huge impact on educational facilities. Most public schools in New Orleans were destroyed or severely damaged, and colleges and universities were devastated. Dillard University's campus was under water; Xavier University was flooded as well. The University of New Orleans was not as badly affected as original reports had it, but it suffered serious flooding and wind damage. The medical schools in New Orleans were wiped out; the teaching hospitals and laboratories were submerged, and most of the research animals drowned. Many seriously ill and/or elderly patients were taken out by helicopter from hospital rooftops, after dangerous days in dark and fetid rooms (the generators these facilities had were located in basements that were flooded).

In Baton Rouge, Louisiana State University (LSU) suspended classes for a week, and the campus became a field hospital and morgue. Helicopters were landing constantly, bringing in the sick, the wounded, and the elderly, who were treated in makeshift triage facilities in the major athletic buildings and elsewhere. Students and faculty volunteered in droves, and many athletes in particular played leading roles in the medical facilities. A particularly dramatic moment came when it was reported that missing musical legend Fats Domino, whose home had been inundated in the lower Ninth Ward, was indeed alive and had taken shelter, along with twenty others, in the two-bedroom apartment of JaMarcus Russell, the quarterback of the LSU football team whose girlfriend is Domino's granddaughter. When classes resumed, LSU took in thirty-five hundred extra students; the university had already been bursting at the seams, with a record thirty-two thousand students. The campus was packed, gridlocked with automobile and foot traffic. New Orleans and southwestern Louisiana students who had condominiums or apartments were forced to put up their extended families. Stores and major thoroughfares were jammed, and there were shortages of many commodities. Almost everybody in Baton Rouge sheltered friends or relatives, sometimes for months. But other Louisiana cities, and towns in adjoining states, acted similarly, particularly Houston, which welcomed hundreds of thousands of evacuees. Texas is now where most Katrina victims who haven't made it home yet reside.

Baton Rouge, the state's capital, is now also the state's largest city, with approximately eight hundred thousand people in the metropolitan area. Louisiana itself, however, which had already been losing citizens to other states, suffered a catastrophic loss of more than two hundred thousand people, which will affect its congressional representation, federal funding formulas, and economic future for years to come.

Everyone knows by now that Katrina alone didn't destroy New Orleans; it was the collapse of the levees. Certainly the Corps of Engineers has the responsibility of providing protection from a catastrophic storm. It seems clear, in 2007, that many former citizens and businesses are waiting to see if the levees are going to be adequately rebuilt and reinforced before a decision is made to return. In the meantime, massive hikes in both insurance premiums and rents are keeping evacuees where they are. Clearly, funds need to be used creatively to bring back the displaced citizens; some of them are poor financially, but rich culturally, and they love New Orleans and want to return. But we also need to restore the wetlands that have historically formed a buffer for South Louisiana. Ruthless oil exploration, cutting ship channels, and the notorious Mr. Go outlet created funnels for rising waters. If Congress would pass laws granting Louisiana its fair share of offshore oil revenues, we could start this process ourselves. But Americans need to be reminded how precious and unique our centuries-old New Orleans and Gulf Coast cultures are—and that is the prime purpose of this book. The gulf South is steeped in history and tradition, and especially in African American, French, and Caribbean elements that form the rich gumbo of our culture and is manifest in music, vernacular architecture, cuisine, folkways, and just plain joie de vivre. The Dutch would never abandon Amsterdam if it flooded; we cannot afford to abandon New Orleans. It is a national and world treasure.

We completed this collection before the hurricanes hit, but we felt it would be remiss not to consider their effect in this book, so this introduction was expanded and Ruth Salvaggio's concluding essay was added. We firmly believe, however, that the disasters Louisiana has recently suffered only confirm the validity of the other essays, which make a strong case for the exceptional nature of our state and its cultures, a fact more salient now than ever before, when so much of our heritage seems endangered. The nation, following the gaze of our surviving Pelicans, needs to cast their eyes back to Louisiana, this time going beyond the spectacle of destruction that so gripped Americans in August and September 2005. Using a multicultural and interdisciplinary approach, and a new, urgent register, *Louisiana Culture from the Colonial Era to Katrina* attempts a resurrection of that ancient shibboleth of southern studies, place. Recent work by Michael Kreyling and Patricia Yaeger has scoffed at this as a tired, indeed, worn-out, notion. However, building on Eudora Welty's words, which began this essay, we propose a new concept of place that proceeds from recent theoretical work, such as that of Edouard Glissant, who notes that the old way of thinking about at least part of Caribbean "space" was to link Cuba, Puerto Rico, and the Dominican Republic with Latin America: "But Haiti is a peasant-based culture just like Columbia. The African presence, so long suppressed, forms a fringe around the Caribbean, from Brazil to Panama in the west (the coast), and from Venezuela to Cuba in the east (the islands)" (116). Louisiana and the coastal South fit seamlessly in this configuration as well; the circumference and center of this Caribbean world are thus returned to physical form and link people through an agricultural and racial past that continues to reverberate in new ways in our mostly urban but still hybrid, new century.

We pursue this new imperative through reconceptualizing the region's origins. From beginnings in the oral tales of Indians, the letters and journals of the early European explorers, and the spiritual memories of nuns and priests, Louisiana has had a literature directly generated by its locales and events. Much of it remains untranslated from the original native languages, French, or Spanish. Before the Louisiana Purchase, English was a foreign language. But throughout the state's rich history, the clash of many kinds of cultures, races, and nationalities has inevitably produced a literature that is exotic, dramatic, and different and yet, in many ways, paradigmatic of American culture as a whole. Its sagas of first contact, immigration, settlement, religious controversy, linguistic mixing, racial struggle, the Cajun diaspora, the Civil War, Reconstruction, the twentieth-century advent of industry, new forms of shipping and new ports, the discovery and exploitation of oil, the rise of the backwoods messiah Huey Long, the Great Depression, and the boom-to-bust oil patch years of the fifties to eighties have produced great writers such as George Washington Cable, Lafcadio Hearn, Kate Chopin, Alice Dunbar Nelson, Arna Bontemps, Tennessee Williams, Lillian Hellman, Lyle Saxon, Robert Penn Warren, Walker Percy, John Kennedy Toole, Pinkie Gordon Lane, and Shirley Anne Grau. Most recently the civil rights movement, the rise of the New New South, and a new interest in the ethnic cultures of the state have produced writers such as Ernest Gaines, Rebecca Wells, James Wilcox, Richard Ford, Tim Gautreaux, Nancy Lemann, Ellen Gilchrist, Brenda Marie Osbey, Yusef Komunyakaa, Robert Olen Butler, and Ernest Hill. Writers from the state who chose other topics to explore have often turned back to their roots, as the Pulitzer Prize–winning playwright Tony Kushner has done in his recent Broadway musical, *Caroline, or Change,* which interrogates the troubled history of Louisiana's racial and domestic systems.

Culture, however, is comprised of more than literature. Louisiana has also contributed unique traditions in cuisine, music, linguistics, folklore, agriculture, politics, and popular culture. Its peculiar rituals—jazz funerals, hoodoo ceremonies, Mardi Gras, Mardi Gras Indians, All Saints' Day practices, Saint Joseph's Day altars, football tailgating, parades, crawfish boils, cochon du laits, fais do-dos, the rough male culture of the oil rigs and river ports—all these things seem to be endlessly reinvented by a dynamic and creative culture that revels in novelty and putting its own stamp on everything. Its mythic moments—some real, some fictional—have resonated for all Americans, from the heroic Battle of New Orleans and Evangeline's tragic exodus in the swamps to the notorious governor's race runoff between David Duke and Edwin Edwards.

These latter two figures are two of a long declension of politcos, for the state's solons have charted a starry course. The early French and Spanish governors fought with the frontier wilderness, the Native Americans, and each other; the Florida Republic attempted a new nation; and later Louisiana joined the Confederacy's similar attempt in an effort to prop up the appalling "special institution" of slavery, which the state's cotton and rice fields seemed to demand. In the modern era we have had colorful figures such as the "Kingfish," Huey Long, his gravely voiced brother, Earl K., and the aforementioned

Duke and Edwards. We have produced colorful and dynamic women politicians too, such as congresswoman Lindy Boggs, Governor Kathleen Babineaux Blanco, and our current senator, Mary Landrieu, the daughter of a legendary and charismatic New Orleans mayor.

These are some of the specifics of Louisiana's history; for most Americans, however, the images are hazier. The word "Louisiana" has an exotic ring to it, conjuring up humid swamps, gators, Spanish moss, and grand but fading plantation mansions. New Orleans, a subset of the mental construct, also emerges, with images of the French Quarter's lacy ironwork, seedy bars, and raucous Mardi Gras celebration. The River Road plantations have been the stuff of dreams for Hollywood productions since the industry's startup days, from films such as *Jezebel* to *Interview with the Vampire*. But Louisiana is more than a set of visuals; the word conjures tastes: blackened redfish, gumbo, jambalaya, Dixie beer, crawfish étouffée, oyster po'boys, the piquancy of Tabasco, and the lusciousness of bread pudding. For the ear there is zydeco, Creole ballads, gospel, crank-a-chank Cajun, Dixieland, New Orleans jazz, and redneck rock and roll.

To state this in another way, Louisiana used to be a vast domain and then became a rather small state, but one with a unique history and culture, anchored in both a special landscape and climate. Raymond Williams has commented, "We are *born* into relationships which are typically settled in a place. This form of primary and 'placeable' bonding is of quite fundamental human and natural importance. Yet the jump from that to anything like the modern nation-state is entirely artificial" (Williams i). Louisiana's particularity was never more evident than in 1803, when its own special qualities—rather than its French, Spanish, or African foundations—became sharply visible under the pressure of becoming American. George Washington Cable's *Old Creole Days* (1879) repeatedly delineates the sense of colonial oppression that swept over the people as they adjusted to the imperatives of their new national identity, which did indeed to them seem "entirely artificial." No matter that Cable himself was despised by the Creoles even as he was limning their pain—after all, he was viewed as an outsider, a voyeur and opportunist who "distorted" old Creole families in contrast to their new American compatriots by having his fictional Creoles speak what actual Creoles deemed demeaning dialect.

In their objection to the linguistic—and thus cultural—image that Cable constructed, Louisiana's Creoles demonstrated both a sense of pride and heritage and, alternately, paranoia and fury. But the contrast he was drawing between them and other Americans had been patently evident for decades on the streets and docks of the city, where bargemen, traders, farmers, and slaves from the surrounding South and farther afield in the fledgling nation formed a usually rough contrast to the citizens of francophone Louisiana, mostly Catholic, hedonistic, European Caribbean, or African in orientation who often hated English, backwoods Protestantism, and the vulgar parochialism of nonaristocratic fellow southerners.

And it was New Orleans, after the cultural ascendency and waning of centers such as Charleston and Savannah, that came to define southern achievement and elegance in the antebellum era and beyond; Scarlett and Rhett, after all, spent their honeymoon in Louisiana, not Birmingham or Nashville. As a great port, as gateway to the Caribbean and to the Atlantic beyond, but also to the upper reaches of the Mississippi, the Missouri, the Midwest, and the Great Plains, New Orleans has simultaneously been the locus of the migrant and the metropolitan.

At the same time, Louisiana functioned, from 1803 onward, as a microcosm of America—especially in its polyglot, dynamic culture, more Caribbean, European, and African than virtually any other place in the nation—and a counternarrative to the national script, one that has continually ruptured the sense of boundary that has always been crucial in the conceptualization of any nation. Most other Americans are surprised to learn that Louisiana attracted thousands of Italian, German, and Caribbean immigrants in the nineteenth century and more recently has been a magnet for South Asians, Vietnamese, and Lebanese immigrants.

But from the beginning, Louisiana's linguistic identity affiliated it with a transatlantic, Caribbean, and African world, as did its strongly French and, to a lesser extent, Spanish heritage, which involved many strikingly different modes of self-presentation and performance as well as a dominant Catholicism shared only, for a time, by Maryland. Its tropical climate linked it to the Caribbean, Florida, and South America, another rupture of boundary made visible by trade routes and paths of immigration, especially after the revolution in Santo Domingo.

Louisiana Culture from the Colonial Era to Katrina forcefully demonstrates the limited nature of many popular perceptions of the state and its broader cultures while, more importantly, exposing the artificial nature of sheerly national boundaries in an attempt to bring out Louisiana's rich and complex history of relationships with the peoples and cultures of the Atlantic and the Caribbean. This study has been generated by conversations among a number of scholars who have cooperated to establish the Program in Louisiana and Caribbean Studies at LSU. Appropriately, in 2003, the bicentennial of the Louisiana Purchase, the Louisiana Board of Regents provided funding for the program, and a major conference, "Beyond the Islands: Extending the Meaning of Caribbean Cultures" took place in Baton Rouge in April 2004 to inaugurate the program. The conference was jointly sponsored by the Center for Francophone Studies and the Comparative Literature Program. This joining of forces finds expression in Louisiana Culture from the Colonial Era to Katrina as well, where a battery of interdisciplinary approaches are applied to Louisiana's spectacular multiculture. Three more conferences have been held in successive years: "Creole Connections: Linking Louisiana and the Caribbean," "After Katrina: Rebuilding Landscapes, Rebuilding Cultures," and "The Black Diaspora in Louisiana and the Caribbean." Both this book and these ongoing annual conferences on Louisiana and the Caribbean are intended as extensions of the bicentennial of the Louisiana Purchase.

The Program in Louisiana and Caribbean Studies was built on sturdy foundations. During the 1990s the interdisciplinary area of cultural studies appeared on many United States campuses. At LSU, several departments developed new courses dealing specifically with Louisiana and/or the Caribbean, and faculty across the disciplines came to realize the signal potential of interdisciplinary research and collaboration. The Center for French and Francophone Studies, for instance, which was founded in 1983, has for some years sponsored research, teaching, discussion, and debate of diverse aspects of French and Francophone cultures, transcultural exchanges involving the uses of language, the production and interpretation of literatures, and the formation and intermixing of cultures. This center's ongoing work has in many ways been extended through the broader program of Louisiana and Caribbean studies, which has brought together ongoing and parallel work being done in English- and Spanish-language studies. The tripartite study of the linguistic heritage of the region facilitates interdisciplinary and multicultural projects such as a broad consideration of creolization, slavery's history and enduring effects, the formative influence of plantation culture, the intermixing of diverse ethnic populations with a major African component, multilingualism and the extensive role of oral traditions, and the various ways all of this was carried out through social mobility, immigration, trade, war, exploration, colonization, industrialization, the rise of media, and so on. Parallel involvement of the history, religion, anthropology, and linguistics professors doing work in the region's history, cultures, and languages has fostered interdisciplinary commerce and the consequent expansion of individual faculty knowledge of the region, resulting in new kinds of research and exciting, new discoveries.

The African American Cultural Center and the minor in African American studies have stimulated interest in our state and region's unique and rich African heritage and have helped attract more students of this ethnic background to the University. The excellent cultural programs sponsored by the center have been of immense benefit to all students and led to increased enrollment of non–African American students in relevant courses, better relations among campus constituencies, and an increased awareness of our shared heritage. *Louisiana Culture from the Colonial Era to Katrina* draws from the state's complex practice of slavery in Daniel Littlefield's analysis of the peculiar ways in which Louisianans of French ancestry approached the system, from Gallic times to the 1803 takeover of the state through the Louisiana Purchase. Carolyn M. Jones's essay on former state poet laureate Pinkie Gordon Lane, current poet laureate Brenda Marie Osbey's two contributions, and John Lowe's discussion of race and ethnicity are other places where this vital component of state and national culture finds consideration and interrogation, but the African American contribution to Louisiana figures significantly for most of the scholars included here.

The various language departments on campus have a joint linguistic program that also includes faculty from the Departments of Psychology, Communications Sciences and Disorders, and Geography and Anthropology. Studies in bilingualism and second-language learning, Louisiana Creole, Cajun French, black English, English-based pidgins and Creoles, language and culture, and theories and practice of second-language acquisition are important to the work of the program.

The Department of English already has many courses in place, in folklore and in southern, African American, diasporan, ethnic, and Louisiana literature, and it recently added new classes in Caribbean literature. Women's studies has many joint courses with English that intersect with Louisiana-Caribbean studies. Cultural studies courses often overlap here as well.

The language departments—especially French and Spanish—offer many courses that reflect the literature and languages of the region as well as cultural studies classes and women's studies topics. The Program in Louisiana and Caribbean Studies will soon include German and Native American projects, as we plan translations of the literary products of Louisiana and the region that were not originally written in English. Our conversations with the Longfellow Institute at Harvard University should prove useful here; it has already published *Creole Echoes: The Francophone Poetry of Nineteenth-Century Louisiana* (2004).

Since 1928 LSU has been an important catalyst for public cultural and art programing in the region. Plays, concerts, and operas have been integral parts of the university's extended mission of public education, and thousands of citizens not enrolled in classes have come to campus to be entertained and instructed. This tradition continues forcefully today; the School of Music and the Department of Theater—and here we include the innovative Louisiana-centered work of Swine Palace Productions—are increasingly being noticed in the national and international arts community, primarily for their special strengths in jazz, gospel, and dramatic performances that feature the work of Louisiana and Caribbean musicians and playwrights. Swine Palace and LSU Theater Department have mounted fascinating treatments of traditional plays in Louisiana settings, as in playwright/director Femi Euba's stage productions of a *Hedda Gabbler* set in New Orleans, Maryse Condé's *Tropical Breeze Hotel,* and his own engrossing black diaspora drama set off the Louisiana coast, *The Eye of Gabriel.* There have also been wonderful staged adaptations of Louisiana novels, such as *All the King's Men* and *A Confederacy of Dunces;* even Lyle Saxon's folklore collection *Gumbo Ya-Ya* found new life as a musical. A 1941 Irving Berlin Broadway show, *Louisiana Purchase,* was revived and rethought for a celebratory set of performances during the bicentennial year. Similarly, the New Orleans opera commissioned a new opera from composer Thea Musgrove, *Pontalba,* based on the dramatic life story of the Baroness Pontalba, whose tragic but creative life played out in both Paris and New Orleans, culminating in her construction of the historic Pontalba buildings on Jackson Square.

In spring 2007 the LSU Department of Music mounted a major new production of Carlisle Floyd's opera *Willie Stark,* which was based on Robert Penn Warren's *All the King's Men,* a Pulitzer Prize–winning novel that was written while Warren was on the faculty at LSU. It has been made into two films; the first won the Academy Award for best picture, and the second, released last year, was filmed in Baton Rouge and features an all-star cast, including Jude Law, Kate Winslet, Anthony Hopkins, and Sean Penn in the central role of Willie. Louisiana, in fact, has become one of the major venues for film production, with extensive studios, experienced technicians, sound stages, and generous tax breaks for Hollywood production companies. This promising new industry has continued to thrive even after Katrina.

As this perusal of the recent cultural events and the current situation in

Louisiana and Caribbean studies suggests, the time has come for the work of connection and for interdisciplinary, cooperative work between and among existing programs, and not just at LSU. The Center for Louisiana Studies at the University of Louisiana at Lafayette, the Deep South Humanities Center at Tulane, and the Creole Heritage Center at Northwestern State University are just three of many related units that join us in this work of rediscovering our state and reconfigured region's complex heritages.

It is our hope that students and scholars who develop an awareness of the multicultural riches and traditions of our state and region will naturally be better equipped to relate to people outside their own ethnic enclave and to see the potential in democratic endeavor in every realm. A linkage of the ethnic history of the region and that of the Caribbean should inspire interest in other languages, especially French and Spanish but also pidgin languages, Cajun French, and secondary group languages such as German, Italian, and Vietnamese. Louisiana and the Caribbean have created one of the world's most fascinating and diverse literatures, yet we have only begun to study these traditions side by side. Indeed, much remains to be done in both areas while the work of connection begins, for we lack primary studies of some of the most important figures in the field, such as Ernest Gaines of Louisiana and Maryse Condé of Guadeloupe.

Nevertheless, this book offers a tantalizing set of readings of some of the most distinguished writers of Louisiana, a dazzling array of artists any state would be proud to claim. Peggy Prenshaw provides a helpful overview of the Louisiana literary firmament; Carolyn M. Jones concentrates on the lyric poetry of Louisiana's former poet laureate, Pinkie Gordon Lane, whose work speaks to the rich history of the state's African Americans. John Lowe gives a rambunctious reading of the complex, locally infected ethnic humor of perhaps the funniest book ever written, John Kennedy Toole's *Confederacy of Dunces;* Margaret Bauer explores Ellen Gilchrist's New Orleans.

These literary and cultural readings are extended differently through the related field of folklore, which often provides the foundation for great literature. In recent years scholars have conducted important research into African American linguistics and folklore; African survivalisms in language, architecture, and dance; gospel traditions; vernacular architecture of Louisiana and the Caribbean; and southern, Louisianan, and Caribbean folklore. Accordingly, folk culture receives an important treatment here from a distinguished Louisiana folklorist, Marcia Gaudet, who looks at Huey Long's relation to the state's folk culture. As she indicates, Louisiana has a fabled political history, one that is closely connected to powerful families and factions that have held sway for extended periods of times. This is epitomized in the sixty-year reign of the Long family, from Huey to his son Russell, who only retired from the U.S. Senate in the 1980s. Huey Long, the ultimate populist governor of the New South, is recalled here as a trickster figure extraordinaire, one in line with some of the greatest trickster traditions in American folk culture.

Of particular interest for the Program in Louisiana and Caribbean Studies is an ongoing examination of French in the African diaspora, French and the emerging cultures of the Caribbean and the postcolonial world, multilingualism and translation as means of transcultural communication, and the study of the construction and circulation of francophone cultures and their interaction and mixing (*metissage* or creolization) with other cultures as local and global phenomena. LSU's aforementioned Center for French and Francophone Studies has in the past sponsored international colloquia on topics such as "The Plantation System in the Americas"; the plantation economy; slavery; forms of culture, music, architecture, oral expression, and other manifestations of the plantations of the American South and the Caribbean; "Experiencing Languages in Louisiana," and the problems and perceptions "foreign language speakers" in Louisiana, such as Native Americans, Vietnamese, Spanish, Cajuns, and Creoles. *Louisiana Culture from the Colonial Era to Katrina* offers a taste of this in Germain Bienvenu's engrossing and original research into the history of early French explorer/writers, who detail the nature of relations between France and the New World but also particulars of the intricate encounters between the French and the Native Americans.

In recent years, historians of African American and Caribbean history have taken new approaches to the always vexed and continually fascinating attempts, by many constituencies, to define "Creoles" and "creolization." This book brings together two different yet complementary studies of these issues, one by the distinguished German historian Berndt Ostendorf (a frequent visitor to the Pelican State) and Sybil Kein, a literary professor who is also a talented musician and historian of the Creoles of color of New Orleans, from whence she originated.

Louisiana and the Caribbean have enjoyed a rich mix of religions; the interior of the continental part of the region has been mainly Protestant, as have the British-dominated islands of the Caribbean. Southern Louisiana, however, and most islands (certainly the Hispanic and francophone ones) have been centers for a Roman Catholic tradition, one highly charged, in the case of people of color, with remnants of African religions, resulting in fascinating amalgams such as hoodoo, Voudun, Santeria, and other hybrid faiths. The powerful and unique sense of death in the city of New Orleans is hauntingly evoked by Louisiana Poet Laureate Brenda Marie Osbey's second essay for this collection, "I Want to Die in New Orleans." Her essay, written before Katrina, took on new levels of meaning after the waters rose. Osbey, like all New Orleaneans, had to flee the city in the aftermath of the storm, and her university, Dillard, was shut down. She subsequently took a position as writer in residence at LSU and embarked on an ambitious lecture and reading tour of the nation, helping to explain why Katrina was a wound suffered by all Americans. She is currently writing a new collection of poems about the catastrophe, tentatively titled "Death by Water Suite."

A by-no-means-exhaustive list of issues we attempt to address in *Louisiana Culture from the Colonial Era to Katrina* begins with the larger problem of how to reconnect Louisiana's peoples with the region that has so powerfully shaped their heritage and with which they continue to interact. Next on the list is overcoming the disciplinary balkanization that has prevented the cooperative development of area studies in the past. We hope *Louisiana Culture from the Colonial Era to Katrina* will demonstrate a need for increased funding of regional studies everywhere, for the local is inextricably related to the global and the transnational. Evidence is ready at hand for what collections like this and programs like Louisiana and Caribbean Studies can mean for communities. The most salient examples of the regional centers are the Center for the Study of Southern Culture at Ole Miss and the Center for the Study of the American South at the University of North Carolina–Chapel Hill. The Ole Miss center has garnered an international reputation for its pioneering work in the study of region and has become well known through its many conferences and programs, which have been extensively publicized and reported on, such as the annual William Faulkner Conference, the Conference on the Book, the Southern Writers Conference, the Elvis Conference, and a myriad of other programs dealing with issues such as civil rights, the southern environment, southern women, and so on. The many publications of the center have gained wide fame as well, particularly the award-winning *Encyclopedia of Southern Culture,* which has been a best seller and an often-referenced research tool for scholars and laypeople alike. The center has been a dynamo for research grants, and the staff over the years has achieved an enviable success at bringing donors into the university. Many times those who contribute to the center become interested in other programs and possibilities at Ole Miss, and everyone here at LSU will profit in a similar manner from interest initially expressed in the Program for Louisiana and Caribbean Studies.

I mention all these things because books like *Louisiana Culture from the Colonial Era to Katrina* are not isolated publishing events; they are vitally connected to the necessary work of stimulating citizen interest in their own local culture, for interest often leads to dynamic involvement and thereby to the extension and innovation of culture. We feel a special responsibility to the citizens of our state and base our commitment on an old African proverb: "No people should be hungry for their own image." We also believe the work of physical and cultural restoration after the recent catastrophes cannot hope to be successful without an informed vision of our state's past, present, and future.

Concurrently, our conversation about Louisiana joins the wider one about transnationalism and global cultures. Much has been made lately about the myriad new connections between cultures permitted by the Internet, new forms of global commerce, jet-age travel, and the development of a universal popular culture—one dominated by American forms, particularly from Hollywood and hip-hop culture. Yet Louisiana, always at the crossroads of transatlantic, pan-Caribbean, and hemispheric trade routes, has always been connected to global culture; its peoples have always spoken more than English.

We also intend for this collection to inspire a new meditation on history. The first part of this book draws on the exciting work that has been done in the last decade by scholars on the age of first contacts between Native Americans and Europeans in the lower Mississippi Valley, the peculiar forms of slavery in francophone Louisiana, and the little known story of German explorers and writers who came to the bayous. At one point the vast area just west of Lake Pontchartrain was designated on state maps as "the German coast." The story of Charles Sealsfield's relations with Louisiana offers fascinating testimony to this unknown but central component of Louisiana's ethnic history. Alexander Ritter, a prominent German scholar, demonstrates the fascination Germans in general had with the Pelican State and makes an extraordinary sets of transatlantic connections, just as his subject did so many years ago.

The Program in Louisiana and Caribbean Studies expects to stimulate research into the region's constantly shifting musical patterns; surely this area has produced more distinct forms of musical expression than virtually any other place on earth, for spirituals, gospel, blues, jazz, Cajun, Creole, zydeco, salsa, reggae, rap, Latin jazz, hip-hop, and many other forms continue to thrive and mutate. The program features panels and symposia on these topics and has included musical performances as part of its annual conferences. Two of our essays here reflect this interest. Wilfried Raussert, who has done extensive research at the Blues Archive of the University of Mississippi, considers "Hollers, Blue Notes, and Brass Sounds" as manifestations of the amazingly diverse musical and cultural influences on jazz in Louisiana, and New Orleans' Brenda Marie Osbey, Louisiana's poet laureate, zeroes in on the musical and metaphysical ambiance of one of her city's most treasured and intricate musical/religious/social forms, the jazz funeral. New Orleans alone has functioned as the cradle for blues, jazz, gospel, and Dixieland; the state as a whole has contributed to those traditions, and Cajun and Zydeco strains have emanated from Acadian homes and hamlets. Although it is beyond the scope of this study, dance forms have been generated by all these musical traditions as well, at events such as the celebrated fais do-do and at the celebrated performances of the "Louisiana Hayride" broadcasts in northern Louisiana.

In all these essays, we have attempted to open up existing parameters of discourse about region, cultural identity, and particularity. And we have sought to demonstrate how culture overflows all kinds of boundaries, particularly when that culture is unique and vibrant. In his speculations on border lives, Homi Bhabha has urged us to use subject positions to guide us to a new sense of group identities. As he states, we need to "think beyond narratives of originary and initial subjectivities and to focus on those moments or processes that are produced in the articulation of cultural differences" (Bhabha 1). As he develops this position, Bhabha eventually urges a consideration of what he calls "counternarratives of the nation," which "continually evoke and erase its totalizing boundaries—both actual and conceptual—disturb those ideological manoeuvers through which 'imagined communities' are given essentialist identities. For the political unity of the nation consists in a continual displacement of the anxiety of its irredeemably plural modern space—representing the nations' modern territoriality is turned into the archaic, atavistic temporality of Traditionalism" (Bhabha 149).

The African American contribution to Louisiana culture has been enormous, and black New Orleans has probably been the most significant cauldron (along with New York City) for the creation of African American cultural expression. New Orleans, of course, was a primary port for the slave trade, which shifted from African ports to the Caribbean over time as the export of Africans was banned. The massive exodus of Haitian planters, along with their slaves after the Haitian Revolution (which began in 1791), had a profound effect on New Orleans black-white relations and Creole cultures. There were always more free men and women of color in Louisiana than in any other southern state, and the unique cultures developed by this group of peoples had myriad ramifications for both Louisiana and southern culture as a whole. The dispersal of thousands of black New Orleaneans to other states after Katrina poses a severe threat to the continuance of precious cultural and social traditions that heretofore have been seamlessly interwoven into the fabric of the city and state's history and daily life.

There are many aspects of Louisiana that are not covered here. The state contains, for example, our nation's largest, most importantly productive, and most menaced wetlands. The aquaculture industry has some of its most extensive operations there. Contemporary Native Americans have vibrant, postmodern cultures, especially since monies derived from the relatively recent gambling industry on reservation lands has enabled cultural revivals of all sorts. The state also has one of the most important series of festivals that occur year around, where local crops, crafts, and cultural practices are celebrated and used to revitalize local economies.

The complicated, often tragic history of the timber industry in Louisiana took a special form as loggers destroyed huge tracts of ancient cypresses, a parallel to the destruction of the great forests of Michigan, Wisconsin, and other states. The petroleum industry, though responsible for much of Louisiana's wealth in the twentieth century, has also despoiled the wetlands and coastline, contributing forcefully to coastal erosion through the creation of many channels used for wetland and offshore drilling. There is no question that this situation made the effects of the recent storms more devastating. The related petrochemical industry has polluted the Mississippi River delta and the skies above it, and yet it too has created jobs, taxes, and entree into transnational trade. Tourism has figured as one of Louisiana's most significant income-producing industries and has increasingly been fueled by its partnership with historical societies and local chambers of commerce, which now understand cultural heritage can mean cold cash. But Katrina shut down the port and the cruise ships for some time, and much business was lost permanently to other venues. It remains an open question whether the booming tourism before Katrina can be restored, especially in New Orleans, where so many of the service jobs associated with visitors—dishwashers, chambermaids, laundry personnel, waiters, and so on—were filled by people who lived in the devastated neighborhoods that have not been rebuilt. Cruelly, the city had been riding a wave of increased traffic before the storm. The "Age of Jefferson and Napoleon" show at the New Orleans Museum of Art, assembled to celebrate the bicentennial of the Louisiana Purchase, brought affluent tourists to New Orleans hotels, restaurants, and casinos. Each year more and more luxury liners steamed out of the Crescent City on Caribbean and South American cruises; conversely, tourists from those places sailed for New Orleans.

But what we have left undone, and what now, post Katrina, needs to be done, can have its beginning in these conversations and in the crucial cultural discussions that have preceded and accompanied it. Certainly the question of the future of African American New Orleans lies at the heart of these conundrums. In his paradigm-shifting study *The Black Atlantic* (1993), Paul Gilroy explodes national boundaries to reveal an intricate world of black life that spanned (and continues to span) the Atlantic, uniting all people of color in the Western Hemisphere. He asserts that our "past nationalist paradigms for thinking about cultural history fail" when confronted by boundary-crossing cultural configurations. As he demonstrates, many prior studies of state, region, and nation have been notably constrained by artificial boundaries and often have ignored concerns such as race and ethnicity (Gilroy ix). We believe our essays here richly confirm his observations in a focused manner.

In a different but nevertheless complementary study, *Cities of the Dead* (1991), Joseph Roach has posited a new way of looking at performance traditions over the centuries in New Orleans by linking them, again across the Atlantic, with those practiced in London. His study factors in the critical connection of slavery as it was practiced by these two urban poles and shows conclusively how Native Americans and immigrants played critical roles in shaping all forms of New World performance scripts and traditions. His findings take on a new urgency as Mardi Gras Indians, African American painters, sculptors, quilt makers, creative cooks, photographers, musicians, writers, and artists of all types lost manuscripts, costumes, instruments, works of art, studios, performance spaces, and homes to the storms. Many of them are now scattered across the nation. I recently attended a conference in Philadelphia and dined at a famous restaurant there. The entertainment for the night was a noted New Orleans brass band, whose home base, at least for now, is the City of Brotherly Love rather than the City that Care Forgot—now a cruelly ironic soubriquet.

Following the examples of Gilroy and Roach, and that of other scholars of transnationalism, our essays break the old molds of traditional regionalism, but without disavowing the myriad southern aspects of Louisiana and its cultures. Yes, the Mississippi is the South's greatest waterway, but it is also its essential link to the Gulf of Mexico and the Caribbean, the Panama Canal and the Pacific, the Western Hemisphere and world trade. In concurring with Edouard Glissant ("The Caribbean Sea is not an American lake. It is the estuary of the Americas" [139]), we by implication make a central case for Louisiana as hub and generator of a new cultural configuration, but one with a rich, hybrid, and varied past. Properly read and reinterpreted, that past can help guide us into the future as we navigate around the wreckage to rebuild, rethink, and restore a land and culture unique in all the world, yet one that on so many registers speaks to and nourishes the souls of all people across the globe.

NOTE

1. The hurricane and its aftermath have been extensively studied already, and other books and articles are being written daily. The three most significant early book-length studies were by Brinkley, Van Heerden and Bryan, and Dyson. Spike Lee's television documentary, *When the Levees Broke: A Requiem in Four Acts,* has been seen by millions. A recent special edition of *Callaloo* has some compelling interviews and firsthand accounts of the flood, the evacuation, and the aftermath, along with an array of photographs.

WORKS CITED

Bhabha, Homi. *The Location of Culture.* London: Routledge, 1994.

Brinkley, Douglas. *The Great Deluge: Hurricane Katrina, New Orleans, and the Mississippi Gulf Coast.* New York: William Morrow, 2006.

Dyson, Michael Eric. *Come Hell or High Water: Hurricane Katrina and the Color of Disaster.* New York: Basic, 2006.

Gilroy, Paul. *The Black Atlantic: Modernity and Double Consciousness.* Cambridge: Harvard University Press, 1993.

Glissant, Edouard. *Caribbean Discourse: Selected Essays.* Charlottesville: University Press of Virginia, 1989.

Kreyling, Michael. *Inventing Southern Literature.* Jackson: University Press of Mississippi, 1998.

Roach, Joseph. *Cities of the Dead: Circum-Atlantic Performance.* New York: Columbia University Press, 1991.

Rowell, Charles, ed. *American Tragedy: New Orleans Under Water.* Special issue of *Callaloo* 29.4 (2007).

Said, Edward. *Reflections on Exile and Other Essays.* Cambridge: Harvard University Press, 2000.

Van Heerden, Ivor, and Mike Bryan. *The Storm: What Went Wrong and Why During*

Hurricane Katrina—the Inside Story from One Louisiana Scientist. New York: Viking, 2006.

Williams, Raymond. *The Year 2000.* New York: Pantheon, 1983.

Yaeger, Patricia. *Dirt and Desire: Reconstructing Southern Women's Writing, 1930–1990.* Chicago: University of Chicago Press, 2000.

PART 1 INDIAN, FRENCH, SPANISH, AFRICAN, GERMAN

The Early Origins of a Unique Culture

The Beginnings of Louisiana Literature

The French Domination of 1682–1763

GERMAIN BIENVENU

For the most part, the writings in French from the first phase of Louisiana's colonial history, the French domination of 1682–1763, have not been studied as Louisiana or New World literature—that is, as writings by native or naturalized residents of Louisiana or the other Americas. Instead of being read as literature of the Western Hemisphere, these histories, travel narratives, journals, poems, plays, and other compositions have been viewed as Continental French writings *about* Louisiana. They have not been designated as a body of literature distinct from European works about the Americas, works by such authors as Antoine-François Prévost and François-René de Chateaubriand, two of the most famous eighteenth- and nineteenth-century French writers to bring fiction set in Louisiana to an international audience.

As late as the 1950s scholars such as Richebourg Gaillard McWilliams, who wrote on André Pénicaut, were still pioneering a consideration of Louisiana's colonial authors as American (i.e., New World) writers. In 1954 Auguste Viatte pointed out in *Histoire littéraire de l'Amérique française* that the poetry and prose written in the French colonies of the New World should be viewed as both Franco-American literature and Continental French literature even though the literature of Europe and that of the New World were, in essence, inseparable at the time (2–3). Although it is true that French colonists of Canada, Louisiana, and the Caribbean were French men and women in the same way that Anglo-American colonists were British subjects or Hispano-Americans were Spanish before revolutions of independence rocked the world, it would not be anachronistic to distinguish long-term colonists who committed themselves to and were changed by their second home from compatriots who performed stints in the colonies and then returned to Europe. By the same token, it is not an insupportable imposition of present-day perceptions onto earlier discourse to distinguish New World literature in a given language from Continental literature in the same.

Clearly, the French who merely passed through Louisiana or worked in the region for only a short time (as in temporary service to the Crown, with no intention of making the colony a second home) and then wrote about their brief experiences should not be considered Louisiana writers but, rather, writers about Louisiana. On the other hand, those who were fervently engaged in the development of the colony, who wanted to make the territory their second home, who resided in the region for a considerable and significant part of their lives, and who wrote about their experiences in hopes of promoting the place should be thought of primarily as Louisianians, as members of a socio-regional grouping of French subjects "Americanized" by their particular New World home.

These Louisiana colonists' writings—whether of the same or different genres, composed by persons who knew each other or did not, or created at the beginning of French occupation or at the end—are remarkable for the common themes and concerns that connect them over spatial and temporal distances. The similarities derive in large part from experiences held in common by the authors in their New World home. These similarities color the writings to such an extent that together the compositions must be viewed as forming an individual body of literature. It is a literature written in French, but not French literature, even though comparisons may obviously be made between Louisiana authors and other writers of the French-speaking world. It is a literature of one of the colonial Americas that subsequently became part of the United States, which had its origins in a separate colonial America.

Until recently, the critical consensus had been that Louisiana French literature as distinguishable from Continental French literature about Louisiana had remote beginnings in Louisiana's Spanish colonial period (which followed the first French domination) but that this literature did not flourish until the United States' acquisition of Louisiana after 1800. Everything composed during the founding years of French rule was dismissed as writings by Continentals or Canadians who had spent time in the Louisiana colony. The actuality, however, is that many of these Continentals and Canadians had become naturalized to a geographic and political entity that was developing its own identity, evolving in its own fashion, and becoming so distinguishable from other Americas that much of its differentness persists to this day. Not surprisingly, then, the writings from the area and the era—works that are sometimes as unique as the authors and the region itself—must be viewed as constituting a distinct body of literature, one still in need of classification, definition, and delineation through creation of a canon.

Over the years, the above-suggested criteria for the formation of a separate literary canon have not generally been considered by those commenting on colonial Louisiana writings. Thus, as indicated earlier in this essay, a much later consensual date than the one currently being proposed has been assigned to the naissance of an identifiable Louisiana literature. Generally, Louisiana literature has been discussed as beginning with Julien Poydras's poetry in the 1770s, the decade after the colony had passed from French to Spanish rule.

In their 1981 *Anthologie,* Mathé Allain and Barry Ancelet break with convention when they claim, "It may be said that the French literature of Louisiana was born at the same time as the colony. Indeed, from the time of the first French explorations, discoverers wrote reports, letters, and travel journals in a language lacking rhetorical artifice, but not charm and vigor" (1; trans. Germain Bienvenu). By ascribing the possible beginnings of Louisiana literature to the colony's very date of birth, Allain and Ancelet make a bold proposal. After all, at the time that the first explorers and colonizers were writing they had not yet established a permanent settlement in lower Louisiana to call home. Founding fathers and authors such as Henri de Tonti and Nicolas de La Salle were then still operating from bases in the Illinois region of upper Louisiana (the place where the Louisiana colony actually began), from Canada, or from France. Not surprisingly, therefore, in the section of their anthology titled "Les débuts: 1682–1814," Allain and Ancelet quickly move from excerpting accounts of the activities of René-Robert Cavelier, Sieur de La Salle and Pierre Le Moyne, Sieur d'Iberville at the turn of the 1600s and 1700s to highlighting Antoine-Simon Le Page du Pratz's *Histoire de la Louisiane* (1758) as a showpiece specimen for the collection's next section, "Les premiers colons et leur littérature" ("The first colonists and their literature").

Nevertheless, it is not until the appearance of Poydras's poems in the Spanish colonial period (1763–1800) that Allain and Ancelet detect the first works written for a literary purpose (4), a view the two anthologists share with most of the critics before them. Further, in accord with their scholarly predecessors, Allain and Ancelet hold up Paul-Louis Leblanc de Villeneufve's play *La fête du petit-blé, ou L'héroïsme de Poucha-Houmma* (1814), produced after Louisiana's acquisition by the United States in 1803, as Louisiana's first play. More recent research reveals, however, that both Poydras's and Leblanc's claims to primacy no longer hold. Rather, the two poets may now be viewed as actually emerging at the end of a century of colonial Louisiana compositions in both prose and verse.

The views of critics preceding McWilliams, Allain and Ancelet formed the lasting consensus that colonists writing before Poydras were more French subjects writing about Louisiana for compatriots back in Europe than Louisianians creating a literature about themselves, a literature based on their unique New World experiences to be shared with Continentals as well as fellow colonists. But the fact is that by the time they began to write their accounts, many of these New World French men and women had actually lived in Louisiana longer than Poydras had done before he composed his poems. This reality notwithstanding, because these colonists did not publish their works in Louisiana or did not end their lives in the colony, they have been deprived the type of recognition lavished upon Poydras by virtue of his being the first littérateur published in Louisiana.

Beginning with *Louisiana Studies* (1894) by Alcée Fortier, who asserted, based on the limited material available to him, that during the French domination there was "no literary enthusiasm" and "no works written in Louisiana except the reports of officers," critics have tended to refer to Poydras as "the author of the earliest work in our literature" (6–7). To his credit, however, Fortier does acknowledge that another "document is . . . of great importance; it is the celebrated 'Mémoire des Négociants et Habitants de la Louisiane sur l'Événement du 29 Octobre, 1768,' written by Lafrénière and Caresse, two of the chiefs of the revolution of 1768, which was so heroic and ended so unhappily" (7). Although preceding Poydras's work, Nicolas Chauvin de La Frénière's protest over Louisiana's new ownership was composed after the colony had been transferred from France to Spain and, hence, after the works of the authors now being proposed as Louisiana's first. Obviously, Fortier upheld as a requisite for "our literature" that works be both composed in their entirety in Louisiana and then published in the colony, a twofold stipulation that many later critics seem to have used but one that few eighteenth-century Louisiana writers met. For although most of the accounts actually were composed primarily in the colony, the texts were invariably taken back to France for publication or manuscript circulation, conditions in Louisiana at the time not permitting printing and distribution of large amounts of reading material.[1]

The strength of Fortier's critical legacy is evident in the views of scholars after him. In her 1929 annotated bibliography appended to *The French Literature of Louisiana,* Ruby Van Allen Caulfield lists writers such as Tonti, Marie-Madeleine Hachard, Pénicaut, Jean-François-Benjamin Dumont de Montigny, Le Page du Pratz, and Jean-Bernard Bossu alongside the likes of Pierre-François-Xavier de Charlevoix and the infamous Louis Hennepin under the heading "Journals and Accounts of Voyages by Explorers and Travelers in Early Louisiana," thereby placing the former outside of her discussion of true Louisiana literature. And though she does include Louisiana patriot La Frénière and the French-born Poydras, Guy Soniat du Fossat, and Leblanc de Villeneufve (the latter two of whom wrote as Louisiana was being tossed among Spain, France, and the United States at the turn of the eighteenth and nineteenth centuries) in the section titled "Louisiana Writers," Caulfield only reluctantly places Louisiana-born dramatist, academician, and classical scholar Étienne Viel there, maintaining that the latter is really out of place due to his moving to France at an early age for schooling and his beginning a career there before returning to Louisiana.

Viatte, in *Histoire littéraire de l'Amérique française,* also sees Louisiana literature as beginning in the Spanish period and cites Soniat du Fossat's *Histoire de la Louisiane* and Poydras's "La prise du morne du Bâton-Rouge" as examples of two or three texts that presage a beginning of literary activity (223). Later, in his *Anthologie littéraire* (1971), Viatte, dividing Louisiana francophone literature into three periods (1800–1840, 1840–1865, and 1865–1930), ascribes the commencement of Louisiana literature to an even later date: the appearance of Leblanc de Villeneufve's tragedy *Poucha-Houmma,* performed in New Orleans in 1809 and published in 1814 (251).

In his 1932 bibliographic study *Les écrits de langue française en Louisiane au XIXe siècle,* Edward Larocque Tinker, still the most handy guide to nineteenth-century Louisiana francophone literature, overlooks the fact that many eighteenth-century colonists began and even completed writing in Louisiana, not in France. Tinker states, "Initially, there was no literature. The pioneers never produced literary works before ceasing to be pioneers. These hardy colonists were too busy fighting Indians, taming a new land, and struggling to survive to find time to write, even if they had had the background sufficient for it" (1–2; trans. Germain Bienvenu). A closer look at the writings of the "pioneers" predating Poydras, none of whom Tinker mentions as forerunners of the nineteenth-century writers included in his study, shows that the early colonists were not as busy fighting Indians as might first be believed and that many were well enough versed in classical works and contemporary literary conventions to vie with the average Continental writer in quality of production. And although Tinker allows any French journalist who happened to pass through New Orleans in ante- and postbellum years entrance into his bibliography of Louisiana-French authors of the 1800s, his disregard of 1700s writers who spent years carving out the civilization to which later French exiles could flee revolutions and political oppression in Europe is puzzling. In sum, Tinker concludes, "In truth, it may be said that it was only after Louisiana had been separated from France by thirty-four years of active Spanish rule and then come under American domination that a Creole literature began to flourish" (3; trans. Germain Bienvenu).

Tinker is correct in asserting that a *Creole* literature—that is, a body of writings by *natives* of Louisiana—did not result until acquisition by the United States, for the great majority of writers of French and Spanish colonial Louisiana (Viel being the major exception) were émigrés from France. In addition, these European-born residents of Louisiana who anteceded Poydras attempted publication of their writings on the Continent, with primarily but not exclusively a European audience in mind. The desired readership notwithstanding, the tall tales, assorted anecdotes, historical events, and wealth of information that the colonial authors recorded were part of a body of oral lore and learning that naturalized Louisianians held in common even when they did not know each other personally. Writings by Creoles, published in Louisiana mainly for Creoles, did not become commonplace until Louisiana was a United States possession. Nevertheless, the Creole literary flowering of the 1800s did not mark the first era in which a group of writers identifiable as Louisianians shared their strikingly similar views on the same subjects, subjects that pertained to their lives in Louisiana, that were of concern to French readers in both Old and New Worlds, and that even appealed to nonfrancophone audiences to such an extent that translations of some of these texts into English occurred in the authors' lifetimes.

Although most of these writings spanning a century of colonial activity cannot be easily grouped into the same literary school (written for the most part independently, separated by many years as well as by their authors' ignorance of each other and employment of varying forms of composition), some were created by colonists who knew each other, who borrowed information from each other, and who then offered different versions of occurrences that had already become local oral legend before having been put to paper. For example, Pénicaut, Dumont, and Le Page (with Bossu following closely) offer exclusive reports on the one hand while on the other they record some of the same historical events, the same Indian anecdotes, and the same experiences of colonists. Furthermore, the aforementioned authors and others expand upon the life of the first great hero of Louisiana literature, Louis Juchereau de Saint Denis, creating in their treatment of this explorer, commandant, trader, and negotiator Louisiana's first historical fiction.

Saint Denis, a historical figure idolized for fair and beneficial dealings with French, Spanish, and Amerindian populations of the Louisiana frontier, concretized a twofold myth held by the colony's first writers: that French, Amerindian and other non-French and nonwhite groups could live harmoniously under French rule or even as politically different neighbors and that those who ruled could govern in such a way that all would prosper or at least be content with the degree of independence and material possession possible and appropriate to their station in life.

Excepting Viel and Poydras, neither of whom writes about Native Americans, the French-language writers of French, Spanish, and United States Louisiana show a consistent acceptance and sympathetic treatment of Amerindians. The Louisiana writers' favorable disposition toward indigenous groups predates the movement in Anglo-American literature from neoclassical Christian prejudice against what was viewed as aboriginal uncouthness and recalcitrance to romantic pity and nostalgia for disempowered and nearly extinct Native Americans.

Concern for the masses of all colors living under the dominance of the few—for their right to prosper economically, live relatively freely, and be spared abusive authority—also permeates the writings of Franco-Louisianians throughout the eighteenth century. This concern links poets such as Poydras and Viel, neoclassical rhymers who have the least in common with colonials who write about Amerindians and occurrences in the colony, to their fellow Louisianians.

During the golden age of Louisiana francophone literature before and after the U.S. Civil War, the concerns and interests set forth by the colonial writers of the preceding century continue to express themselves and even extend to other areas of life.

In part it was a common Gallo-Catholic background that contributed to the humanitarian spirit binding Louisiana writers together regardless of when or where they composed. But "Americanization" (or "Louisianization," to be more specific)—that is, the change in thinking, believing, and behaving brought about by accommodation of Continental lifestyles and attitudes to existence in the New World—also informed and thereby connected the naturalized authors and their writings to each other, to later Creole writers, and to New World literati in general. Such a shared Americanization is especially noticeable in the treatment of Amerindians (even though many persons of the New World, unlike the early Louisiana authors, proved to be decidedly antinative over the ages) and in the overall depiction of life in the Western Hemisphere. In fact, many of the writers openly state that they composed their works specifically to correct Continental misconceptions about the Americas—above all, unfavorable notions concerning indigenous peoples.

Undoubtedly, the necessity of people from all ranks of life in fledgling societies to depend upon each other and even upon members of other societies simply to survive also encouraged the Louisiana writers' more or less democratic spirit and tolerant outlooks, traits that even Viel, a Creole who chose to make the Continent his home, displays. These writers—most of whom envision a colony in which persons of all levels and colors may work together for individual and collective well-being, albeit the work and well-being matching each person's station in life—could appreciate, perhaps more than their peers on the Continent could, a society built upon the horizontalizing interdependence of its constituents.

Three themes are common in the writings of Louisiana's first authors: the development of the Saint Denis legend; the treatment of Amerindians and, later, the treatment of blacks; and the interest in universal welfare, which entails discussions of what is believed to be the proper relationship between those who rule and those who are ruled (i.e., between the monarchy and its representatives and the masses).

The third area links practically all of the writers of the first and later colonial periods. The second area, dealing with relations between people of different colors, figures in a great majority of the compositions as well, Viel's and Poydras's being major exceptions. The first area, the expansion of the Saint Denis myth, involves fewer but nonetheless a substantial number of writers. It is also more temporally confined, whereas concerns about color and ruler-ruled relations span the entire first French era, becoming more pronounced, of course, as colonial society becomes more defined. A discussion of the colony's very first writers (those of the late 1600s and early 1700s) may emphasize more than anything else a prefiguring of characteristics that become commonplace only as the eighteenth century progresses.

An observation of Edward Said in *Culture and Imperialism* applies wonderfully to Louisiana history as reflected in Louisiana colonial literature: "All cultures are involved in one another; none is single and pure, all are hybrid, heterogeneous, extraordinarily differentiated, and unmonolithic" (xxv). Said's remarks, which may be used to describe the overlaying of peoples and cultures in prestatehood Louisiana, may be applied as well to the country into which Louisiana was eventually subsumed, thanks as much to U.S. expansion into territories beyond the original thirteen colonies as to wave after wave of immigration to the United States from all parts of the world. As Said further notes, "The fact that the United States contains so many histories, many of them now clamoring for attention, is by no means to be suddenly feared since many of them were always there, and out of them an American society and politics . . . were in fact created" (xxvi). Just as U.S. academia should not fear to give attention to cultural contributions coming from without white, Anglo-Saxon, Protestant spheres, so it should also not hesitate to acknowledge and appreciate fully that groups and regions not originating in the Thirteen Colonies but presently making up part of the United States likewise have histories and developments separable from those of the Union. Furthermore, these persons and places possess legacies deserving of analyses that do not necessarily have to be linked to the study of the United States' evolution. The study of the literature from Louisiana's first colonial period must be placed within both the examination of Louisiana's contributions to the national fabric and the analysis of Louisiana's separate development.

The canon of Louisiana literature from the first French domination should include the works of the following writers. Henri de Tonti and Nicolas de La Salle, companions of Cavalier de La Salle at the very birth of the colony, record both French penetration into what would become Louisiana as well as initial extension of a French presence from the Great Lakes to the Gulf of Mexico through alliances with indigenous tribes. The missionary priests Mathurin Le Petit and Pierre Vitry offer views of the colony from an ecclesiastical perspective, as does Ursuline nun Marie-Madeleine Hachard, who also adds a female dimension to early Louisiana literature. Bernard Diron Dartaguiette and Jérémie Jadart de Beauchamp serve as fine examples of settlers who wrote in order to report on specific colonizing ventures rather than to make a mark in literature but whose accounts afford informative and entertaining reading nonetheless. Pénicaut, Le Page, Dumont, and Bossu may be considered the main writers of Louisiana's first French domination because of both the scope of their work and its consistent manifestation of the major characteristics of Louisiana-French colonial literature. With Bossu serving as a transition from French to Spanish rule, later authors such as Julien Poydras, Étienne Viel, Soniat du Fossat, and Leblanc de Villeneufve move from the preoccupations of the first writers (who were actively engaged in wresting a new civilization from a "new" world) to novel yet similar concerns as Louisiana became Spanish, French again, and then part of the United States. Along with the works of these authors, many other documents by colonial writers of lesser importance should be examined for a deeper appreciation of life during the first phases of Louisiana history.

Of the three themes most common to the literature of Louisiana's first colonial period, the discussion of Native Americans is the most pervasive. Jean-Bernard Bossu, writing as Louisiana passed from French to Spanish possession, manifests all three themes in his writings, but most noteworthy, perhaps, is that he consistently displays an emotional attachment to, a humanitarian concern for, and a scientific interest in Native Americans. As such, Bossu may be offered as a showcase author of 1700s Louisiana.

In many respects, Bossu should be examined as much with authors of Louisiana's second colonial period (the Spanish possession of 1763–1800) as with writers from the first French domination. After all, the first of Bossu's two books, *Nouveaux voyages aux Indes occidentales,* was not published before 1768, the year Louisiana was bucking Spanish attempts finally to begin governing the colony. However, in light of the fact that the book concerns Bossu's stays in Louisiana from 1751 to 1762 (and hence, the additional fact that its contents touch on many of the same events treated in texts of the first French domination), *Nouveaux voyages aux Indes occidentales* fits well alongside the literature from Louisiana's first colonial period. The same themes that figure in Bossu's first book continue in his second, *Nouveaux voyages dans l'Amérique septentrionale,* published in 1777 and relating the author's third stay in the colony in 1770–1771, right after Spain had forced Louisiana into submission and while the new rulers were enacting changes that would bring a well-being and prosperity to the territory that French governance could never provide.

By virtue of his dates in the colony both well before and well after the transfer from France to Spain, Bossu was able to leave a lasting record of Louisiana as a French and then a Spanish colony. Thus the writings of this one author provide a good transition from Louisiana literature of the first French domination to that of the Spanish regime. Like writers before and after the transfer, Bossu concentrates to a great extent on Franco-Amerindian relations and on the relationship between rulers and the ruled. In addition, Bossu, along with Le Page, devotes more attention than most of the first Louisiana authors do to an increasingly important aspect of life in the colony—black slavery.

Jean-Bernard Bossu (also known as Jean-Baptiste le Bossu and Nicholas Bossu) was born in Baigneux-les-Juifs, France, in 1720.[2] Coming from a prominent medical family of Burgundy, Bossu added a military career to his credentials, distinguishing himself in the Italian wars. In 1750 he was sent to reinforce the garrison at New Orleans. Arriving in Louisiana in 1751, he ventured up the Mississippi River to an assignment in the Illinois country. Along the way, he was "adopted" by the Arkansas Indians. Suffering from old war injuries, Bossu returned to New Orleans from upper Louisiana in early 1757. He sought treatment in France but was back in Louisiana in 1758.

Aboard ship during his second voyage to the colony, Bossu befriended Vincent-Gaspard-Pierre du Rochemore, Louisiana's newly appointed *commissaire ordonnateur.* When Rochemore and the colony's governor general, Baron Louis Billouart de Kerlérec, entered into a feud, Bossu sided with Rochemore. As a result, Bossu did not receive the expected command of the Illinois post when it became available. Bossu asked to return to France, but Kerlérec sent him to Mobile and to Fort Toulouse in the Alabama region instead. There he became friends with the Alabama Indians. In 1762 he accompanied the recalled Rochemore to France. Upon arriving in Europe, the two learned that Kerlérec had filed complaints against them. In 1769 the Rochemore-Kerlérec controversy was settled in favor of the late Rochemore.

Letters to the Marquis de l'Estrade de la Cousse concerning Bossu's first two travels and sojourns in the New World were published in 1768 as *Nouveaux voyages aux Indes occidentales; contenant une relation des différens peuples qui habitent les environs du grand fleuve Saint-Louis, appellé vulgairement le Mississippi; leur religion; leur gouvernement; leurs moeurs; leurs guerres et leur commerce.* Kerlérec's infuriation over several passages in the book resulted in Bossu's arrest for libel and imprisonment in the Bastille. After a month of investigation, Bossu was cleared and set free. The seals that had been put on his book were lifted.

Before Seymour Feiler's 1962 edition, titled *Jean-Bernard Bossu's Travels in the Interior of North America, 1751–1762,* another English translation of Bossu's first book appeared in London in 1771.

After Louisiana had changed from French to Spanish possession, Bossu made a third trip to the colony in 1770–1771 to attend to personal business and to visit the Arkansas Indians. A second book of letters, these addressed to Bossu's friend "M. Douin" and describing the third venture, appeared in 1777 as *Nouveaux voyages dans l'Amérique septentrionale, contenant une collection de lettres écrites sur les lieux, par l'auteur; à son ami, M. Douin.* Samuel Dorris Dickinson offered the first published English translation in 1982 as *New Travels in North America by Jean-Bernard Bossu, 1770–1771.*

Bossu died in France on May 4, 1792. Cumulatively, he spent twelve years in Louisiana during the two decades spanning 1751–1771. Although the combined length of his three separate stays in the colony falls short of the years spent by other émigré authors in Louisiana, Bossu's active participation in colonial development, his interest in red, white, and black inhabitants, his desire for societal reform, and his affectionate attachment to the New World tie him and his writings inextricably to Louisiana's colonial history and literature.

Feiler and Dickinson allude to a romanticization of Amerindians on Bossu's part, a treatment of indigenous Americans that connects Bossu to Rousseau and Bossu's Amerindians to the Noble Savage (Feiler x–xi; Dickinson x–xi). Such views notwithstanding, it could also be argued that in his desire for accurate depictions of native peoples, Bossu resembles Pénicaut and other Louisiana writers as much if not more than he does contemporary Continentals who had never been to the New World or seen a Native American. The achievement of some of the more realistic depictions in Bossu's books occurs through the author's presenting Amerindians as he believes they are, with "good" and "bad" qualities as judged by European norms, Native American standards, or the author's own values. Bossu, like Pénicaut and Le Page, points out the terrors and the beauties, the benefits and the drawbacks of life in the Native Americas. Further resembling the other Louisianians who write about Amerindians, Bossu makes distinctions between different indigenous groups and does not fail to criticize what he views as flaws in Amerindian individuals when he deems it necessary. In truth, Bossu's Native Americans are too complicated and too distinct from one another to fit easily into one stereotype.

Despite what Bossu concedes to be their harmonious communion with nature and insights deriving therefrom, most of Bossu's Amerindians are still plagued by ignorance and external dangers. Bossu notes that long before the arrival of Europeans, indigenous peoples had to deal with moral corruption within their own communities as well as constant harassment from neighboring tribes. To remedy these and other woes afflicting Native Americans, Bossu, again like Pénicaut and Le Page, suggests European scientific and religious correctives. More forcefully than even Pénicaut and Le Page do, Bossu proposes genuine conversion of both whites and nonwhites to Christianity as a means to reform society. Bossu firmly believes that the best of all possible futures for Amerindians lies in their embracing Catholicism and swearing allegiance to the king of France, the former affording a more enlightened code by which to live and the latter granting the protection and rights of a more powerful nation.

If Bossu's often favorable portrayals of Amerindians in their original state link his writings to the Noble Savage convention, the resemblance is due primarily to the fact that Bossu observed Native Americans displaying what could be judged by any culture to be very noble qualities indeed, even if manifested along with unsettling behavior. Of only secondary importance is the possibility that the likeness of Bossu's works to Noble Savage literature occurred as a result of Bossu's possibly wishing to associate his writings with those of authors influenced by or operating from the same milieux as Rousseau. If the thoughts and behavior of indigenous persons in Bossu's two books reflect novel intellectual considerations of later eighteenth-century Europe, the coincidence does not occur simply because some characterizations may have been contrived to correspond to the views of trendy writers and thinkers; rather (and more important), Bossu found and wished to share with his peers attitudes and actions preexisting in aboriginal American societies that validated the developing theories of European intelligentsia.

Although Bossu's writings indicate the preoccupations of scholarly Continentals of the late 1700s, their primary value may rest more in their depicting thoughts and actions of European subjects working in the colonial Americas. In presenting the colonies and their inhabitants as he finds them (thereby leaving valuable records of specific peoples at given times), Bossu comments on colonial life in ways that reveal insights gained not solely from French "enlightenment" but also from Americanization. That is, Bossu's knowledge of and compassion for Amerindians, Anglo-American patriots, black slaves, and French and Spanish colonists; his criticism of European conquest of the New World and trafficking in African captives; his interest in future development of the Western Hemisphere; and his insistence upon Continental adaptation to the New World and reformation of the Old result as much from travel and residence in Louisiana as from any other influence.

If, as Dickinson states, not all of the contents of Bossu's work were composed on the dates or at the spots the author claims, then as early as the first letters (dated 1751 but not published before 1768) Bossu may well have patterned/repatterned his writings after reading Rousseau's *Discours* (1750 and 1754) and becoming acquainted with his Noble Savage and social contract. In any event, French political, intellectual, and artistic ideas preceding, concurring with, and culminating in Rousseau's work are reflected in Bossu's writings. Although significant Continental influence is undeniable, Bossu, because of his formative New World experiences and his choice of New World subject matter, cannot be viewed as a typical eighteenth-century

French writer. The author was too profoundly shaped by residence in the New World not to be transformed into an American writer.

The foreword to Bossu's first book introduces Amerindians as primary focuses of the narrative. It states that Bossu spent twelve years traveling through Louisiana in hopes of allying Native Americans more closely to the French (Feiler 5). In the process Bossu's increased familiarity with native peoples resulted in a diminishing of certain personal prejudices that had been acquired in Europe as a result of hearsay and lack of contact with Amerindians. The foreword states early on that Bossu was "surprised to discover the oratorical talent and order which are evident in the speeches of these men whom we call savages" (ibid.). This and many other revelations of greater significance to the author fostered such a positive outlook on Amerindians that Bossu soon became one of their leading spokespersons both in practical matters and in literature.

Perhaps nowhere are Bossu's esteem for Native American oral artistry, his respect for indigenous persons, and his approval of Franco-aboriginal mixing on all levels more apparent than in the romantic anecdote involving Rutel-Attikaloubémingo in the Sixth Letter of the second book. In a footnote, Bossu explains that Rutel-Attikaloubémingo "was the son of an *Akanças* chief and the grandson of a lower Brittany sailor named Rutel who was lost in 1683 when La Salle came down the Mississippi making a reconnaissance of this famous river" (Dickinson 106). Bossu then reports on the Arkansas bard's amorous advance on a French girl:

> In 1756 when I was detailed for duty in the *Illinois* country an *Akanças* orator named *Rutel-Attikaloubémingo,* which means chief of the language that affects the heart, came in behalf of his nation *en calumet,* in other words, as ambassador, to M. de Macarty, French commandant of Fort de Chartres, to renew the alliance between our nation and the natives of that district. The Indian was young and handsome. As for his intellect, you never will have a doubt after the anecdote I am going to tell. He was welcomed at the post with all possible honors and M. de Macarty gave a brilliant ball in his honor at which *Rutel-Attikaloubémingo* was the king, because they had him open it with Mademoiselle Manon Robert, a young lady fourteen years old, daughter of one of the richest French settlers among the Illinois, with whom he fell madly in love at first sight. The American ambassador made a very graceful bow to her and embraced her with his eyes (he copied the French). He would not leave her for a moment during the ball that lasted all night. She was seated close to him at the most stylish cold collation. The

> assembly was infinitely amused by the native and passionate manner with which he confessed to her (with interpreter's help) how he felt toward her.
>
> Finally, in an ecstatic mood, he tried to persuade Mlle. Manon to remove a light scarf which covered her bosom. The belle blushed; he insisted. He said not a word in reply to the expostulations that each country has its customs, and that it would be the vilest impropriety for a French woman to expose her bosom, although it was very natural for an *Akanças* lady to do so. He lowered his head and remained in deep thought for about a quarter of an hour. Then, after having collected his thoughts, he rose and with a noble and sensitive demeanor, he gave the little speech which he had just planned. I was so struck with the novelty of the Indian's ideas that I took my notebook and rapidly wrote the poor prose that the Indian interpreter gave us in very bad French, and I tried as much as possible to preserve the form and especially the spirit of the original. (106–7)

Bossu then offers his "translation of the delightful Elegy of the Indian Envoy *Rute1-Attikaloubémingo.*"

Several aspects of Bossu's portrayal of an Amerindian man's pursuit of a white girl in this episode are worth noting. First of all, Bossu speaks only favorably of the Franco-Amerindian male's appearance, intelligence, and creativity, almost offering these qualities as the logical outcome of Franco-aboriginal union. Furthermore, it hardly matters to Bossu and the other white personages in this account that the Arkansas ambassador-bard is culturally more Native American than he is Euro-Amerindian. Accepted as he is, Rutel-Attikaloubémingo is honored and allowed into intimate circles of French society in upper Louisiana. Neither Mademoiselle Manon, her French company, nor Bossu considers it wrong that Rutel-Attikaloubémingo makes advances on the white-female object of his desires. Even when the Arkansas Indian oversteps French boundaries of propriety, he is not chased away or chastised. Rather, the French allow him to deliver (and Bossu rushes to record) an impassioned, poetic plea for the juvenile Mademoiselle Manon to bare her breasts. The happy, tolerant encounter between French people and Amerindians—replete with overt sexuality—in the Rutel-Attikaloubémingo account is one of the best idealized representations of the peaceful, accepting interactions that Bossu, along with other Louisiana writers, wishes to be commonplace between Euro- and Native Americans. Bossu and his peers believe, after all, that such interactions would lead to the forging of the truly Euro-Amerindian societies that the authors would like to see populating the Americas. However, although Rutel-Attikaloubémingo (who may be viewed as standing for all Native Americans in this story) is appreciated for what he is, he is held in check by Euro-Americans, who, Bossu and the other Louisiana writers ultimately uphold, must govern and enlighten, but with leniency and understanding.

In addition to recording what Bossu views as Amerindian creativity and other strengths, what he would like to believe are preexisting favorable French attitudes toward Native Americans, and what he proposes as a model for Euro-Americans' and indigenous peoples' coming together, Bossu's tale has further importance in its rendition of Rutel-Attikaloubémingo's verse. The fact that Bossu perfected this and another poetic translation of Indian oratory before his second book's 1777 publication causes Julien Poydras to share the distinction of being one of Louisiana's earliest poets with yet another author who composed verse earlier than Poydras penned his. Bossu dates the Sixth Letter "In the *Akanças* country, April 1, 1771." Although Bossu may have finished his poem then, he did not publish it before 1777, the year Poydras's first two poems also went to press. Here it must be remembered that Dumont de Montigny (now being considered a Louisiana poet) created his lengthy *Poème en vers, touchant l'établissment de la province de la Louisiane* long before Bossu and Poydras composed their verse, starting the text in 1728 in Louisiana and completing it in 1742 in France, where it was published, but not before Poydras's and Bossu's works. Likewise, Viel produced his verse play *Evandre* in 1769 in France, but it did not attain publication before 1991. Whereas Viel's poetical drama was printed posthumously in Louisiana (his other works having been published in France while he was still alive), Poydras published in Louisiana in his lifetime. Thus although Poydras may no longer be called Louisiana's first poet, first littérateur, or even first published author, he is still the first belletrist to publish *in Louisiana*.

Bossu's "translation of the delightful Elegy of the Indian Envoy Rutel-*Attikaloubémingo*" (taken from Dickinson's publication) reads:

À MANON

Pourquoi, jeune MANON, tenir emprisonné
Avec tant de rigueur ce blanc sein nouveau né;
Que nul mortel n'a vu, dont nulle main encore
N'a su cueillir la fleur, qui ne vient que d'éclore?
Quelle barbare loi te force à resserrer
Ces jolis prisonniers? Laisses-les respirer.
Tendres êtres, hélas! innocentes victimes,

Pourquoi vous étouffer? quels furent donc vos crimes?
Usez de tous vos droits; laissez à l'avenir,
Si vous en abusez, le soin de vous punir
Jeunes infortunés! Lorsque MANON respire,
Voyez leurs mouvemens, que le dépit inspire,
Le peu que j'entrevois de leur joli contour
Fait naître dans mon coeur le désir & l'amour.
Que j'ai peine à le voir, ce sein que j'idolâtre,
Lancer contre un mouchoir ses deux globes d'albâtre!
Telqu'un tendre chevreau, jeune, vif & charmant,
Ils voudroient lutiner & bondir librement.
Exempts de préjugés, ils redoutent la gêne;
Les captiver ainsi, c'est être une inhumaine.
A peine sont-ils nés, vous pensez bien, MANON,
Que, plus jeunes que vous, ils ont moins de raison.
De l'austère vertu ils ignorent l'usage.
Et vous-même étiez-vous plus prudente à leur âge?
On n'emmaillote point les enfans au berceau;
Ce qui n'est pas gêne n'en devient que plus beau:
Mais si tu crains, MANON, de troubler la cervelle
De quiconque verra cette gorge si belle,
Si, pour de tes amans prévenir les malheurs,
Tu veux punir leur vue en épargnant leurs coeurs,
Voile donc tes beaux yeux, voile donc cette bouche
Dont l'éclat nous enflamme & dont le son nous touche;
Et, certaine des coups qui portent tes attraits,
Aux regards des mortels ne te montre jamais. (107)

Dickinson translates Bossu's rendition of Rutel-Attikaloubémingo's poem:

TO MANON

Why, young MANON, do you keep imprisoned
With so much sternness, this new-born white breast
Which no mortal has seen, of which no hand as yet
Has plucked the blossom, that only has just bloomed?
What barbarous law forces you to keep
These pretty ones prisoners? Let them breathe,
Tender creatures, alas! Innocent victims,
Why should you smother? What were your crimes then?

Exercise all your rights; leave to the future
If you are led astray thereafter, concern for punishing yourselves,
Young unfortunates! When MANON breathes
See their movement that vexation inspires.
The little that I glimpsed of their pretty contour
Gives birth in my heart to desire and love.
How I grieve to see it, this bosom that I adore,
Thrusting against a scarf two globes of alabaster!
Like a tender doe, young, lively and charming,
They would like to tease and caper freely,
Free from prejudices, they dread constraint;
To enslave them in this manner is to be inhuman;
They are hardly born, you are right, MANON,
That, younger than you, they have less judgment,
They are not aware of the custom of austere virtue.
And were you yourself more discreet at their age?
Babies are not swathed in the cradle;
What is not fettered only becomes more beautiful;
But if you fear, MANON, to disturb the mind
Of whoever will see such a beautiful breast,
If, to forestall unhappiness for your lovers,
You wish to punish their sight by sparing their hearts,
Then cover your beautiful eyes, cover this mouth
Whose luster sets us on fire and whose sound moves us;
And certain that your charms deal blows,
Never show yourself to the eyes of mortals.

I end my letter here, and am, etc.,

(In the *Akanças* country, April 1, 1771, 108)

As evinced in Bossu's and other Louisiana writers' treatments of Amerindians, Louisiana-French attitudes toward indigenous peoples corresponded in many ways to Anglo-American and Hispano-American alternatives to the much-studied and much-criticized approaches of Puritans and conquistadores. Just as the Louisiana literary consensus concerning Franco-Amerindian relations derived from Catholic and French humanitarian sentiments and led authors at times to counter official policies of the military and the state, so the opposing views within British and Spanish American political structures and literatures often came from religious writers.

Bartolome de Las Casas and Thomas Morton in particular are often highlighted as two of many voices at variance with the views dominating the governments and the writings of the Anglo- and Ibero-Americas.

Las Casas, a fifteenth- and sixteenth-century Americanized Spaniard who combined his priestly and literary vocations when speaking out against abuses of enslaved indigenous peoples in the Spanish colonies, not only forced Spaniards to look at the dark side of their New World enterprises but also provided the impetus for the Black Legend, a medium through which Spanish activity was condemned in various literatures.

Tzvetan Todorov's summation of Las Casas's approach to Native Americans also applies to the stance of Louisiana writers vis-à-vis Amerindians: "Submission and colonization must be maintained, but conducted differently; it is not only the Indians who stand to gain (by not being tortured and exterminated) but also the king and [the mother country]." Thus "the ideology assumed by Las Casas and by other defenders of the Indians is certainly a colonialist one" (171, 173).

Las Casas's and the Louisiana writers' views reflect Euro-American debates on the nature of Native Americans that not only place the writers at variance with others involved in the colonizing process but also cause the authors to explore, confront, and contradict personal attitudes concerning indigenous peoples. What Todorov observes in the evolution of Spanish considerations of New World peoples also fits the development of French concepts regarding Amerindians:

> From its first formulation [the] doctrine of [nonwhite] inequality will be opposed by another, which affirms the equality of all men; hence we are listening to a debate, and we must pay attention to the two voices in contention. Now, this debate does not only oppose equality to inequality, but also identity to difference; and this new opposition, whose terms are no more ethically neutral than those of the preceding one, makes it more difficult to bring a judgment to bear on either position. . . . Difference is corrupted into inequality, equality into identity. These are the two great figures of the relation to the other that delimit the other's inevitable space. (146)

The internal debates involving concepts of "the other" as delineated by Todorov explain perhaps better than anything else the self-contradicting statements that even the best and most favorably inclined of Louisiana's authors make when treating Native Americans in their writings.

Thomas Morton, the notoriously Indianized sixteenth- and seventeenth-century Englishman of Merrymount fame, offered an alternative approach to colonizing and interacting with Native Americans that so offended the Puritan establishment that he could not be tolerated by New England church and state. Although his views earned him the opprobrium of his peers, Morton's comparing what he viewed as Amerindian virtues to what he considered Continental vices and his advocating the mixing of Native American and Euro-American groups on all levels have many counterparts in the colonial Louisiana literary canon. In fact, Morton's channeling of opposing views into derogatory yet entertaining fiction finds a fitting complement in Dumont's scathing poem, both works remaining ripe to this day for an analysis of the angry colonial artist at odds with his or her colony's administration.

Although Anglo- and Hispano-American literatures feature some positive alternatives to negative attitudes toward indigenous peoples that culminate in the pale and the requerimiento, possibly no American colonial literature manifests as total and positive a consensus toward Native Americans as does the canon of writings from Louisiana's first French domination. The favorable views of Louisianians with regard to Amerindians was born in great part of necessity between the 1680s and the 1760s. Because they were stretched thin over vast geographical expanses and poorly supported by France, the French, Canadian, and later Creole residents of Louisiana needed Native American involvement in their colonial enterprises perhaps more than any other Euro-Americans did. Nevertheless, the reasons for cooperation on the part of both Amerindians and colonists, for the sharing of cultures on such a large scale and at so many levels, and for the ultimate advocation of Franco-aboriginal fusion in the establishment of a new civilization do not lie simply in French need. Other factors contributing to the type of acceptance and interest that would manifest themselves in Franco-Amerindian undertakings of all sorts and in the crafting of tales such as that of Rutel-Attikaloubémingo are sure to be gleaned through renewed and intense examination of Louisiana texts written during French rule.

What became of the Franco-Amerindian Louisiana highlighted by many colonial writers, a prosperous mixed society that seemed to be resulting from the situations mentioned above? The neglect of the much-touted Euro-aboriginal communities of Illinois during the Company of the West (1717–1731) and Company of the Indies (1718–1731) years, the continued "official" discouragement of miscegenation, and the arrival of European men and women whose tastes watered down Euro-Americans' openness to union with natives weakened the upper Louisiana establishments that were to many writers the models of the colony's future. When France ceded western Louisiana to Spain in late 1762 and eastern Louisiana to England in early 1763, the area that would retain the name given by La Salle to the southern half of New France (hispanicized as Luisiana) would not include most of the regions (Arkansas being a major exception) that authors had been fond of highlighting for possessing prosperous hybridized societies. Even before France's relinquishment, the portion that would become Spanish Luisiana had received the shift in importance and population from Illinois, Biloxi, and Mobile, where many acculturated Amerindian communities had settled in the first years but which would no longer be part of Louisiana. The Amerindian population, both slave and free, of New Orleans, which had become the colony's major city after its 1718 founding, dwindled following the 1729 Natchez Massacre. The colonists' ensuing paranoia and mistrust of nonwhites in the wake of the Natchez uprising (which Louisiana writers blamed on French leaders) resulted in not only the extermination of at least one small and innocent tribe near New Orleans but also the breakdown of other longstanding Franco-Amerindian bonds in lower Louisiana.

In addition to all of these factors, the same sad story repeated throughout the Americas—one of decimation by European disease and removal through wave after wave of encroachment by outsiders—dealt additional blows to vestigial Franco-Amerindian Louisiana. However, the neglect of once prosperous centers of cultural mixing and the growing lack of appreciation for Native Americans did not totally eliminate the process of transculturation begun when the very first Europeans (Spaniards in the 1500s) entered what would become Louisiana. Groups such as the United Houma Nation, denied federal recognition as a Native American tribe in part because of its French heritage but nonetheless discriminated against for generations because of its indigenous origins, preserve centuries-old practices of cross-cultural mixing and borrowing that were pushed from the forefront of Louisiana society and literature to the backwaters because of the prejudices and ignorance of increasingly racist and intolerant powers that came to control what has evolved into the state of Louisiana.

In ways that have yet to be fully acknowledged, Americans of all countries of the New World are what they are today in part because of the indigenous persons who inhabited their sections of the globe. In the writings from Louisiana's first French domination, at least, there is an awareness and appreciation of this fact.

Auguste Viatte asserts that the literatures of the French-speaking world outside of France began with history narratives *(Histoire comparée* 18; *Histoire littéraire* 509). Looking at the beginnings of Louisiana francophone literature alone, one may judge the truth of Viatte's assertion, shared by many scholars. From Tonti's and Nicolas de La Salle's travelogues to those of Bossu, the bulk of the literature from Louisiana's first colonial period consists of "relations"—historical and travel journals, diaries, and letters relating to military campaigns, to exploratory/speculative expeditions and peace/war negotiations with Native Americans, and to past, present, and projected progressions of colonial activity. Sprinkled throughout are anecdotes and other artistic passages featuring unique and often strange episodes from colonial life.

In practically all of these narratives from Louisiana's first colonial experience Amerindians figure prominently, an attestation to the importance of Native Americans in Louisiana society, an importance deriving in large part from French need of indigenous cooperation in the colonial enterprise. So vital were Amerindians to French colonialism (and, increasingly, vice versa) that an entire mythology grew out of the symbiotic relationship. Journals, histories, travelogues, diaries, letters, and occasional poetry consistently expound the benefits of such a mythologized symbiosis. The myth, permeating a century of Louisiana writings, holds that French and native peoples are good for each other, that under French king and French law and united by French religion the two are able to work for the improvement of each other and develop a society that is not Europe or Native America but something sprung of both. For the birth of the new civilization to happen, whatever "barbarity" exists in Amerindian beliefs and practices must be modified through the embracing of Christianity. Blinded by their idealism and even aware at times of the hegemony inherent in their agendas, Louisiana writers gloss over the reality that French penetration and subsequent control of the Native Americas ultimately means the complete subjugation of Amerindians' prerogatives to those of European newcomers.

As a final word, it must be noted that Jean Morisset's observations of North America's Gallic diaspora reflect in part the situation of Franco-Louisiana, which from its inception to the present has been a collection of marginal societies into a fragile yet viable and recognizable general entity. Morisset states that

> throughout the French colonial period there was always a multitude of Americas that, largely unconsciously, overlapped: Native America, French America, Black (Slave) America, and a fourth America, dominant but ambivalent and vague, born of the first three. We of the fourth America were called then, and we continue to be called today, French, but we know only too well that we are not and have never been French, nor indeed French

> Americans, but something very different: mixed-race people without a clear name and, by virtue of that, bearers of a multitude of names. In other words, we are an anonymous America that has given its soul to the entire continent. (339)

Although Louisiana-French writings testify to the fact that in many respects "our" America has given its soul to an entire continent, Louisiana-French Americans and their literature can hardly be said to be part of an "anonymous America." From the earliest days of the colony to the present, French-speaking people living in Louisiana (be they of Continental, Canadian, Caribbean, African, or Native American origins) have been associated by outsiders and by themselves with a separate, clearly identifiable "other" America—Louisiana, a hybridized collection of societies within a specific geographic location and with a particular political status, linked to and incorporating persons and practices from other Americas and other continents, but always transforming these elements by a unique legacy begun in its French colonial past. Still distinguishable today from the other forty-nine states by its laws, customs, and inhabitants, still maintaining special cultural and educational ties with the French-speaking world that the other forty-nine states do not, the multicultural collection of people in Louisiana has been and remains different above all because of its Gallic roots. This difference, evident today in the daily way of living, thinking, and governing of several million people on the northern coast of the Gulf of Mexico and projected to national and international attention by unusual self-expression through music, cuisine, seasonal ritual, and politics, was discernible even in the founding years of the colony, when Europeans, Canadians, Native Americans, and Africans quickly began establishing a new homeland by combining varying world views and everyday experiences on the same ground, under French rule. The literature that coincides with the birth, growth, transfer, and transformation of that hybrid society attests to an individuality born of cultural conglomeration under French orchestration. Whether expressed today in English or in French, Louisiana literature, like much of contemporary Louisiana life, owes its uniqueness to the fusion of cultures that was allowed, needed, hoped for, and enjoyed by the state's first French-governed residents.

NOTES

1. As noted in *Louisiana: A History,* "Denis Braud became the colony's first printer in 1764. *Le Moniteur de la Louisiane* became New Orleans' first newspaper in 1794" (O'Neill et al. 82).

2. The biographical information on Bossu comes from Feiler's and Dickinson's introductions to their translations of Bossu's two books.

WORKS CITED

Allain, Mathé, and Barry Ancelet. *Anthologie: Littérature française de la Louisiane.* Bedford, N.H.: National Materials Development Center for French, 1981.

Caulfield, Ruby Van Allen. *The French Literature of Louisiana.* New York: Institute of French Studies, Columbia University, 1929.

Dickinson, Samuel Dorris, ed. and trans. *New Travels in North America by Jean-Bernard Bossu, 1770–1771.* Natchitoches, La.: Northwestern State University Press, 1982.

Feiler, Seymour, ed. and trans. *Jean-Bernard Bossu's Travels in the Interior of North America, 1751–1762.* Norman: University of Oklahoma Press, 1962.

Fortier, Alcée. *Louisiana Studies.* New Orleans, 1894.

McWilliams, Richebourg Gaillard, ed. and trans. *Fleur de Lys and Calumet: Being the Pénicaut Narrative of French Adventure in Louisiana.* Baton Rouge: Louisiana State University Press, 1953.

———. "Pénicaut as Alabama's First Literary Figure." *Alabama Review* 5 (1952): 40–60.

Morisset, Jean. "An America that Knows No Name: Postscript to a Quincentenary Celebration." *French America: Mobility, Identity, and Minority Experience across the Continent.* Ed. Dean R. Louder and Eric Waddell. Baton Rouge: Louisiana State University Press, 1993. 337–47.

O'Neill, Charles Edwards, et al. *Louisiana: A History.* Ed. Bennet H. Wall. Arlington Heights, Ill.: Forum Press, Inc., 1984.

Joe Gray Taylor, William Ivy Hair, Mark T. Carleton, Michael L. Kurtz. *Louisiana: A History.* Ed. Bennet H. Wall. Arlington Heights, Ill.: Forum, 1984.

Said, Edward W. *Culture and Imperialism.* New York: Vintage, 1994.

Tinker, Edward Larocque. *Les écrits de langue française en Louisiane au XIXe siècle.* Paris: Librairie ancienne Honoré Champion, 1932.

Todorov, Tzvetan. *The Conquest of America: The Question of the Other.* Trans. Richard Howard. New York: Harper and Row, 1984.

Viatte, Auguste. *Anthologie littéraire de l'Amérique francophone.* Sherbrooke, Québec: CELEF, 1971.

———. *Histoire comparée des littératures francophones.* Poitiers, France: Nathan-Université, 1980.

———. *Histoire littéraire de l'Amérique française.* Paris: Presses universitaires de France, 1954.

Louisiana—the New Egypt

Charles Sealsfield's Report from the 1820s

ALEXANDER RITTER

I

On May 10, 1823, thirty-year-old Karl Postl (1793–1864), a Catholic priest and secretary of the Prague order Kreuzherren mit dem Roten Sterne (Masters of the Cross with the Red Star)[1] was on an official administrative tour near the health resort of Karlsbad. Postl suddenly decided not to return to his cloister and embarked for the New World, winding up in Louisiana, with a new career as a novelist, using a new "British" name: Charles Sealsfield.[2]

The beginning of his career as a writer of novels is marked by the travelogue *Die Vereinigten Staaten von Nordamerika nach ihrem politischen, religiösen und gesellschaftlichen Verhältnisse betrachtet . . .* (*The United States as They Are by Their Political, Religious, and Social Conditions . . .*). Published in 1827 by Cotta in Stuttgart, it is one of the earliest descriptions of the United States. Karl Postl/Charles Sealsfield, now pretending to be an American, attempted to follow what he hoped would be a sophisticated strategy of self-assertion. This meant that he had to confront his own cultural heritage, which became the starting point for his perception of America. Consequently, Sealsfield found himself in a situation of a doubled search for identification; his own, and the national one—the identity of America. Combining both searches, he followed the already established tradition in American thought that the nation's birth was a monoethnic construct, a predestined development occurring in the world's ideal society in time (history) and space (global geographical destiny). This search was directed ideologically by the principles of the Declaration of Independence, the first election of a president in 1789, and the subsequent operation of a "sophisticated machinery of identification" (Lubbers 84) of the national character.

These factors, which center on Sealsfield's possibilities and limitations as he experienced the New World, influenced the book's quality of information. Together with his desire for publicity, literary success, and economic profit, they directed the literary transformation he made of the "travelogue," a genre positioned between the documentary and the fictional. Sealsfield's report was by conception, content, and ideology a significant presentation of the United States at that time, one made impressive by the breadth and ambition of its two volumes. Properly considered, the book constitutes a landmark in America's continuous search for identity.

II

The radical changes in the author's curriculum vitae must be considered to understand the way the book developed. Three basic conditions are important.

First, there is the biographical dimension. When Postl disappeared in May 1823 the case of a vanished priest, friar, and order secretary was a sensational event, annoying and embarrassing for the Austrian orthodox Catholic and restorative political administration (Lorenz 92–95).

Second, his emigration became a journey of no return, so he chose to change his passport identity and become an American citizen. That meant ignoring and hiding his family background, forgetting his home and his friends; it meant defying the order in Prague, violating his vows as a priest, and in every way wiping out his Austrian-Moravian background and living under cover until his death in 1864. Because of this psychic drama, he continually felt forced to stabilize his new existence by seeking official documents of identity. This culminated in his attaining American citizenship in 1858, but also in his relentless determination to behave consequently as an "American citizen."[3] But in his mind there remained the heritage of social and mental education in his home country, one loaded with the tension of contrasts and implicated conflicts: the orthodox Catholic education he received from his peasant background, his theological studies, and the pressures of his religious order and his priest's vows versus the philosophical, theological, and political enlightenment of his university teacher Bernhard Bolzano's (1781–1848) lessons in theology and philosophy.[4]

Having traveled throughout the United States during his stays in 1823–1826, 1827–1830, 1837, and 1853–1858, he had gathered a sound knowledge of the country, especially of the South, which led to his decision to make Louisiana his home state. He lived in New Orleans during wintertime, presumably as a plantation owner and slaveholder,[5] and from the state's landscapes, its aristocratic "King Cotton"society, and the southern ideology of an agricultural organization of social and political life he drew the material for his travelogue and most of his novels.

After arriving in New Orleans he went to Pennsylvania, which had many German-speaking inhabitants. Here he learned English and adopted the name Charles Sealsfield and the pseudonyms "C." or "H. Sidons." When he asked on his way back to Europe 1826 at the State Administration of Louisiana for a safe conduct passport, he stated a false year of birth—he was thirty-three years old, not twenty-something. His alleged trustworthiness was no doubt assured by a Pennsylvania paper that had referred to him as "Charles Sealsfield, Clergyman, native of Pennsylvania." The Louisiana document acknowledges him, though provisionally, as an inhabitant of Louisiana, traveling under protection of the United States.[6] From now on he introduced himself as "Charles Sealsfield from the U.S. Louisiana," as we know from publisher contracts, even though he had not been naturalized. He used this document until 1837, when he got a new one, which he exchanged in connection with a grant of American citizenship in 1858, proved "By the Court" of the "State of New York, City & County of New York." Looking at Postl/Sealsfield's successful search for change of identity, his relationship with Louisiana is crucial on both the official and the psychological level; Louisiana provided a home for a harassed loner.

The third dimension is Sealsfield's stunning achievement of establishing himself as an American freelance writer in the United States and Europe, something he managed to do in the span of only a few years. We hardly know anything about the people he dealt with and the specific places he stayed in the state. Nevertheless, his frequent presence in Louisiana caused him to learn and accept southern ideology as part of his philosophy of life and society; he passed it on to European readers, for in his publications he presented the American South as a model of future society, one in contrast to the monarchies in the Old World. It is significant that in his autobiography Sealsfield separated his way of life into a practically unknown private sphere bound to Louisiana and into a public one conducted in the northern business region, with its speedy industrialization, journals, and publishers.

In 1829, Sealsfield sent a remarkable letter (one of the very few he wrote in English) to the famous German publisher Heinrich Brockhaus (1804–1874; Castle II, 149–51). This letter demonstrates his self-conscious pose as a pretended U.S. citizen; nothing is left from Sealsfield's former life. In the full version of the letter, he hides his original identity by mobilizing several credible circumstances: the employment of the English language; the use of both his new names, the supposed original and the pseudonym; and the emphasis on his comprehensive knowledge of Americans and their political affairs, including his admiration for Andrew Jackson and his anti-British attitude. Other passages suggest cooperation with a New York publisher and a pretended successful publication of a book dealing with the United States in German and English. Further, he hides his home, which is very likely located in a southern area of wealth und political power,[7] the region of the "cotton-nabobs," on the banks of the Mississippi between Natchez, Baton Rouge, and New Orleans. Other aspects of his strategy here are his inference of his smart dealing with business interests and the promotion of his career as an author; he mentions the famous European publishers Cotta (Stuttgart) and Murray (London) to convince Brockhaus of his importance as a writer, neglecting to mention the economical failure of both projects and his cooperation with the publisher Carey, Lea and Carey in Philadelphia.[8] He follows this with the commercial proposal of an up-to-date project in connection with rising numbers of emigrants from Europe and the specific publisher's program (travel guides), aided by a professionally detailed offer for the publisher's calculation. Finally, one notices the coaxing and calculated way he addresses the publisher in order to win his sympathy.

Bearing in mind Sealsfield's personality and his position concerning the political and literary conditions of his time, we should consider how he integrated this ideology of American identity into the mythological tradition of the Golden Age, thereby configuring a triadic understanding of mankind's progress in the sense of a rediscovered idea of modern utopia.[9] Indeed, this philosophical position of historical development must have converged with the theological perspective remembered by the former priest Postl, as he developed the metaphor of a visionary "Louisiana—Egypt of North America" (Castle 1955, 183).

On the biographical level the pretended American constructed an identity as a southern planter, one radically different from his actual heritage as an educated citizen of the Austrian Empire, a priest, and member of a strict religious order. On the educational level we have an anticlerical, learned, bilingual person, highly informed about the present and historical development of both the Americas and Europe versus the man who had received an orthodox clerical education as a priest. On the business level there is the pragmatic freelance writer taking advantage of the industrialization in the American North, both as wealthy shareholder and as writer for the northern publishing houses, as well as for those in Europe; this role is opposed to his overall philosophical condemnation of industrialization and European absolutism. On the level of literary history we find an open-minded writer who developed from a journalist and travelogue author into a novelist who would eventually use and combine the poetic concepts of the southern plantation novel (William Gilmore Simms, John Pendleton Kennedy), American romanticism (Henry Wadsworth Longfellow, James Fenimore Cooper), the British Gothic and historical novel (Walter Scott), German romanticism, early realism, and the political-didactic poetics of Young Germany writers while rejecting the stylistical and ideological hermetic requirements of the Catholic Church and its rhetorical tradition. On the level of history and state-philosophy, Sealsfield is an ideological writer who connects aspects of the late Austrian enlightenment ("Josephinismus") with the ideas of an early European liberalism in the prerevolutionary phase between 1815 and 1848 ("Restoration"and "Biedermeier" versus Young Germany [1820–1850] and the radical liberal "Vormärz" [pre–March 1830–1848]). He also accepts the Manifest Destiny idea, coupled with the romanticized agricultural concept of southern aristocratic-democratic society, a vision based on the ideas of Crèvecoeur, Jefferson, and Jackson. By contrast, Sealsfield rejected the European restorative monarchism and the rising specter of an industrialized society of the American "Yankee"states.

For Sealsfield, Louisiana's geographical and political reality became the metaphoric projection of a New World, but in the doubled sense of its pragmatic and philosophical meanings. The author's point of view is tied to his time; originally labeled the Era of Good Feeling, it had become a time of flux, rapidly changing already into an era of bad feeling, because, as Gretlund puts it, the "outlines of the solid South were clearly visible; the southern states were united in defense of states' rights, Christian orthodoxy, and the institution of slavery," turning "inward in consideration of its own society" and leading to "a state of changelessness," ignoring "the fact that the rest of the nation was changing fast" (121–22). The congruent vectors of regionalism, nationalism, and southern recalcitrance had created a political situation quite similar to that of Europe; the different constitutional circumstances in the United States and Europe consequently have much to do with Sealsfield's understanding of politics and history.

III

When Sealsfield left the United States in 1827 for Europe, he decided to become a traveling author whose publications and appearances would publicly instruct; he would be a kind of political missionary, shuttling between two continents and fulfilling his self-made mission of furthering the enlightenment in the New World.

As a writer he developed a threefold career during his stay: (1) as correspondent, serving periodically different papers in the United States, Great Britain, and Germany between 1827 and 1830 (Castle 1955, 290); (2) as travelogue author; and (3) preparing his career as a novelist. He had two travelogue manuscripts in his luggage. One dealt with the actual situation in the United States, the other with that in the Austrian Empire. The first one was written in favor of the young transatlantic republic and pleads for democracy; as such, it constitutes a virtual confession of Sealsfield's deepest yearnings. The second one is a fictitious travelogue set in Austria, a pamphletlike lampoon criticizing the empire and the monarchy in general, which constitutes a type of personal yet public revenge.[10] Both manuscripts are programmatic documents for his dialectical view of an antiabsolutist, proliberal society. He placed the American travelogue with firms in Germany and Great Britain and the Austrian piece in Great Britain; both essays were published in 1827.

The prospects in middle Europe for publication of a travelogue dealing with America were ambivalent in those days. There was a general but limited interest in the development of the United States because the political and mental consequences of the 1815 Congress of Vienna (Restoration) led to an attitude of abstinence in public affairs and to a retreat into a private sphere, a period leading up to 1848 called Biedermeier. America was thereby reduced to a literary metaphor, one signifying an exotic, far-off region for basic human longings and an escape from the insufficient conditions of present life. On the other hand, liberal intellectuals calling themselves Junges Deutschland (Young Germany) accepted the United States as a historical metaphor for their own political activities, which sought liberalization of society.[11] Press managers and publishers asked for eyewitness accounts; at the same time, however, they mistrusted even these reports because only a few publishers had actually seen the United States themselves, so control of accuracy was nearly impossible. Still, the beginning of mass migration generated a need for travel and migration guides, but this need was not yet intensive enough to merit the printing of large editions. So Sealsfield, employing the Sidons pseudonym, published his travelogue *The United States of North America Looked at for Their Political, Religious, and Social Relations. Together with a Journey Through the Western Part of Pennsylvania, Ohio, Kentucky, Indiana, Illinois, Missouri, Tennessee, the Territory of Arkansas, Mississippi and Louisiana. By C. Sidons, Citizen of the United States of North America. In two Volumes. Stuttgart and Tübingen, printed by J. G. Cotta's bookstore. 1827* with a minimal chance of economic success.[12]

While Sealsfield went to Great Britain to find a publisher for the English translation, Johann Friedrich von Cotta, his careful German publisher, printed 750 copies but sold less then 400. After rather lukewarm, if not negative, reviews, and following Sealsfield's failure to send him promised information for newspapers, Cotta canceled the contract.

Meanwhile, in London, Sealsfield succeeded in persuading John Murray to publish an English translation in 1827. Murray, as careful as Cotta, printed only the first volume in 750 copies; he soon realized the political and economic risk bound to the pro-Jackson and anti-British tendency of the book and passed 588 copies on to the publisher and retail bookseller W. Simpkin and R. Marshall, who had sold only 162 copies by 1834. In 1828, 502 had already been turned to waste paper. Since Murray and Simpkin showed no further interest in the second volume, Hurst, Chance and Company, which printed Sealsfield's Austrian travelogue (*Austria as it is*) in 1828, published the second volume of *United States of North America* in the same year, very likely with a similar poor result. Although most writers would view such a situation with the three publishers a disaster, Sealsfield was unconcerned. He earned very little, but his name won publicity among German and British intellectuals, as well as with French and Dutch readers, because of unauthorized translations done in 1828. So in future literary transactions he could point to his international reputation as well as to his dealings with two of the most renowned publishers in Europe.

Sealsfield's first publication dealing with the United States is a sort of travel report, combining geographical information of social, political, and economical conditions with chronologically organized impressions of an eager traveler. The prose was complemented by sketches depicting special events. The entire work, moreover, was written from a specific political viewpoint.[13] The first volume presents the informative report and the second the travel report. In the introduction, signed "30th October 1826. Sidons" (Castle 1952, viii), Sealsfield provides information on how to understand the message of the book. First of all he asserts its veracity, claiming it is written by a "citizen of the United States," one who was an eyewitness without pursuing a "systematical scholarly conception" (Castle 1952, vii). His intention is to pass on a "distinctly written lesson" that will enable the "European reader" and the "immigrants of all classes . . . to judge the status of the U.S., not looking at phantoms but at reality."

He details the fiftieth jubilee of July 4, 1826, which "saw the exorbitant performance when more then eleven million of free citizens between Boston and

Pensacola, Detroit and New Orleans, Washington and St. Louis celebrated the big ceremony . . . of mankind's victory over tyranny, superstition, and prejudice." On the other hand, we have the "declaration by President Monroe" in 1824. Both events demonstrate that "the United States have . . . proved that man is able to live free and nevertheless in social and legal conditions" in the "the most free and independent nation" (1952, iii–iv). These passages show that Sealsfield sees himself within the ideologized historical discourse of a nation's development, demonstrated by the mythicized date of the nation's birth, its liberal principles, and the statement of the president's responsibility. From his euphoric point of view there is only one "dark spot" attached to America's glory. The Tories and President Adams are seen by the author as "a symptom of this time which will vanish again . . . a plant from a foreign hothouse, which will not and can not flourish in America" (1952, 5).

Sealsfield articulates himself as part of the mainstream, which has shaped an answer to Crèvecoeur's question, "What then is this American, this new man?" (1782). He repeats the pattern of America as the first nation in world history which has developed an monoethno-cultural community independently. He joins the public consensus that the United States presents a political paradigm based on universal principles of freedom and equality, individualism and the ethic of labor, liberal principles guaranteed by Euroamericans, following the conditions of democracy, constitutionalism, and capitalism. And he shares the American dream of Manifest Destiny, somewhat unaware of potential conflicts that might arise because of the way so-called liberal ideas, republicanism, and Puritan elements of tradition will relate to the fate of the Indians, Afro-American slaves, industrialization, and the onset of multiethnic mass immigration; his blindness results from his wholehearted adoption of Americanization, which he intends to teach the European people.

Transforming his image of the United States into a report of ideological authenticity, he creates a document reflecting the spirit of his time. He employs a rhetorically functional language and a didactic organization of facts. The travelogue points to his belief in the "power of eloquence in a free country." He sees himself in the rhetorical tradition of "Cicero and Demosthenes" (1952, viii) and as someone acting for the progress of mankind, a movement started in classical times. The reader has to be aware of the narrator's manipulation of facts by means of judgment, exaggeration, manipulated combination, particularity, and omission.

The German edition's volume 1 offers a relatively complete survey of the country's attributes. The first seven chapters deal with domestic and foreign political affairs, followed by chapters introducing social patterns of education, the media, private and public lifestyles, religion, the legal system, economics, agriculture, agriculture, the militia, medical care, industrial development, and the life of artists. All this was supplemented by five pages of custom tariffs levied in 1824. Still, the book offers a very selective view of the United States. The matters most obviously of importance to Sealsfield may be found in the extensive explanations of political life (nearly one-third of the text), religious life, and agricultural economy. We will therefore concentrate on these three topics.

Sealsfield's dominant interest in affairs of the "Yankee" states, including the administration in Washington, is obvious. But his intentional neglect of the South actually aims at indirectly presenting that society as the social-political paradigm for the United States. He criticizes the federal government by pointing to the depravity of the political class and its fatal influence on the nation's progress, which has culminated in the disastrous election of John Quincy Adams. Sealsfield anticipates that the United States will soon face a crisis, one "which will lead towards the decision whether the republican or the monarchic principle will dominate [. . . . Justice and freedom" will be threatened by "depravity and corruptibility" and lead to the separation of the New England states (Castle 1952, 49). He claims to foresee the danger of a constitutional change to "monarchy" and "oligarchy" because of two circumstances: the origin of most presidents has been dynastic (most have come from Virginia) and now there is the baleful influence of the Adams "dynasty" (1952, 56). If the nation succumbs to these dangers—particularly in the form of a New England dominated "monarchy"—it will make the "slave states of the Union . . . its most bitter enemies" (1952, 49).

Sealsfield understands himself as someone who has joined the mainstream of early-nineteenth-century thought through his belief in the essentials of "moral values," the urgent need to push for the general progress of mankind, and a need for a romanticized dominance of reason. Because of his personal background he shares the hidden but widespread fear in the United States "of France, fear of Europe, fear of the Negro, fear of popular passion" (May 358); similarly, he largely ignores signals of coming change, such as religious revivals, mass immigration, multiethnic conflicts, and industrialization, adhering to the traditional conservative model of aristocratic-democratic agricultural society of Louisiana and the South.

This presentation does not result in a well-balanced survey of American history. His argument proceeds by contrasting universal ideas for a liberally orientated society accepted by the Constitution with the present crisis, which he feels has been caused by the morally misled political class. Still, "world history does not have another example of a state which within the short time of 50 years could have made such giant steps than the United States of North America" (1952, 1). The reasons for this triumph are said to be the geographical advantages of a large country, a long coast, many streams, fertile soil, and a temperate climate, all usefully accessed by immigrants, "the descendants of the privileged nations, who transferred sciences and experiences from all over the world on to a new ground." Sealsfield see these practices in fruitful interaction with "the most free constitution which ever has existed" (1952, 3). On the other hand, he does not believe that these positive suppositions of autochthonous Euro-Americans, liberal principles, and vast space for cultivation have been continually promoted by the presidents and their administrations, although Sealsfield agrees that Washington, "Jefferson, Madison, Monroe . . . were men, whose remembrance the United States has reason enough to bless" (1952, 6). But despite U.S. political achievements, the author criticizes the badly fought American-British War of 1812, a too-close relationship with the states of South America, a Washington establishment tending to centralization, and an exaggerated nationalism, ironically coupled with a fixation on Europe; all this has led to a general deterioration of political culture and an unfortunate and forced support of industrialization, twin developments that neglect the people in the backcountry, on the frontier, and in the South.

For him this crisis is personalized by the Adams family. Ignoring Adams's outstanding education, eloquence, and political experience, he sees him as a mediocre person "dangerous for the freedom of the people," acting neither as "democrat nor federal," and as a chief executive not attentive to welfare of the nation (1952, 17). From Sealsfield's point of view, Adams is a "Tory by birth, a Tory by education, an absolute Tory like his father was" (1952, 16). Therefore Adams emerges as a "most dangerous man" (1952, 18), a threat to the freedom of the United States and a figure who acts like the "British and European great people" (1952, 19). He seems unable to practice "wise politics" (1952, 47) by keeping away from an "unholy alliance" with the "military-oligarchic" countries of Central and South America (1952, 42); nor, Sealsfield charges, does Adams bear in mind the "delicate relationship between the Southern slaveholding states and the Union"(1952, 47). Sealsfield's conclusion is that the American people show a "deep disgust at the present administration" (1952, 22–23).

When Sealsfield talks about the American North and its betrayal of the essentials of American democracy, he displays his preference for the West, Louisiana, and the southern heartland, where such concepts are still honored. It is part of his European-inspired dialectical thinking and the Continent's corresponding romantic view of agricultural society to contrast the Old World with the New, the New England states and their growing industries with the frontier of the West and the agrarian society of the South. In conjunction with his distaste for Adams, Sealsfield believes that a regeneration of the politically spoiled system has to be started from the South in order to gain a "salutary cleaning from a secretion developed for fifty years, which has established in the interior of the state's body" (1952, 57). The only person to overcome the crisis successfully will be Jackson, the "second Washington" (1952, 14), the "hero of New Orleans" for whom the southern "people had pleaded clearly" (1952, 11).

Introducing Jackson in a special chapter, Sealsfield underlines his sympathy for this politically dazzling Tennessee planter, lawyer, general, and republican politician (1952, 57–69):

> Perhaps never before there have been so contradictory opinions said of a man like Jackson. While one of the parties (Adams) see him as a tyrant, military chieftain, a passionate and furious man, others exalt him into the position of a hero, who darkens even Washington. He is the head of the opposition and therefore of course the ruling party has any reasons to grovel him in the dust like others who praise him to the skies. . . . Violence joins in him with republican sense of equality. This man, who opposes Tories and persons whose patriotism seems to him suspect, can be a tyrant, but at the same time treat poor farming people as his equals. (1952, 58)

Following this estimation, Sealsfield sums up Jackson's career, picking those aspects that are favorable for the narrator's intention, emphasizing his actions as "Brigade-General" (1952, 60), when he was the first and only one "since the revolution . . . who battled against the Indians successfully" (1952, 62). During this fighting he "punished the Seminoles . . . took Pensacola by storm, chased the British and the Spanish administration. . . . The results of the fighting dated 8th January 1815 are well known. Leading his 5000 American militia he won a brilliant victory over 16,000 British soldiers [and] liberated Louisiana" (1952, 62, 66). As a presidential candidate, in contrast to Adams, he appeared to *not be*

> conditioned by the infiltrating poison of European diplomacy cultivated at the two Machiavelli academies in Paris and St. Petersburg, which could spoil republican principles at the roots, seduce some to criminal activities near to treason, neutralize the differences between the parties . . . and [lead] the nation finally to the conviction that it will accept a hereditary sovereign as benefit. (1952, 68–69)

Sealsfield also urges the United States to change from a republic to a democracy, which leads directly to the southerner Jackson and his democratic-autocratic attitude. He also calls for true separation from Europe (nationalism) (1955, 59ff., 62ff.) and the removal of trouble-making people such as the Indians (1955, 59ff.), combined with the integration of European immigrants into a monoethnic population. Because these are acknowledged principles of the nation's progress, Jackson's penchant for force—"punishing and chasing"—is deemed right.

Sealsfield's Catholic education led to his anticlerical and antiabsolutistic convictions, so it is interesting to see how he presents Catholicism as part of the state's religious culture (1952, 118–44). Bound to his view of a correspondence between the liberal Constitution and its political realization, he praises "the perfect freedom of conscience and the equality of all religions" (1952, 118), but these sects must be separate from the state; accordingly, "religion changed from a source of income for the caste of preachers . . . to the property of the people." His basic belief is that "religion of the people has normally a direct relationship with the status of its enlightenment" (1952, 131) and therefore "does the spiritual power rest in the free will of the people" (1952, 140). The widespread religiosity of the Americans (1952, 119) can be seen, therefore, by the many churches and believers, their frequent churchgoing, the vast variety of denominations, sects, and parishes steadily growing and privately driven. Sealsfield himself distinctly favors the Anglican High Church. Judged by these principles, he sees no need for the Roman Catholic Church: "The catholic does not get any recognition for his belief. Everybody considers him as somebody who has not yet found his spiritual freedom. . . . The American preacher realizes the independence of the people, the catholic one that of the Pope. The American preacher has to . . . enlighten . . . his congregation, for the catholic preacher . . . the task [is] to keep it in mental obscurity. The catholic preacher . . . sees himself monarchical, the American is republican." Sealsfield foresees the erosion of the Catholic Church in America; driven by obsolete ideas, it is doomed by the revival of other religions, which together counterbalance clerical heritage and immigration from Catholic countries such as Ireland and France. Sealsfield supports moral standards presented by Protestant religion: "The court of Rome will be forced to be content with the southern hemisphere of America" (1952, 140–41).

Finally, looking at the aspect of "agricultural society" as the third main parameter of Sealsfield's concern, it is again remarkable that he avoids talking about Louisiana, southern slaveholding plantation society, or the ideology of agrarianism (1952, 163–84).[14] He does, however, introduce the reader to farming activities in the northern states. Aiming at potential immigrants, he deals with pragmatic details; he describes frontier land speculation and tells how to buy farmland, build and furnish houses, raise cattle, market crops and animals, and manage taxes and income. Slaves appear as a functional part of society yet exist outside social relations.

When talking of the South Sealsfield does it the way he deals with Jackson, by criticizing present developments that are not following a liberal Constitution. Speaking didactically, he names the state of Virginia—the home of many presidents—as the worst-case scenario. "The aristocratic farmer lives on the banks of the St. James River in Virginia hospitably and proudly as a tobacco planter surrounded by a crowd of slaves. Since his acres show symptoms of exhaustion because of a continuous cultivation by tobacco planting, he being a genuine aristocrat starts to sell them [the slaves] to Louisiana." Property, power, and money "have given him an idea of importance, which reduced the values of republican freedom [he becomes] convinced that he is allowed to act absolutely independently, and . . . society has to accept everything he likes to do." He considers the "conversion of his plantation into a lordship (aristocratic supremacy) . . . and openly he announces that Virginia and the United States—from his point of view only a supplement to his own state anyhow—are doubtless the 'head' of the Union and will never again satisfaction until there will be no success in introducing the British constitution at least the Lords and Commons" (1952, 165). Because of a mainly negative description of the North, and a very selective discussion of the South, Louisiana, the latter region's center, is presented as the paradigmatic frontier, where the great themes of political leadership, ethnic purity, and national independence may best be studied.

IV

In the second volume of Sealsfield's travelogue, the narrator invites the reader to travel through the United States from North to South in the 1820s. Whereas the first volume gives rather systematic geographic and background information on administration and society, and its development in time, this volume focuses on the "machinery of national identification and integration" by following the second parameter—the expansion in space. Composed as a diary, it provides circumstances of Sealsfield's travel, descriptions of the landscape and people, facts of general interest, anecdotal episodes, and reflections by the narrator. Sealsfield uses the knowledge he gathered from two journeys he took between New York and New Orleans over the period from 1823 to 1826, but especially from his time spent in Louisiana, "where I stayed a whole year and therefore know half the plantations" (1955, 157).

The account begins, "I left my hometown Kittaning on the banks of the Allegheny River, 35 miles north of Pittsburgh, to come back to the so-called paradise in the Southwest of the United States of North America in order to settle my business and to regain my health, which has not been fine for some time" (1955, 1). This opening presents an established and well-off American eyewitness who guarantees an authentic account of his impressive ride of about seventeen hundred miles through a vast landscape. The table of contents gives further details about the topography en route and a forecast of the twenty chapters that follow.

It is significant that for this second part of the book "Louisiana" becomes the central motif and symbol; Sealsfield names it "the so-called paradise" (1955, 1). The two discourses, of the spiritual paradise and the political ideal, merge in the metaphor of the "best of all possible worlds." Continuing the philosophical conceptions of earthly paradise that range from Thomas More's *Utopia* (1516) to Bernard Bolzano's *Vom besten Staate* (*The Ideal State;* 1933 ed.), from Johann Schnabel's utopian novel *Die Insel Felsenburg* (*The Island Rocky-Castle;* 1731–1743) to Goethe's description of a philanthropic society heading for America in *Wilhelm Meisters Wanderjahre* (1821), Sealsfield explains his understanding of history in the tradition of the eighteenth-century enlightenment bound to a deep belief in mankind's progress. He combines this idea with aspects of the then-current discourse in German countries about independent national territory and its individual development (Johann Gottfried Herder) and the ideas of liberalism. These concepts had been limited to a merely theoretical realm among European intellectuals since the Congress of Vienna. These circumstances led to a romanticized seeking for an independent nation, one based on an agricultural conception of society coupled with a growing and irrational refusal of industrialization.

This mixture of ideas influenced Sealsfield's idealized projection of European hopes onto the reality of the United States. On the one hand, he agrees with the principles represented by the New World and its myth of manifest destiny. On the other hand, he experienced a reality very different from this ideal and posits an ideal United States based on the concept of a paradisiacal Louisiana, which in turn is representative of a possible Edenic South. Sealsfield defines the state and region as "the free Egypt of the West" and "North America" (1955, 161, 183). His argument proceeds from a geographical, theological, and historical-philosophical position. Obviously, "Louisiana is very similarly positioned to Egypt, on the same degree of latitude. And the importance of the river Nile is the same that the Mississippi has for Louisiana" (1955, 224). This comparability leads to a theological connotation that transfers both the positive and negative qualities of biblical Egypt onto Louisiana. In the history of salvation Egypt is presented as a place of sanctuary several times. The patriarch Abraham saved his family from starvation by escaping from Canaan to Egypt (ca. 1700 B.C.) into the "Garden of the Lord" (Gen. 13:10); the patriarch Joseph, son of Jacob, became a member of the Pharaoh's court, leading to the treaty between Jahweh and the people of Israel (Gen. 37–50). The holy family escaped the threat of Herod by heading for Egypt (Matt. 2:13–15). Furthermore, the former priest Sealsfield is also acquainted with the negative connotations of Egypt as the "house of slavery" for the Hebrew people; however, he sees them initiating their escape (Exod. 20:2; Deut. 5:6; 6:12), bound to a vision of the "promised land" as a "new Egypt." Louisiana is seen as part of a positive reflection in the tradition of a return to the Garden of Eden, and it becomes a metaphor within the discourse about mankind's progress.

Sealsfield's itinerary proceeds to Ohio; boating down the river valley into Kentucky, Indiana, and Illinois, he reaches the confluence of the Ohio and the Mississippi at a place called Trinity. After a trip up the river to St. Louis, the narrator heads southwards by steamboat and passes Tennessee, the Arkansas territory, and Mississippi, finally arriving in Louisiana. Along the way, Sealsfield tells the respective states' histories and describes periodic excursions from the river bank into the country's interior. The fact that eight of twenty chapters deal with the South indicates Sealsfield's preference for that region.

Without any doubt the upgrading of historical Louisiana to a visionary land of hope and happiness stems from the author's belief in the state's allegiance to the principles of liberalism and democracy. Sealsfield points to the historical importance of Louisiana: this "state is indeed only a small part of a large territory . . . but this area [has become] the keystone-state to the geographical situation of the United States and has changed its situation decisively, which is not less important than that of the revolution" (1955, 226). The effect of the Louisiana Purchase in 1803 was to connect the North to the South via the Mississippi (1955, 228). Therefore, this state "is doubtless the most important one, determined by its nature to play an excellent role in the history of America" (1955, 227). Thus the Mississippi becomes a metaphor for the South itself and a symbol of nature reflecting the idea of both the everlasting power of life and the might of God. Following the river from north to south, from source to mouth, parallels civilization's progress through space, culminating in Louisiana. And this mythic river is "the center of Louisiana's culture" (1955, 224–25).

The Mississippi, also representing nature itself, gives man the chance to act for the progress of civilization by facilitating the "exploration of the West and Southwest." Therefore the steamboat is recognized as the most important technical aid for men's conquest of vast areas. Consequently, Sealsfield provides copious information on steamboat development, technical items, transportation, social life on boats, schedules, and accounts of accidents, all the while combining facts with emotional reactions (1952, 136–40). He praises Robert Fulton (1765–1815), the inventor of the steamboat, as one of the American "pioneers and heroes" who inaugurated commercial steam navigation: "America is in debt to Fulton so much it should erect marble memorials for him, especially by the people [who live on] the banks of the Mississippi. Their situation of living has been changed by this man enormously" (1955, 137–38). Sealsfield intends to emphasize and celebrate the outstanding genius of American engineering but also to stimulate people to explore the country, prosper economically, and establish the United States as an exceptional country. The term "steamboat era" becomes a symbolic formula of nearly mythic quality.

Passing by Vicksburg and Natchez (Mississippi), the author compares the latter and New Orleans to illustrate the two aspects of rural and urban life in Louisiana. Natchez becomes synonymous with plantations and slavery. After having introduced the inhabitants as "planters, businessmen, lawyers and medical doctors together with a few craftsmen" (1955, 150), he describes the view from the bluff into Louisiana. It is sketched as pastoral scenery "across the 12 mile wide Mississippi, presenting itself in a majestical bend; beyond this the banks of Louisiana with the small town Concordia and many plantations, the pleasant looking home of the planter in the center of fifteen to twenty Negro cabins. Stretched to both sides are the unlimited cotton plantations, and in the background the cedar woods of Louisiana seem to be absorbed by the earth" (1955, 149–50).

The plantation Sealsfield describes belonged to a Mr. Davis from Kentucky; the tract was "two miles north of Natchez, five miles below Palmyra." The plantation history includes "getting slaves from Kentucky by flatboat" and the inception of cultivation of the "wilderness" for cotton, corn, and cattle raising. Since cotton is the primary crop and New Orleans' economy depends on it, the circumstances of plantation-management afford indicators for the further welfare of society, which will depend on soil fertility, weather conditions, a monocultural crop, slaves, the acquisition of fertile land, and the capital and agricultural/economic acumen of the landlord (1955, 154–56).

We find no reflections on humanitarian or liberal principles when the narrator turns to workers; he insists on the necessity of slaves by the pragmatic argument that only they "are able to bear the hot climate" (1955, 164). Slaves are considered as merchandise when it is said that "at the moment Negroes are about 400 to 700 dollars" in Louisiana compared "to lower prices in the northern slave states from where they are transported down the Mississippi by flatboats"(1955, 218). This attitude is supplemented later when Sealsfield provides a formula for setting up plantations in the recommended areas "on the banks of the Mississippi or the Red River"; one should reckon on "10,000 dollars equaling 1,500 acres and eight to ten slaves," a formula that will assure the owner a surplus of "40–60%" from the third year on (1955, 215–19).

The author posits the cotton plantation owners, with their understanding of life, economy, and politics, as the sociological, political, and moral exemplars for the recommended framework of an aristocratic-democratic southern society, thereby supporting a society of classes, one that integrates slavery and marginalizes poor whites, Indians, and any immigrants that do not fit into a sociological homogenic population.

Coming to the description of New Orleans, Sealsfield filters it through his ideological view of positive basic suppositions. He takes care to provide information important to immigrants, criticizing problems and appealing for solutions that will help achieve the destiny of the city. Because he does this through details and statistics, we become interested in the outlines of the city's image he has in mind, since we can only follow the selective topics of his discourse (1955, 173–224).

He starts with a kind of verbalized city map, mentioning the size of the town, its position beneath the river's water level, the necessity of levees, its precincts and streets. He characterizes the architecture of brick buildings and wooden cottages and notes the enormous undertaking of constructing houses, pavements, and street lighting. He gives a convincing estimation of the city's outstanding importance as the economic and political metropolis of the South: By depending entirely on cotton and its successful export, New Orleans defines itself as a virtual El Dorado for plantation owners and cotton traders. And yet this outstanding city has been achieved through the work of immigrant Americans, who changed it from "a former shabby hideout for criminals from France and Spain . . . situated amidst swamps and alligators, to one of the prettiest cities of North America . . . connected to half of the world" (1955, 166–67). The present prosperous situation, dating from 1803 and the Louisiana Purchase, is the consequence of American influence, which has wiped out "the miserable pressure of ridiculous tyranny"and will lead this city "despite some circumstances of disadvantage and the enormous egoism of its inhabitants, to its [destiny as] the main place of stores and trade of America. The extraordinary wealth of its state, this Egypt of North America, and the fertility of the states along the Mississippi valley . . . bound to exportation, will inevitably develop it to one of the largest and richest cities. There is no other place on earth which is better suited for trade" (1955, 183).

Sealsfield's dialectical presentation follows the fading optimistic attitude at the end of the "era of good feeling," that is, the still-vivid, naïve belief in a never ending economic progress based on the agricultural product cotton and the common vision of an ideal society. And for that demonstration the narrator follows the simplified pattern of the interdependencies of nature and civilization, plantation culture and economic growth, monoethnic population, and a wealthy Euro-American high society.

From this point of view Sealsfield turns New Orleans into the coming economic and culture center of the world, not just of the United States. He is convinced of this development because the city thrives "on the exterior part of the longest river in the world"; it constitutes a catchment area for a stretch of land from "Lake Erie and New York" to the gulf, comprising "more then one million British square miles." To the other side there is "the Gulf of Mexico, its coast, the West Indies, South America, and to the left Europe, in the North the sister-states of the Union. . . . New Orleans will develop without any doubt into the most important city of trade in the world." For proof Sealsfield offers statistics that locate over one thousand steamboats and sea going vessels in the city's harbor (1955, 182). For him this dimension of shipping is symptomatic of the wealth of the city, where "many families own at least a hundred thousand dollars, and there are several families who earn fifty thousand dollars a year and most of the plantation owners have 25,000 dollars of income. Nowhere else is one able to win easily . . . so much money as in Louisiana" (1955, 188). Naming rich entrepreneurs such as "Mr. Reliaux at the corner of Tchoupitulas and Poydras Road," owner of the most modern cotton gin, the German wholesale seller "V. Nolte," and others (1955, 180), Sealsfield underlines that prosperity is bound to cotton production. And he sees this economic importance supplemented by a corresponding political power because of the links of the local consulates of "Great Britain, France, Russia, Spain, Portugal, Denmark, Netherlands, Prussia, Sweden and Norway and Hamburg" (1955, 182).

Following these idealized images and concepts of the city, the narrator looks at the local administration and the city's public institutions. In contrast to his positive, sometimes glowing view of the metropolis in general, the city's organization, buildings, and institutions are mainly criticized. By naming their deficits, he calls for improvement as vitally necessary because of the current and anticipated importance of the city. Looking at the "public buildings" and mentioning the "City Hall," the residence of the mayor, the "Presbytere," seat of the Louisiana High Court of Justice and of the New Orleans Court of Justice, and the Capitol building, his opinion is that they are not comparable with those in the northern states "by architecture and structure . . . [and that none are] dignified except the Capitol" (1955, 175, 181). He shows a similar critical attitude when considering the small number of churches and notes their weak influence on social life. Notable exceptions: the activities of the renowned "bishop of Louisiana, Mr. Dubourg" and "father Antoine, a Capuchin" (1955, 203–4). He finds both education and medical care badly neglected, considering the city's wealth (1955, 200–202). Sealsfield's comments on banks, insurance companies, Freemasons, market halls, and newspapers are presented as matters of fact. Referring to the theaters, the narrator's indifferent attitude reveal the author's position as an outsider and former priest. The reader smiles when he is informed about New Orleans theaters, "where in the time of carnival the only fancy-dress balls in the United States are celebrated," yet Sealsfield claims "there is nothing imaginable more boring than a fancy ball in New Orleans. Everybody acts solely as a businessman and even the fourteen year old Miss asks, during the first hour of having met somebody, whether he is rich and how many warehouses filled with cotton and tubs of sugar he could build" (1955, 179–80, 204–7).

Led by his preference for a monoethnic and homogenic society, the narrator is more interested in statistics documenting the growth of the city's population and its sociological structure. The figures point at two facts. One is the rapidity of population growth between 1820 (twenty-seven thousand) and 1826 (forty thousand; actually thirty thousand), which is offered as an argument for the attraction of New Orleans. The other is the number of black slaves, which has stayed constant at the high level of about seven thousand plus twenty-five hundred free people of color (1820). The statistics are given without any comment, confirming that slavery is looked at as a natural attribute of society, unfettered by any moral aspects, and not at all irritating in a monoethnic society (1955, 182). A similar attitude emerges when the narrator analyses the sociological structure. His perspective is mainly trained on ethnic and class stratification. This presentation of a sociological structure, dictated by social status and rank, reminds the reader of European orders.

The first class, dominant only in numbers, is made up of Creoles. Their favorable status is made possible solely by the positive influence of the newly arrived "restless and masculine" Americans (1955, 189–91). Although these "Yankees" represent only three-eighths of the white population and thus constitute a minority, they are the leading and exemplary class because they embody the ideal attributes the South, Louisiana, and New Orleans need for a prosperous future: mobility, activity, intelligence, morality, and stable families. Therefore they occupy "most of the leading jobs, having become very rich by running plantations and trade within a short time" (1955, 192–98). The "immigrated French" constitute the third class; a few of these are respected lawyers and merchants but most of them are "adventurers, hair and music artists, maitre de dances, parfumeurs, dentists, etc. From all nations the French are the worst acquisition for a young state. . . . They are without any morality, principles, education, and concerning religion, the most frivolous people" (1955, 196). The fourth class, the Germans, live under circumstances of "self-contempt and an awareness of uselessness for society." Many of them were "being sold as white slaves." Without any comment the narrator summarizes, "Englishmen, Scots, and Irish normally get on fine"(1955, 196–97), obviously avoiding details and judgment because of the intended publication of his book in Great Britain. The narrator finishes his sociological analysis by saying that "the . . . rest of the population represent the colored people and the slaves. . . . Among this lowest class . . . are some, who are honest and reliable and get the respect of their landlords. But there are thousands who show all the malignity of a slave." Looking at the poor status of the Afro-Americans, which he justified earlier, the author points out that anyone turned into a slave would develop the same negative character. Therefore any slave rebellion would be an affront to a monoethnical society, and must lead to justified punishment "as it happened recently in the upper region of Louisiana . . . to regain law and order" (1955, 198–99).

Another classification of inhabitants is bound directly to origins, either internally or from overseas, but also is based on occupation. "The first and privileged class comprises those immigrants who intend to stay in the country," Sealsfield states, and are rich enough to obtain large areas to start cotton planting by slavery and make their fortune within a short time (1955, 215–20). The second class are "the planters or farmers who own less than 10,000 dollars and are not able to get slaves." They settle west of the Red River and east of Lake Pontchartrain and thus face a risky economic future (1955, 220–21). "A third class of immigrants are tradesmen, people of average image pushed by their greed. . . . Attracted by [a desire] to make money . . . the town became the rallying point of the bad guys from Europe and America to seek their fortune . . . Generally, the industrious tradesman coming over from Europe will prosper" because of the most profitable importation "of European made objets d'art and manufactured goods" (1955, 221–22). "Craftsmen can count in a slave state . . . only on half of the population as customers." Although "butchers, bricklayers, tilers, bakers, and farriers—mostly German—do very good, the order is not respected well and it ranks a little above free slaves" (1955, 222–24).

This classification enables the narrator to give a systematic survey. But more important, he presents a hermetic sociological and political structure of a society following two parameters of systematic organizations. Meeting demands for social stability, easy control, and a clear hierarchical distribution of economic and political power required an autocratic leadership, one distinguished by its property, wealth, and political function. There is thus no doubt that Sealsfield speaks in favor of a property orientated, democratically limited organization of society, regionalized and relatively independent from a central administration. It is an arrangement that will stabilize an agricultural conception of southern society, differentiating it from that of the North, and damning industrialization as a negative development of modern societies.

Sealsfield concludes the second volume with the twentieth chapter. But he does not complete his original plan to have the narrator's 1825 journey follow the entire flow of the river. Titled "The Battle of New Orleans," chapter 20 presents a short history of Andrew Jackson's campaigns against the British and the Seminoles in 1815, which ended in the great victory that regained the status quo established by the Treaty of Ghent of 1814 (1955, 240–47). The reader learns that "the eighth of January, the anniversary of the victory over the Britains" meant the "rescue of the nation's honour and military glory." This event compares in significance to the battles of "Waterloo, Leipzig, Marengo, Jena etc." Sealsfield presents a single incident from the nation's history and turns it into a dominant factor in world history, upgrading it through comparison with Europeans' struggle for freedom against Napoleon. Integrating it into the American traditions of national heritage, it becomes part of the sequence of events that include the Fourth of July 1776, the presidential elections of 1789, and the Monroe Doctrine of 1824. At the same time, Sealsfield signals the desired regeneration of the nation can only be carried out by the hero of New Orleans, the triumphant Andrew Jackson. Thus a heroic movement proceeds from the providentially protected southern metropolis New Orleans and from a rescued southern society, and for all this Jackson is the symbol. He is presented as the future president and a metaphor of the nation's predestinated political power and social welfare. For Sealsfield's report on the United States, Jackson is the commanding and closing figure of the book, the personification of the narrative's ideological discourse, and a personal guarantee for the anticipated glorious future of the United States, which in turn will provide the model for mankind's development.

In this second volume, Sealsfield reports from a decidedly American point of view. This description is bound to a spatially oriented conception of the nation. The movement of the talking traveler follows a firm direction: from the northern states to the southern states, from the figurative beginning of the Mississippi to its mouth and the open sea, from the industrial center of Pittsburgh to the agricultural center of New Orleans. The flowing direction of the river and the moving position of the narrator correspond with the development of a national identity, one shaped by the tensions among natural, cultural, and philosophical-historical circumstances and Sealsfield's intention. Therefore the report is a repetition of the specific American process of understanding nature as destined for continuous cultivation, thus turning wilderness into civilization. Aware of the emergence of the nationalistic doctrine of Manifest Destiny, the end of the Era of Good Feeling, and Adams's controversial presidency, the author offers southern society as a social paradigm for the necessary regeneration of the Union and the European monarchies.

V

Looking at Louisiana and its biggest city as pastoral paradise, Sealsfield's mapping of an idyllic land reflects his deistic understanding of physics and metaphysics and corresponds with the topic and intention of his travelogue. The respective first and last sentences of both volumes provides the reader confirmation of Sealsfield's intent. The first volume starts with the statement that the development of the United States is a unique phenomenon in "world history" (1952, 1), and it is closed by the opinion that "nowhere man can live as comfortably, free, and happy as in America" (1952, 201). Corresponding to this, the second volume begins by transforming historical circumstances to philosophical perspective, by claiming Louisiana is the "paradise of the United States of North America" (1955, 1). The conclusion refers to both the exceptional historical and ideal designation of the American nation and its equality among the family of nations looked upon from the South (1955, 247).

Methodologically Sealsfield's approach is dialectical. Pointing at the principles of liberalism and democracy (constituting his thesis), he gives a critical analysis of the present national climate, observing the change from an "era of good feeling" to an "era of bad feeling" (antithesis). The third step is his perspective for a possible ideal society in the future (synthesis). Since he sees the historical paradigm in his conception of southern society and Louisiana, he offers the latter as both reality and metaphor. All this is filtered through his view of state development, which in turn is indebted to the philosophy of enlightenment, especially Johann Gottfried Herder's ethnonational interpretation of history and Austro-German ideas of national liberalism. This leads to a static conception of society, bound to a limited understanding of democracy. It appears in his formula of "democratic-aristocratic" or "aristocratic-democratic" character. He uses it throughout his work until 1848; he stopped writing as the national debate over slavery, which would culminate in the Civil War, revealed the inadequacy of his vision (Castle 1955, 287, 323).

Considering his fixed and Utopian vision for mankind, one sees why Sealsfield presents a restrictive selection of facts, offering heroic archetypes of the farmer, the political leader, and aristocrats while neglecting items that do not fit into his hermetic concept of society, such as industrialists, poor whites, slave markets, burgeoning mass migration inside the Union and from Europe, and so on. The book thus turns out finally as a manufactured and partial documentation and discourse, one that purports to characterize the spirit of the 1820s but actually reflects only stereotypes.

Sealsfield's book is a political report with a certain message. For him the liberal Constitution is essential for a democratic society in a republic. Politicians are those who serve and guarantee it. The United States is the only country in the world that installed the liberal essentials by means of a successful revolution. In creating this vision for an absolutist Europe, Sealsfield shares a view common in his time, one that conceived Europe as the heritage of America and America as the future of Europe.

NOTES

1. Any citation from Sealsfield's works and letters originally done in German are translated into English to support a better understanding by English-speaking readers.

2. Introductions in English: Walter Grünzweig, *Charles Sealsfield,* Boise State University Western Writer Series No. 71 (Boise, Idaho: Boise State University Printing and Graphic Services, [1985]); Jeffrey L. Sammons, "Charles Sealsfield (Karl Postl)," *History of Literary Biography,* vol. 133, *Nineteenth-Century German Writers to 1840,* ed. James Hardin and Siegfried Mews (Detroit: Gale Research, 1993) 248–56; Alexander Ritter, "Charles Sealsfield (1793–1864): German and American Novelist of the Nineteenth Century," *Mississippi Quarterly* 47.4 (1994): 633–44.

3. Alexander Ritter, "Grenzübertritt und Schattentausch: Der österreichische Priester Carl Postl und seine vage staatsbürgerliche Identität als amerikanischer Literat Charles Sealsfield. Eine Dokumentation," *Freiburger Universitätsblätter* 38.143 (1999): 39–71.

4. Bernhard Bolzano, philosopher and mathematician, was one of the leading Catholic priests and professors in Prague who publicly represented ideas of enlightenment. Together with other teachers he had to leave university in 1819 (the year of the so-called Karlsbader Beschlüsse [Orders of Karlsbad]) due to the introduction of a strict censorship for universities and press concerning "demagogical activities." Because of interventions by the Vatican, the Vienna government, and local authorities, there were legal proceedings against Bolzano accusing him of alleged false doctrine.

5. There is no verification yet concerning his properties in Louisiana. But we can presume that he had a plantation in the area of the Red River or between St. Francisville and Baton Rouge. In a letter to his publisher Erhard dated July 17, 1854, he speaks about "selling my lands" in order to "buy a comfortable respectable farm" in New York, Pennsylvania, or Maryland (Castle 1955, 297, 300).

6. Compare his autobiographical sketch, where he says that during his first stay in the United States he "let himself admit to this republic's union of citizens" (Castle 1955, 290). The information about his passport from Pennsylvania is a misunderstanding passed on by his biographer Castle and is based on a wrong interpretation of the notice made by the Austrian chargé d'affaires Philip von Neumann (Castle 1952, 175). In 1833 "Charles Sealsfield from Louisiana" signed the contract with his publisher, Orell, Füßli and Company (Zurich), and he became a naturalized citizen in 1858 (Castle 1955, 156–58).

7. We do not know for certain whether he owned a plantation in Louisiana, but the many direct and indirect references in his letters and novels justify the assumption that the South was his home, that his home included plantation property, and that he was a slaveholder. Compare, for instance, Sealsfield's letter to Erhard dated July 17, 1854: "I like . . . to sell my plantations in order to get a comfortable large farm in New York State, Pennsylvania, or Maryland where I will lay down my tired head after having ended my career as novelist" (Castle 1955, 297; see also 156–58, 283, 285–86, 301).

8. Carey, Lea and Carey published his first novel in English: *Tokeah; or, The White Rose,* 2 vols. (Philadelphia: Carey, Lea & Carey, 1829).

9. Compare Hans Galinsky, *Naturae cursus: Der Weg einer antiken kosmologischen Metapher von der Alten Welt in die Neue Welt. Ein Beitrag zur historischen Metaphorik der Weltliteratur* (Heidelberg: Carl Winter, 1968) and Klaus H. Borner, *Auf der Suche nach dem irdischen Paradies: Zur Ikonographie der geographischen Utopie* (Frankfurt: Jochen Wörner, 1984).

10. Compare the edition recently published: Charles Sealsfield—Karl Postl: *Austria as it is, or Sketches of continental courts, by an eye-witness, London 1828. Österreich, wie es ist oder Skizzen von Fürstenhöfen des Kontinents. Wien 1919,* ed. Primus-Heinz Kucher, Literatur in der Geschichte—Geschichte in der Literatur 28 (Vienna: Böhlau, 1994).

11. Compare for the literary reception of "America" by German literature: *Amerika in der deutschen Literatur: Neue Welt-Nordamerika-USA,* ed. Sigrid Bauschinger, Horst Denkler, and Wilfried Malsch (Stuttgart: Philipp Reclam, 1975); *Deutschlands literarisches Amerikabild,* ed. Alexander Ritter, Germanistische Texte und Studien 4 (Hildesheim: Georg Olms, 1977).

12. Alexander Ritter, "Charles Sealsfields frühe Publizitätssuche bei den Verlegern Cotta (Stuttgart) und Murray (London). Biographische und buchgeschichtliche Umstände als Ursachen des Publizitätsverlustes nach 1848," *Literarisches Leben in Österreich, 1848–1890,* ed. Klaus Amann, Hubert Lengauer, and Karl Wagner, Literaturgeschichte in Studien und Quellen 1 (Vienna: Böhlau, 2000) 561–600.

13. Many writers in his day, in Germany as well as in the United States, started as journalists, then turned to travelogue writers, and ended up as novelists. Cf. Percy G. Adams, *Travel Literature and the Evolution of the Novel* (Lexington: University Press of Kentucky, 1983).

14. Edwin Adams Davis, *Louisiana: The Pelican State* (Baton Rouge: Louisiana State University Press, 1959) 173–84.

WORKS CITED

Castle, Eduard, ed. *Der Große Unbekannte: Das Leben von Charles Sealsfield (Karl Postl).* Vienna: Manutius, 1952.

———. *Der große Unbekannte: Das Leben von Charles Sealsfield (Karl Postl), Briefe und Aktenstücke.* Vienna: Karl Werner, 1955.

Gretlund, Jan Nordby. "1835: The First *Annus Mirabilis* of Southern Fiction." *Rewriting the South. History and Fiction.* Ed. Lothar Hönnighausen and Valeria Gennaro Lerda. Tübingen: A. Francke Verlag, 1993. 121–22.

Lorenz, Willy. *Die Kreuzherren mit dem roten Sterne.* Königstein im Taunus: Königsteiner Institut für Kirchen- und Geistesgeschichte der Sudetenländer e.V., 1964.

Lubbers, Klaus. Modelle nationaler Identität in amerikanischer Literatur und Kunst, 1776–1893." *Nationales Bewusstsein und kollektive Mentalität: Studien zur Entwicklung des kollektiven Bewusstseins in der Neuzeit 2.* Ed. Helmut Berding. Frankfurt: Suhrkamp, 1994. 82–111.

May, Henry F. *The Enlightenment in America.* New York: Oxford University Press, 1978.

[Sealsfield, Charles.] *The Americans as they are.* London: W. Simpkin & R. Marshall, 1828. Reprint, Charles Sealsfield. *Sämtliche Werke.* Ed. Karl J. R. Arndt. Vol. 2. Hildesheim: Olms, 1972.

———. *The Americans as they are; Described through a tour through the valley of the Mississippi. By the author of* Austria as it is. London: Hurst, Chance, St. Paul's Church Yard, 1828. Reprint, Charles Sealsfield. *Sämtliche Werke.* Ed. Karl J. R. Arndt. Vol.2. Hildesheim: Olms, 1972.

———. *The United States of North America as they are in their political, religious and social relations.* London: John Murray, 1827.

Sidons, C. [Charles Sealsfield.] *De Vereenigte Staten van Noord-Amerika, in hunne staatkundige, godsdienstige en maatschappelijke betrekkingen beschouwd.* Leeuwarden: Steenbergen van Goor, 1828.

———. *Die Vereinigten Staaten von Nordamerika, nach ihrem politischen, religiösen and gesellschaftlichen Verhältnisse betrachtet. Mit einer Reise durch den westlichen Theil von Pennsylvanien, Ohio, Kentucky, Indiana, Illinois, Missuri, Tennessee, das Gebiet Arkansas, Mississippi und Louisiana.* Vol. 1. Stuttgart: J. G. Cotta, 1827. Reprint, Charles Sealsfield. *Sämtliche Werke.* Ed. Karl J. R.Arndt. Vol.1. Hildesheim: Olms, 1972.

———. "Voyage de M. Sidons, Citoyen des États-Unis, dans le partie occidentale de la Pennsylvanie, des états d'Ohio, Kentucky, Illinois, Missouri, Tennessee, le territoire d'Arkansas, les états du Mississippi et de la Louisiane, en 1826." *Journal Nouvelles Annales des Voyage,* Deuxième Serie 7 (1828): 322–42; 8 (1828): 59–80, 175–217. Abbreviated version.

Slavery in French Louisiana

From Gallic Colony to American Territory

DANIEL C. LITTLEFIELD

On January 9, 1811, terrified planters fled into New Orleans from German Coast County, Louisiana, which straddled the Mississippi River thirty-six miles northwest of the city.[1] They reported an uprising of slaves, which turned out to be the largest ever within the United States. On the night of January 8, under the leadership of Charles Deslondes, reputedly a mulatto slave from St. Domingue, slaves numbering between 180 and 500 rose in the neighborhood of Manuel Andry's plantation in St. John the Baptist Parish, where Charles was employed. The insurrection had been planned in concert with runaways and bondsmen in the immediate area and moved along the River Road in the direction of New Orleans. The rebels destroyed several plantations, and, having moved about fifteen miles ("five leagues") by the next morning (June 9), they stopped at the plantation of Jacques Fortier to eat, drink, and celebrate. Meanwhile, Andry, present during the upheaval and wounded by "the stroke of an axe" while his son was killed, went to raise the alarm. He was, as he reported to the governor, "able to collect a detachment of about eighty men, and although wounded," he took command. "We have been so happy as to meet the brigands, who were in the neighbourhood of the plantation of Mr. Bernoudi, colors displayed and full of arrogance. As soon as we perceived them we rushed upon their troops, of whom we made considerable slaughter. The spot was unfortunately unpropitious to cut off their retreat, so that many have been able to take to the woods, and the chiefs principally being on horseback, have made their escape with greater facility" (Carter 916). But military forces under the command of U.S. General Wade Hampton in New Orleans and Major Homer Milton from Baton Rouge converged on the region, and the rebels, heavily outgunned, were quickly overcome. Sixty-six were killed in battle or executed on the spot. Total slave casualties were somewhat greater, however, for patrols reported the discovery of many more bodies not part of the count (Dorman 397–98). Several were captured, tried, and sentenced to death by firing squad, "without any preceding torture." But their heads were cut off and set on poles to decorate the road between New Orleans and Major Andry's plantation "as a terrible example to all who would disturb the public tranquility in the future" (Conrad, "Summary" 472–73).

Several questions suggest themselves from these events, such as what were the precipitants of the rebellion, what did the rebels hope to accomplish, and what peculiarities of Louisiana prompted the largest slave rebellion in United States history? Since no extended record of the reasoning of the participants, similar to that accompanying Nat Turner's insurrection, has come to light, the answer to the second question one can only surmise. One leader expressed his purpose quite simply as "to kill whites" (détruir le Blanc) (Dorman 398). General Hampton thought that the plan was "unquestionably of Spanish origin" and that it had a more "extensive Combination" than appeared (Carter 917). But eight days after Hampton's comment (January 20), when the governor declared the insurrection at an end, he reported, "It does not appear to have been of extensive combination, and the mischief done is by no means as great as was at first apprehended" (Rowland 5:113). One historian figured that only about 8 percent of the slaves in the county took part (Dorman 402). Moreover, some slaves alerted their owners to the revolt, local free blacks fought against it ("with an indefatigable zeal and intrepid courage" that deserved "l'estime publique," one observer recalled [Dorman 402]), and black troops called to suppress it performed enthusiastically and received the governor's thanks (Everett 394).

The leaders must have been aware of their relative lack of support among the slave population. Or, to put it another way, they must have known how many they could count on, and even if they expected to gain more followers if the initial outbreak was successful, they must still have had an idea about what was reasonable to expect under the circumstances, which, in the upshot, was relatively little. If Charles Deslondes was disappointed in his expectations of the servile reaction, it may be that he was misled by a St. Domingue experience whose essential features were not replicated in Louisiana. Of course, the fact that he was a foreigner might not only have clouded his perceptions but vitiated his ability to lead as well. Slaves often separated along lines of ethnicity and nativity. Indeed, such divisions regularly hampered cooperation among slaves in early Louisiana, especially during conspiracies in the 1730s and 1790s (Hall, *Africans* 97–118, 317–74). It is quite clear, however, that in a few instances, at least, great hostility existed between blacks and whites in 1811. One of the few white people killed in the uprising, Jean-François

Trépanier, evidently was claimed by his own body servant. Moreover, another rebel "donné un coup de hache à M. François Trépanier lorsque celui-ci était déjà mort" (struck M. François Trépanier with an ax when he was already dead) (Dorman 399n), indicating either intense dislike, bravado, or both. (Trépanier was reported by one source to have defied the rebels when others ran, perhaps sparking extra vindictiveness.)[2] But just as clearly, hostility was not widespread enough, or intense enough, to galvanize more of the oppressed into active opposition, or even to encourage them to silent collaboration. Or could it be that repression was severe enough that few dared entertain serious thoughts of resistence? This essay will not begin to answer the questions it will pose. Nevertheless, the 1811 incident furnishes a convenient point from which briefly to consider slavery in Louisiana. I have chosen to interpret the phrase "French Louisiana" in geographical rather than temporal terms—thus essentially taking it to mean "southern Louisiana"—and to follow the region from initial settlement to American acquisition, noting some of the changes that occurred under each administration.

Although I have consulted published and unpublished primary sources, constraints of time and space determined that I undertake an interpretative rather than an archival effort, depending on recent scholarship. Moreover, I offer a simple introduction rather than an extensive exploration. I have relied heavily on Gwendolyn Midlo Hall's, Daniel Usner's, and Carl Brasseaux's descriptions of the early French period. While other national groups helped settle the region, the "ancienne population" remained basically French in language, culture, and outlook, and numerically dominant until the 1830s (Rogers 53). That consideration caused American officials distinct concern, but French heritage still distinguishes the area.

One way of judging the character of a slave society or of assessing its distinctive features is to look at the nature of opposition to it—to look at the extent to which it fostered or contained slave rebelliousness and to determine the ingredients and characteristics of servile unrest when and if it occurred. The United States is generally noted for the degree to which large-scale slave uprisings are lacking, certainly in comparison with the violent unrest, occasionally successfully concluded, on the part of slaves in St. Domingue, Suriname, Jamaica, Cuba, and elsewhere in the Caribbean. Brazil, the largest slave society in South America, was chronically plagued by revolts. Although the relative quiescence of slave society in North America is not to be taken to mean that slaves there were satisfied with their situation—there is plenty of evidence to the contrary—it does suggest that something about that society differentiated it from others. To explain that difference is to explain much about the society and its institutionalized bondage.

"Everywhere in the Americas," Eugene Genovese has stated, "a correlation existed between concentrations of African-born slaves and the outbreak of revolts" (Genovese, "Rebelliousness" 307). The fact that one of the largest slave rebellions in the United States occurred in eighteenth-century South Carolina and involved relatively recently imported Angolans is consistent with that assertion, as is the fact that significant slave unrest, featuring particularly, but not exclusively, the Bambara, followed increased African importation at both the start and end of the period in eighteenth-century Louisiana. Frequency of rebellion, however, may say relatively little about its scale or seriousness, and scale or seriousness is a matter of definition or interpretation. In terms of destructiveness, for example, it may be that more white people were killed in Nat Turner's rebellion in Virginia than in some "larger" slave rebellions in Brazil—defined in terms of the number of slaves involved.[3] On the other hand, the number of white deaths in Nat Turner's rebellion were so arresting partly because they were so unusual. This was in striking contrast, perhaps, to the situation in Brazil. In any case, both the Turner incident and South Carolina's Stono Rebellion destroyed more white people than the event on Louisiana's German Coast. Between sixty and eighty blacks killed fifty-five whites in Virginia in 1831; sixty to one hundred blacks killed twenty-one whites in 1739.[4] As many as 500 blacks killed three whites in 1811. In all of these cases, black lives lost exceeded white.

The ending of the slave trade, necessitating better slave treatment, partially explains the absence of large-scale slave unrest in nineteenth-century North America. That, however, is only one of several determinants. Conspiracies involving mainly native bondsmen were organized, and, in contrast to Gabriel Prosser's Virginia conspiracy in 1800, Denmark Vesey's 1822 plot involved a significant component of foreign-born—African and West Indian—participants.[5] Vesey himself was born in Africa or the West Indies and had recently gained his freedom. Both of these intended insurrections depended upon careful planning and silent adherence to be successful, and both were betrayed before they could be carried out. The Turner affair, though contemplated for some time by its instigators, took place with some spontaneity, which, according to Marion Kilson, helps to explain both its success and its failure: success in that it actually took place but failure because it had no long-range purpose and was relatively easily crushed (176). In a country where the white population outnumbered the black, monopolized the sources of power, and possessed the will to use it, where, in a word, insurrection had no real chance of success—either in establishing black domination or as a viable means of escape—quiescence, as Genovese argues in *From Rebellion to Revolution,* made good sense. Without debating the merits of the "paternalistic compromise" as an explanation, Thomas Fiehrer, following that reasoning, comments that "with some exception in the Carolinas and Louisiana, where French planterdom accounted for a different social pattern, slaves of the Old South rather completely internalized the hierarchical-racist ethos of the larger society. Servility and conformity, which typify the subordinate caste in North American slavery, became in some measure established in Louisiana only with Americanization" (Fiehrer, 18). The existence of Turner and others of his ilk casts doubt on the extent to which slaves "completely internalized" this "hierarchical-racist ethos"; growing evidence on the slave community indicates that they had alternative perspectives. At the same time, it must be conceded that successful planters everywhere achieved their aims by getting bondsmen to identify their interest with that of the master class, and North American planters may have been more successful than most in doing so. This purpose was partly accomplished by assuming greater responsibility for the slaves' livelihood. Major Amos Stoddard, an American who visited Louisiana soon after the purchase, compared the condition of slaves in the new acquisition with that of those in the adjoining American territory:

> In no part of the world are slaves better treated than in the Mississippi Territory, where the planters generally allow them salted meat, as much corn meal as they can consume, cows to furnish milk for their families, land for gardens, and the privilege of raising fowls. They also allow them one suit of clothes for summer, and another for winter. Their slaves are active and robust, and enabled to perform their allotted portions of work with ease. . . .
>
> When we pass into Louisiana we behold a different and more disgusting picture. The French and Spanish planters treat their slaves with great rigor. . . . Few of them allow any clothing to their slaves, or any kind of food, except a small quantity of corn; and even this they are obliged to pound, or grind, while they ought to be at rest. The consequence is, that the slaves are extremely debilitated, and incapable of much labor. (332–33)

The depiction of conditions in the "Mississippi Territory" is somewhat idealized: most slaves did not have cows or milk, and they may or may not have had gardens or fowl. Yet they received adequate subsistence, and anything else was supplemental. But if Stoddard exaggerated about conditions in

Louisiana, he did not do so by much; his description accords well with that of other observers. The basic dissimilarity is accurate. Anglo-American planters attempted to supply the essential needs of their slaves in a way that Louisiana planters did not, and the consequences were psychological as well as physical. But whatever the myriad components of their reasoning, Anglo-American slaves could not help but accept the obvious disproportion of power, a situation that, before the American period, was not always absolute in Louisiana.

Settled by French and Spaniards, Louisiana was governed by civil law, a fact that distinguished it from the common-law nation to which it was joined. The outlook of colonists there was distinctive. The *Code Noir,* or Black Code, introduced in 1724, was retained by the Spanish with modifications that re-enforced its humane provisions, though these clauses were as often honored in the breach as in the observance. Eugene Genovese has argued that the code was "notoriously a dead letter" in St. Domingue, while Gwendolyn Hall adduces evidence to suggest that French colonial authorities there tried consistently to enforce it (Genovese, "Materialism" 373; Hall, *Social Control* 87–89). In Louisiana, the situation varied with the level of material development and the locus of political control—that is, whether power proceeded from the metropolis or had shifted to the colony. In the early days of French settlement, when the colony was at a low level of development and was in the process of adopting a labor system, colonists brought with them a paternalistic ethos that governed relations between superiors and inferiors—lords and peasants, fathers and families—in France.[6] This relationship involved mutual obligations and responsibilities but also mutual caring, if not affection. More than one historian has warned against confusing paternalism with kindness, and Carl Brasseaux cautions that "relations between lord and peasant, and, indeed among French family members, were frequently poor, and, by modern standards, brutal. The landholder, nevertheless, felt obligated to guide and, when necessary, discipline his workers as he would his children" (140). Bringing this cultural background intact, early landholders and officials operated within its framework and attempted to provide food, clothing, and shelter to their workers without apparent distinction as to color or status. Governor Bienville, for example, exerted himself to reunite a slave family, and another official nullified an important military regulation because two slaves were—unjustly, he felt—flogged in an attempt to carry it out. These events occurred before the Black Code—which reaffirmed rather than established a paternalistic outlook toward blacks—was applied to Louisiana. The code was guided by practical rather than humanistic considerations, however, and planters obeyed those articles that fit their attitude and purpose and disregarded those that did not. The government was not strong enough to enforce the code, and adherence was largely voluntary. Nevertheless, planters "exhibited a remarkable degree of paternalism toward their black laborers," and this was true without regard to plantation size. The majority of slaveholdings, however, was small (Brasseaux 140). It is worth noting, too, that the ways in which the code was disregarded were not always to the slave's disadvantage.

The Black Code established that slaves had to be properly housed, clothed, and fed, even when old and disabled, and authorized them to bring suit against masters who failed to comply with the regulation. They could also bring suit if they were physically abused. Slave families were not to be broken up before children reached the age of puberty, nor could slaves be forced to marry. Slaves were to be instructed in the Roman Catholic faith and were to observe Sundays and holidays. Concubinage between slaves and free people, whether white or black, was forbidden. Interracial marriages between whites and blacks were also forbidden. (Mathé Allain argues, however, that that prohibition had less to do with a concern for racial purity than with the preservation of royal authority. Faced with obstreperous colonists in the West Indies, the French government feared that interracial unions would create a community of interest between whites and free blacks in opposition to the crown, an alliance it designed, in the islands and on the continent, to prevent [Allain, "Slave Policies"134; Allain, *"Not Worth a Straw"* 81–82]).

In fact, the nine- to eleven-hour day the slaves worked in early Louisiana compared favorably with the ten- to sixteen-hour day of French textile workers in the same era (Brasseaux 143; Hall, *Africans* 128). Moreover, they were allowed a two-hour lunch break, during which they could work for themselves. Although slaves occasionally ran away, none of the published depositions Brasseaux examined gave overwork as a cause; Hall, however, asserts that slaves did run away as a result of being overworked (Brasseaux 143; Hall, *Africans* 128). It even seems that their medical needs were considered, albeit to what effect is moot. More than one contemporary commented on the deplorable state of the medical profession in the colony (M. Wood 681; Robin 41; Duffy 1–6). But at least the situation was no worse for blacks than for whites. And to the extent that they practiced herbal medicine brought from Africa or learned from Indians, medical care may even have been better for blacks than for whites (Usner, "From African Captivity" 33). So to some extent, at least, both the letter and the spirit of the *Code Noir* was observed. It should be emphasized, however, that more than one source indicates that slaves occasionally were overworked and underfed (in view of the sketch Hall draws of disorder it could hardly have been otherwise), and one historian places responsibility for the relatively short workday on black *commandeurs* rather than white planters (Usner, "From African Captivity" 38; Brasseaux, 143n). In addition, when slaves did run away, punishment could be ferocious (Usner, "From African Captivity" 42). Still, none of this was inconsistent with paternalism.

According to Brasseaux:

> The attitude of these early Louisiana masters is best reflected in [Jean de] Pradel's personal correspondence. In a letter to his brother, dated 1755, Pradel relates the manner in which St. Louis, his slave to whom he frequently entrusted minor business matters, had unfortunately betrayed his master's confidence. St. Louis was charged with the responsibility of transporting sheep each morning from Pradel's Cannes Brulees indigo plantation, "Montplaisir," to the New Orleans slaughterhouse; but, instead of departing at dawn, as directed by his master, St. Louis, accompanied by two young black oarsmen, regularly left the Pradel concession as soon as the chevalier had retired for the evening. According to Pradel, St. Louis then "danced all night at free Negroes' homes with Negroes and Negresses from town [New Orleans], [at which] he furnished fiddle music and light meals worth 150 livres." The source of St. Louis' generosity, however, was his thriving illicit operation in sheep and poultry pilfered from "Montplaisir." While Pradel had no apparent objection to his slave's carousing, he was most concerned about the thefts. Nevertheless, Pradel confided to his brother that ". . . without speaking to him nor having him flogged, I told my commander to take him to the Negro quarters and make him work with them." (144)

If this case represents an example of a kindly-hearted patriarch, it also furnishes evidence of the extent to which violation of the Black Code was not always to the slave's disadvantage, for "Pradel's slave traveled freely without proper authorization, sold livestock and poultry without written permission, kept the proceeds of the sales, used the profits to purchase merchandise for himself, visited free men of color during his unauthorized absence from 'Montplaisir,' and danced the calinda with slaves from several concessions—all of which were expressly forbidden by existing slave regulations." (Brasseaux 144–45).

Of course, the contraband trade in which St. Louis engaged resulted partly from the attempt, following West Indian practice, to make Louisiana slaves, as much as possible, support themselves. They were given plots of ground to cultivate for their own use and were permitted Sunday and sometimes Saturday to work for themselves. While service was supposed to be suspended during Mass, all places of business were open on Sundays and holidays (Dart 35; J. Robertson 1:75). Slaves also used their lunch breaks to work for others to gain extra money, and some sold fruit, vegetables, or firewood (Usner, "From African Captivity" 39). Their contribution became part of the market economy, whose restriction would have been detrimental, though their earnings, too, were in violation of the Black Code. This obligation for slaves to feed themselves and the resulting self-sufficiency was one aspect of a distinctive planter outlook in Louisiana, in contrast to Anglo North America, though a unique labor practice—the task system—led to the development of a similar market economy and similar independence among slaves in lowland South Carolina, where it was likewise contrary to law (Littlefield). The task system appears to have been used somewhat in Louisiana as well—in the Spanish period if not the French, but probably in both (Robin 238). Its chief characteristic and advantage was that after an assignment was completed, the laborer had the rest of the day to himself. Slaves preferred this arrangement though not all labor was suited to it. Régine Hubert-Robert comments that planters preferred the raising of indigo because, among other reasons, its seasonal character left slaves periods of freedom to perform other duties, such as making shingles, lintels, and other construction materials that were readily marketable (248). These skills would appear to be imminently suitable to the task system, and slaves may also have appreciated this aspect of indigo farming, despite the fact that woodworking entailed the exacting (and exhausting) process of gathering wood in cypress swamps. With independent time-management came a corresponding lack of planter control.

There were not many free blacks during the French period; one count has only 165 in 1763, and some think that their impact has been exaggerated (Fiehrer 14). But as the Pradel incident illustrates, they were an added element complicating planter control, however slightly, by providing slaves an opening. In the French as in the Spanish period, the majority of those emancipated were likely the progeny of interracial sex, since the majority of those freed were of mixed race. (Most nonmixed blacks who were freed were women.) According to one source, the Spanish in 1769 counted seventy-three free blacks and ninety-two free mulattoes, a likely undercount considering the work of Kimberly S. Hanger (Sterkx 33n; Hanger 18). And while Ira Berlin argues that the disproportion between free blacks and mulattoes increased during the

Spanish period, Hanger, in an argument hinging on the interpretation of those terms, suggests the contrary (Berlin 110; Hanger 29).[7] The Spaniards expanded opportunities for freedom, introducing *coartación,* or self-purchase, among other things, and also expanded miscegenation and the fruits thereof (Fiehrer 21n). And there were still other ways for slaves to obtain freedom: faithful service to a master and meritorious service to the colony were two. The Superior Council freed some slaves for their loyalty during the Natchez War (Sterkx 26–27), and others achieved emancipation after years of quiet bondage. In a few instances, as, for example, in the case of the sixty-year-old Françoise (Lugano 603), self-interest as well as gratitude may have sparked the beneficent action, for the owner was relieved from the responsibility of caring for an aged and decrepit charge. On the other hand, slaves already bore a large share of the obligation for their own maintenance, and remaining enslaved was no guarantee of adequate support. Notwithstanding the rifts that developed between blacks and mulattoes involving color and status—and perhaps between free blacks and slaves over status—there was still greater ground for common sympathy and interest during the French regime than might later have been the case.

In fact, there was extensive interaction among all three of the races—black, white, and Native American—during most of the French era. James T. McGowan, Gwendolyn Hall, and Daniel Usner all write about the extent to which American Indian customs had significant influence on early French settlers before the adoption of slavery. While some officials favored intermarriage between French and Indians as a solution to problems of settlement, others opposed it because of the fear that French culture in the region would be subsumed into Native American culture rather than the reverse. Colonists adopted Indian foods, medicines, and ways of dress. "Frenchmen," for example, "shed their traditional costumes and moved through the forest with loose leggings and a cloth around their waist. French women dispensed with shoes and sometimes with dresses; at work in the humid heat, they often wore only a petticoat around their lower body, leaving their breasts completely bare" (McGowan 11). Even building patterns reflected local influence (McGowan 10–12, 15–17; Hall, *Africans* 1–27; Usner, *Indians* 13–105). After 1718, when planters increasingly chose to own slaves rather than employ indentured servants, they were still forced into intense relationships with native peoples. Authorities had now to prevent possible collusion between slaves and Indians. Thus, during the Natchez War, Governor Perier sent blacks to attack an unoffending native group near New Orleans, setting an example that "kept in check all the small nations higher up the river" (Gayarré 1:423). But it reenforced antipathy between black men and red, which had already been encouraged by the offering of bounties to Indians for the return of runaways (Gayarré 1:422–23; Brasseaux 155; Usner, *Indians* 73–76). By 1727, blacks outnumbered whites in southern Louisiana, a pattern that may have moderated somewhat in the 1740s and certainly had by the 1760s (Sterkx 33n; Brasseaux 157; Gayarré 2:11–12; Hall, *Africans* 177; Lachance, "Growth" 230).[8] As slavery increased, crop production advanced, and Indians were defeated or removed, stratification led to greater social distance between masters and slaves and between black and red and brown.

The attorneys general through most of the French period were natives of the mother country and followed a policy of selective enforcement generally consistent with the humanitarian impulse of the *Code Noir* but also in accordance with the wishes of slaveholders, who dominated the Superior Council. The prohibition against cruelty to slaves, for example, was enforced only to the extent that owners brought suit for damages if their property was mistreated by someone else. It was thus a civil rather than a criminal matter, although the code provided for criminal punishments. The slaves' right to adequate food and clothing was ignored, as was the provision for religious instruction. The ban against interracial cohabitation was notoriously flouted. While it declined somewhat as the number of white females increased, it remained a prevalent practice that, in violation of the Black Code, the Superior Council condoned by freeing the mixed-race children and the mistresses of planters. The code even anticipated this result by forbidding gifts or donations to freedmen in an apparent attempt to preserve the inheritance of the "legitimate" family (Allain, *"Not Worth a Straw"* 135; Brasseaux 147–49).[9]

This relatively mild regime, consistent with paternalism if not the Black Code, was reversed beginning in the 1750s and continuing into the 1760s. Coincident with increasing *marronage* (escaped slaves banding together to form their own societies); the recognition of blacks as a threat (which had previously been overshadowed by the danger from aboriginal groups); the acquisition of a native-born attorney general versed in, and fearful of, antislavery activity in France; and a concern about the disproportion of blacks to whites, conditions tightened. The colony enacted stricter regulations, provided harsher punishments, and restricted outside influence (Brasseaux 155–58). With the power of the local planters ascendant, the initial guiding paternalism, whether legal or cultural, was modified and planter authority solidified. The slaves' condition deteriorated not merely because the code was less likely to be enforced—

it never had been completely—but because the tenor of society had changed, for the worse from the slave's point of view. The treatment of slaves in French Louisiana had evolved toward the absolute planter control often considered predominant in Anglo North America. In fact, it followed the trend of the planter class's treatment of slaves everywhere. Still, certain aspects of slaveholding society in Louisiana provided slaves with greater autonomy than usual among Anglo North American slaveholding society; slaves in Louisiana still had part of the weekend free to work for themselves and were able to participate in the local market economy, their contribution to which was essential. Of course, these distinctions were not necessarily or solely attributes of Latin or Gallic cultural conditioning. Such practices in Louisiana had counterparts in South Carolina and the British West Indies. Along with Louisiana slaves' greater economic freedom went a more open attitude among whites toward miscegenation.

When the Spanish assumed control, the *Siete Partidas* (Seven Parts) code supplemented the Black Code. Its ideals were at least as protective of the slave as the Black Code's, if not more so, and the Spaniards came out of a tradition that was no less paternalistic than that of the French. But they had to establish administrative control before they could proceed with any meaningful regulation, whether of white people or black. They immediately faced a white rebellion that Alejandro "Bloody" O'Reilly put down with expulsions and executions, but Spanish authority remained somewhat tenuous. To say, then, as Fiehrer does, that the code was more rigorously enforced under the French than the Spanish is perhaps to miss the point. It may be true in general, as Fiehrer summarizes Gwendolyn Hall, that the Spanish system was "vague, pompous, abstract, unreal, slow to formulate adaptations and . . . indifferent towards slaves until the advent of Bourbon reforms" (Fiehrer 16; Hall, *Social Control* 88), but faced with hostile colonists opposed to their rule in Louisiana, the Spanish could not afford to be more antagonistic by obtruding their power between masters and slaves. That is to say, they could not do so in any brutal way. The slaves benefitted because the Spanish followed the earlier Gallic practice of keeping elements in the colony divided. In the same fashion that French authorities forbade interracial marriage to divide whites from freedmen and played off blacks and Indians against each other, so Spanish officials balanced blacks and mulattoes against French settlers. Within the interstices of this society rent by differences, slaves found room to maneuver, although, for other reasons, their overall situation may well have continued to decline. Among Genovese's criteria is that of day-to-day living conditions, including such things as food, clothing, housing, length of workday, and working conditions ("Treatment" 203). By this standard, the slaves were not doing well. Spanish missionaries who came to replace their French counterparts complained that "the generality of slaves here, . . . are furnished by their masters but with one barrel of corn per month, which is less than is given to a horse. This barrel of corn is to be both food and clothing to them; and, as this is impossible, their necessities drive them into prostitution and other shameful vices" (Gayarré 3:65). Others have pointed out that this barrel of corn was in ears, or on the husk, which amounted to no more than a third of a barrel in grain. Moreover, it had to be husked, shelled, and pounded before it could be used, costing valuable time and effort that was charged to the slave's account (J. Robertson 1:181–84). While there may have been few documented cases of slaves running away because of overwork in the early French period, even then the same could not be said about slaves absconding because of inadequate food (Brasseaux 154).

Spanish missionaries were also upset that slaves cohabited together without benefit of marriage and, worse, that they did so with the knowledge of their masters. When admonished, slaves responded "that they are exposed to be sold by their masters and to be thus separated" (Gayarré 3:63), which, if true, indicates that the prohibition against separating married slaves was not followed. This may have been only an excuse, however, for some scholars think that the rule against separating married slaves was the one most strictly observed (Allain, *"Not Worth a Straw"* 135; Brasseaux 147). What is important is that, under the Spanish, slaves continued to have a great deal of autonomy in arranging their social lives. Evidence presented at a trial following the murder of Juan Baptiste Cézaire Lebreton in 1771 makes it clear that their freedoms in this regard had scarcely eroded. Some blacks, at least, had guns and escorted their women between neighboring plantations without authorization. Temba, whom Lebreton employed as hunter, was scolded for sleeping away from the plantation, but he continued to do so despite the threat of punishment. It would seem, in fact, that on Lebreton's plantation slaves commonly slept away from home (Porteous). That this case was not isolated is apparent in C. C. Robin's comment that the nightly peregrinations of the slaves regularly woke him at one place where he occasionally stayed (Robin 245). Louisiana slaves' relative freedom of movement relates to Genovese's second criterion, referring to general conditions of life and including "family security, opportunities for an independent social and religious life and . . . cultural developments" (Genovese, "Treatment" 203). In this instance, with some possible reservations concerning family life, conditions may not have changed. "It seems to me," one missionary to Louisiana advised, "that the most effective way to prevent the commission of such sins [as unwed cohabitation], is to impose upon the masters the obligation of watching over the morals of their slaves" (Genovese, "Treatment" 203). But this obligation the Black Code had already imposed. The planters' respect for it (or lack thereof) remained as it always had been.

When the specter of rebellion in St. Domingue cast its shadow on the Gulf Coast, the Spanish acted to provide protections guaranteed by law in the hope of avoiding the evident consequences of violent slave unrest. Certainly, bad treatment of slaves in the first sense (i.e., in terms of day-to-day living conditions), a concomitant partly of economic decline, was involved in a planned uprising in Pointe Coupee Parish in 1795, and the governor was sympathetic to the slaves (Fiehrer 16). Governor Carondelet confessed, however, that he could not act without the support of the Cabildo (the New Orleans city council), which was controlled by landowners opposed to his intentions. The Cabildo had earlier protested to Spain against humane provisions enacted in the *Código Negro Español* (1789) and forced Carondelet to minimize its effects (Arena 32–34; Holmes 343–44; Fiehrer 16). Yet, on the other hand, the Cabildo had prevented executions of slaves involved in a conspiracy in 1791—executions that the governor favored in order to help maintain order—because its members objected to the financial loss they would impose on the slaves' owners (Holmes, 343). It is clear that Spanish authority attempted to balance the concerns of masters and slaves, with the metropolis promulgating ideal regulations and the local governor, sympathetic to these aims, nevertheless operating within the limits of practical realities.

One of the practical realities was that Spanish authority depended in part on the support of black and mulatto troops, some of whom had come over from Cuba with Alejandro O'Reilly (McConnell 16). The French had also used black troops, and so their presence in itself did not herald a precedent. Under the French, however, these troops had been used against Indians, while under the Spanish they posed a threat to white colonists. The Spaniards also recruited local blacks, who, obviously dependent upon them for their position, could be expected to be loyal (McConnell 17). Under the circumstances, Spanish authorities had less reason than French colonials to regard every black man as a potential enemy. To the contrary, they had good reason to establish a working relationship with the black population. "Mulattoes and negroes are openly protected by the government," one visitor charged. "He who was to strike one of those persons even though he had run away from him, would be severely punished" (J. Robertson 1:71). Carondelet encouraged slaves to complain to him about their masters' conduct though he denied the charge that he upbraided planters in the presence of their slaves (Lachance, "Politics" 174). Along with more liberal manumission policies went more extensive miscegenation and an increase in the number of free blacks and mulattoes. Travelers commonly remarked on the pervasiveness of concubinage between white men and black women, and one even commented that "white women at times esteem well built men of color" (J. Robertson 1:71). This intimacy was beneficial in maintaining Spanish control over the colony but not in solidifying the master's control over the slaves.

Concubines might be either slave or free and those who had been slaves could, as a result of the relationship, become free, along with their children. But whether they were freed or not, they still had ties to the slave community. The free black or mulatto community was not so large that it could afford to divorce itself entirely from the slaves, even when it wanted to do so. For example, dances designed for free men of color were frequently invaded by slaves—so the "coloreds" complained. They asked authorities to prevent the intrusion. Such events doubtless occurred most often in New Orleans, where there were freedmen sufficient to envision separate gatherings. In the countryside, where the number of free coloreds was small, they sometimes attended slave affairs. Dances held on a plantation or in the woods catered to the whole black community without regard to status or color even though such distinctions existed. No matter how light-skinned, coloreds could not attend affairs with white people and were left either to their own devices or to relationships with blacks. Connections between the two, sometimes denied, were not forgotten. "I have noticed," C. C. Robin averred, "especially in the city that while the funerals of white people are attended by a few, those of colored people are attended by a crowd, and mulattoes, quadroons married to white people, do not disdain attending the funeral of a black" (248).

Contemporaries observed that "colored" women frequently took up with white men and that sometimes young girls were placed in such relationships by their mothers when they were as young as fourteen years old (J. Robertson 1:85); that their attachment to these men was transitory and based on pecuniary considerations; and that colored men discreetly vacated the homes of their mothers and sisters when white men came to call and that they often married women darker than themselves because women with lighter skin would not have them (J. Robertson 1:87; "Observations" 168). Then there were the fabled "quadroon" balls, confined to white men and colored women. Before these balls were organized, white men attended black balls, despite some opposition from authorities (Morazan 310–15). While none of these trends would necessarily predispose colored people favorably toward blacks, they would not conduce to an extraordinary regard for white people either, since they underlined a sense of their own inferiority and whites' domination. The visitor Berquin Duvallon thought that colored women "only affect[ed] a fondness for whites" and that, in reality, their sentiments were "with men of their own colour" ("Observations" 168). This antipathy of mulattoes to whites, on the one hand, or to blacks, one the other, would suit Spanish authorities. But whatever the range of conflicts and emotions, contacts between this class and the slaves and of the Spanish with both could not help but benefit the most enterprising among the bondsmen. One is sometimes tempted to equate mulatto with free person and black with slave even though the equation was not absolute, and the extent to which it was not is part of the extent to which slaves benefitted. Miscegenation served to demystify the planters, if mystification ever obtained, and to prevent the formation of an impermeable social system entirely separating blacks from whites and freemen from slaves in such a way as to contribute to an unquestioned mythology of white supremacy. This process of demystification continued at taverns and gaming tables, described as promiscuous gatherings of men regardless of status or color (J. Robertson 1:216; Dart 42–45).

The Spanish gave sanction to the variations of color gradation in Louisiana. The French there had practiced more racial openness, and the "colored" wives of white men were often identified as white. It is possible, however, that this attitude was a function at an earlier stage of what Paul Lachance describes for a later period, when marriages were enrolled on either a black or a white register, obliging a white man to choose one or the other and bringing them somewhat closer to their Anglo North American counterparts in more sharply defining racial lines, providing only the outlet of mixed-race people's "passing" as white. Certainly in the West Indies the French were close to English practices, though Hall insists that Louisiana colonists were more flexible than their Caribbean compatriots (Foner 406; Lachance, "Formation" 213–14; Hall, *Africans* 239–42). There may not have been enough of a mixed population, at least as a cohesive unit, for the French to have made much distinction among *gens de couleurs* in the early days of settlement. But the Spanish brought with them their own complexity of perceptions and expressions, somewhat simplified, as when they transported from Cuba *moreno,* or "dark," and *pardo,* or "light," regiments of colored troops (McConnell 16). It was the Spanish who introduced the "quadroon" balls and established or reinforced a preference for that class of women (Morazan 310). Of course, tastes varied. Amos Stoddard remarked that the Spanish preferred black to colored women and that they carried "their impure connexions to a much greater extent than any other description of inhabitant" (328). But even Stoddard noted the normal practice of whites' establishing relationships with lighter-skinned women of color.

Gerald Mullin and Mechal Sobel, among others, write about the different sense of time reckoning and other concepts that divided Africans from Europeans, and Fiehrer uses these cultural distinctions as important considerations in distinguishing blacks from *gens de couleurs.*[10] But Sobel points out that some of these outlooks had a common base in peasant society on both continents, and while European culture changed among the elite, earlier concepts still had resonance among the peasant class. Along these lines, such cultural divergence as existed between blacks and mulattoes was probably more significant in the nineteenth century in a more settled society than it was in the eighteenth century, despite the larger African component at the earlier stage. Moreover, these people would have been bicultural as they were biracial, instilling within the group, and within individuals, a span of attitudes from one end of the racial-cultural spectrum to the other. Finally, even blacks and whites began at some point to develop a degree of cultural commonality in some respects.

One evidence of this is in blacks' and whites' outlooks on sex and marriage. As the Spanish missionaries complained about extramarital sex among the slaves, they likewise criticized the practice among planters. Many white men remained unmarried and relied on black or colored women for sexual release. If they married, they might not change preexisting habits. There were various reasons for the initial choice, having primarily to do with the sexual disproportion among whites. But if miscegenation declined at some point during the French period, with a growing immigration of white females, it did not cease. Indications are that it increased under the Spanish. In their penchant for extramarital sex, and in their disinclination toward marriage in general (assuming reports were correct), black men and white men were alike (J. Robertson 1:101–2, 111, 200; Hall, *Africans* 128–29, 235–74). The fact that, in some sense, they desired the same women, created ostensible similarity within basic distinction: similitude in that they shared a common object of desire divergence in that white men had the upper hand and competition could not help but create conflict. In addition, white men had a choice that black men did not, in that white women normally were unattainable to blacks as, practically, were many women of color. Indeed, as Winthrop Jordan suggests, white men's very interest in black women carried implications of racism and dominion. Similar activities, therefore, carried different imports for black and white men and were at once uniting and dividing. Still their common interest in black and "colored" women created a distinctive cultural milieu and opportunities in Louisiana. Among the opportunities, however, were those for revolt, especially if "good" treatment in Genovese's second sense (general conditions of life) was coupled with "bad" treatment in the first (day-to-day living conditions). There was, Paul Lachance points out, a "dialectical relationship" between frequent interracial cohabitation and both cruelty and repression ("Politics" 174). This dynamic was by no means inconsistent with paternalism and continued to operate as the province moved steadily in the direction of materialism. "Even observers from Saint-Domingue," Lachance reflects, "notorious for the callous treatment of slaves, commented on the brutality of Louisiana slaveholders" ("Politics" 174n).

The decade of the 1790s may be taken as the watershed separating whatever was left of an older, paternalistic ethos from a more exploitative economic and social mentality, provided one bears in mind that these qualities are not necessarily absolute. One could find aspects of each throughout the antebellum period. But in the 1790s, the staples of tobacco and indigo began to be replaced by sugar and cotton (though the latter had been grown earlier). Sugar cultivation in particular is labor intensive and traditionally associated with a deterioration in the physical well-being of the slave.[11] The revolution in St. Domingue spurred slave unrest in Louisiana and prompted planters to adhere more closely to some of the harsher features of the Black Code. Reopening of the slave trade, although supposed to be restricted to African rather than West Indian sources, nonetheless provided an opening for the importation of those infected with the revolutionary virus. Other slaves came with successive waves of refugees from St. Domingue. Harsher labor conditions, a spirit of insubordination, and a growing slave population created an explosive mixture. When the United States acquired Louisiana in 1803 and followed the usual American practice of placing all power in the hands of the planters, they responded in 1806 with one of the strictest slave codes in the nation. It purged the Black Code of all its benevolent features and left those clauses that ensured the master's authority. The slave owners now had uncontested power in a government that, in terms of its ability to suppress slave unrest, was stronger than ever it had been. The ultimate fate of a rebellion now could never really be in doubt.

The 1811 revolt took place in an area settled primarily by German-speaking farmers—mainly from Baden, Alsace, and the Palatinate—among whom French officials also settled (Conrad, *St.-Jean-Baptiste* vii; Conrad, *German Coast* vii). It served as a breadbasket for New Orleans, producing dairy products and garden crops along with the staples of rice, indigo, corn, and cotton (Deiler 62; M. Wood 671). It was, for most of the eighteenth century, an area of yeomen farmers who worked alongside the few slaves they possessed, a situation normally associated with considerate slave treatment. At the turn of the century, some in the region switched to sugar planting, requiring larger units of production, and while it may be described as largely a general farming region as late as 1811, it was clearly an area in transition by that time (Conrad, *German Coast* viii). In St. Charles Parish, the southeastern part of the county, closest to New Orleans, the census of 1810 revealed 35 planters with 20 or more slaves, comprising an aggregate of 1,870, or 81 percent of the 2,321 slaves in the parish. St. John the Baptist Parish had not yet reached that level of development. There, 21 planters had 731 slaves, or 48 percent of the 1,518 in holdings of 20 or more. Most of these were in holdings of less than 30, and only 7 had more than 40; the largest was Manuel Andry's, with 86 (United States, Census Office, *Aggregate* 82; United States, Census Office, Third Census). Andry almost certainly raised sugar, and it was at his plantation that the insurrection began.

In a region such as the German Coast, there would be many ways to explain both the number of slaves who supported the rebellion and the number who did not. The county might be considered a microcosm of the province, or at least of its southern portion, exhibiting the full range of slave treatment in its various permutations. The extremes of slave treatment could be found in other places, but the average range of treatment was probably greater in the county and in the province than in other areas of the United States. Thomas Fiehrer has related slavery in Louisiana to the institution in the West Indies, and in both places it had a violent history. It is possible to view the 1811 incident as part of that tradition. But is it also part of the history of slave resistence in the United States, suffering all the disadvantages such opposition encountered on the continent. Outside of the unique environment of Louisiana it may not have occurred at all. In one sense, however, to inquire into the reasons for the revolt is to beg the question. For as Herbert Aptheker once said, the reason for slave revolts was slavery.

NOTES

1. One of the best accounts of the 1811 rebellion is James Dorman, but it will likely be superceded by Paquette. There are also accounts in Aptheker, *American Negro Slave Revolts* 249–51; Gayarré 4:266–68; Fortier 3:78–79; Taylor 212–14; and Young 208–10, among other places.

A slightly different version of this essay appeared in Wolfgang Binder, ed., *Creoles and Cajuns: French Louisiana–La Louisiane Française* (Frankfurt am Main; New York: Peter Lang, 1998), 91–114. I have modified some of my earlier assertions in accordance with recent scholarship but have not entirely reconceptualized the piece.

2. Gayarré 4:266–67. Gayarré reported the incident of Trépanier alone holding off a crowd of blacks with a shotgun, but, adopting a white supremacist stance, the historian used it simultaneously as evidence of the extent to which white people in Louisiana really had nothing to fear from blacks and as a reason blacks ought to remain suppressed. He did not report Trépanier's fate.

3. For Brazil see Kent; Schwartz; and Genovese, *From Rebellion to Revolution.*

4. For Nat Turner see Aptheker, *Nat Turner's* 48–49; Oates; French; and Greenberg. For the Stono Rebellion see P. Wood 308–26; M. Mullin 12; Olwell, 21–29; Morgan, 455–56; Smith; and Thornton, 1101–13.

5. For Gabriel Prosser see Sidbury; and Egerton, *Gabriel's Rebellion.* For Denmark Vesey see Lofton; D. Robertson; Egerton, *He Shall Go;* and Walker and Silverman.

6. The following three paragraphs largely follow Brasseaux. Obviously, he is not responsible for the way I use the information.

7. Kimberly Hanger offers a more sophisticated, or at least more extensive, terminology of race mixture than suggested by the terms "black" and "mulatto" and assuming "moreno" and "grifo," which phenotypically refer to the "dark-skinned" can be counted as "black." Hanger defines morenos and grifos as "slaves with more than half African blood" (29), and by her count 56.7 percent of those freed in New Orleans between 1771 and 1803 were "black." However, they would still be mixed race. Hanger also offers an extended treatment of manumission in Spanish New Orleans (17–54).

8. Paul Lachance ("Growth") provides the most recent, complete, and dependable statistics for early Louisiana though his regional aggregations do not always coincide with my conceptualization. But also see Pitchard.

9. Schafer explores the issue of miscegenation and the legal concerns that developed, particularly in the nineteenth century.

10. Smith in both *Mastered By the Clock* and "Political Economy" discusses the distinctive perspectives on time that separated even the northern and southern United States.

11. See McDonald for details about sugar cultivation in Louisiana, including the possibility of material accumulation by slaves and development of an internal market system along with the harsh regime of cultivation.

WORKS CONSULTED

Allain, Mathé. *"Not Worth a Straw": French Colonial Policy and the Early Years of Louisiana*. Lafayette: Center for Louisiana Studies, University of Southwestern Louisiana, 1988.

———. "Slave Policies in French Louisiana." *Louisiana History* 21 (1980): 127–38.

Aptheker, Herbert. *American Negro Slave Revolts*. 1943. Reprint, New York: International Publishers, 1983.

———. *Nat Turner's Slave Rebellion*. 1966. Reprint, New York: Grove, 1968.

Arena, Richard C. "Landholding and Political Power in Spanish Louisiana." *Louisiana Historical Quarterly* 36 (1955): 23–39.

Berlin, Ira. *Slaves without Masters: The Free Negro in the Antebellum South*. New York: Pantheon, 1974.

Brasseaux, Carl A. "The Administration of Slave Regulations in French Louisiana, 1724–1766." *Louisiana History* 21 (1980): 139–58.

Carter, Clarence E., comp. *The Territorial Papers of the United States*. Vol. 9, *Territory of Orleans, 1803–1812*. Washington, D.C.: Government Printing Office, 1940.

Conrad, Glenn R. *The German Coast: Abstracts of the Civil Records of St. Charles and St. John the Baptist Parishes, 1804–1812*. Lafayette: Center for Louisiana Studies, University of Southwestern Louisiana, 1981.

———. Ed. *St. Charles: Abstracts of the Civil Records of St. Charles Parish, 1700–1803*. Lafayette: University of Southwestern Louisiana, 1974.

———. *Saint-Jean-Baptiste des Allemands: Abstracts of the Civil Records of St. John the Baptist Parish, with Genealogy and Index, 1753–1803*. Lafayette: University of Southwestern Louisiana, 1972.

———. "Summary of Trial Proceedings of Those Accused of Participating in the Slave Uprising of January 9, 1811." *Louisiana History* 18 (1977): 472–73.

Dart, Henry P. "Episodes of Life in Colonial Louisiana." *Louisiana Historical Quarterly* 6 (1923): 35–46.

Deiler, J. Hanno. *The Settlement of the German Coast of Louisiana and the Creoles of German Descent*. Philadelphia: Americana Germanica Press, 1909.

Dorman, James. "The Persistent Specter: Slave Rebellion in Territorial Louisiana." *Louisiana History* 18 (1977): 389–404.

Duffy, John. "Slavery and Slave Health in Louisiana, 1766–1825." *Bulletin of the Tulane University Medical Faculty* 26 (1967): 1–6.

Egerton, Douglas. *Gabriel's Rebellion: The Virginia Slave Conspiracies of 1800 and 1802*. Chapel Hill: University of North Carolina Press, 1993.

———. *He Shall Go Out Free: The Lives of Denmark Vesey*. Latham, Md.: Rowman and Littlefield, 2004.

Everett, Donald. "Emigres and Militiamen: Free Persons of Color in New Orleans, 1803–1815." *Journal of Negro History* 38 (1953): 377–402.

Fiehrer, Thomas M. "The African Presence in Colonial Louisiana: An Essay on the Continuity of Caribbean Culture." *Louisiana's Black Heritage*. Ed. Robert R. McDonald, John R. Kemp, and Edward F. Haas. New Orleans: Louisiana State Museum, 1979. 3–31.

Foner, Laura. "The Free People of Color in Louisiana and St. Domingue: A Comparative Portrait of Two Three-Caste Slave Societies." *Journal of Social History* 3 (1970): 406–30.

Fortier, Alcée. *A History of Louisiana*. 4 vols. New York: Manzi, Joyant & Co., 1904.

French, Scot. *The Rebellious Slave: Nat Turner in American Memory*. Boston: Houghton Mifflin, 2004.

Gayarré, Charles. *History of Louisiana*. 4th ed. 4 vols. New Orleans: F. F. Hansell & Bro., 1903.

Genovese, Eugene D. *From Rebellion to Revolution: Afro-American Slave Revolts in the Making of the Modern World*. Baton Rouge: Louisiana State University Press, 1979.

———. "Materialism and Idealism in the History of Negro Slavery in the Americas." *Journal of Social History* (1968): 371–94.

———. "Rebelliousness and Docility in the Negro Slave: A Critique of the Elkins Thesis." *Civil War History* 4 (1967): 293–329.

———. "The Treatment of Slaves in Different Countries: Problems in the Application of the Comparative Method." *Slavery in the New World: A Modern Reader in Comparative History*. Ed. Laura Foner and Eugene Genovese. Englewood Cliffs, N.J.: Prentice-Hall, 1969. 202–10.

Greenberg, Kenneth S., ed. *Nat Turner: A Slave Rebellion in History and Memory*. New York: Oxford University Press, 2003

Hall, Gwendolyn M. *Africans in Colonial Louisiana: The Development of Afro-Creole Culture in the Eighteenth Century*. Baton Rouge: Louisiana State University Press, 1992.

———. *Social Control in Slave Plantation Societies: A Comparison of St. Domingue and Cuba*. Baltimore: Johns Hopkins Press, 1971.

Hanger, Kimberly S. *Bounded Lives, Bounded Places: Free Black Society in Colonial New Orleans, 1769–1803*. Durham, N.C.: Duke University Press, 1997.

Holmes, Jack D. L. "The Abortive Slave Revolt at Pointe Coupée, Louisiana." *Louisiana History* 11 (1970): 341–62.

Hubert-Robert, Régine. *L'Histoire merveilleuse de la Louisiane française; chronique des XVIIe et XVIIIe siècles et de la cession aux États-Unis*. New York: Maison Française, 1941.

Jordan, Winthrop. *White over Black: American Attitudes Toward the Negro, 1550–1812*. Chapel Hill: University North Carolina Press, 1968.

Kent, R. K. "African Revolt in Bahia: 24–25 January 1835." *Journal of Social History* 3 (1970): 334–56.

Kilson, Marion D. deB. "Toward Freedom: An Analysis of Slave Revolts in the United States." *Phylon* 25 (1964): 175–87.

Lachance, Paul F. "The Formation of a Three-Caste Society: Evidence from Wills in Antebellum New Orleans." *Social Science History* 18 (Summer 1994): 211–42.

———. "The Growth of the Free and Slave Populations of French Colonial Louisiana." *French Colonial Louisiana and the Atlantic World.* Ed. Bradley G. Bond. Baton Rouge: Louisiana State University Press, 2005. 204–43.

———. "The Politics of Fear: French Louisianians and the Slave Trade, 1786–1809." *Plantation Society in the Americas* 1 (1979): 162–97.

Littlefield, Daniel C. "Continuity and Change in Slave Culture: South Carolina and the West Indies." *Southern Studies* 26 (1987): 202–16.

Lofton, J ohn. *Denmark Vesey's Revolt: The Slave Plot That Lit a Fuse to Fort Sumter.* Kent, Ohio: Kent State University Press, 1983.

Lugano, G., trans. "Records of the Superior Council of Louisiana, LXXXIII." *Louisiana Historical Quarterly* 23 (April 1940): 589–634.

McConnell, Roland C. *Negro Troops in Antebellum Louisiana: A History of the Battalion of Free Men of Color.* Baton Rouge: Louisiana State University Press, 1968.

McDonald, Roderick. *The Economy and Material Culture of Slaves: Goods and Chattels on the Sugar Plantations of Jamaica and Louisiana.* Baton Rouge: Louisiana State University Press, 1993.

McGowan, James T. "Planters without Slaves: Origins of a New World Labor System." *Southern Studies* 16 (1977): 5–26.

Morazan, Ronald R., ed. and trans. "'Quadroon' Balls in the Spanish Period." *Louisiana History* 14 (1973): 310–15.

Morgan, Philip. *Slave Counterpoint: Black Culture in the Eighteenth-Century Chesapeake and Lowcountry.* Chapel Hill: University of North Carolina Press,1998.

Mullin, Gerald W. *Flight and Rebellion: Slave Resistence in Eighteenth-Century Virginia.* New York: Oxford University Press, 1972.

Mullin, Michael, ed. *American Negro Slavery: A Documentary History.* New York: Harper and Row, 1976.

Oates, Stephen B. *The Fires of Jubilee: Nat Turner's Fierce Rebellion.* 1975. Reprint, New York: Harper and Row, 1990.

"Observations on the Negroes of Louisiana." *Journal of Negro History* 2 (1917): 164–85.

Olwell, Robert. *Masters, Slaves, and Subjects: The Culture of Power in the South Carolina Lowcountry, 1740–1790.* Ithaca, N.Y.: Cornell University Press,1998.

Paquette, Robert L. "'A Horde of Brigands'? The Great Louisiana Slave Revolt of 1811 Reconsidered." *Historical Reflections/Réflexions Historiques* forthcoming.

Pitchard, James. "Population in French Louisiana, 1670–1730." *French Colonial Louisiana and the Atlantic World.* Ed. Bradley G. Bond. Baton Rouge: Louisiana State University Press, 2005. 175–203.

Porteous, Laura. "Torture in Spanish Criminal Procedure in Louisiana, 1771." *Louisiana Historical Quarterly* 8 (1925): 5–22.

Riddell, William R. "Le Code Noir." *Journal of Negro History* 10 (1925): 321–29.

Robertson, David. *Denmark Vesey.* New York: Knopf, 1999.

Robertson, James A., ed. and trans. *Louisiana under the Rule of Spain, France, and the United States, 1785–1807: Social, Political and Economic Conditions, . . . as Portrayed in Hitherto Unpublished Contemporary Accounts* . . . . 2 vols. 1910. Reprint, New York: Libraries Press, 1969.

Robin, C. C. *Voyage to Louisiana, 1803–1805.* Trans. Stuart O. Landry Jr. New Orleans: Pelican, 1966.

Rogers, Tommy W. "Origin and Cultural Assimilation of the Population of Louisiana." *Mississippi Quarterly* 25 (1971–72): 45–68.

Rowland, Dunbar, ed. *Official Letter Books of W. C. C. Claiborne.* 6 vols. Jackson, Miss.: State Department of Archives and History, 1917.

Smith, Mark, ed. *Stono: Documenting and Interpreting a Southern Slave Revolt.* Columbia: University of South Carolina Press, 2005.

Schafer, Judith Kelleher. *Slavery, the Civil Law, and the Supreme Court of Louisiana.* Baton Rouge: Louisiana State University Press, 1994.

Schwartz, Stuart B. "The Mocambo: Slave Resistance in Colonial Bahia." *Journal of Social History* 3 (1970): 313–33.

———. "Resistance and Accommodation in Eighteenth-Century Brazil: The Slaves' View of Slavery." *Hispanic American Historical Review* 57 (1977): 69–81.

Sidbury, J ames. *Ploughshares into Swords: Race, Rebellion, and Identity in Gabriel's Virginia, 1730–1810.* New York: Cambridge University Press, 1997.

Smith, Mark M. *Mastered By the Clock: Time, Slavery, and Freedom in the American South.* Chapel Hill: University of North Carolina Press, 1997.

———. "The Political Economy of Time in the American South: The Evolution of a Southern Time Consciousness, 1700–1900." Diss. University of South Carolina, 1995.

Sobel, Mechal. *The World They Made Together: Black and White Values in Eighteenth-Century Virginia.* Princeton: Princeton University Press, 1987.

Sterkx, H. E. *The Free Negro in Ante-Bellum Louisiana.* Rutherford, N.J.: Fairleigh Dickinson University Press, 1972.

Stoddard, Amos. *Sketches, Historical and Descriptive, of Louisiana.* Philadelphia: Mathew Carey, 1812.

Taylor, Joe Gray. *Negro Slavery in Louisiana.* Baton Rouge: Louisiana Historical Association, 1963.

Thornton, John. "African Dimensions of the Stono Rebellion." *American Historical Review* 96 (October 1991): 1101–13.

United States. Census Office. Third Census, 1810. Louisiana.

———. Census Office. Third Census. *Aggregate Amount of Persons within the United States in the Year 1810*. Washington, D.C.: Government Printing Office, 1811.

Usner, Daniel H., Jr. "From African Captivity to American Slavery: The Introduction of Black Laborers to Colonial Louisiana." *Louisiana History* 20 (1979): 25–48.

———. *Indians, Settlers, and Slaves in a Frontier Exchange Economy: The Lower Mississippi Valley before 1783*. Chapel Hill: University of North Carolina Press, 1992.

Walker, Lois A., and Susan R. Silverman, comps. *A Documented History of Gullah Jack Pritchard and the Denmark Vesey Insurrection of 1822*. Lewiston, N.Y.: Mellen, 2000.

Wood, Minter. "Life in New Orleans in the Spanish Period." *Louisiana Historical Quarterly* 22 (1939): 642–709.

Wood, Peter H. *Black Majority: Negroes in Colonial South Carolina from 1670 through the Stono Rebellion*. New York: Knopf, 1974.

Young, Tommy R., II. "The United States Army and the Institution of Slavery in Louisiana." *Louisiana Studies* 13 (1974): 201–22.

PART 2 THE CREOLE CONTROVERSY

Creole Cultures and the Process of Creolization

With Special Attention to Louisiana

BERNDT OSTENDORF

This essay pursues three interests. First, it charts a genealogy of the terms "Creole" and "creoleness" on the basis of the available documentation codified in encyclopedias and dictionaries.[1] This gives us what linguists call a full semasiological description and a documentation of established usage in situ. Second, it historicizes the accumulated social and political mortgages therein by taking a long view of the debate over definitions. It further helps to clarify which specific historic conditions led to the construction of tacit background assumptions and how these, at certain moments, congealed into dogma, much of it defensive. This diachronic reconstruction of the sites of meanings will enable us to position the historical uses of "Creole" as a descriptive *and* prescriptive concept in an asymmetrical system of circum-Atlantic power relations among Europe, Africa, and the Americas. Third, this essay scrutinizes recent efforts at reconceptualizing the term "creolization" for an understanding of processes of culture formation across transatlantic or racial divides and in asymmetrical settings. The wider horizon and conceptual frame of this essay are circum-Atlantic, but my focus is on Louisiana.

The meanings that these terms cover, it will soon appear, are themselves victims of the dynamics of creolization. Their semantic charges will change depending on who uses them, where and when—in that asymmetrical power relationship between metropolis and colony on the one hand, and in that new, postcolonial Atlantic or diasporic space between Africa, Europe, and the New World on the other (Trouillot "North Atlantic"). Today creolization certainly partakes of a tendency of theory to travel fast; it has become a new buzzword of theory cartels in the age of globalization discourses (Hannerz "World in Creolization"). There is overlap but little agreement on specific meanings because the terms are pliant and have at all times been hotly contested. They are, unavoidably, part of a colonial identity discourse trying hard to become postcolonial; in fact, the battle of meanings proceeds along the lines of older colonial contradictions (Palmié "Creolization"; Lambert). Today the Manichean fault line between the "subaltern" colonial and the "liberated" postcolonial condition inspires the morality play enacted by cultural critics of the postcolonial debate. Buried under the ongoing debate is the process of self-authentication by hitherto marginalized groups in the New World against the powers of the Old World. This debate continues the self-liberationist and emancipatory agendas set by Franz Boas, Melville Herskovits, and Frantz Fanon. Yet it is dogged by familiar political contradictions.[2]

I. Dictionaries and Encyclopedias: Between Prescription and Description

Any reconceptualization of the term "creolization" involves a reconsideration of the actual historic uses of the term "Creole" as both a noun and an adjective. First, I will assemble the semasiology of the term and its history as recorded in major dictionaries and encyclopedias; second, I will discuss articles and monographs that deal with the discursive settings of the term.[3] The latter cover most of the semantic range of the term, which is considerable. We should use the documented public evidence with some caution because it tends to privilege the literate sides of the colonial ruling class, thus favoring what Jürgen Habermas called a "literate imperialism." Against them, the more elusive local and oral traditions have little chance of recognition or semantic survival. One should also take an implied bias in favor of a conceptual order into account, a tacit yearning for grammaticality. Wherever necessary, therefore, I will introduce circumstantial evidence. Drawing on all these sources I will attempt to create—for heuristic purposes—a taxonomy of latent background assumptions that have gone into the term and have at various times in history determined its meaning.[4]

All sources believe that the word "Creole" is some form of "colonial" (*Oxford English Dictionary* [*OED*]) or "Negro" (*Encyclopaedia Britannica,* 11th ed. [*EB11*]), a corruption of either the Spanish word *criadillo,* the diminutive of *criado* (brought up, reared, produced, bred, domestic), or, more directly, the verb *criar* (to create).[5] The history of its morphology, then, begins in creation, but under the cloud of "corruption." This captures the colonial moment well. For the word "Creole" springs from that same metaphorical imagination that gave us the word "culture," with its roots in agricultural processes of growing and nurture. Both words refer to man's creative and active involvement with a changing nature, as either "cultivation" or "rearing." Indeed, it is this heritage of mediation between nature and nurture that makes the term "creolization" attractive to the cultural historians who love to draw on organic metaphors. It may also explain why so many popular expressions for the process of creolization are drawn from agriculture or cooking—melting pot, salad bowl, jambalaya, gumbo, *ajiaco*—or why Brazilian theorists in trying to define a national culture have used metaphors of eating and even of cannibalism (anthropophagy) to conceptualize cultural appropriation across ethnic and colonial fault lines.[6]

The term was first used in the context of Spanish and Portuguese colonialization as a function of "boundary maintenance." It marked the boundary between two sets of experience and thus between two "socially constructed realities," the Old and the New Worlds. It served to distinguish people born and firmly rooted in the Old World who had moved to the New World as founding fathers, from the generation born, raised, and rooted in the New World. Here the suspicion of degeneracy or corruption was an early trope in the Spanish empire, later applied to North America by Abbé Raynal, Comte Buffon, and Cornelius de Pauw in the late eighteenth century (Chinard). What distinguishes the two sets of experience was not only the locus of their roots but also their access to power. The center held on to power and was loath to cede it to the periphery. Thus the genesis of the term and its subsequent use is inextricably bound up with the control over colonial expansion and its social order to the Americas and hence with the histories of imperialism and racism.

The *OED* prefaces its long entry on "Creoles" with an interesting and, perhaps in view of the later restrictive usage of the term, telling opinion: "According to some 18th c. writers originally applied by S. American negroes to their own children born in America as distinguished from negroes freshly imported from Africa; but D'Acosta, I:90, applies it to Spaniards born in the West Indies" (1163).[7] In recent years this eighteenth-century view has been buttressed by many earlier sources. The early presence of the African in the term's history would continue to "haunt" its purist users in later centuries and would account for its continued racialist ambiguity.

The noun "Creole" is then defined in the following manner: "In the West Indies and other parts of America, Mauritius, etc.: orig. A person born and naturalized in the country, but of European (usually Spanish or French) or of African Negro race: the name having no connotation of colour, and in its reference to origin being distinguished on the one hand from born in Europe (or Africa), and on the other hand from aboriginal" (ibid.). Its subsequent history, so continues the *OED*, reduced this larger and inclusive sense to denote "white creoles," or "descendants of European settlers, born and naturalized in those colonies or regions, and more or less modified in type by the climate and surroundings." The sources, which are given here as quoted in the entry, range from E. Grimstone, trans., *D'Acosta's History of the West Indies,* to *Juan y Ulloa's Voyages* of 1760–1772,[8] to Washington Irving's *Astoria* of 1836. However, some sources do not make racialist distinctions or are colorblind. *Earthquake of Peru,* published in 1748 (no author), states, "Criollos signifies one born in the Country; a Word made by the Negroes, who give it to their children born in those Parts," and the aforementioned source *Juan y Ulloa's Voyages* subdivides not only whites but also Negroes into Creoles and non-Creoles. One source from 1863 that limits the term to Negroes is quoted. Hence the overlapping consensus agrees on "born in the New World" as a common marker. Racial specification is a secondary distinction that over the years will become increasingly controversial.

Unlike the more substantive noun, the adjective is rarely essentialized and is thus not grounded in blood or nature. It is saddled with fewer distinctions and includes the effects of New World "nurture" on whites, Negroes, animals, plants, and architectural styles. Anything imported to and raised in the New World may be called Creole, including Creole sugarcane or Creole horses. Indeed, the difference between noun and adjective mirrors the difference between nature and nurture, between essence and social construction, between bloodline and acculturation. This provided much later a way out of the racialist dilemma: The noun was reserved for whites and denoted essence, whereas the adjective could be attached to any person, animal, or plant that had been nurtured in situ.[9]

The *EB11* is adamant that the term does not originally mean mixture of races: "The use of the word by some writers as necessarily implying a person of mixed blood is totally erroneous; in itself 'creole' has no distinction of colour; a creole may be a person of European, negro, or mixed extraction—or even a horse." So much for the horse sense of the *Encyclopaedia Britannica* at the height of imperial and colonial expansion.

The *EB11* also makes much of local variation: Whereas in the West Indies the term is applied to descendants of any European race, in Louisiana it refers to those with French or Spanish blood. To wit, interjects the author, neither French Canadians nor South Americans of Spanish or Portuguese extraction are referred to as Creole. Only Mexicans of Spanish background use the term. In countries with black majorities Creole refers to the entire population—as in Réunion or Mauritius.[10] The rigorous exclusion of Acadians (Cajuns) from the term certainly has to be modified for Louisiana, where there is some overlap between Creoles and Cajuns;[11] similarly, the use of *criollo* as a generic term for all South Americans is documented.

The American *Webster's New International Dictionary of the English Language, Second Edition* of 1953 is stricter in observing the color line. The original sense of the term, so begins the first section of the entry, refers to people of European descent born and bred in the colonies. The second definition begins, "In the United States, a white person descended from the French or of Spanish settlers of Louisiana" (623). At this point George Washington Cable is given a long quote to confirm the myth of origin, that is, of *pur sang* and of class distinction ("excellence of origin"), that was to become so dear to the white Creoles of New Orleans from the latter nineteenth century onward:[12]

> The title (*Creole*) did not first belong to the descendants of Spanish, but of French, settlers. But such a meaning implied a certain excellence of origin, and so came early to include any native of French or Spanish descent by either parent, whose nonalliance with the slave race entitled him to social rank. Later, the term was adopted by, not conceded to, the natives of mixed blood, and is still so used among themselves.[13]

Only the third definition mentions the possibility of African descent: "A Negro born in America;—more properly, *creole negro*." And the misappropriated or "stolen" meaning implying miscegenation is presented as number four: "A person of mixed Creole and negro blood speaking a dialect of French or Spanish; a half breed." The fifth definition refers to language: "In Haiti, and some other West Indian islands, the language of the people. It is a degenerate French with admixture of native West African and Carib and sometimes, Spanish words." On balance the *OED* and *EB11* grant both priority and more space to "black" meanings as compared to the *Webster's* of 1953.[14] Ironically, Cable, who in this entry supports the *pur sang* myth, became persona non grata in New Orleans for his support of civil rights and chose to remove himself to New England.

Georg Friederici's *Amerikanistisches Wörterbuch* (219–20) presents three major meanings with copious quotes from original Spanish, Portuguese, Dutch, English, and French sources. "Creole" first applies to *all* people born in the Americas of Old World parents, including blacks. The quotes are from sources gathered in Puerto Rico, Suriname, Louisiana, and parts of the Spanish empire and range from 1602 to 1909. The term applies, second, to the children of pure blood European parents. Here most quotes are from Mexico,

L'Isle de France, and parts of the French dominion dating from 1570 to 1883. Third, in the early colonization of Brazil, the term referred to all blacks either from Africa or born in the New World who, in opposition to Portuguese, Brazilians, and Mamelukes, were referred to as "creoulos," and here Friederici quotes sources from 1540, 1634, and 1711. Friederici includes one source from 1720 that—general consensus notwithstanding—speaks of "Les Canadiens, c'est-à-dire les *Créoles* du Canada."

The *Encyclopaedia Britannica* of 1975, much less prescriptive in temperament, stresses above all the geopolitical distance between metropolis and colony and makes much of regional variants. Creoles were generally excluded from high office in Spanish colonial America, whereas immigrants from Spain, called "peninsulares" or, with contempt, "gachupines" (Mexico) or "chapetones" (South America), enjoyed privileges in business and high office. Only after national revolutions in the early nineteenth century in which Creoles played a leading role did these constitute a new ruling class. Recent usage in the West Indies includes "all the people whatever their class or ancestry—European, Asian, Indian—who are part of the easygoing, lively Caribbean culture." In an interesting variant in French Guiana the term refers to all people, regardless of skin color, "who have adopted a European way of life."[15] This usage also is found in parts of Latin America and rural Louisiana, where urban Creoles kept their country cousins or Cajuns at a safe social distance.[16] By another turn of the semantic screw,

> in such countries as Peru, the adjective creole describes a certain spirited way of life. Important expression of this way of life are the abilities to speak wittily and persuasively on a wide range of topics, to turn a situation to one's advantage, to be masculine (macho), to exhibit national pride, and to participate in fiestas and other sociable activities with a certain gusto—in sum to be *muy criollo* ("very creole").

Richard A. Long, an African American scholar from Atlanta, begins his two-column entry on Creoles in the *Harvard Encyclopedia of American Ethnic Groups* by stating that the term refers to people, culture, food, music, and language. After pointing out the various regional differences in South America and the Caribbean basin, he focuses on Louisiana. After the Louisiana Purchase of 1803, Louisianians of French and Spanish descent, he avers, referred to themselves as Creoles to distinguish themselves from the new Anglo-Saxon masters. Indigenous whites used the term in an exclusive sense of *pur sang,* which, Charles Gayarré and Alexander Dimitry notwithstanding, is most unhistorical. Today's Creoles of color are "the product of miscegenation in a seigneurial society." Long stresses the self-conscious sense of this group, who are perceived by other groups as separate and sometimes standoffish. Many near-white Creoles have passed either into white America or for the sake of political solidarity into the larger African American population.

By the twentieth century the North American myth of pure origin was so much in place that a Louisiana appeals court could rule in 1906 that "when a person is called a 'creole' this evidences an absence of any negro blood" (Dominguez 94). And a newspaper editorial in the *New Orleans Item* of March 26, 1922, demonstrates the shortness of historical memory:

> Here in Louisiana a "creole" has never been anything but a descendant of the original French and Spanish settlers born in Louisiana instead of in France or Spain. . . . One dictionary says that the term was once applied to negroes born here to distinguish them form negroes brought from Africa. We have never heard it used in that sense. Such usage must have died out as soon as the slave trade closed. (Tregle "On that Word," 68)

Surely by that time the term had become weighted with racist presuppositions. In her historical survey of the term, Virginia R. Domínguez cites a death certificate of 1745 that identifies a person as "the first Creole in this colony." In the early period, she claims, the adjective "Creole" was used as the equivalent of native. However, in this period of ethnogenesis, New World identities of the charter generation were not yet in place; hence it is a period of unfocused terminology with the attendant lack of conceptual rigor. According to Dominguez, blacks were referred to as "sauvage," "esclave," "negresse," "mulatress," "negrion," "negritte," and "nègre libre" (97). And although "Creole" was used to describe the generation born of Old World parentage, there was little political or social meaning attached to the term. This "casual" use persisted until the end of the century.

The first political event that "integrated" the French or native population into a more coherent Creole identity was the cession of the colony to the Spanish Crown in 1763 and the advent of the first Spanish governor, Antonio de Ulloa, in 1768.[17] Many citizens who identified themselves as "inhabitants and merchants of the province of Louisiana" suddenly discovered their allegiance to the French flag, but, it seems, for practical and local rather than cultural motives. In previous decades the merchants had enjoyed a period of economic deregulation since the French government had taken little active interest in the colony. Dominguez suspects that these "enemies" of Spanish rule would not have been so pro-French if the French had followed a stiff mercantilist colonial policy and run a tighter economic ship (99). Their sense of Creole togetherness was prompted by a desire to maintain those *local* rights and freedoms that had grown as a consequence of benign neglect. In other words, a new localism is articulated as "creolization," an assertion of local and native privilege and power against the central powers. Moreover, in the Spanish period (1768–1802) we note the beginning of the Creole/American opposition. Marked economic and demographic changes occurred under Spanish rule, setting the stage for what I would call a politicization of Creole identity: (1) the city grew in size as did its subgroups of whites, free people of color, and black slaves; (2) Anglo-Americans began to push westward to the Mississippi and became a threat to francophone Louisiana; (3) sugarcane became profitable and identity acquired an economic basis; (4) the Spanish actively solicited settlers, among them Acadians and Canary Islanders (Isleños); (5) Spanish authority encouraged leniency in the manumission of slaves, which increased the population of free Creoles of color and added a racist threat; (6) Louisiana became a haven for political refugees from France and St. Domingue; (7) through land grants a caste of landed aristocracy and with it a social class division emerged; (8) New Orleans in 1795 granted port privileges to Anglo-American merchants, which increased commercial traffic with America and made the port of New Orleans attractive to both river and sea trade; and (9) French, Spanish, and American cultural and political choices could be played off against each other by the creolized populations. Creole had become a category that could be instrumentalized for boundary maintenance in support of local power and privilege.

Dominguez dates the first use of "Creole" in reference to blacks from 1779, which has since been faulted (107). And her point, that the term carried little "political or social" connotation, must be taken with a grain of salt, particularly as concerns the social dimension. Gwendolyn Midlo Hall, Jerah Johnson, and Joseph Tregle have amply demonstrated, for Louisiana at least, that although the white population may still have been suffering from a certain fragmentation so typical of early colonial societies, by the time the Spanish arrived in 1768, a substantial Afro-Creole-Indian charter culture was in place.[18]

The second political event that forged a Creole identity in the public sphere was the Louisiana Purchase. The previous decade had already seen a drastic increase of the English-speaking traders who had used the port of New Orleans for commerce with the Midwest. Now the tug-of-war between the "ancienne population" and the newcomers over matters of culture and politics began. American governor Claiborne, in his dispatches to Washington, admitted to puzzlement that conflicts would arise between Creoles and Americans over which dances were to be played at masked balls, French or English, or which holidays were to be honored, Bastille or Independence Day. As these skirmishes multiplied, cultural enmity became increasingly ideologized and fetishized, even though in matters of governance many Creoles accommodated to the principles of American republicanism.[19] From the Louisiana Purchase to 1836, the date when the city split into three municipalities, there were marked economic and demographic changes: the total population of New Orleans rose from 8,056 in 1803, to 17,242 in 1810, to 27,176 in 1820, to 46,082 in 1830, and to 102,193 in 1840, an increase caused first by a relative growth of the francophone charter group due to fugitives from the Haitian revolution but then due to the massive growth of a multiethnic, typically American immigrant population. After the arrival of the refugees from St. Domingue, which was responsible for the doubling of the population between 1803 and 1810 and had strengthened the Creole contingent, most new arrivals thereafter were either Americans or immigrants and most of these were white and speakers or learners of English. Self-selected settlement patterns in the city contributed to the widening gulf between the various groups. The Americans settled primarily in Faubourg St. Mary (Second District), whereas the Creoles and incoming immigrants moved to Faubourg Marigny (Third District) or remained in the Quarter (First District). After the split in 1836 the American district experienced rapid growth and economic success whereas the Creole and immigrant sectors suffered decline and severe recessions. In this climate of attrition Creole identity took on a new defensive urgency. Auguste Lussan wrote a play in 1836–1837 titled *La famille créole,* which emphasized the French connection. At about the same time the "myth of Creole womanhood" emerged in the pages of a new journal, *Louisiana Créole; gazette des salons, des arts et des modes.*[20]

Yet a loose and casual use of the term "Creole" beyond national and racial categories persisted. In fact, not only those of French or Spanish extraction but also the local-born descendants both of Negroes and of Anglo-Saxons were on occasion called Creole in the antebellum period. As the gulf between Creole culture and American culture widened after the Civil War, fewer Anglo-Americans would refer to themselves as Creole:

> As locally born Anglo-Americans grew more and more visible and sociopolitical tension between French and English speakers mounted, the meaning of *Creole* began to shift. Cultural attributes of the descendants of French and Spanish colonial settlers who had been calling themselves Creole for a number of generations became criteria for Creole identity. Language became crucial, and social customs were frequently mentioned and compared. Southern Louisiana society was polarized into Creoles and Americans. (Dominguez 125)

More and more "Creole" was adopted also as a marker of local color or folkloric legitimation and as such was popular among German and Irish immigrants who elected "Creole queens" or ate "Creole Ice Cream." It is perhaps an indication of the relative latitude of the term (or of its declining significance in the postbellum period) that even George Washington Cable, a teetotaler and Protestant of New England and German extraction (viz. the original family name Kabel), would refer to himself as Creole. Most often such usage would imply an act of self-authentication or self-entitlement, in the sense of "I am one of us, I have local knowledge." Dominguez also quotes a number of usages between 1830 and 1860 that apply "Creole" to blacks. At this time neither Creoles of color nor Acadians were excluded from the Creole category. However, as the "ancienne population" went into deep economic and social decline after Reconstruction, the racial identity of creoleness became an issue of high priority for white Creoles. At the same time, and as a consequence of New Orleans' deserved reputation as a place of lax racial mores, outsiders began to associate Creole with miscegenation. This made the white Creole population defensive, though it had been instrumental in giving substance to this image. They could either drop the term as a hot potato (and some did and consequently stressed a "French origin") or try to limit its semantic range to pure white European parentage. As Dominguez notes, "The abolition of slavery, the polarization of North and South over the issue of slavery, the economic disarray of the immediate postbellum years, the enfranchisement of the numerically dominant colored population, and its recruitment into Northern carpetbagger administrations all served to create racial polarization" (134).

But it was most of all the high visibility of Creole *gens de couleur* in the public sphere (journals, political activism, etc.) that dichotomized the subsequent debates (Logsdon "Americans and Creoles"). For the Creole/American dichotomy also affected the black population. Creoles of color were fighting on two fronts: They had to deal with Afro-American and Protestant resistance to their Creole and Catholic leadership, and they had to deal with the fear that both white Creoles and Americans would impose negro "supremacy" in Louisiana. On one hand the race question brought white, francophone Creoles and Americans together; on the other, the emerging color line turned the tripartite social system into a binary one.[21]

II. Background Assumptions

It is helpful to identify certain key tropes operative in the larger debate over Creoles or creoleness and thereby create a sort of semantic geography in a circum-Atlantic setting. By laying bare the various structural and historical layers of meaning, it is possible to determine which tacit background assumptions dominate its usage at any given time and in different places of the Old and New Worlds. Structurally speaking, the fragments of meaning, which we have collected, may be put into quite different synchronic hierarchies or diachronic sequences. Which partial meaning is given priority over others and by whom, and which meaning is allegedly older or sounder—according to whom? Historically speaking, we see that over time simple human interest and political expedience transforms meaning into custom or, in the case of Louisiana, into law. And the battle goes on. We might ask why the controversy is so often bitter. The answer is simple. It concerns people's cultural and personal identity in a racialist setting, and thus the definition game is matter of existential urgency and, sometimes, a last-ditch defense of acquired privileges.[22] Gary B. Mills suggests a "Louisiana compromise": "A Creole can be anyone who says he is one" ("Creole" 427). And yet only people with a safe sense of self can afford to be so generous or casual. Contest over the term is choreographed by a colonial topography. I would therefore differentiate a colonial and postcolonial usage, and both of these are embedded in a circum-Atlantic tug of war between achievement and ascription.

The meaning of the term has an existential, a temporal and local dimension. Or it depends on *who* uses it *when* and in *what* context. And all cultural or linguistic meaning is negotiated between inside achievement (being a body) and outside ascription (having a body). In this particular case the metropolis (London, Paris, Madrid) tend to use "Creole" as a colonial term of ascription, whereas the colonies used it as a postcolonial term of achievement. The term has therefore become important in postcolonial identity politics.

The constitutive elements advanced in the definition of "Creole" concern both the basis and the ideological superstructure, that is, they are objective and subjective and include (1) movement in space, (2) generational sequence, (3) bloodlines, (4) soil and climate, (5) evolution of a language, and (6) ethnic or national consciousness. It is worthwhile to look at each one of these discursive settings separately and understand Creole first as a positive achievement and second as negative ascription. The positive charge is found mostly in the New World as a function of self-liberation from colonial powers; the latent negative charge confirms the colonial usage of the metropolis.

Due to the asymmetrical power relation between dominant Old World culture of the metropolis and dependent New World culture of the colony there is a tug-of-war over the semantic charge of the term "Creole," and consequently there is a permanent process of resemantization (Lambert 107). Indeed, there is a dialectic switch along a binary fault line between the metropolis and the periphery. Whereas in the New World the term has, in time, acquired a positive ring, albeit in a defensive spirit, in the metropolis its connotations remain mostly negative. It is hard for the colony to meet the exacting norms and standards of the metropolis that looks down upon the colonial boondocks. Hence the positive and defensive self-entitlement of the colony is built upon a foundation of negative charges laid and inspired by the metropolis. This may also explain why in so many instances decolonization processes begin on the symbolic level by recoding the negative projection of the metropolis into positive counterimages. According to JanMohamed and Fanon, there is a Manichean divide between the colonial and postcolonial experience that affects political semantics. Hence a binary switch from positive to negative may be run through the same changes, depending upon the point of view of the periphery or the metropolis.

Spatial Transfer: Movement, Distance, and Power in Geopolitical Space

The most important element in the definition of "Creole" is that of transfer from a place of origin to a place of new settlement, in this case from the Old World (Europe and Africa) to the New World or from the political center (the metropolis) to the periphery (the colony). The term is central for the asymmetrical relationship of the Old and New Worlds. It is part and parcel of the heritage of colonization and imperialism. This is the most basic layer of semantic energy in the term. It is a term of negotiation between these worlds. Most of all, by marking the triangular range it also creates a new diasporic space: the Atlantic rim.

Previous to the Atlantic slave trade the negotiation between Europe and Africa had created an in-between space for indigenous negotiators, traders, and translators, many of whom were of mixed descent. They were speaking an earlier version of what later would be develop into full fledged "Atlantic creoles" (Holm 11). As Ira Berlin suggests, these Creoles were in place rather early. They enjoyed a measure of independence and success and became founding or charter families of creolizing cultures along the Atlantic rim.[23]

For the metropolis, leaving the Old World is associated with cultural defection, cultural loss, or even degeneracy (Chinard). This projection of the metropolis was internalized by the colonies so that certain Creole families would send their daughters and sons to London, Paris, or Madrid to "recharge" batteries or "decreolize" them. A *locus classicus* of the fear of going to seed by going native is the following description by a Mrs. Duncker (an Englishwoman living in Jamaica) of Englishmen becoming West Indians:

> Although there were some people who came to the West Indies and refused to conform, the power of the society to mould new-comers was strong. However oddly constructed West India Society might appear in England, for the English People coming to the West Indies it was only a short time before they were caught up in the system. J. B. Moreton observed of men from other countries when they became inured to the West Indies "how imperceptibly like wax softened by heat, they melt into their manners and customs." Perhaps it was because the standards were laxer than in the society from which the newcomers came that they were so easy to acquire. Even a strong willed person faced with . . . loneliness, heat and probable fever would find it hard to resist the consolations of the island. (Brathwaite 296)

First Generation vs. Second Generation

Generational boundary maintenance plays a major role in the founding phase of new societies. Hence the "normal" generational break between a parent generation and their children is confounded by a break in socialization, and this difference in nurture is precisely what makes one *criollo.* The fathers and mothers are bound by socialization to the old country; the sons and daughters are tied by socialization to the new country. The latter have "gone native." Common blood ties but different socializations—this is the crucial semantic difference that first of all the parents observed in their children and gave a name to *criollo.* It is perhaps not unimportant that naming begins as a unilateral process that runs from the parents to the children and, implicitly, from the parent country to the dependent country.

All too often suspicion runs from the first to the second generation ("You are going native, you do not remember the old ways!"), a defensive stance from the second to the first ("Leave us alone with your tales of the old country!"). One may hypothesize that these changes would also have affected family life: Instead of the older traditional vertical integration of generations into one extended family (from grandfather to father to son), the New World experience ruptures the generational sequence and would encourage a horizontal orientation by peer groups. New types of local loyalty developed among the "creolized" cohorts.

Viewed from the metropolis, suspicion would run from the first to the second generation, most drastically expressed in the English colonies by the halfway covenant. Implied was the fear that the old stamina of the founding fathers was no longer guaranteed (Sollors).

Blood: Ethnicity by Descent

As Creoles acquired a measure of self-confidence and power in the New World, the continuity of bloodlines played a decisive role: Occasionally there was an insistence on noble, good blood. Soon, however, anyone who was non-native, that is, not Indian, and born in the New World, was referred to as Creole. People of *mixed* African-European parentage were by virtue of their Old World descent automatically included. This introduced, surreptitiously as it were, the notion of mixture into the term. This is true of French Louisiana, where early documents use the term to denote anyone born in the New World. Later, with the rise of racism, "unmixed" or "uncontaminated" blood would be advanced as the "essential" element in the noun "Creole." The key factor here is that "indigenous populations" are excluded. Though Creoles may intermarry with Native Americans, the latter are by definition not Creole. The new bloodline has to come from the Old World. Here the Creoles of Sierra Leone, free blacks who returned from the New World to Africa, provide a curious subplot. The key notions, however, remain in place: The transfer of bloodlines from one soil to the other and an active boundary maintenance vis-à-vis the indigenous population (L. Spitzer).

The metropolis used the term to isolate and disenfranchise the Creoles from power. In the Spanish dominions Creoles were barred from higher office. In the American colonies the governing class was most often drawn from native-born Englishmen, which was one of the root causes of the revolution. The second generation, the Creole (American) generation, is seen as unreliable because

(1) they had no automatic loyalty to the crown;
(2) their bloodline was weakened, according to physiocratic beliefs, by the new soil and climate (they were seen as sanguine, foolish, incontinent, and lazy, and in some early documents a verb, "to creolize," appears, used to denote sloth and degeneracy) (Chinard); and
(3) the metropolis very early noted with revulsion that Creoles were sexually incontinent, and consorted and mated with natives. Thus the anxiety of white Creoles in denying that "Creole" connotes "race-mixing" arose from a negative ascription and reflects one of the oldest fears of the metropolis, which was internalized by the colony: mongrelization.

Soil, Climate, and Breeding: Acculturation or Degeneracy

Settlement and growing up on a new soil is the innovative fact, the fact that "changes" the bloodline. In other words, the difference between a Spaniard and a Creole is not in any difference of blood but in the "breeding" of old blood on a new soil. The oldest definition of culture derived from agriculture: In keeping with physiocratic beliefs of the eighteenth century, creoleness marked those changes in physiognomy and character, which were the consequences of acculturation or Americanization. The new exigencies of survival changed everyday lifestyles and even patterns of reproduction. Later a difference was made between noun and adjective, or between "biological essence" and "acquired character" or "race" and "culture." Whereas a Creole had to have the right blood (or essence), a "Creole" horse, slave, or tomato could be any horse, slave, or tomato grown on the new soil. In this minority view the factor of nature (blood) defined the noun but the factor of nurture defined the adjective.

Acculturation is seen by the metropolis not as a gain but as a loss. Going native is a form of degeneracy. Creoles are referred to as "perdidos." The New World climate, physiognomy, and character are in the view of the metropolis of a lesser quality. Creoles are seen as "effeminates," whereas the metropolis is "masculine." This gendered decline is in tune with a geopolitical gender ascription in the anthropological discourse of the Enlightenment: Europe was always regarded as the masculine continent, the colonial world as feminine. One of the founders of the Chicago School of Sociology, Robert E. Park, referred to the Negro as "the lady among the races" (Ellison 294). This effeminization process, so says the metropolis, is enhanced by Creole dietary habits, the languid climate, and a general sense of self-indulgence—in short, it is responsible for the laid-back posture of Creoles. French physiocrats thought that the American colonists due to the wretched climate had of necessity a weaker constitution (Chinard).

Language: From Pidgin to Creole

Cultural autonomy is often based on a new and distinctive language spoken by a new people. Creole languages in general and Louisiana Creoles in particular are interesting test cases.[24]

Pidgin languages arise in a hegemonic (colonial) and asymmetrical system as a result of language contact between a dominant language (e.g., English or French) and native or local languages (e.g., African or Indian). Hence in the colonial world there are English-, French-, and Spanish-based pidgins. Pidgins are not yet "autonomous" or "independent" languages; they work with a simplified and reduced lexicon and grammar in the context of a hegemonic situation and exist side by side with the dominant and local languages. They are, tectonically speaking, lean-to languages. When this hegemonic situation and the need for pidgin communication is terminated, they may collapse. Therefore, the situation is linguistically very unstable.

Creoles are languages that may or may not have begun as pidgins but have become linguistically less dependent on the original donor languages. Creole is spoken by that charter generation that grew up in the new linguistic space prepared and created by pidgin language contact. Creoles are therefore full-fledged but not yet codified languages. This does not mean they are politically, socially, or culturally as "independent" as English or French. Creoles as language systems have greater stability than pidgins, but there is great fluidity within the language for two reasons:

(1) A lack of established standards (which has more to do with social than linguistic factors). Creoles are immensely flexible and changeable. They are marked by ongoing processes of creolization, that is, a movement towards greater independence and autonomy, particularly in isolated, rural regions (Neumann). This very lack of grammatical

stability and the situational adaptability of the Creole moment, however, may explain the thesis of a "rapid early synthesis" (Palmié "Creolization").

(2) If the original dominant language continues to play a hegemonic role, as French did in Louisiana or in Haiti among the educated, urban elites, there is also a constant drive toward "decreolization" (Holm). Within a Creole continuum there are two opposite drives, creolization and decreolization, which constantly destabilize "standards." When there is no "received standard" of Creole but instead there is, depending on the distance of its speakers from the metropolis, a dynamic process of creolization or decreolization, there will be a multitude of Creole idiolects or individualized and local Creoles. Class may also play a role in the stratification of the linguistic continuum; many individuals in a Creole setting will speak several variants of Creole dialects, or some may be able to speak both received French and several Creoles. In other words, there is high linguistic viscosity and code switching is de rigueur.

From the high perch of the Académie Française a French Creole is considered "petit nègre," a "gutter dialect," a deviation and a "corruption" of proper usage, or in Creole, "fransé bannann." It is said to be infantile and restricted in its range of expression. Early French and Spanish theories of Creoles subscribe to a "baby talk" theory or speak of the infantilization of grammar and vocabulary. It is interesting that in presenting the linguistic career of the term "Creole" the dictionaries employ a rhetoric of "corruption." Why should the formation of "Creole" be called a "corruption" of *criar* when the evolution of Old World languages are rarely explained that way?

Creole Nationalism: New World Ethnicity by Consent

Next to primary determinants of ethnicity such as blood, soil, and spatial transfer, which are objective factors in culture creation, there may develop a subjective local feeling of togetherness and belonging among the groups so defined. Here independence movements and nation building play an important part. This feeling usually is grounded in primary bonds, on generational cohorts, but may also develop as a result of custom and political will. To choose to be Creole by free will and consent may at certain political moments be more important than bloodlines and may signal a liberal insurrection against imperial hegemony or monarchy. Often this type of New World insurrection stems from a feeling of being forgotten or wronged by the metropolis, a sense of nationhood by defensive consent: "It was an identity. . . that found expression in terms of anguish, nostalgia, and resentment. From the start, creoles appear to have conceived of themselves as dispossessed heirs, stripped of their patrimony by an unjust Crown and the usurpations of recent migrants from the Peninsula. . . . The creole was an American Jacob, robbed of his birthright by a peninsular Esau" (Brading 293, 296).

In Louisiana right after the Louisiana Purchase the word "Creole" becomes the term of choice for the "ancienne population" (regardless of bloodlines). Even some Englishmen or Americans who had settled in New Orleans before the purchase are now on the basis of their political consent included among the Creoles. The litmus test here is loyalty to the culture and political goals of the local population which sets itself off from intruders as being non-Creoles. It is a curious fact that all ethnic groups that were present in Louisiana during the ethnogenesis of a Creole culture and the local-born population claim the term as their own, including blacks and free people of color. The local problem is compounded by racism and class; the question of who has the right to define the local culture becomes increasingly political after 1803. Late in the nineteenth century the "white Creoles" fight a losing battle trying to prove their *pur sang* creoleness, which, as everyone agrees, is a genealogical myth. By this time all other groups seem to agree that creolization, in contrast to its early etymological history, involves mixing of cultures and races. Within this process of creolization the hegemonic structures tacitly persist in the tacit values attached to somatic norms.

The new emerging nationalism of Creole societies (or colonies) is seen as a threat by the metropolis (or the colonizers). As a rule, revolutions were started by populations that had become creolized. Both Spain and France attempted repeatedly to recharge the Spanish or Latin cultural batteries. A *locus classicus* is the attempt to restore monarchy in Mexico as a bastion against local Creole, liberal insurrections on the one hand and the hegemony of Yankeeism on the other. In Trinidad most of the insubordinate passions during Carnival were attributed to Creole African Americans (Cowley).

III. Current Reconceptualizations

As could be demonstrated, "creolization" and "Creole" are terms of an ongoing transatlantic and (post)colonial debate that has tried to capture and address processes of culture formation in a contact situation in the colonized spaces of Europe, Africa, and America. The question is how to conceptualize cultural change and processes of realignment in an area of instability and fragmentation. Linguists first operationalized the term "Creole" and lifted it from its agricultural connotations (Holm). Although the common agricultural origin gives Creole and culture their usefulness, it also causes conceptual ambiguity, thus creating certain problems of tautology as far as cultural studies is concerned. In that sense Creole is, onomasiologically speaking, too close to culture (and acculturation) to make any real difference. In linguistics the term refers to the completion of a self-referential linguistic or cultural system or, in other words, to the achievement of a functioning, dominant "grammar." This yearning for a normative grammar that both regulates our behavior and provides a key for its interpretation may explain the term's attractiveness for cultural studies. The problem is this: Will the linguistic paradigm not inevitably systematize and overdetermine cultural behavior along the lines of grammaticality? Does culture have a syntax as languages such as Creoles do? Is there a semantic or a phonetic equivalent in culture?[25] Less burdened by theoretical aporias it seems to me is the concept of creolization, which accentuates permanent process, thereby negating any stable norm. This conceptual tension between Creole and creolization or between construction and reconstruction deserves to be examined.

In Louisiana any professional meaning is overshadowed by echoes of sin and miscegenation that have inspired the popular usage of "Creole" to this day. However questionable these semantic resonances may be, they point to deeper sociohistorical layers of historical meaning that reach beyond the merely semasiological debate. In the context of Louisiana studies creolization refers to the fusion of fragmented traditions into a new and ongoing cultural pluralism, whereas the term "Creole" instantly evokes the strange genealogical career of the Creoles of New Orleans. Indeed, most of the mythmaking in New Orleans history has to do with the semantic overcharge of the word. It has acquired the popular meaning of miscegenation (with that titillating frisson evoking tragic mulattoes and octoroon balls). The history of this charged meaning, some would say misconception, is therefore part of the social, demographic, and ethnic history of New Orleans.

It will have become clear that the processes and changes the term "Creole" has gone through encompass the entire New World experience. For each Spanish example one may find myriad "Anglo-American" examples. In my view it is therefore fruitful to investigate the *dynamics* of creolization (in the sense of a historic process of cultural give-and-take over a long period of time) that affected all groups in a similar manner and to include in it factors of transfer, blood, soil, climate, language, and consciousness. It is in this sense that Daniel Crowley has proposed a dynamic notion of creolization that merits attention:

> Creolization today describes more generally the process of adaptation Herskovits synthesized as retention, reinterpretation and syncretism, and that the concept it represents is applicable not only in . . . the Caribbean, Southern Louisiana and the west coast of Africa, but also in any area where a culture neither aboriginal nor alien but a mixture of these two, with retentions on both sides and ample borrowing from other outside sources is in the process of becoming dominant. (Whitten and Szwed 38)

And yet this sounds too peaceful and orderly to be true. In view of the conflict-ridden usages of the key terms we may ask why the concept of creolization has in recent years moved from the margin to the center of attention. Its revaluation has to do with the discovery of the Caribbean as an *oikoumenê* worthy of serious anthropological study (Mintz "Enduring Substances"). The context in which it was revalorized was the new interest in culture contact, culture formation under conditions of historic hegemony—usually associated with the rise of an Atlantic slave-based economy. It also touches the national and personal identity of "new people," the recognition of the hitherto unrecognized, a centering of the marginalized, and the inclusion of the excluded. In short, the new focus is a sort of salvaging effort of "maroon cultures" (Mintz and Price). In cultural anthropology the term "Creole" has been used to reconceptualize what Melville Herskovits called the reinterpretation, adaptation, and syncretism of cultures usually subsumed under paradigms of assimilation (*Life* xxii–xxiii). Indeed, the entire controversy over what he referred to, in 1941, as "the Myth of the Negro Past" (Herskovits, *Myth of the Negro Past*) is in this post–civil rights age a powerful motive for its revalorization. The Cuban debate over *transculturación* led by Fernando Ortiz addresses a similar problematic (Ortiz; Palmié *Wizards;* Mintz "Enduring Substances").

Two trends increased the attractiveness: First, globalization and the economic range of and interest in world systems has deparochialized the historiography of the New World. Second, the rise, after the national emancipation of African and Caribbean countries, of a sense of local perspective and of local merit has brought into focus the many local, creolized cultures of the

Atlantic system. Hence the discourse of creolization articulates a remapping of diasporas between Europe, Africa, and the New World, and trying not to privilege either of the three centers, it also takes a new look at the in-between new spaces of the Atlantic rim (Gilroy; Berlin "Free People of Color"). Ulf Hannerz suggests that one aspect of globalization may be creolization, which has triggered a new global interest in flux, culture contact, and diversity. As James Clifford has it, we may all be Caribbean now in our urban archipelagos. Hence there is a new need of finding terms that would conceptualize such multicultural diversification. Creole as a concept was found useful in domesticating diversity, in making pluralism lose its otherness and go native.

In literary studies the deconstruction of the Eurocentric or phallocentric canon has revalorized the margin, the border, and favored concepts such as *metissage* or hybridity. In Haiti and the French Antilles *créolité* has become a postcolonial agenda advanced by poets who are trying to throw off the shackles of a francophone *négritude.*

But habits die hard. As the debate over Eurocentrism, Afrocentricity, and American exceptionalism indicates their positionality remains defined by Europe, Africa, and America, by their respective absence or presence. The first problem, as has become clear in the review of its usages, is the position, perspective, and thrust of interest (*Erkenntnisinteresse*) under the weight of hegemonic, colonial, and, subsequently, counterhegemonic, postcolonial habits of thought.

Basically, three ideal type perspectives, each one of them with their particular reification and essentialization, which usually implies a privileging of Eurocentrism, Afrocentrism, and exceptionalism, are at work. But in fact the triangular relation is overlayered or weighted down by a binary, Manichean racial division that—in the context of the United States—is an exceptional habit of the heart. Indeed, there are two habits here that work as conceptual traps. I will call them the binary trap and the purity trap.

It is interesting that a sort of morality play between Eurocentrism and Afrocentrism is being enacted in America as a reflex of Manichean disposition, an ideological checks-and-balances system in which the two partners need each other for their own identity construction. Behind it we see the tacit logic of and working of the color line: a Manichean handling of a racialized identity politics in the United States. Indeed, in the United States an acceptance of the fact of creolization would be useful in that it would move from a binary either/or notion to a multilateralization of the color line through multiple ethnicities, to a hybridization and metissage of what used to be rigid categories of belonging. The newest theoretical object of desire or theoretical utopia is a fluid, in-between perspective, that of Atlantic Creoles or of a circum-Atlantic Creole mind-set as evoked by Berlin or Gilroy. Its problem is that it lacks focus and therefore it is difficult to instrumentalize as cultural politics.

Equally stubborn is the purity trap. Even in the thin air of theory the notion of creolization has to labor against the privileging of purity. In much of Western philosophy there is a tacit background assumption that postulates the superiority of purity over any mixture; hence the notion of biological miscegenation or cultural mixture does not have a good press, particularly from the point of view of the classic metropolis, the bastion of "good blood." This epistemological blindness combined with the power game of ascription is particularly problematical in countries where cultural mixture was the norm. The 1980 *Harvard Encyclopedia of American Ethnic Groups* treats 106 American ethnic groups as if they were discrete and separate groups loyal to the notion of biological and cultural purity. Mixture between the groups, which, unmeltable ethnics notwithstanding, has been rampant in American history, tends to get avoided in group entries and is merely referred to in passing in a few of the survey articles. Even Afrocentrism holds on to the dogma of purity by merely reversing the charges.

Since then a veritable revolution has occurred: Today's fashionable terms "hybridity" or "metissage" may be shorn of their negative charge, but they too operate from a prior notion of purity and, by default, from a conscious positive revaluation of mixture. There is an element of the pastoral in such binary switches. As Nietzsche already noticed, the anti-Platonist who in trying to separate from Plato by reacting to Plato continues to define himself through Plato and thus reaffirms him. Boundary maintenance between the pure and impure is deeply rooted in academic epistemologies within the Manichean disposition of American exceptionalism. Even when purity becomes metissage, racial danger continues to animate the semantics.

There are a number of epistemological shifts and political reversals in the reconceptualization of creolization at this postcolonial moment. The first moves from universal to local narratives, but also from a mere national perspective to a global system of networking. The second thrust is from holism (or wholeism) to fractal thinking. The third moves from essence to process, from stasis to dynamics, from national text to circum-Atlantic performance (Roach). All this is necessary because these turns are concerted efforts to move from master perspectives to subaltern perspectives, from master speech to creolized speech, from the colonial to the postcolonial or diasporic. Implied is a move from the written, codified "grammar" to a dynamics of creolization of local and preferably oral language use. Implied is also a shift from purity and norm to a conscious corruption of norm on the one hand and from purity to creole hybridity and metissage on the other. Cornell West captures the new preference in a nutshell. The new theories try "to trash the monolithic and homogeneous in the name of diversity, multiplicity, and heterogeneity; to reject the abstract, general, and universal in light of the concrete, specific, and particular; and to historicize, contextualize, and pluralize by highlighting the contingent, provisional, variable, tentative, shifting and changing."[26]

This creates a conceptual terrain of high viscosity in which any sort of historical fact or truth becomes *ideologieverdächtig.* This situation of ambivalence is hard to keep up and creates an identity and a power vacuum. One ethnocentric knee-jerk reaction will be a renewed essentialization at the Others' expense, that is, when it involves a positional or political advantage. Then there is the post-structural refusal to accept any but local knowledges. To posit local knowledge, then, depends ultimately on an act of *individual* will or faith. Due to the historical mortgage of power relations and due to the caveats of theory, creolizing cultures may be defined easier *ex negativo*—by what they are not rather than by what they are. Postcolonial Brazilian culture is harder to define than the colonial Portuguese norm enshrined in museums, cathedrals, and documents. Cuban culture, as Ortiz found out, has a harder time than the Spanish metropolis. But new nations keep trying. There is a danger that "creoleness" becomes codified and instrumentalized for purely nationalistic purposes, as in the Brasileiridade and Cubanidad movements, which have petered out into folklore or pop culture. On the other hand, without creating such national identities and without asserting a national cultural purpose, such new states are weaker as agents in the international arena. Thus postcolonial desires may also solidify the very power relations they tries to unseat. Ambivalences multiply. To paraphrase Henry Louis Gates, just as blacks are constructing their identity for political reasons, they are told by the agenda setters that identity politics is out (Gates).

Conclusion: Creolization and Socialized Ambivalence

The habit of the heart to differentiate between "them and us" in asymmetrical terms continues into the age of pluralism. Even after the negative ascription associated with creolization was dropped and it had become chic to be ethnic, writes Barry Jean Ancelet, the outside perception of creolized cultures remain charged with "colonial" projections that fit the abovementioned patterns. He lampoons the expectations of visitors from both the metropolis and other parts of the diaspora to southern Louisiana. The difference between their expectations of fantasy Cajuns and what actual Cajuns do is an exact measure of the effects of the colonial prejudice and its asymmetrical relations:

> French Canadians, for instance, who seek in Cajuns a symbol of dogged linguistic survival in predominantly Anglo-Saxon North America, find virtually no Anglo-Franco confrontation and an absence of animosity in cultural politics. The French who seek vestiges of former colonials find instead French-speaking cowboys (and Indians) in pickup trucks. They are surprised that the Cajuns and Creoles love fried chicken and iced tea, forgetting this is the South; that they love hamburger and Coke, forgetting this is the United States; that they love cayenne and cold beer, forgetting this is the northern top of the West Indies. American visitors usually skim along the surface, too, looking in vain for traces of Longfellow's Evangeline. (Ancelet 422)

How about the locals themselves? Edward Brathwaite for one celebrates the cultural choices involved in creolization processes and closes his study *The Development of Creole Society in Jamaica, 1770–1820* with the following summary:

> My own idea of creolization is based on the notion of an historically affected socio-cultural continuum, within which (in the case of Jamaica), there are four inter-related and sometimes overlapping orientations. From their several cultural bases people in the West Indies tend towards certain directions, positions, assumptions, and ideals. But nothing is really fixed and monolithic. Although there is white/brown/black, there are infinite possibilities within these distinctions and many ways of asserting identity. A common colonial and creole experience is shared among the various divisions, even if that experience is variously interpreted. These four orientations may be designated as follows: European, Euro-creole, Afro-creole (or folk), and "West Indian." (Brathwaite 310)

Edouard Glissant would agree. He prefers creolization to creolism, claiming that the latter suggests essentialism whereas the former reflects "the idea of a continuous process capable of producing the identical and the different" (2). Brathwaite's and Glissant's words on the Caribbean sociocultural continuum apply just as well to New Orleans. Indeed, given New Orleans' complex history, one could easily expand the list of *local* orientations. As we have seen, there is a Euro-American, Euro-ethnic (divided into Italian, Irish, German, French, and Spanish), Euro-Creole, Euro-Cajun, zydeco-Cajun, Afro-Creole, African American (divided into Afro-cosmopolitan and Afro-folk), and, usually, on occasions such as Mardi Gras, an integrative N'awlins (or South Louisianian) orientation all of them embedded in processes of creolization. Melville Herskovits proposed in a discussion of Haitian culture that the acculturation process should not be seen as an amalgam of two traditions but as "two sets of counterposed values or behavioral alternatives," one African and the other Euro-American. The fourfold choice involved—affirmation or rejection of the respective traditions—makes for a rather complex socialization process. Herskovits named the behavioral results of these processes "socialized ambivalence," noting that this ambivalence is as "responsible for the many shifts in allegiance that continually take place as it is for the change in attitude in everyday association" (Herskovits 1971, 299; Ostendorf). In the production and interpretation of culture it is, I believe, is a constitutive element of the creolization processes described above. As the contradictions of New Orleans history increased and the orientations for its agents multiplied, the willingness to agree on one version of its history has largely atrophied. Creolization, then, may also be understood as a mind-set for not wanting to write *one* New World master narrative and for keeping the interpretive options open.

At the level of everyday cultural praxis one may observe in each one of the ethnic groups in New Orleans a perpetual process of a realignment of their cultural memory to current needs or, indeed, an ongoing process of creolization. Their local myth making is not overly burdened by any agreed-upon or canonized version of history. Historiography remains a free for all, an open proposition without a master narrative. There are now as many popular and oral histories of New Orleans Creole culture as there are groups, but there is not as yet a dependable history of southern Louisiana or, rather, a history that has found the approval of all groups.[27] Applying Michael Walzer's concept, there are a number of overlapping spheres of local cultures. Indeed, such a history would, in view of the mythmaking so dear to many groups, be impossible to write. Instead, the most favorite historiographical genre is the popular, anecdotal history, such as Robert Tallant's *Voodoo in New Orleans* (1946) or Herbert Asbury's *French Quarter* (1936), inspired by nostalgia without memory and replete with historiographical canards and myths.

Hence cultural change may proceed unburdened by the weight of a divisive historical past, and processes of creolization are encouraged by the workings of what linguists call "structural amnesia" (Goody and Watt 314).[28] And yet there is also a common creolized experience based on a vaguely articulated sense of whatever passes for history, "even if that experience is variously interpreted" (Brathwaite 310). Despite all this fragmentation and fractal cultural knowledge there is in New Orleans a cultural common denominator, most readily expressed in what might be called a "second line culture" of trans-ethnic celebration: parades, festivals, picnics, and other Caribbean pleasures in which members of all groups mix and meet and eat together (Smith). It stands to reason that the chamber of commerce and the tourist trade have been more interested in the integrative power of current celebrations than in the divisive history that lies buried under multicultural fictions of a forever-creolizing cultural gumbo.

NOTES

1. An earlier, short version appeared as an in-house publication of Odense University, Denmark, in 1999 under the title "Creoles and Creolization: The Concepts and their History." It has been expanded and updated. The assistance of Stephan Palmié in compiling this documentation is gratefully acknowledged.

2. "You can empower discursively the native and open yourself to charges of downplaying the epistemic (and literal) violence of colonialism; or play up the absolute nature of colonial domination, thus textually replicating the repressive operations of colonialism" (Gates). JanMohamed, following Fanon, postulates a Manichean divide in race relations. Palmié, "Model in the Muddle?"

3. These will include *The Encyclopaedia Britannica,* 11th ed. of 1910 (*EB11*) (7: 409), the *Oxford English Dictionary* of 1933 (*OED*) (1163), *Webster's New International Dictionary of the English Language, Second Edition* (623), George Friederici's *Amerikanistisches Wörterbuch* of 1960 (219ff.), the *Harvard Encyclopedia of American Ethnic Groups* (Cambridge: Harvard University Press, 1980) (247), and longer articles and books that address the question of Creole identity in the Caribbean basin.

4. Cf. Hartmut Lehmann and Melvin Richter, eds., *The Meaning of Historical Terms and Concepts* German Historical Institute Occasional Paper No. 15. Washington, D.C., 1996.

5. Salvador de Madriaga considers the *OED* derivation from *criadillo* absurd and insists on a Spanish derivation, *criollo,* from *criar.* François Chevalier, French historian of South America, proposes the Portuguese origin *crioulo,* since *criollo* would be an unusual formation on the basis of *criar* (Nègre 39).

6. The poet Oswald de Andrade published the *Manifesto Antropófago* in 1928, using cannibalism as a metaphor for the incorporation of other cultures; cf. Julia Podeschwa, *Untersuchung zum Kulturkontakt zwischen den USA und Brasilien in der populären Musik unter spezieller Berücksichtigung der Tropicalismo-Bewegung* (Munich: Magisterarbeit, 1995). Al-

though cultural theorists use "cooking" as a metaphor of culture formation, specific cooking traditions and eating habits could be a rich source and focus for the study of "creolization."

7. This lean bibliographical reference of the *OED* in all likelihood refers to Juan d'Acosta's *História natural y moral de las Indias.* Garcilaso de la Vega commented in his history of the Incas of 1580 that white Spaniards had taken over the word from African Negroes, who called their American offspring "criollo" or "criolla" (Nègre 39ff.). Nègre also quotes slave invoices from Guadeloupe, Martinique, and St. Domingue in 1767 and 1789 that distinguish Africans and "Créole."

8. This skimpy reference probably refers to Antonio and Jorge Juan de Ulloa, *Relación histórica del viaje a la América meridionel,* 5. vols. (Madrid, 1748).

9. Thomas Pettit reminds me that the term "vernacular" has a parallel, even similar history. Derived from Latin *verna* (slave), it refers to indigenous language and culture formation. Like "Creole," the vernacular stands in opposition to the high and dominant traditions. Cf. *OED,* 3614.

10. This is contested by Eriksen.

11. Neumann found a group of "petits Blancs" in St. Martin Parish near the Atchafalaya basin who speak a variant of black Creole (63ff.).

12. Joseph Tregle charts the genesis of the myth of pure-blood creoleness. It was according to him the last-ditch attempt of French-speaking New Orleaneans to hold on to cultural and political power within a generally racist climate determined by the Anglo-Saxon world around them: "But the creole added to the common white man's rejection of the black this additional spur to hatred: he might be confused with him. Even more dreadful than a sharing of power with the Negro was the possibility of being identified as his half-brother, a sort of mixed breed stripped of blood pride as well as any claim to social or political prestige. For the creole knew the world he now lived in to be one obsessed with the no-longer-settled issue of racial supremacy, in which the very suspicion of mixed racial inheritance was a ticket to opprobrium, contempt and ostracism. He knew it because he had helped make it so. In such manner was the cardinal tenet of the now familiar myth born: for those so threatened, henceforth to be creole was to be white" ("Creoles and Americans" 55). George Washington Cable's *Grandissimes* did not exactly allay those fears.

13. Reading between the lines we may sense a certain caution on the part of Cable. Indeed, Cable's novel *The Grandissimes,* first published in *Scribner's Monthly* in 1879, had caused an uproar over the proper definition of "Creole" in Louisiana. His parable of the Creole brothers divided by race might have caused less furor had he remained a mere regional writer. After all, other "Creole" authors such as Alfred Mercier had said far less flattering things about Creole society. But with Cable's growing national and international fame the issue became politicized. When he published "Freedman's Case in Equity" (1885), which argued for black rights, even his older friends and informants such as Charles Gayarré and Alexander Dimitry (the latter is credited by Cable for the story of Bras Coupé) turned against him. The culmination of this battle was an English-language address by Gayarré titled "The Creoles of History and the Creoles of Romance" (1885), which puts the myth in place (Dominguez 143).

14. The entry on "creole" in Webster's *New Twentieth Century Dictionary of the English Language* of 1976 marks a subtle shift, in that the more inclusive general meaning is given

first, the more exclusive Louisiana meaning second (emphasis added): "1. originally, a native, especially of the West Indies, Central America, tropical South America, the Gulf States, or Mauritius, of *nonnative descent;* 2. a person of French or Spanish descent born in the Americas; 3. a person of Negro descent born in the Americas; usually a creole Negro, 4. a person descended from or culturally related to the original French settlers of Louisiana and New Orleans; hence, French as spoken by such people; 5. loosely, anyone from Louisiana; 6. a person descended from or culturally related to original Spanish settlers in the Gulf States, especially Texas; 7. loosely, a person of mixed Creole and Negro stock; and 8. (from Sp. Criollo) in parts of tropical South America, the child of a white father and a mestiza mother."

15. It is a curious fact that in Africa "Creole" initially referred to those liberated Africans who came back from the Americas. By this time and for Africans at least, the New World had become part of the Old World. It is even more telling that the difference in class and urbanized lifestyle of these westernized Africans soon affected the definition and marked the border to rural folk: "The Creole community always included, and still includes, persons of black-African stock. . . who emulated the "Creole way of life" by adopting the habits, standards of behavior, and outlooks with which Creoles identified" (N. Spitzer 12–13).

16. Gary B. Mill's study of the Cane River Creoles of color *(Forgotten People)* makes a similar point for rural Louisiana. Next to urban Creoles there were a considerable number of rural Creoles who kept their distance from Cajuns. The difference was one of class and culture, but also of descent. Cajuns had come to Louisiana by way of Canada and therefore did not meet the requirements of direct Old World descent. In a belated revenge the culture and history of these country Creoles, particularly black Creoles, were displaced or overlayered by the Cajun revitalization movement. The Creole origins of zydeco culture got lost. Zydeco is claimed as a Cajun derivative, which is a gross simplification. This history needs to be unpacked.

17. Circumstantial evidence of the process of "creolization" lies in the curious fact that the leader of the French insurrection against Ulloa was Karl Friedrich D'Arensbourg, the commander of the German militia. Of Swedish extraction, he commanded German settlers who had emigrated to the colony in 1721 under John Law's colonization scheme and who, after a rough beginning, had settled on the so-called Côte des Allemands and acculturated quickly. Mostly of poor farming background, they had come to stay and had by this time created a viable local community. Hence they came out to defend their New World home with particular vengeance. Their current descendants have creolized names such as Oubre (Huber), Zeringue (Zähringer), Vicnaire (Wichner), Chauffe (Schaf), or simply LaBranche (Zweig) (Kondert).

18. See my "Urban Creole Slavery and Its Cultural Legacy: The Case of New Orleans," in Binder. It would be useful to differentiate between a private/cultural and public/political Creole identity. The private Creole identity preceded any public and political articulation. We may also assume that creolization in the sense of cultural fusion was a salient factor in the making of the Afro-Creole-Indian bond long before there was a name for the new identity. See Berlin "From Creole to African"; Fiehrer; and Foner.

19. A typical instance is the wrecking of the French theater on July 4, 1838, which Henry Kmen reports. As a special treat for the Fourth of July the orchestra played the overture to

"La Dame Blanche": "The conductor was Louis Hus Desforges, a veteran musician who had been associated with opera in New Orleans virtually from its start. M. Desforges was also a veteran of the battle of New Orleans and as a result had been nearly deaf for 15 years. Now therefore he was happily unaware of the uproar behind him, hearing only what he took to be a gentle murmur of approval. While he put his heart into his work with supreme vigor, the audience began to tear up chairs and benches. The old conductor came to a halt only when the distraught Caldwell reached the podium and shouted in his ear to stop. The audience wanted 'Yankee doodle'! Turning with hurt dignity to the unruly Americans, Desforges dressed them down: 'You want Yankee Dude? Well, you no have Yankee Dude. Because Why? Because not necessair'" (194–95).

20. The myth had its European audience. Charles Baudelaire's *Les Fleurs du Mal* pays tribute to "Une Dame Créole."

21. The privately printed pamphlet by Aline St. Julien, *Colored Creole: Color Conflict and Confusion in New Orleans* (New Orleans, 1977), follows this deep conflict into our day: "But when I decided to step out of that "Creole bag" I became a Negro. . . . But being a Colored Creole-Catholic Negro-Afro-American has brought me through the struggle of finding my true identity." See also the article by Wonk, which stirred up much controversy.

22. The most recent, post–Hurricane Katrina éclat was caused by an article of the food critic of *GQ*, Alan Richman, who badmouthed New Orleans Creoles and their cuisine. He not only called Creole identity into doubt but also claimed that their cuisine "had the stodgy stink of 1950s French hotel food and might not be worth saving" (cited in Severson).

23. Berlin "From Creole to African," 251–88.

24. See Holm for a succinct survey of the linguistic debate.

25. An example of such mythmaking is Owen and Murphy, the product of a CETA Artists in the City of New Orleans Project. See Brenda Marie Osbey's critical review in *New Orleans Tribune* 3.11 (November 15–December 15, 1987): 31. See also Wonk. Useful introductions to New Orleans and its history are Conrad; Logsdon and Hirsch.

26. "The New Cultural Politics of Difference," *October* 53 (1990): 93–109, 93.

27. Lawrence Powell is under contract with Harvard University Press to undertake this delicate and complicated task.

28. Goody and Watt write that "in each generation, therefore, the individual memory will mediate the cultural heritage in such a way that its new constituents will adjust to the old by the process of interpretation that Bartlett calls 'rationalizing' . . . ; and whatever parts of it have ceased to be of contemporary relevance are likely to be eliminated by the process of forgetting" (314). It seems to me that forgetting and mythologizing are two of the most important factors in the historiography of this conflict-ridden concept.

WORKS CONSULTED

Ancelet, Barry Jean. "Cajuns and Creoles." Wilson and Ferris 421–23.

Berlin, Ira. "The Free People of Color of Louisiana and the Gulf Ports." *Slaves without Masters: The Free Negro in the Antebellum South.* New York: Pantheon, 1974. 108–132.

———. "From Creole to African: Atlantic Creoles and the Origins of African-American Society in Mainland North America." *William and Mary Quarterly* 3rd. ser., 53.2 (April 1996): 251–88.

Binder, Wolfgang, ed. *Slavery in the Americas.* Würzburg: Königshausen & Neumann, 1993.

Brading, D. A. *The First America.: The Spanish Monarchy, Creole Patriots, and the Liberal State.* Cambridge: Cambridge University Press, 1991.

Brathwaite, Edward. *The Development of Creole Society in Jamaica, 1770–1820.* Oxford: Clarendon, 1971.

Buisseret, David, and Steven G. Reinhardt, eds. *Creolization in the Americas.* College Station: Texas A&M University Press, 2000.

Chinard, Gilbert. "Eighteenth Century Theories on America as a Human Habitat." *Proceedings of the American Philosophical Society* 91.1 (1947): 27–57.

Collier, Gordon, and Ulrich Fleischmann, eds. *A Pepper-Pot of Cultures: Aspects of Creolization in the Caribbean.* Amsterdam: Rodopi, 2004.

Conrad, Glenn R., ed. *Readings in Louisiana History.* New Orleans: Louisiana Historical Association, 1978.

Cowley, John. *Carnival, Canboulay, and Calypso: Traditions in the Making.* Cambridge: Cambridge University Press, 1996.

D'Acosta, Juan. *Historia natural y moral de las Indias.* Mexico: Fondo de Cultura Económica, 1962.

Dominguez, Virginia R. *White by Definition: Social Classification in Creole Louisiana.* New Brunswick: Rutgers University Press, 1986.

Ellison, Ralph. Review of *An American Dilemma,* by Gunnar Myrdal. *Shadow and Act.* New York: Signet, 1966. 290–302.

Eriksen, Thomas Hylland. "Tu dimunn pu vini creol: The Mauritian creole and the concept of creolization." Lecture, Transnational Connections, Oxford, England. Available online at http://folk.uio.no/geirthe/Creoles.html.

Fiehrer, Thomas Marc. "The African Presence in Colonial Louisiana: An Essay on the Continuity of Caribbean Culture." *Louisiana's Black Heritage,* ed. Robert R. MacDonald, John R. Kemp, and Edward F. Haas. New Orleans: Louisiana State Museum, 1979. 3–31.

Foner, Laura. "The Free People of Color in Louisiana and St. Domingue." *Journal of Social History* 3.4 (Summer 1970): 406–30.

Friederici, Georg. *Amerikanistisches Wörterbuch.* Hamburg: Cram, de Gruyter, 1960.

Gates, Henry Louis, Jr. "Critical Fanonism." *Critical Inquiry* 17 (1991): 457–70.

Gilroy, Paul. *The Black Atlantic: Modernity and Double Consciousness.* Cambridge: Harvard University Press, 1993.

Goody, Jack, and Ian Watt. "The Consequences of Literacy." *Language and Social Context.* Ed. Pier Paolo Giglioli. London: Penguin, 1972.

Hall, Gwendolyn Midlo. *Africans in Colonial Louisiana: The Development of Afro-*

Creole Culture in the Eighteenth Century. Baton Rouge: Louisiana State University Press, 1992. (Cf. review in *Africa* 64 [1994]: 168–71.)

Hannerz, Ulf. "American Culture: Creolized, Creolizing." *American Culture: Creolized, Creolizing.* Ed. Erik Asard. Upsala: Swedish Institute for North American Studies, 1988.

———. "Culture Between Center and Periphery: Toward a Macroanthropology." *Ethnos* 54 (1989): 200–216.

———. "The World in Creolization." *Africa* 57 (1987): 546–59.

Herskovits, Melville. *Life in a Haitian Valley.* 1937. Reprint, New York: Anchor, 1971.

———. *The Myth of the Negro Past.* 1941. Reprint, Boston: Beacon, 1958.

Holm, John. *Pidgins and Creoles.* Cambridge: Cambridge University Press, 1988.

JanMohamed, Abdul. "The Economy of Manichean Allegory: The Function of Radical Difference in Colonialist Literature." *"Race," Writing, and Difference.* Ed. Henry Louis Gates Jr. Chicago: University of Chicago Press, 1986.

Johnson, Jerah. "Colonial New Orleans: A Fragment of the Eighteenth-Century French Ethos." Logsdon and Hirsch 12–57.

———. "New Orleans' Congo Square: An Urban Setting for Early Afro-American Culture Formation." *Louisiana History* 32 (Spring 1991): 117–57.

Joyner, Charles. "Creolization." Wilson and Ferris 147–49.

Kmen, Henry. *Music in New Orleans: The Formative Years, 1791–1841.* Baton Rouge: Louisiana State University Press, 1966.

Kondert, Reinhart. "Germans in Louisiana: The Colonial Experience, 1720–1803." *Yearbook of German-American Studies* 16 (1981): 59–61.

Lambert, David. *White Creole Culture: Politics and Identity during the Age of Abolition.* Cambridge: Cambridge University Press, 2005.

Logsdon, Joseph. "Americans and Creoles in New Orleans: The Origins of Black Citizenship in the United States." *Amerikastudien/American Studies* 34.2 (1989): 187–202.

Logsdon, Joseph, and Arnold Hirsch, eds. *Creole New Orleans: Race and Americanization.* Baton Rouge: Louisiana State University Press, 1992.

Lussan, Auguste. *La famille créole: Drame en cinq acts et en prose.* New Orleans: Fremaux et Alfred Moret, 1837.

Mercier, A. "Étude sur la langue créole en louisiane." *Comptes rendus de l'Atheneé louisianais* 1 (1880): 378–83.

Mills, Gary B. "Creole." Wilson and Ferris 426–27.

———. *The Forgotten People: Cane River's Creoles of Color.* Baton Rouge: Louisiana State University Press, 1977.

Mintz, Sidney W. "Enduring Substances, Trying Theories: The Caribbean Region as *Oikoumenê.*" *Journal of the Royal Anthropological Institute* new ser., 2 (June 1996): 289–311.

———. "Melville J. Herskovits and Caribbean Studies: A Retrospective Tribute." *Caribbean Studies* 4 (1964): 42–51.

———. "The Socio-historical Background of Pidginization and Creolization." *Pidginization and Creolization of Languages.* Ed. Dell Hymes. Cambridge: Cambridge University Press, 1971.

Mintz, Sidney W., and Richard Price. *The Birth of African American Culture: An Anthropological Perspective.* 1976. Reprint, Boston: Beacon, 1992.

Nègre, André. "Origines et Signification du Mot 'Creole.'" *Bulletin de la Societé d'Histoire de la Guadeloupe* 5–6 (1966): 38–41.

Neumann, Ingrid. "The Créole des blancs en Louisiane." *Études créoles* 6.2 (1984): 63–78.

Ortiz, Fernando. "Los factores humanos de la cubanidad." *Revista Bimestre Cubana* 45 (1940): 165–69.

Ostendorf, Berndt. "Double Consciousness in Afro-American Oral Culture." *Amerikastudien/American Studies* 20 (1975): 209–59.

Owen, Lyla Hay, and Owen Murphy. *Créoles of New Orleans: People of Color/Gens de Couleur.* New Orleans: First Quarter, 1987.

Palmié, Stephan. "Creolization and Its Discontent." *Annual Review of Anthropology* 35 (October 2006): 433–56.

———. "Is There a Model in the Muddle? 'Creolization' in African American History and Anthropology." *Creolization: History, Ethnography, Theory.* Stewart 178–200.

———. *Wizards and Scientists: Explorations in Afro-Cuban Modernity and Tradition.* Durham, N.C.: Duke University Press, 2002.

Richman, Alan. "Yes, We're Open." *GQ,* November 2006. www.men.style.com/gq/features/full?id=content_5165&pageNum=1.

Roach, Joseph. *Cities of the Dead. Circum-Atlantic Performance.* New York: Columbia University Press, 1996.

Severson, Kim. "Faerie Folk Strike Back with Fritters." *New York Times,* December 6, 2006.

Smith, Michael P. *Mardi Gras Indians.* New Orleans: Pelican, 1994.

Sollors, Werner. "First Generation, Second Generation, Third Generation . . : The Cultural Construction of Descent."*Beyond Ethnicity.* By Werner Sollors. New York: Oxford University Press, 1986. 208–36.

Spitzer, Leo. *The Creoles of Sierra Leone: Responses to Colonialism, 1870–1945.* Madison: University of Wisconsin Press, 1974.

Spitzer, Nicholas. "Monde Creole: The Cultural World of French Louisiana Creoles and the Creolization of World Cultures." *Journal of American Folklore* 113.459 (2000): 57–72.

Stewart, Charles. E., ed. *Creolization: History, Ethnography, Theory.* Walnut Creek, Calif.: Left Shore Press, 2007.

Tregle, Joseph. "Creoles and Americans." Logsdon and Hirsch 131–85.

———. "On That Word 'Creole' Again: A Note." *Louisiana History* 23 (1982): 193–98.

Trouillot, Michel-Rolph. "The Caribbean Region: An Open Frontier in Anthropological Theory." *Annual Review of Anthropology* 21 (1992): 19–42.

———. "North Atlantic Universals: Analytical Fictions, 1492–1945." *South Atlantic Quarterly* 101 (2002): 839–58.

Whitten, Norman, and John Szwed, eds. *Afro-American Anthropology.* New York: Free Press, 1970.

Wilson, Charles Reagan, and William Ferris, eds. *Encyclopedia of Southern Culture.* Chapel Hill: University of North Carolina Press, 1989.

Wonk, Dalt. "The Creoles of Color." *New Orleans* 10.8 (May 1976): 47–57.

One-Drop Rules

Self-Identity and the Women in the Trial of Toucoutou

SYBIL KEIN

The 1858 case of Anastasie De Sarzant, known as Toucoutou, was the first New Orleans case of slander and defamation that involved a woman who sued her neighbor for publicly stating that she was a person of color. There were two earlier cases filed in New Orleans for slander by men who were accused of being colored. The earliest was that of *Cauchoux v. Dupuy et al.* in 1831 and *Pandelly v. Wiltz* in 1854. These three cases do have some things in common. Pierre Soulé, the attorney for the appellant in the 1831 case, was also the attorney for the defendants in the Toucoutou case, and George Pandelly, who filed the 1854 case for slander, was the clerk for the fifth justice of the peace in the Toucoutou case.

Before the original records of the Toucoutou case were discovered by Greg Osborn in August 1999 at the New Orleans Public Library, the only record available was the song titled "Toucoutou," which was written by a free man of color, Joseph Beaumont (Desdunes 87). According to Desdunes, Beaumont, a barber by trade, wrote many songs about the case (85). But Desdunes did not fix a date to the song or the full name of the plaintiff. He also only supplied slight information to the case. *Toucoutou,* the 1928 novel by Edward L. Tinker, has been seen as a purely fictitious account of what may have been the story of the woman and her case. As it turns out, both Beaumont and, especially, Tinker used the first names of just about every person involved in the story and trial and recounted the incidents very close to those recorded in the testimony of witnesses in the case. Although a century apart, Beaumont, who lived at the time of the trial, and Tinker, who lived into the following century, did give a fairly good account of what actually happened. One of Beaumont's songs, which Desdunes says was the most popular of the songs Beaumont wrote about this case, contains a very biting refrain and a "moral" at the end that was sure to frighten anyone else who considered Toucoutou's tactics. The songs were sung in Louisiana Creole:

REFRAIN:

Ah! Toucoutou, yé conin vous,
Vous cé tin Morico.
Na pas savon qui tacé blanc
pou blanchi vous lapo. (87)

Ah! Toucoutou, they know you,
You are a black.
There is no soap
white enough to bleach your skin.

THE ENDING MORAL:

Mo pre fini mo ti chanson
Pasqui manvi dormi:
Mé mo pensé que la leson
Longtemps li va servi. (88)

I've almost finished my little song
because I want to sleep:
But I think that the lesson
will serve for a long time.

The "whiteness" in this song refers to the social status that was in question because testimony from the trial states that Anastasie, like her mother, was very fair with large blue eyes and curly hair (OCR, testimony of Eugenie Saizer and Justine Bourgois). Although not an eye witness, Rodolph Desdunes offers pertinent insight to the response of the Creole community to this trial:

> Une decision adverse, . . . était désastruse, fatale, car elle entrainait le perte de tour prestige pour la victime, qui ne pouvait plus alors vivre dans les mêmes conditions sociales. . . . La population de couleur était sérieusement divisée sur cette question *d'usurpation ethnologique.* Les unes approuvaient, les autres désapprouvaient la conduit des gens de couleur qui voulaient se glisser dans la société des blancs. Les dissidents étaient en majorité. (84)
>
> An adverse decision . . . would be disastrous, fatal, because it would mean the lost of all prestige for the victim, who will never again be able to live in the same social conditions. . . . The population of color was seriously divided on this question *of ethnological usurpation.* One side would approve, the other side would disapprove of the people of color who would wish to slip into the society of the whites. The dissidents were in the majority.

The response from the people of color in the Faubourg Marigny, where Toucoutou lived, was very harsh. Their lives were especially complicated because of their use of the system of plaçage as well as other problems of their caste. Plaçage began in the mid-1700s, created by mostly wealthy free women of color who belonged to a social club known as La Société du Cordon Bleu. They formed this organization to protect their daughters from being sold as slaves. European men were contracted to provide financial security for the women and their resulting offsprings for life in exchange for a romantic relationship with the woman. This was both a romantic and business arrangement. La Société du Cordon Bleu presented the first of their balls or debutante parties in the eighteenth century in New Orleans. Their balls were elegant private affairs for which one needed an invitation to be admitted. The young women chose the European men. A woman could reject a man by merely refusing to dance with him more than once. Later, other parties became known as "quadroon balls." They were imitated by white businessmen who hired prostitutes of all races to preside over public dances designed to profit from the original. (Kein 81–82). A review of the Toucoutou case reveals some of the intricacies of self-identity and social status involved here. The facts in this case are complicated, so the Louisiana Supreme Court summary (including the verdict) follows:

> Is she a white or a colored person? She claims to be the daughter of Jean Desarzant and Françoise Martin, both natives of Switzerland; whilst on the part of the defendant, countered that Jean Leizaire, a white person was her father and Justine Bacquié *alias* Françoise Martin, a free woman of color was her mother. It is worthy of notice , however, that as a matter of public notoriety, the plaintiff has been court ordered here to fore as a person of color; but this is accounted for by the latter's counsel, from the fact, as stated in his brief, "that the defendant's witnesses have confounded the plaintiff with a child Justine Bacquié."
>
> One fact is well established, that Justine Bacquié, a free woman of color went by the name also of Françoise Martin; and in several deeds and documents on file, she is invariably styled a free woman of color, and her name given as either Françoise Martin, Françoise Justine Martin, or Justine Bacquié. The duplicity of name of this person being shown, it remains to be ascertained whether at the same time and in the same neighborhood lived a free white woman bearing the same name of Françoise Martin to whom the plaintiff can trace her filiation.
>
> The plaintiff rests her case principally upon two documents—the one a certified list of the white passengers arrived at New Orleans on board of the

Brig Davis from San Domingo, and the other her certificate of baptism. In the above mentioned lists are to be found the following entries: "Francoise Martin aged 20 years, from Switzerland, an inhabitant." "Jean Desarzant, aged 25 years, from Switzerland, an inhabitant." In the Certificate of Baptism, she is stated to be the natural child of Jean Desarzant, a native of Dormeloge in Switzerland, and Francoise Martin, a native of San Domingo. Apart from the discrepancy to be found as to the place of nativity assigned to Francoise Martin in the list of passengers and in the certificate of Baptism, it is obvious that the former document does not show the *status* of Francoise Martin but merely that a person so styling herself came from San Domingo to New Orleans as stated in the instrument. There is no proof in the record that Francoise Martin was of European birth but it appears that she came from San Domingo and so does Justine Bacquié, even if she be considered as a different person from the Francoise Martin whom the plaintiff claims as her mother.

Justine Burgoin says that she was acquainted with both Justine Bacquié and Francoise Martin; that the latter who had four children, including the plaintiff confided them to Jean Leizaire before her death; that Jean Leizaire after the death of Francoise Martin placed them under the care of Justine Bacquié. Strange to say that this witness, who does not know herself whether she is a white or a colored person, is aware of the maternal filiation of the plaintiff, knows nothing of her father, nor whether Justine Bacquié ever had any children, although they lived in the immediate neighborhood. The testimony of Mrs. Cooper is in keeping with that of Mrs. Burgoin. The declarations of these witnesses, even though they stood uncontradicted, would not show that the person whom they point out as the plaintiffs mother, was a white person, and indeed the filiation itself would be left somewhat involved in doubt. But the documentary and oral evidence found in the record prove sufficiently that the pretenses of the plaintiff to be a white person are an afterthought, and that the person that she claims to be her mother is the identical Francoise Martin *alias* Justine Bacquié. The proof is direct that Justine Bacquié gave birth to the plaintiff, nor can it be doubted that Jean Leizaire was her father. In his will, Jean Leizaire says that the place of his nativity was Switzerland, and that his deceased mother's name was Margarite Desarzant; a circumstance that would tend to explain the fact that the plaintiff and her brothers and sisters assumed the name of Desarzant, the more so as Leizaire was at the time a married man, rearing a family in the City of New Orleans.

> Two children of the plaintiff by an unlawful connection with one Mr. A. Abat, were registered in the office of the register of births and deaths as the grandchildren of *Mme Justine Martin.* The dates of this register are the 26 and 27 of June AD 1847. On the 6th day of October Armand Desarzant one of the plaintiff's brothers was baptized a colored person, the certificate of baptism stating that his father was Jean Desarzant of Switzerland, and Francoise Bacquié of San Domingo. Subsequently, three children of Louise Desarzant or Marie Louise Bacquié plaintiffs sisters, were baptized as free colored persons.
>
> The voluntary statement made under oath several years past by Justine Bacquié before Justice Lugembuke, that she could not be the mother of Anastasie Desarzant, but had been only foster-mother; and that Francoise Martin, a native of Switzerland was in reality the mother, is not entitled to any weight. Her subsequent statements on this subject corroborated by abundant documentary and oral evidence place this matter in its true light. It can no more be doubted that the plaintiffs real *status* is that of a person of color, and that she has been endeavoring to usurp that of a white person. It is therefore ordered, adjudged and decreed that the judgment of the court below be affirmed with costs.

At question, then, was whether Toucoutou's self-identity as a white was legal, that is, approved by the law. This would have meant that she would be able to keep her self-labeled status and forever belong to the privileged class or status of whites. Further, since interracial concubinage was a felony during the time of the trial (1808 to 1872), she and her lover, who was white, could have been saved the pain of being arrested for committing that felony. Evidently, both the lower court and the state supreme court did not deem her self-identity legal. She lost both cases. Therefore, as she identified herself as being white or of strictly European heritage, the law as well as the custom (witness the opposition of the majority of Creoles in her neighborhood) was against her right to self-identify. Also, by extension, the right to self-identify by others like her was denied by law. This served to retain the status quo, which at that time was three-tiered, with whites or Europeans as the privileged, wealthy, or preferred class and caste; free people of color, who were mixed people or Creoles, constituting the second class or caste; and black slaves making up the third. True to Bernier's class distinction theory of 1648 based on color, Louisiana held this class/caste system in place by passing rules and regulations and by promoting customs, all of which served to keep the Europeans or whites in control.

Early in the history of the state, laws were passed to control the growth of the free people of color population and their ability to accumulate wealth. For instance, according to the territorial legislation of 1806, free blacks must never "conceive themselves equal" to whites. The law prohibited free persons of color from insulting or striking a white person "under penalty of fine or imprisonment" (Bell 75). Also, in 1858, the year of the trial, "mounting public concern over the increasing size and frequency of gathering of persons of color led city officials to enact a severe new ordinance. The law prohibited "assemblages of either free blacks or slaves . . . without white supervision" (Bell 84). The division of free people of color into a number of categories according to the amount of African blood they possessed was done in order to stop the rise in population and hold back their progress as economic competitors. A 1982 article in the *New York Times* on the Susie Guillory Phipps case cites Munro Edmonson, who was at that time a professor of anthropology at Tulane University, in this regard:

> In an interview Dr. Edmonson said of the so-called black Creoles: From the time of the Louisiana purchase the Anglo-Saxons have done their dead-level best to wipe out this group of people and the way they've done it is to reclassify them as black. That's what this one-thirty-second law is all about, and that's what laws in this state have been about since before the Civil War. Beginning in the 1820s restrictive laws were passed against the group. In the 1840s it was against the law for anyone free and colored to emigrate here. (Jaynes)

In the same article a black professor of sociology at Dillard University, Dan Thompson, was quoted on the Phipps case, a twentieth-century version of the Toucoutou case:

> "I am cheering Susie Phipps on for two reasons," Dr. Thompson said. "First, she is emphasizing something we've said all along: It is a great advantage to be white in American society. It costs several thousand dollars a year to be black. Schools, clubs, economic advantages are still to this day much better if you are white." "Secondly," he said, "I hope her case will dramatize the foolishness of race as a criterion in our society. I would like to see this distinction abolished. I would like to see racial designation gone. When you apply for a job and somebody asks you your race, it's demeaning. What the hell difference does it make? You're an American citizen, period."

In the nineteenth century laws and other factors were in place that in total seemed to inspire women such as Toucoutou to change their self-identity to that of a white person. The position of free women of color was tenuous at best. Laws forbade them to marry slaves or whites and they outnumbered free men of color two to one (Hanger 94). Thus the system of plaçage was in place at the time of the trial. Toucoutou, her mother Justine, Eglantine Demasilere (the neighbor she sued), and many of the women of color who testified at the trial were surviving as mistresses under the system of plaçage.

The legacy of Toucoutou then was that of a child of plaçage. Slavery, with all of its inherent evils, had created this third caste of people. For some of them an escape route toward a better life was through the long-standing method of *usurpation ethnologique,* or *"passe blanc"* in Creole, which was forbidden by law and custom.

Toucoutou's mother, Justine Bacquié, tried to help her daughter "passe blanc." Her testimony was taken by Guy Duplantier, the justice of the peace. In 1853 Justine Bacquié testified that Anastasie was not her daughter but a child she had raised since 1828 for European parents who died of yellow fever. She did not seem to have a problem with her own self-identity as a free woman of color, although she was "very fair with large blue eyes." However, according to other testimony Justine "regretted that she lied before the Evangelists" because her daughter refused to allow her to see her grandson even as a servant and "put her out the house," treating her "like a slave" and calling her "an old mulatress" (OCR, testimony of Margaret Menard). However, she did lie to help her daughter escape the stigma she herself lived with and accepted as her place. She died before she could contradict her own testimony.

Another woman who testified in this case was fifty-six-year-old Delphine Dupre, a witness for the defendants who identified herself as a "Creole" of New Orleans. She testified that she has always known those children and their mother in her class as "colored persons" (OCR, testimony of Delphine Dupre). Delphine Dupre, then, did not question her own identity as being a woman of color. Her initial identity at the beginning of her testimony was that of a Creole, and according to her, "Creole" and "colored" meant the same thing.

A somewhat similar situation was revealed in the testimony of Margaret Menard, a witness for the defendants who was about sixty or sixty-five years old. She said that she came from St. Domingue then went to Cuba, where Mr. Bacquié "took Justine to Santiago de Cuba and had a child by her called Zelime Bacquié." There he left Justine and married. She also said that she saw Toucoutou at the St. Philip balls, which were for colored people, and that Toucoutou "before the cholera . . . used to exclusively frequent colored people altogether" (OCR, testimony of Margaret Menard). Mme Menard's self-identity is implied rather than stated. It is implied in her remarks to Lucien, a colored man who comes to tell her to testify in favor of Toucoutou, "who is a Creole of your country. Witness answered no. Eglantine has more sense than Toucoutou and moreover, when I die Eglantine I'm sure will come to my funeral but Toucoutou would not" (OCR, testimony of Margaret Menard). It can be assumed from this last reply that she felt more comfortable as a Creole or colored person, which was also Eglantine's identity. It is again implied in her answer regarding whether or not she ever visited the house of Toucoutou: "Witness never went to plaintiffs house. She does not frequent white people and plaintiff claims to be white" (OCR, testimony of Margaret Menard). Margaret Menard, then, implies that she self-identifies as a colored person, not a white.

Another witness, Eugenie Saizer, said she was white and the daughter of Jean David Saizer. She testified that her mother told her that "Justine Bacquié was the concubine of J. D. Saizer" and that "Anastasie Desargant always said that she was the daughter of J. D. Saizer" (OCR, testimony of Eugenie Saizer). This witness, as well as the other white women who testified, seemed to have no self-identity problems because they knew their status as members of the ruling class was secure. Some of the white women who testified did so for the plaintiff. Emilie Moreau, the wife of François Vaussan, swore that Françoise Martin was a white person: "Witness being asked, was Françoise Martin a white or a colored woman answers she was from Switzerland and how could she be a colored woman?" (OCR, testimony of Emilie Moreau). Two of the white women testified that Toucoutou was a white woman (OCR, testimony of Nancy Lazard and Miss Roach). On the other hand, when another witness for Toucoutou, a ninety-three-year-old woman, Justine Bourgois, was asked in cross-examination whether she was "a person of color [she] answers that she does not know, that she was born in San Domingo and knows not who her father was nor who her mother was" (OCR, cross-examination of Justine Bourgois). The lawyers did not press her on this point. She testified that Justine Bacquié was white. Of all the women who testified on either side of this case, Justine Bourgois was the most intriguing because she did not belong to either group. At ninety-three years old she had lived without an identity that was sanctioned by custom or law in New Orleans. Was she representative of many of the immigrants from St. Domingue? Did she move in either social strata, changing her class and caste as she went from one to the other? Or did she self-identify as a white and join the ranks of the privileged? Does her noncommittal answer in court and the fact that there were no witnesses there who contradicted any of her statements and no lawyer who pressed the issue of her nonstatus indicate a kind of acceptance? Did the people and the court approve of people like Madam Bourgois who in effect did fit into this sharply divided community in the Faubourg Marigny? What is most curious is that this woman with no self-identity regarding color testified for Toucoutou that "she never knew Justine Bacquié to have any children nor had she ever saw her pregnant or in a family way" (OCR, testimony of Justine Bourgois).

The only other witness who did not know whether she, the witness, was a white woman was Josephine St. Germain Cooper: "Being asked whether she's a white woman she answers that she does not know. She could see that Mme. Françoise Martin was white from the whiteness of her skin. Being asked how it happens that she could say that Françoise Martin was white, and is not able to say whether she is white herself. She answers that she is a colored but doesn't see what her color has to do with this case" (OCR, cross-examination of Mrs. Cooper). Thus Cooper has an ambivalent attitude toward her identity as a woman of color. It could be that she did not say what she was so that she could move about the city without a badge of shame to prohibit her well-being. Or, if one is to judge from the flippancy of her answers to the lawyers, she may have ignored whatever people thought of her and went about her life as she pleased.

It would have been interesting to watch the body language of Toucoutou as the above-mentioned witnesses testified for or against her suit. She knew that Justin Bacquié, alias Françoise Martin, was her mother not long after she brought suit against the Lablancs but continued the suit anyway because she saw that her mother was in very ill health. Besides, Justine had already testified that she was not her mother. It had been recorded. The reason for the continuation of the trial? Perhaps she had heard of the Pendally case in which George Pendally won a judgment in 1854 in his favor and as a result had thereafter continued to live as and enjoy the privilege of being white. Perhaps she truly loved her lover and her son so much that she simply wanted to continue to enjoy the fruits of the life she had began with them within the higher social status. This is what Tinker suggests in his novel. But her pain was evident (Tinker 198). Toucoutou asks, "Why, why had Claircine brought her up as a white girl, to ruin it this way? It would have been kinder to have her grow up a little nigger wench? Was she? . . . 'Mo pas negue! Mo pas negue!' she sobbed dropping into the gombo French of her childhood" (190). "Terrible retch-like sobs wracked her slender body." "Nigger! Nigger! pounded through her brain, each repetition giving her physical pain. Was she or wasn't she? Clarcine had always told her she was white" (189).

Toucoutou's self-identity? Did she feel she was white because she was told this was her identity or did she simply want a life free of her society's legal and customary restrictions, constraint, and plain hatred of persons of color and slaves? New Orleans society in 1858 was a three-caste, two-race one. If you could prove that you belonged to what Tinker called the "dominant race" (214), you were free to live as you pleased and as well as your economic and educational levels permitted. However, if you had any amount of African blood, you were given the social status of "colored or "black" and were only a small step above slaves, even though you were free. The larger question of African slavery for Toucoutou and others like her became one of less importance than that of survival of self. Although at different points in history many free people of color participated in and in fact led slave revolts in many areas of the state, including New Orleans, some had to devote their energy to day-to-day living and surviving by whatever means they could with all of the laws and customs against them. Those free people of color who were wealthy and could contribute to the larger cause of freedom and civil rights did so, and on a grand scale.

A perusal of the history of these free people of color will show that the majority of those who could lead did, and they were major "movers and shakers" of their time. For instance, Thomy Lafon and Sister Henriette DeLille, who was recently nominated for sainthood because of her good life and works, are only two of the examples from this legacy. The wealth and benevolence of both these free people of color lives on even today in the education and health care their institutions provide in the city of New Orleans and elsewhere. Toucoutou was not one of these extraordinary people but an ordinary person struggling to survive and make a place for herself and her son. She sought from the courts the opportunity for a better life, and she lost. The legal documentation overwhelmed the courts. Moreover, according to the evidence of the trial and to Tinker's account in his novel,

> the balance of public opinion went against Anastasie. None of them seemed to bother their heads much about whether she was actually white or colored, they merely let their prejudices form their opinions. The whites felt it was a preposterous impertinence for any person, about whom there might be a question, to attempt to invade the sacred ranks of the Nordics. The majority of the negro population, whose kinkiness of naps and darkness of coloring marked them ineradicably for what they were, resented equally keenly that a woman of black blood should desert her color in an attempt to steal all the superior privileges of the ruling race. (213)

However, many free people of color and their descendants did join the ranks of the ruling race. There is a traceable diaspora of free people of color and their descendants that started very early in the state of Louisiana but especially after the annexation of the state in 1804. Free people and their descendants have migrated to other states as well as to Europe, Canada, Mexico, South America, and the Caribbean. However, at the time of Toucoutou's case, not all of the free people of color of the city, as Tinker has suggested, abandoned their communities. Many remained in New Orleans and became leaders in the fight to gain freedom for their slave brothers and sisters and continued to work for legislation to correct the evils of slavery and promote the rights of women. Their story is just now being told as a result of new research and scholarship, some of it by descendants of the *gens de couleur libres.* Now, although the one-drop rule still exists, as custom though not law, the social status once given to whites or blacks according to their percentage of white or African blood seems to have been somewhat de-emphasized. At least for the middle and working classes in Louisiana, one's level of education and economic status seems to be more of a determinant of social class, though not totally. Unfortunately, however, the message from the nineteenth-century case of Toucoutou, as well as the message from the twentieth-century case of Susie Guillory Phipps, rings true for the twenty-first century: It is still far better in the United States to be labeled white than black, even though we now know that these labels have no meaning and could easily be replaced by less divisive cultural identities.

WORKS CITED

Bell, Caryn Cosse. *Revolution, Romanticism, and the Afro-Creole Protest Tradition in Louisiana, 1718–1868.* Baton Rouge: Louisiana State University Press, 1997.

Desdunes, Rodolphe. *Nos hommes et notre histoire: Notices biographiques accompagnées de reflexions et de souvenirs personnels, hommage à la population créole, en souvenir des grands hommes qu'elle a produits et des bonnes choses qu'elle a accomplies.* Montreal: Arbour & Dupont, 1911.

Hanger, Kimberly S. *Bounded Lives, Bounded Places: Free Black Society in Colonial New Orleans, 1769–1803.* Durham, N.C.: Duke University Press, 1997.

Jaynes, Gregory. *New York Times.* September 30, 1982..

Kein, Sybil. *Creole Journal: The Louisiana Poems.* Detroit: Lotus, 1999.

Original court records (OCR). 1858 case of *Anastasie Desarzant vs. Pierre Lablanc and Eglantine Desmazillier.* Third District Court of New Orleans, #9808, Supreme Court of Louisiana, Docket #5868. No. 1846–61.

Tinker, Edward L. *Toucoutou.* New York: Dodd, Mead, 1928.

PART 3 LOUISIANA LITERATURE

The Tradition and Three Contemporary Writers

Louisiana and the American Literary Tradition

PEGGY WHITMAN PRENSHAW

Louisiana, both as a home of writers and a subject of literature, occupies a secure place in the history of American letters. The literary heritage of the state exists in some respects, however, as buried treasure—acknowledged but not yet fully discovered by a general public made more aware of a Louisiana that draws its celebrity from politics, sports, food, music, plantations, swamps, Mardi Gras, the Mississippi River, and catastrophic hurricanes. That Louisiana's literary treasures rival these cultural markers may surprise some, and yet in the power of books to embody life in forms that survive even Lafitte's bounty, such treasures reflect the human spirit in its full reach of imagination and memory. Indeed, our books replenish the imagination time and time again as we return to them in a search of understanding—and delight. They endure.

When Barbara Ewell wrote the introduction to the important volume on Louisiana women writers that she and Dorothy Brown edited in 1992, she began by acknowledging the state's literary wealth. But she went on to observe that "few readers actually realize how many writers, male or female, are associated with the state. Not recognizing this literary legacy seems to us a failure of vision, a neglect of the past that distorts our present conceptions of who we are."

In preparing an overview of the literary history of the state to present at a 1995 symposium celebrating the founding of the Louisiana Center for the Book, a project sponsored by the State Library of Louisiana and associated with the Library of Congress, I was reminded of the breadth of experience, the variety of literary forms, the language diversity, the literary prize winners, the sheer number of writers, and the sweep of centuries represented in the vast library holdings of "Louisiana books." There were many works known and enjoyed, but many more yet untapped, a thrilling and somewhat daunting discovery. And every week or so I continue to learn of a writer formerly unknown to me or of a new book just published—and am made aware of the state's literary tradition actively in the making.

Having accomplished this sort of jet ride (or channel surfing) across a broad literary terrain, I came away with two distinct observations. The first has to do with the extent to which Louisiana literature has been centrally part of the tradition and canon of southern and American literature. To illustrate the representativeness of the state's literary contributions, one might begin with a nineteenth-century story that belongs to the genre of the frontier tall tale, "The Indefatigable Bear Hunter" from *Odd Leaves from the Life of a Louisiana Swamp Doctor,* an 1850 collection by Henry Clay Lewis or, using his pseudonym, Madison Tensas. The story's main character, Mik-hoo-tah, whose name means the "grave of bears," is a bragging but courageous frontiersman, a master of flamboyant language, a loner who loves to talk. The story is typical of the old southwestern humor tales so popular in the early nineteenth century, a strain of writing that eventuates later in such work as Mark Twain's *Huckleberry Finn* and "The Bear" by William Faulkner. A man with a wooden leg, this old yarn-spinner tells the doctor of an unforgettable fight with a bear:

> I'd worn the old leg pretty well off to the second jint, when, jest 'fore I made a lick, the noise of the boys and the dogs cummin' sorter confused the bar and he made a stumble, and bein' off his guard I got a fair lick! The way that bar's flesh giv in to the soft impresshuns of that leg war an honor to the mederkal perfeshun for having invented sich a weepun! I hollered—but you have heered me holler an' I won't describe it. I had whipped a bar in a fair hand to hand fight—me, an old sickly, one-legged bar hunter! The boys come up and when they seed the ground we had fit over, they swore they would have thought 'stead of a bar fight that I had been cuttin' cane and deadenin' timber for a corn patch, the sile war so worked up. They then handed me a knife to finish the work.
>
> Doc, les licker. It's a dry talk. When will you make me another leg? Bar meat is not over plenty in the cabin and I feel like tryin' another!

Lewis's contribution to the tall tale is shortly followed by a representative work in the tradition of the slave narrative, Solomon Northup's *Twelve Years a Slave* (1853), an account of Northup's years as an enslaved man, wrongly captured by villainous slave traders and brought from his home in the North to the Louisiana cane fields. There is also the significant contribution of Louisiana writers—such as George Washington Cable, Kate Chopin, Grace King,

Ruth McInery Stuart, and Alice Dunbar-Nelson—to the fiction of regional and domestic realism in the late nineteenth century. Ben Forkner concentrates upon Cable in his introduction to the anthology *Louisiana Stories,* calling him "the founding father of the modern Louisiana short story." Cable is a powerful voice in American fiction, not so well known now as his contemporary, Mark Twain, but widely read in the 1880s and 1890s, and he once shared stage billing with Twain on a tour in which they presented public readings of their work. Cable expressed his contempt for racial injustice in the South but also his admiration for certain virtues he found in the traditions of the antebellum South. Indeed, he offers us a complex vision in some extraordinary fiction.

Cable's "Jean-ah-Poquelin" from *Old Creole Days* (1879), for example, is as haunting a story as Poe's "Fall of the House of Usher." The central figure, a former slave trader living in a swamp with an old African man who is mute, is regarded by the New Orleans townspeople as strange and bitter, even dangerous, and is victimized by harassing mobs of Irish and Creoles. Cable characterizes the civil unrest as a cultural upheaval set in motion by modernist and American forces, a social change sharply diverging from the dictatorial and absolutist days of the French regime but threatening and oppressive in a different way. The urban development supporters in the city want to appropriate Poquelin's land, drain the swamp and build new houses. They are motivated, it would seem, by progressive values with which most of Cable's readers would likely sympathize. The progressive citizens are oblivious, however, to Poquelin's rights or needs. After his death at the conclusion of the story, he is revealed to be a man who for years has faithfully tended a leprous brother, a man who has honored ties of personal commitment over principles of progress and change. Cable offers an unsettling narrative that interrogates many glib assumptions about progress and justice, expressing here a profound vision of the cultural and moral anxiety that was so deeply embedded in American domestic realism of the late nineteenth century.

In *The Grandissimes,* a long novel of antebellum Louisiana published in 1880, Cable brings an even more intense vision to the complex fate of the southerner, both the white southerner, who was increasingly trapped between a national ideology of individual freedom and a local/familial ideology of white supremacy, and the black or biracial southerner, who was trapped with a double consciousness, that of African and American, a consciousness W. E. B. Du Bois would analyze later in *Souls of Black Folk.* In the novel Cable contrasts two brothers of the same name, Honore Grandissime, the one white, burdened with family pride and great debt, the other, a free man of color, burdened by racial humiliation but possessing material wealth sufficient to rescue the white Grandissimes from their impoverishment, a depletion that the novel suggests is both material and spiritual.

Cable's characters, much admired by William Dean Howells and other literary contemporaries as well as by a broad national readership of his Creole fiction, include the magnificent African prince, Bras Coupe, mutilated, slain, unyielding to white power; the old street vendor Clemence, so brutally, callously shot down; and Palmyre, a beautiful and powerful woman who dominates with her voodoo knowledge but whose life is finally blighted by intractable social divisions. Cable's white southern belles are clearly of their time, somewhat less interesting and perhaps even ridiculous to some of today's readers, although Howells pronounced Aurora the most "adorable" woman in literature. The young widow, beloved by the white Honore, tells her daughter that the "worst wickedness" a woman can do in the whole wide world is to look ugly in bed.

The originality and impact of Kate Chopin's fiction, first published in the decade just following Cable's early work, bespeak Louisiana's major contribution not only to domestic realism but also to the canon of American feminist writing. The subject of enormous critical attention and interest in the past quarter century, Chopin is read for her literary artistry and for her penetrating and subtle portrayals of character, particularly that of Edna Pontellier of *The Awakening* (1899).

Like Chopin herself, who in 1870 came to Louisiana from her St. Louis home when she married, Edna comes to New Orleans from her Kentucky home as the bride of Léonce Pontellier. She is described as "an American woman, with a small infusion of French which seemed to have been lost in dilution" (6). An outsider, she encounters the Louisiana Creole culture with ambivalence—curious but guarded, admiring of the easy expressiveness but too attached to her own "American" independence to become one of the "mother women" whose sexuality and maternity define them. With her two young sons she strives to instill independence rather than foster the kind of close, dependent bond she observes in the Creole families. For herself, she rejects the circumscribed life of upper-class (white) wifedom and motherhood that are her lot, and she seeks fulfillment of her romantic dreams in love affairs and in fanciful thoughts of becoming an artist. In many respects, Edna is an American version of Flaubert's Emma Bovary, a woman driven by romantic visions of a life lived not only independently but also with passionate intensity. Edna is never as pitiful and helpless as Emma, but the obstacles that obstruct her desire are insurmountable. Pregnancy always haunts sexual pleasure, and the merciless requirements of discipline and commitment that mark the artist's life exact as steep a toll.

Ultimately, however, it is the conflict between individualism and motherhood that traps Edna. She puts her dilemma to Doctor Mandelet near the end of the novel: "I don't want anything but my own way. That is wanting a good deal, of course, when you have to trample upon the lives, the hearts, the prejudices of others—but no matter—still, I shouldn't want to trample upon the little lives. Oh! I don't know what I'm saying, Doctor. Good night. Don't blame me for anything" (105). Edna Pontellier's suicidal death is soon to follow (though some readers regard it as unintentional, if despairing). The significance of the death is unambiguous: The striving soul who yearns for free expression and independence is well suited as an American, not well suited as a mother of children.

Chopin's *Awakening* is a major text of American literary realism and a precursor of a century of feminist fiction to follow. In widely used anthologies of American literature, today's college students typically read *The Adventures of Huckleberry Finn* and *The Awakening* as exemplars of the late-nineteenth-century novel. Chopin's and Cable's fiction, along with Grace King's *Tales of a Time and Place* (1892) and *Balcony Stories* (1893) and Alice Dunbar-Nelson's *Violets and Other Tales* (1895) and *The Goodness of St. Rocque and Other Stories* (1899), demonstrates further Louisiana's contribution to American fiction at the turn of the century, a fiction sensitively attuned to diverse expressions of social class, race, and vernacular and dialectal language. Significantly, this fiction depicts an American scene increasingly caught in the throes of change from a rural, agrarian economy to an urban, industrialized way of life. In *The Myth of New Orleans in Literature,* Violet Harrington Bryan describes, for example, the remarkable range of Dunbar-Nelson's New Orleans subjects: "Nuns and praline women, Creole belles and beaux, rejected lovers and musicians, Mardi Gras Indians and fishermen," all of whom speak in "distinctive voices using their diverse dialects" (62).

Turning to the twentieth century, one finds Louisiana writers and Louisiana settings central to many of the main movements of the remarkable literary productivity that has distinguished the United States over the past century, an achievement that has paralleled its rise to material wealth and military power. In the development of critical theory and practice in this country, as well as the formation of protocols for classroom study of literature, perhaps no other influence has been more formative than that of the *Southern Review* and the English Department of Louisiana State University (LSU) in the 1930s and early 1940s. Thomas W. Cutrer has recorded this extraordinary story in *Parnassus on the Mississippi: The Southern Review and the Baton Rouge Literary Community, 1935–1942* (Louisiana State University Press, 1984).

LSU faculty members Robert Penn Warren and Cleanth Brooks, through their example as editors of the *Southern Review* and practicing critics, as well as authors and editors of the influential college textbooks *Understanding Poetry, Understanding Fiction,* and (along with John Thibaut Purser) *An Approach to Literature,* contributed crucially to the dominance of the New Criticism in American literary study during the midcentury. The *Southern Review* figures prominently in the careers of such writers and editors as Katherine Anne Porter, Eudora Welty, Peter Taylor, Robert Lowell, Jean Stafford, Albert Erskine, and John E. Palmer. Warren, of course, was publishing his own fiction during the period. In fact, Cutrer quotes a *Time* magazine article of April 10, 1939, noting that Porter's *Pale Horse, Pale Rider* was the second book (after Warren's *Night Rider*) in three weeks "to come out of the new Southern literary center at Baton Rouge." A native of Kentucky, Warren lived in Louisiana for nine years, leaving only after campus politics and the withdrawal of support for the *Southern Review* blighted the academic climate and prospects for his future. His tenure at LSU had lasting consequences, however, as one sees in such poems as "Bearded Oaks" or in the novel *All the King's Men,* the work for which he is best known and one of the major political-philosophical novels of American literary history.

In addition to Warren the plays of Lillian Hellman, who spent much of her youth in New Orleans, have added a significant dimension to the American theater of politics and social protest. Many other writers of the 1930s to 1950s, not so well known as Warren and Hellman, vastly extend Louisiana's reach in American letters, especially in the depiction of regional experience and domestic realism. I think of Lyle Saxon, Ada Jack Carver, and E. P. O'Donnell, among others.

Representing a different direction of twentieth-century fiction is Louisiana's contribution to the novel of spiritual alienation and psychological dislocation. This fiction, which has so dominated the literary scene, is perhaps best exemplified by the works of Walker Percy. With such novels as *The Moviegoer* (1961), *The Last Gentleman* (1966), and *The Second Coming* (1980), Percy has attracted an intense, devoted readership. And coming just after Percy, a younger generation of writers has further probed the shadowy reaches of contemporary angst and spiritual hollowness—Valerie Martin and Robert Olen Butler, for example. Others have turned similar explorations toward comedy, even satire. I am thinking of John Ed Bradley, James Wilcox, and Tim Gautreaux, among others. In theater there are, of course, few dramatists whose plays have been so often staged or who have so directly influenced the American theater as has Tennessee Williams, a playwright who drew heavily upon a New Orleans he came to know in his youth and that he would return to throughout his life. Of twentieth-century expressions of cultural clashes and dislocations, *A Streetcar Named Desire* (1947) has become one of the preeminent canonical works.

Louisiana's literary artists have also sensitively explored the divisions in our nation arising from race and class and religion and generational misunderstandings. In such works as *Bloodline* (1968), *The Autobiography of Miss Jane Pittman* (1971), *A Gathering of Old Men* (1983), and *A Lesson Before Dying* (1994), Ernest Gaines draws upon a childhood in Point Coupee Parish to capture a distinctive twentieth-century southern African American experience and thereby establish a sure place for his fiction in the collective memory of our times. The poets Pinkie Gordon Lane, Brenda Marie Osbey, and Yusef Komunyakaa have likewise responded to their Louisiana experience in works that draw upon uniqueness but also form part of the wider American mosaic. One thinks, too, of Roger Kamenetz, Christine Wiltz, and many others who have written compellingly of cultural identities that are experienced as an individual otherness.

Among women writers who have memorably traced the tensions and contradictions in social roles that contemporary women often face—the pull toward old patterns in which women are expected always to nurture others, repress their sexuality, and look beautiful at the same time, and the pull toward separate lives and careers toward greater sexual expression and freedom—I turn to Shirley Ann Grau, Sheila Bosworth, Ellen Gilchrist, and Rebecca Wells.

Among these many writers, assembled here with disconcerting brevity, are recipients of the Pulitzer Prize, the National Book Award, and other coveted national and international awards for literary merit. Taking into account both artistic merit and the literary judgment of the market place, one also locates in Louisiana's literary legacy two of the country's most popular writers, Anne Rice and James Lee Burke, major best sellers, still writing, still growing in fame and readership here and abroad. A generation past saw Francis Parkinson Keyes and Gwen Bristow, both of whose novels I read hungrily in my youth, along with a larger popular readership across the country. I remember yet the intense impression *Deep Summer* made upon me.

This admittedly incomplete index of writers who have been significantly associated with Louisiana reflects the remarkable presence of the state in the American literary tradition. The list reveals the many examples of works that have typified the American mainstream in its multiple directions and manifestations and quickly substantiates the State Library of Louisiana's initiative in establishing the Louisiana Center for the Book.

As I mentioned at the outset, though, there is a second and in some way an opposing observation about the image of Louisiana in the American literary mind that I should like to propose. Both in the South and in the nation, Louisiana also occupies the imagination with its difference. It is a place where boundaries seem less distinct than in most other American places, where the lines between water and land, cultures and races tend to blur. When the Mississippian William Faulkner introduces the uncertainty principle that unravels the absolutist Thomas Sutpen in *Absalom, Absalom!* he does so with the character Charles Bon from New Orleans. For George Washington Cable, mysterious tiers of reality, so challenging to his notions of American Protestant morality, embody the inescapable nature of south Louisiana. His character Honore Grandissime—a divided or doubled man—constitutes the fascinating center of his best novel. Similarly, when Eudora Welty invokes the fluid, subtle, mysterious relation between a man and woman in one of her most memorable stories, "No Place for You, My Love," she does so by having the couple depart from Galatoire's restaurant in New Orleans and head south to Venice. The topography of the coastal area, a sort of map of the shifting human psyches of the two characters, gives an image of fluidity, dissolving margins. Land? Water? Swamp?

The image of a primeval, swampy, alligator-ridden land as old as time—the stereotypical image of south Louisiana in the popular media—calls to mind the land's imperturbability, a fixedness that is however vulnerable to hurricanes that transform the landscape in a few hours. Lafcadio Hearn's story "Chita" draws upon and illustrates Louisiana's embodiment of fragility—so at odds with American confidence and domination. Luxury, family solidarity, business, love, human control, and even the land itself—all are gone with the wind in a cataclysmic hurricane in Hearn's story.

In more recent times, of course, in a year that saw the awful spectacles of

New Orleans under Hurricane Katrina's flooding waters and the southwestern parishes raked by Hurricane Rita, the whole world has been witness to Louisiana's vulnerability to nature's threats and levees' limits. Just as the deadly assault of water has aroused the horror of onlookers witnessing televised images of destruction and hopelessness, so has the defiant spirit of survival shown by Louisiana's people inspired admiration and generosity—a spirit fully displayed in the numerous interviews Douglas Brinkley conducted for his account of the post-Katrina flood in *The Great Deluge.* The incredible devastation of the storms will challenge writers, filmmakers, musicians, artists, and others to explore in creative works the human experience of the natural disaster.

Notwithstanding Katrina, the people still celebrate Mardi Gras. The carnival, even in calm years, seems exotic, almost foreign to much of a Protestant United States, allowing, demanding, as it does, that one shed a private identity and responsibility and become something other—transformed by costume and exuberance into a monster or angel, a rabbit, a tree! The separation between church and state seems to be confounded by the presence of Louisiana's parishes in lieu of counties. And the deeply rooted French language and culture, anomalous in most of the English-dominated United States, are manifest throughout the state, especially in the southern parishes, and are preserved in nineteenth-century forms in a sizable body of literature in French. The color line between African and Euro Americans that has seemed so troublingly permanent and distinct in Northern America is often eclipsed in Louisiana by the inclusive designation of "Creole," widely and loosely applied to persons of many racial backgrounds, despite the recurrent controversies that appear from time to time in the popular press about what attributes "legitimately" define a Creole. The "undecidability" of Louisiana has made it a kind of incarnation of ambiguity, a quality that has made it a special gift to the imaginations of many writers. I think it is, in fact, precisely these ambiguities that so challenged the firm, devout Presbyterian George Washington Cable to try to say in fiction what he could not sort out in theology.

At the conclusion of John Kennedy Toole's *Confederacy of Dunces,* Ignatius Reilly, who is another theologian who can't find the absolutes he hungers for, rides out of New Orleans with his girlfriend, Myrna. Those who have read this extraordinary novel will remember that he gets out just ahead of the ambulance coming to transport him to the psychiatric ward of the Charity Hospital. Myrna drives,

> weaving in and out of impossibly narrow lanes until they were clear of the last twinkling streetlight of the last swampy suburb. They were in darkness in the center of the salt marshes. . . . Ignatius rolled down the window an inch or two and breathed the salt air blowing in over the marshes from the Gulf.
>
> As if the air were a purgative, his valve opened. He breathed again, this time more deeply. The dull headache was lifting. (405)

Heading for New York, Ignatius and Myrna are not making their way, however, to a better day. Nothing, in fact, in the whole preceding novel implies that rationalism and materialist efficiency are alternatives that are desirable—or likely even available—in some distant land. For all its uncertain messiness, its swampy, marshy ooziness, its confusion and decadence, even its vulnerability to a flood that would outmatch Ignatius's powers of exaggeration, this Louisiana he is leaving is where life is. It is a fascinating, sensuous place that galvanizes the imagination. It is a good place for writers—and readers.

WORKS CITED

Bryan, Violet Harrington. *The Myth of New Orleans in Literature: Dialogues of Race and Gender.* Knoxville: University of Tennessee Press, 1993.

Brown, Dorothy H., and Barbara C. Ewell, eds. *Louisiana Women Writers: New Essays and a Comprehensive Bibliography.* Baton Rouge: Louisiana State University Press, 1992.

Chopin, Kate. *The Awakening.* 2nd ed. Ed. Margo Culley. New York: Norton, 1994.

Forkner, Ben. Introduction to *Louisiana Stories.* Ed. Ben Forkner. Gretna, La.: Pelican, 1990.

"The Indefatigable Bear Hunter." *Humor of the Old Southwest.* Ed. Hennig Cohen and William B. Dillingham. Boston: Houghton Mifflin, 1964. 353–54.

Toole, John Kennedy. *A Confederacy of Dunces.* 1980. Reprint, New York: Grove Weidenfeld, 1987.

The Carnival Voices of *A Confederacy of Dunces*

JOHN LOWE

Since its rocketlike eruption on the literary scene in 1980, John Kennedy Toole's boisterous novel *A Confederacy of Dunces* has been hailed by many critics and readers as one of the funniest books ever written and a literary masterpiece. The verdict is hardly unanimous, however, as a sizable minority continues to denigrate the novel as a chaotic mess, politically incorrect, or insufficiently focused on moral certainties or political ideologies. Some of these judgments come from the tendency to assess the book through the views of its central character, Ignatius Reilly, thereby missing the considerable distance between him and his supremely ironic creator, Toole, but some critics tend to dismiss comedy in general and certain types of humor in particular, particularly anything that yokes ethnicity with joking.

Critical squeamishness of this type has meant that studies of *Confederacy* so far have largely skirted a problematic area that is paradoxically one of the novel's greatest strengths: its use of ethnic humor. Why is this? Partly because critics to date have been less concerned with the specifics of the novel's ethnic ramifications than with the more familiar task of generic definition. We begin to run into problems, however, when we try to confine this baggy monster to only one of our existing literary categories, such as satire, parody, bildungsroman, and so on. A more productive route might be to think about the book's multiple contributions to American culture as a whole; how exactly does its humor work and does it do *more* than amuse us? Does it offer, as the greatest novels often do, multiple perspectives, tones, and voices? Does it mirror something we need to see about our past, our present, and our future? I believe it does, particularly in terms of the most vexing problem Americans have faced, which is how to deal with our greatest asset but also our greatest difficulty: our creative diversity and apparent dissensus.

America's ethnic groups have always had to deal with their specific variations from the supposed "norm" of mainstream America and to negotiate with that model in an intricate process of acculturation loosely called "Americanization." But as Toole's novel brilliantly demonstrates, that process is dynamic and multipolar; juggling the demands of ethnic survival and acculturation simultaneously, each ethnic group in turn has had an effect on the larger culture, and on the parallel struggles of other groups, particularly when they share the same crowded streets of a city's wards and ghettos. The liberating process of what I call here "ethnic carnival" disrupts boundaries of all sorts, upending hierarchical structures and, ultimately, building new possibilities for community, thereby countering separation, scapegoating, and typecasting. By blurring borders of identity as ethnics keep bumping up against each other, Toole gives us the dynamism of the American kaleidoscope, where distinctly colored "chips" are always there but in play, and when overlaid against other hues they form new hybridities.

Ignatius Reilly, the book's Irish American hero, is an overeducated, lazy, thirty-year-old yet adolescent slob. He would gladly spend all his days abed or in front of the television, eating while writing fragmentary essays in his Big Chief notebooks. His indolence is made possible by his doting and dotty mother. When a pathetic police officer attempts to arrest her darling one day, they try to recover in a seedy French Quarter bar named the Night of Joy, which later becomes one of the novel's centers, functioning openly as a locale for strip shows and covertly as a depot for a pornography ring. Burma Jones, a black New Orleanean, is forced to work there for virtually nothing by the dominatrix Lana Lee, who also abuses Darlene, a would-be stripper who is working on a novelty act involving a cockatoo. Meanwhile, Officer Mancuso is also being persecuted by his superiors on the police force, who toy with him by making him wear degrading undercover costumes at stakeouts such as the men's room at the bus station. Soon he and his aunt Santa Battaglia meet Mrs. Reilly and introduce her to the world of bowling. Over at Levy Pants, absentee owner Gus Levy entrusts everyday management to the slavish Gonzalez, a staff of underpaid black factory workers, and the senile accountant, Miss Trixie. All of these players and many more are united by the seismic force of an unleashed Ignatius, whose mother forces him to seek work when she has to pay for damages to a building she hit with their ancient Plymouth.

These tangled tales are merely the launching pad for an unbelievably complicated plot, a dizzying mechanism with more twists and ups and downs than the Coney Island roller coaster. As Bakhtin demonstrates, all Carnival images are dualistic, uniting birth and death, blessing and curse, praise and abuse, youth and old age, top and bottom, face and backside, stupidity and wisdom. Many things are placed in reverse or inside out, fitting the Carnival category of *eccentricity* in which the usual is violated. There are no bystanders in Carnival, and there are none here. Each ethnic character has a part to play in Toole's symphony/cacophony of American dissensus. Curiously, surely one of the most prominent omissions in the novel is Carnival itself, the annual event those who are lucky enough to live in Louisiana call Mardi Gras. Toole seems to instead want to present the Big Easy as a city in perpetual Carnival, a world where life is turned inside out. Ignatius is the perfect king of Carnival, a fact signified by the name of his much-beloved, now-deceased collie, Rex, the title of the most legendary of the Mardi Gras krewes. Although Ignatius is, in his unemployed, immature, eccentric, even bizarre identity, the most unlikely candidate for king, his role as "Lord of Misrule" sets the novel's multiple plots in motion. As in all Carnival traditions, hierarchical structure and piety are annulled. If the characters here don't want to play, Ignatius forces them to. He cancels distances between himself and others and becomes an agent who deconstructs barriers between others as well. In Carnival "free and familiar contact among people" is extremely important (Bakhtin, *Problems* 123).

Ignoring any kind of boundary, the impetuous Ignatius sometimes seems truly mad, but at other times he seems to illustrate Emily Dickinson's famous line "Much madness is divinest sense." Carnival is "the place for working out, in a half-play-acted form" a *new mode of interrelationship between individuals* (ibid.). The central act of Carnival is the mock crowning and subsequent decrowning of the king. As Ignatius gets and loses one job after another, he is figuratively and repeatedly "crowned" and "decrowned." To be sure, the investitures come about largely through his outrageous appropriations of power and initiative on each job, his violation of working-place protocol, his terrorization of his superiors, and his bizarre schemes to liberate various constituencies within each workplace, but each decrowning sets up the possibility of a new crowning and levels the supposed importance of any one position. Ignatius releases a flood of ritual laughter within each realm he inhabits, laughter that forces crisis and change in each case.

The Body as Comic Text

Historically, carnivalization worked to destroy barriers between genres, systems of thought, and competing styles. For Walker Percy, *Confederacy* is the forced joining of Oliver Hardy, Don Quixote, and St. Thomas Aquinas (Percy 12), and each of the figures he lists is associated with a specific "style." Percy's use of the term "gargantuan," however, suggests an author he doesn't mention by name, for Rabelais, creator of the original Gargantua, leaps out at us from many of Toole's pages, particularly in the employment of body humor, which works closely with the ethnic markers. Both modes of presentation are crucial in democratizing, uncrowning humor, so we might begin our mapping of the ethnic dimension of the book by first examining Toole's portrayal of the body. Like Rabelais, Toole throws the human machine in contrast to American pretensions of all types. He wants to make his tale more tactile, sensuous, and magnetic, even repulsive if need be, to get the reader's attention but also to perversely humanize his characters by making them grotesque. His composite survey of his characters' physicality suggests the human body as a whole, and as such the cast is joined together symbolically. We would do well to remember that Rabelais, Toole's great predecessor in the use of grotesque realism—especially of the body—employed degradation in order to lower "elevated" material to the realm of the people, a "coming down to earth" that ultimately is positive, festive, and fertilizing. As Bakhtin noted, this leads to an emphasis on appetites as well as on apertures, convexities, the phallus, the potbelly, the nose, breasts, and the anus. Bodily excretions are part of this scenario as well (Bakhtin, *Rabelais* 26).

This principle of grotesque realism is everywhere in *Confederacy.* Certainly one of the ways the body and its appetite is initially introduced is through consumption. Eating and drinking are social activities, and the characters in this book, like all Louisianans, live to eat. Mrs. Reilly is initially described not only in terms of her relation to her son but also in grossly physical ones, which unite her body with his in one sentence: We see "her maternal breast" pressed against a glass case of macaroons at D. H. Holmes. With one of her fingers, "chafed from many years of scrubbing her son's mammoth, yellowed drawers," she taps for the saleslady's attention (22). Her physical clumsiness is a motif throughout the book, as in the noises Ignatius interprets from her room "over the years when his mother was preparing to leave the house: the plop of a hairbrush falling into the toilet bowl, the sound of a box of powder hitting the floor, the sudden exclamations of confusion and chaos" (134), a comic litany that recalls Pope's *Rape of the Lock*. Her fondness for wine, which she hides in the oven, is part of her Irish stereotype. Other characters also become comic through their bodies; Officer Mancuso, for instance, is an Italian "bantam," summoning up the whole panoply of short-man's syndrome. Ignatius's obesity is a never-failing source of humor, as is his general appearance. His hands are often described as "paws," while his thighs are likened to

"Smithfield hams." When he's in the tub one hears "whalelike snorts," and when we see him he is like a "pink hippopotamus" (195). His employer in the weenie business calls him a "big ape" (228) on one occasion and a "big baboon" on another (305). When Darlene's cockatoo attacks him he bellows like a moose (352). As we first see him, his blue and yellow eyes (the colors together of course make green, the hopeful color of his hat) are judging the bad taste of passers by in front of the D. H. Holmes store, where a large, freestanding clock still stands on Canal Street (even though the defunct Holmes store is now a boutique hotel). Time and money thus immediately find their opposite in the idle speculations of our obese hero, who feels the pressures of neither. The baggy pants he wears, full of pockets and folds, so handy for the detritus of his many trivial pursuits and nibbles, remind us of the voluminous title garment of Melville's *White-Jacket,* a tragicomic voyage of discovery that this book closely resembles in many ways.

Ignatius claims his mother's growing belligerence makes home like the "den of a lioness" (229). Lana Lee has "hawkeyes" and a "bloodhound nose" (243). In this and several other ways the book's approach bears a resemblance to Laurence Sterne's *Tristram Shandy,* the eighteenth-century comic masterpiece that ruthlessly yet somehow affectionately derides the body and its deficiencies. There the central figure is conceived when his parents have intercourse, as is their habit, when the father winds the clock. Here Ignatius is conceived because his parents have seen Clark Gable and Jean Harlow in *Red Dust:* "In the heat and confusion that had followed their return home, nice Mr. Reilly had tried one of his indirect approaches, and Ignatius was conceived. Poor Mr. Reilly. He had never gone to another movie as long as he lived" (110). Sterne removes romance from the sexual act and in fact relates it to a mechanical function; Toole, however, goes further by equating it to a fumbling accident occasioned by popular melodrama.

Many people have said that they laughed harder reading *Confederacy* than when reading any other book. Might it be because Toole and Ignatius, like Rabelais, never flinch from bodily functions and in fact seem to relish their possibilities? This certainly accounted for the popularity of several twenty-first-century over-the-top films, epitomized by *There's Something about Mary* and, most recently, *Borat,* which similarly rely on "gross-out" physical humor. There, and in *Confederacy,* bodily emissions are especially stressed, particularly semen and gas. The flag Ignatius makes for the Levy Pants demonstration repels his marchers because it is made from one of his semen-stained bed sheets. Toole turns this into a joke, however, for Ignatius claims it to be "'the proudest of banners, an identification of our purpose, a visualization of all that we seek.' The workers studied the stains more intensely," an obvious play on the result of Ignatius's "wet dreams." We actually hear about one of these: Ignatius's masturbation over the thought of his dead collie's fur introduces yet another scandalous metaphor for his onanistic life.

Toole uses such passages to insist on a link between the body and the mind, which often causes disaster for Ignatius's "valve," which is capable of giving off huge outbursts of gas or, conversely, "sealing up" and causing "bloating." Thinking about such modern abominations such as Doris Day or trips aboard the dreaded Greyhound Scenicruiser causes Ignatius to "bloat" with trapped gas, "gas which had character and being and resented its confinement" (48). His pyloric valve is figured as a prophecy, trying "Cassandra-like" or like the oracle at Delphi (which also relied on vapors) to communicate vital messages. Gaseous eruptions in particular or real life in general never embarrasses Ignatius, but phony conventions such as romance disgust him and activate the valve. At the movies he horrifies even little children by roaring out remarks of condemnation toward on-screen lovers: "They probably have halitosis [yet another bodily odor]. . . . I hate to think of the obscene places that those mouths have doubtlessly been before. . . . Oh, my God, their tongues are probably all over each other's capped and rotting teeth" (76). His attitude toward these films is deeply hypocritical, as his journal reveals: "I have sought escape in the Prytania on more than one occasion, pulled by the attractions of some Technicolored horrors, filmed abortions that were offenses against any criteria of taste and decency, reels and reels of perversion and blasphemy that stunned my disbelieving eyes, that shocked my virginal mind, and sealed my valve" (120). These reflections are doubly ironic in that his conception was the direct result of a movie just like this.

There is, however, a more melancholy side to bodily portrayal in the narrative. The list of real and imagined aches and pains of the characters starts to stack up immediately. Both Ignatius and his mother have aching feet; she has a sore elbow and "arthuritis," and he has "frayed nerves," "a heart murmur," and, of course, his notorious "valve" problems. As most of the characters are in financial straits, an inability to afford adequate health care lies behind much of the humor. Again and again Toole slips in a tribute to the ailments of the poor, the elderly, the unemployed, and the forgotten, casting a thin patina of sadness over his usually boisterous characters, thereby replicating the shabby, faded, yet glorious beauty of the fabled city itself.

Reading, Ethnicity, and Cosmopolitanism

Throughout the book, Ignatius defends humanity's physicality with his knowledge of the classics, which often get presented in nationalistic and ethnic ways. When his mother complains about the smell in his room, he replies, "The human body, when confined, produces certain odors which we tend to forget in this age of deodorants and other perversions. . . . Schiller needed the scent of apples rotting . . . to write. . . . Mark Twain preferred to lie supinely in bed while composing those rather dated and boring efforts which contemporary scholars try to prove meaningful" (65). His mother makes similar associations, but not with books: At one point we learn that Mrs. Reilly considers her son's body odor to be like old tea bags.

Invariably, Ignatius relates his activities to novels he has read and admired. During this "Crusade for Moorish Dignity" at Levy Pants, our literary dweeb cannot resist reading the scene through the filter of Conrad's *Heart of Darkness:* "Something from Joseph Conrad sprang to my mind, although I cannot seem to remember what it was at the time. Perhaps I likened myself to Kurtz . . . when far from the trading company offices in Europe, he was faced with the ultimate horror. I do remember imagining myself in a pith helmet and white linen jodhpurs, my face enigmatic behind a veil of mosquito netting" (139). If he were actually thinking of the full implications of the parallel, we might be horrified at his stance, but we laugh because he is only using the novel to set up a costumed tableau vivant in which he stars.

Ignatius also wears a green hunting cap, symbol of his willingness to enter the tangled woods the book sets up, all equivalent, in the European classical tradition, to the Wood of Error. Ignatius is a comic version, not so much of Don Quixote as of Spenser's Red Cross Knight. We get a hint of this in a letter from Myrna detailing a fellow artiste's decision to become a forest ranger in Montana so as to plan a "dramatic allegory set in a dark woods (Ignorance and Custom)." As Myrna says, he "will be a big flop as a ranger, but the allegory, I know, will be challenging and controversial, full of unpleasant truths" (197), clearly a minisummary of Toole's novel itself and a prediction of Ignatius's stint as weenie vendor in the Sodom and Gomorrah of the French Quarter. As he says, "The balconies of the old buildings hung over my head like dark branches in an allegorical forest of evil. Symbolically, a Desire bus hurtled past me, its diesel exhaust almost strangling me" (249). Soon, however, he feels less like a Crusader than a threatened damsel:

> I guessed that the residents of the area were still in bed recovering from whatever indecent acts they had been performing the night before. Many no doubt required medical attention: a stitch or two here and there in a torn orifice or a broken genital. I could only imagine how many haggard and depraved eyes were regarding me hungrily from behind the closed shutters.... Already I was beginning to feel like an especially toothsome steak in a meat market. (250)

One could say that Toole's characters reveal the book-addicted aspect of cosmopolitan New Orleans, which is studded with sometimes moldy but nevertheless well-stocked used bookstores, which is only appropriate for a city that is home to many colleges and universities. Nevertheless, the American habit of random and superficial reading gets needled greatly here, and one might also speculate about Toole's own attitude toward contemporary authors. In a satiric attack on Mrs. Levy's shallow nature, Toole tells us, "Over the years she had given herself freely to bridge, African violets, Susan and Sandra, golf, Miami, Fannie Hurst and Hemingway, correspondence courses, hairdressers, the sun, gourmet foods, ballroom dancing, and, in recent years, Miss Trixie" (204). Apparently, Ignatius—and perhaps Toole himself—sees Hurst and Hemingway as equally superfluous. Mrs. Levy's presumptuous kidnaping of Miss Trixie and her roleplaying as that aged lady's psychiatrist results from casual reading and is all too similar to Ignatius and Myrna's patronizing activities with blacks. At another point, reflecting on the oppression of African Americans, Ignatius realizes he is beginning to sound like "the Beards and the Parringtons," cultural historians he apparently has read.

When his mother complains about the mess in Ignatius's room, he defends the squalor by saying, "My being is not without its Proustian elements" (65), thereby claiming affinities with another author who dramatized his own life while lying abed. Mr. Levy, too, seems to be literate; when his wife cries that his neglect of the pants factory is a tragedy he tells her, "Don't try to make a big Arthur Miller play out of Levy Pants" (116). Myrna, of course, was educated alongside Ignatius, and she too reads life in terms of art. As he watches her join him in the escape-vehicle Renault at the end of the book, Ignatius knows her look at the house is an attempt "to *record* the scene: Eliza crossing the ice with a particularly large genius in her arms. Unlike Harriet Beecher Stowe, Myrna was still around to offend" (413). On the other hand, his melodramatic outbursts betray an interest in pulp magazine narratives; at one point he screams hysterically at Mancuso, "Stop molesting us, you mongoloid.

If you had any sense, you would be investigating dens like that Night of Joy in which my beloved mother and I were mistreated and robbed. I, unfortunately was the prey of a vicious, depraved B-girl" (81).

Psychology and philosophy are glossed too. Mrs. Reilly regularly invades her son's "sanctuary," hilariously conceived by Ignatius as akin to those of great writers, though it more closely resembles a little boy's room with a sign on the door reading KEEP OUT—THIS MEANS YOU. Toole knows as well that he is flirting here with Freud's Oedipal configuration. When Ignatius screams at his mother for standing on his tablets, she replies, "Where I'm gonna stand . . . ? You want me to get in bed with you?" (66). At another point, Ignatius writes, as an inscription to one of his essays, "Books are immortal sons defying their sires—Plato." Later, in an aside about the Mississippi River, Ignatius notes that although the river is a mythic father figure, in reality it is "a treacherous and sinister body of water whose eddies and currents yearly claim many lives." It is polluted and seethes "with sewage, industrial waste, and deadly insecticides. Even the fish are dying. Therefore, the Mississippi as Father-God-Moses-Daddy-Phallus-Pops is an altogether false motif begun, I would imagine, by that dreary fraud, Mark Twain. This failure to make contact with reality is, however, characteristic of almost all of America's 'art'" (138). Ignatius's general disdain for all things American and most cultural production after the medieval period marks him as the most insufferable kind of snob, thereby making his inflated and pompous standards an easy target for Toole's needling satire, especially in terms of the contrast between his literary high-mindedness and his actually infantile daily routines, which revolve around getting or avoiding the attentions of his mother. The several disparaging remarks against Mark Twain have the effect of making us see that Toole has that satirical master's methods in mind, even while using him as the butt of the title character's harangues. We should also remember Twain's devastating attack on medieval chivalry, religion, and philosophy in *A Connecticut Yankee in King Arthur's Court,* which Toole likely admired and imitated.

Myrna knows Ignatius's problem is his "mama's boy" status because she's boned up on Freud too. She tells him in a letter that his paranoia comes from staying sealed up in his room: "A beautiful and meaningful love affair would transform you. . . . Great Oedipus bonds are encircling your brain and destroying you" (201). And at the end of the novel, Ignatius confirms her insight, declaring, "Perhaps my mother has done me a great favor by planning to remarry. Those Oedipal bonds were beginning to overwhelm me" (411). As always, Ignatius's application of the wisdom of famous writers, from Milton to

Freud, are more designed to situate him in a starring performative role than to effect meaningful change.

But then Ignatius, fixated on the stability and order of the Middle Ages, abhors change. The seedy but glamorous New Orleans of the novel seemingly is unchanging, but at the same time it is constantly affected by mildew, decay, and neglect. Sections of the city dissolve aimlessly but are described through romantic poetry; the Reillys inhabit "a neighborhood that had degenerated from Victorian to nothing in particular, a block that had moved into the twentieth century carelessly and uncaringly—and with very limited funds" (54). Their house, with its collapsed fence, dead banana tree, dog grave, and wrecked car, occasions a parody of Keats: "There were no shrubs. There was no grass. And no birds sang" (an echo of "La Belle Dame sans Merci") (55). A jarring mixture of eras is suggested by Ignatius booming out Frankie Valli and the Four Seasons' hit "Big Girls Don't Cry" as Officer Mancuso reads a World War II poster, "A slip of the lip can sink a ship," highlighted by a WAVE pressing her finger to her mouth. Which is worse, the inane propaganda of an earlier but supposedly more heroic age or the mindless banality of the present? Is there any difference, and if not, any sense of cultural progress? New Orleans, at least in this book, seems sunk in the past; few signs of modernization are seen, as Toole, through Ignatius, focuses on decay rather than the real progress that was indeed being made in the business and tourist industries of the city.

This missing sense of "progress" would in any case have to be assessed through the central character, who will never concede advancement over the achievements of his ideal period, the medieval age; his sense of that epoch comes from his rapt reading and revision of Boethius, such as "When Fortuna spins you downward, go out to a movie and get more out of life" (73). Ideas become objects and then weapons, as when Officer Mancuso tries to arrest George in the men's room at the bus station; the adolescent thug brains Mancuso with the book that originally belonged to Ignatius, Boethius's *Consolations of Philosophy.* Later still, Lana Lee uses the book as a prop in some of her obscene photographs.

As these comic uses of the revered book indicate, Ignatius's medieval lodestars are clearly contradictory; he craves the stability of fixed, immutable institutions, but firmly believes at the same time in the vicissitudes of "that bitch" Fortuna, who all too often seemingly turns him under her wheel. Ignatius's theories about Fortuna's wheel of fortune seem borne out in Officer Mancuso's meteoric rise in the department after he exposes Lana Lee's high school pornography ring. As his former tormenter, the sergeant says, "And just a couple days ago I was thinking you was a horse's ass. How's about that?" (366).

Numerous critics have provided astute readings of the novel's base in medieval literature. However, no one has noted how Toole's impressive comic passes at philosophy are inextricably tied to Ignatius's sense of hierarchy and division within his own multiethnic universe of New Orleans and to a sense of the ethnic body. As Lloyd Daigrepont notes, Ignatius's concept of history, inscribed in his Big Chief tablet, sees the "luminous year" of Abelard and Thomas à Becket succeeded by "Fortuna's wheel . . . crushing [humanity's] collarbone, smashing its skull, twisting its torso, puncturing its pelvis, sorrowing its soul. Having once been so high, humanity fell so low. . . . Merchants and charlatans gained control of Europe, calling their insidious gospel 'The Enlightenment.' The day of the locust was at hand" (46). Ignatius goes on to claim that the "Great Chain of Being had snapped like so many paper clips strung together by some drooling idiot [a seeming signification of the Deity himself] . . . [and] death, destruction, anarchy, progress, ambition, and self-improvement were to be Piers's new fate. And a vicious fate it was to be: now he was faced with the perversion of having to GO TO WORK" (47). This seamless and hilarious linkage between the medieval and the modern working man narratives makes us go back and see Ignatius—and perhaps Toole too—playfully stringing together the "paperclips" of cultural objects into a necklace of carnivalized events.

Ethnic Embroidery

Although the basic plot of the novel is set in motion by Ignatius's being cast into the working class and therefore into the mold of a Horatio Alger hero, the basic ground of bodily humor finds ornamentation via ethnic embellishment, which extends to the city itself. The inscription to the book from A. J. Liebling claims that New Orleans is Mediterranean, with allusions to the Greeks, the Italians, the Lebanese, and the Egyptians, a comparison that tellingly takes in three continents and the Afro-Asiatic roots of Western culture. This goes on to subtly parallel the rim of the Old World's lake of commerce with the New World's, the Carribean: "Like Havana and Port-au-Prince, New Orleans is within the orbit of a Hellenistic world that never touched the North Atlantic. The Mediterranean, Caribbean and Gulf of Mexico form a homogenous, though interrupted, sea." This inscription suggests much, especially when we consider the way it annuls boundaries and ethnicity, for Toole's comic and democratizing authorial voice sweeps all before it, leveling pretension and barriers as it hurls a hurricane of laughter across the panhuman landscape. This melting pot also has a special voice; a New Orleans accent is discussed that comes in the German and Irish sectors of the city, that is most like the parlance of areas such as Hoboken, New Jersey, and Astoria, Long Island, both "wards," more or less, of New York City. And in fact it was Toole's genius to make this operatic epic in some ways a tale of two cities, or rather, twin melting pots, casting New Orleans' Ignatius as Tristan and the Bronx's Myrna Minkoff standing in as both *deus ex machina* and as a modern-day Isolde.

Since they are at the pinnacle of ethnic representation in this book, what are we to make of the "Bernie-Bridget" Myrna and Ignatius as a couple? Dr. Talc, who taught them both, offers one view:

> He had had them both in separate classes one grim semester, during which they had disrupted his lectures with strange noises and impertinent, venomous questions that no one, aside from God, could possibly have answered (364). . . . They were like two Huns sweeping down on Rome. Dr. Talc idly wondered if they had married each other. Each certainly deserved the other. Perhaps they had both defected to Cuba. (253)

This idea of ravaging hordes in fact has much to do with the unity and method of the novel. The humor and the chaotic events of the narrative are both designed to lay waste our preconceptions and to clear the ground for a new understanding of the culture around us. Dr. Talc, with his boring, set lectures, *needs* some hard questions, some challenges from his students, just as all the other stagnant figures in the novel need a good psychological shaking.

In terms of Ignatius J. Reilly himself, his name conjures up the popular Irish American hero of radio's *Life of Riley,* a character most memorably rendered in William Bendix's 1950s television show, which depicted American ethnic groups finally achieving the American dream. The show frequently played off of Riley's Irish background (his wife was named Peg), echoing similar approaches on *The Goldbergs, Amos and Andy, I Love Lucy* (Ricky was Cuban, Lucy Scots-Irish), and *Life with Luigi.* As these programs aired during Toole's own youth, they seem to have played a role in the shaping of *Confederacy*'s comic figures and plots, a virtual compendium of ethnic sitcom devices.

I Love Lucy, the most famous of the lot, was the descendent of a long line of dramas that began on the New York stage and focused, sometimes in melodrama, sometimes via comedy, on interethnic marriages. Although Israel Zangwill's play *The Melting Pot* (1914) is more famous, *Abie's Irish Rose* (1922) is perhaps the most pertinent work here, for like *Confederacy* and the 1970s TV sitcom *Bridget Loves Bernie,* it featured an Irish-Jewish couple. Toole's novel, however, ingeniously expands the ethnic marriage exponentially by linking it to region and political and moral philosophy. Ignatius's paradoxical embrace of the womb and his mother's smothering love masks a coiled energy that is waiting for release; the ending of the book, which sets this spring loose, launches him toward Myrna and New York, uniting North and South through a southern Irish Catholic and a northern Jew.

Ignatius himself is acutely conscious of ethnic qualities. Once employed at the Levy Pants factory he sets about "dignifying" employees by affixing important-sounding titles and signs to them, each with a visual emblem of their status/ethnicity. His own lowly status as file clerk becomes, via a boldly lettered Gothic sign, DEPARTMENT OF RESEARCH AND REFERENCE, I. J. REILLY, CUSTODIAN. Interestingly, he affixes to it a regal fleur-de-lis, indicating a consensual adoption of French ancestry, which of course has always added caché in Nouvelle Orleans. On Mr. Gonzalez's sign he paints the arms of King Alfonso, whereas Miss Trixie's receives an old-fashioned nosegay, a signal of her Dulcinea-like status in Ignatius's view.

By contrast to these regal overlays, Ignatius's incredibly provincial attitude toward areas outside New Orleans in the South—the "wasteland"—in fact echoes the famous provincialism of both New Orleaneans and New Yorkers. He feverishly imagines that out of the rolling hills near Baton Rouge "some rural red-necks might toss bombs at the bus. They love to attack vehicles, which are a symbol of progress, I guess" (29). Yet when he describes the "Bronx maiden" Myrna, he claims,

> The parochialism of the ghettoes of Gotham had not prepared her for the uniqueness of Your Working Boy. Myrna, you see, believed that all humans living south and west of the Hudson River were illiterate cowboys or—even worse—White Protestants, a class of humans who as a group specialized in ignorance, cruelty, and torture. (I don't wish to especially defend White Protestants; I am not too fond of them myself.) (144)

Both these great cities as ports of arrival have always featured a polyglot ethnicity. Consequently, Toole's characters often express a distinct ethnic culture, yes, but lines of overlap and connection emerge regularly. The hybrid nature of American culture is suggested in any number of ways. The stripper Darlene, like most Americans, practiced melting-pot cookery when she was married: "I . . . used . . . that canned stuff . . . like that Spanish rice they got and that spaghetti with the tomato gravy" (39). Even inanimate objects enter into this ethnic elbowing; Mrs. Reilly pulls out of a parking place in their vintage 1946 Plymouth, leaving the impression of their bumper in the hood of the Volkswagen behind them. Later still, reflecting on his fellow vendors of hot dogs, Ignatius wonders if their employer realizes how the ironically named "Paradise" hot dogs are subsistence food for vagrants and drifters and defeated ethnics:

> Between the other vendors—totally beaten and ailing itinerants whose names are something like Buddy, Pal, Sport, Top, Buck, and Ace—and my customers, I am apparently trapped in a limbo of lost souls. However, the simple fact that they have been resounding failures in our century does give them a certain spiritual quality. For all we know, they may be—these crushed wretches—the saints of our age; beautifully broken old Negroes with tan eyes; downtrodden drifters from wastelands in Texas and Oklahoma; ruined sharecroppers seeking a haven in rodent-infested urban rooming houses. (246)

Myrna, of course, was educated alongside Ignatius, and she too reads life in terms of art and often casts herself, as in the last scene, as the rescuer of the ethnic downtrodden.

When Mrs. Reilly's Creole suitor, Mr. Robichaux, meets Burma Jones, Toole juxtaposes two languages: broken, French-inflected Creole English and the jive talk of black New Orleans. Just the word "communist" offers play; it's "communiss" to Robichaux, and "cawmniss" to Jones, who can't believe the old man had the nerve to call Mancuso such: "If I call a po-lice a cawmniss, my ass be in Angola [Louisiana's notorious prison] right now for sure" (32). Robichaux and Jones are both New Orleaneans, but they are distinct from each other by race and ethnicity, which is primarily depicted—on the page at least—through dialect. Ethnicity has been rendered through dialect for centuries, and in this country it flourished both on the page (especially in the late nineteenth century, which doted on "eye" humor of strange spellings and punctuation) and on the stage. Gavin Jones has demonstrated the myriad ways in which dialect was used for ethnic caricature in Vaudeville, which was the United States' favorite form of entertainment from the 1870s through the 1920s. Audiences in northern cities were frequently of immigrant/ethnic stock and delighted in seeing their own and other groups depicted through figures called "racial comics." Irish, German, Italian, Jewish, and African American dialects ruled this stage. Jones suggests that the dialect skits had a salutary effect: It "had the power to mediate difference by sustaining multiple interpretations and staging ethnic hybrids" (Jones 163). I argue that Toole's presentation of his ethnic characters continues this technique, creating a constant carnivalization of culture that provides a shifting, kaleidoscopic vision of New Orleans, southern, and national culture, as ethnic traditions collide, merge, and influence one another, as in the exchange I have noted between Robichaux and Jones.

Another dimension of this appears in Ignatius's *Journal of a Working Boy, or Up from Sloth*. The term "satire" means a mixed dish, and as this title indicates, Toole constantly varies the mode of narration as well. This journal mode enlivens the narrative but also mixes genres itself, suggesting both the Horatio Alger stories of the way to wealth and the moral uplift autobiographies such as *Up from Slavery* and classic immigrant autobiographies and novels such as Abraham Cahan's *Rise of David Levinsky*. Here and elsewhere, what makes Toole's ethnic caricatures so interesting is that they have multiple layers. Myrna is not only a Bronx Jewish Maiden but also a trendy revolutionary who has been influenced by the civil rights movement: "Myrna was decidedly masochistic. She was only happy when a police dog was sinking its fangs into her black leotards or when she was being dragged feet first down stone steps from a Senate hearing" (145). Obviously, she and Ignatius have much in common. Both try to help blacks, Myrna going so far as to offer them instruction in folks songs she had learned at the Library of Congress. As Ignatius reports, however, the

> Negroes, it seems, preferred more contemporary music and turned up their transistor radios loudly and defiantly whenever Myrna began one of her lugubrious dirges. Although the Negroes had tried to ignore her, the whites had shown great interest in her. Bands of crackers and rednecks had chased her from villages, slashed her tires, whipped her a bit about the arms. She had been hunted by bloodhounds, shocked by cattle prods, chewed by police dogs, peppered lightly with shotgun pellets. She had loved every minute of it, showing me quite proudly (and, I might add, suggestively) a fang mark on her upper thigh. . . . The subsidiary theme in the correspondence is one urging me to come to Manhattan so that she and I may raise our banner of twin confusion in that center of mechanized horrors. (146)

This valorization of "confusion" reiterates the central comic movement of the book—from order/lethargy to confusion through the agency of Ignatius, the bizarre outsider, whose interventions at the very least, and at the end of all the narrative strands, necessitates change. Once again both he and Myrna are made ridiculous by their absurdly self-centered notions of social activism, whereby they become spectators of their own performative altruism. Thus Myrna, like Ignatius, is effective in this comic role partly because she is "playing" at revolution. More earnest figures could not be so inventive—or so transparently naïve. It should be mentioned that Myrna represents even more than this. In her addiction to psychoanalysis, she offers Toole another opportunity to make delicious comedy out of psychobabble. At one point she tells Ignatius to send her his sex fantasies for analysis, revealing that the members of her group therapy group in New York are all following his case with great interest. Similarly, Mrs. Levy, whose portrait is based in a caricature of the Jewish mother, also employs psychobabble (we remember here that Freud was Jewish), and the following speech directed at her husband suggests the intersection of these two narrative and comic scripts: "So. You're angry all of a sudden. At least you're having a normal response. That's unusual for you" (256). Mrs. Levy's expertise comes from an uncompleted correspondence psychology course, which most importantly leads to her campaign to resurrect Miss Trixie, which we come to see is an effort to recreate an image of her own mother. In a fascinating detail, this is seen clearly when she affixes a large black wig on Miss Trixie's head; a wig like this was worn by orthodox immigrant Jewish women and in fact functions as a comic motif in Abraham Cahan's classic novel *Yekl,* which became the film *Hester Street.* Similarly, Mr. Levy functions as a caricature of both a Jewish businessman and a capitalist exploiter of labor, but he also serves as a parody of the sports-obsessed American male who neglects his wife and daughters.

The book derives much of its humor from such ethnic mixing—and indeed, of mixing opposed elements of all sorts, for as Freud observed, the basic unit of the comic is the forced juxtaposition of opposites. To be effective in this, however, Toole needs to paint a comic portrait of each ethnic group that is robust enough to withstand the encounters with others. He was fortunate to present his portrait of ethnic communities at a time when people were less suspicious of group characterization; as Mahadev Apte has noted, social conditions in America in the late twentieth century changed considerably, with less emphasis on the "melting pot" leading to greater appreciation of ethnic difference, both within groups and in the general population (Apte 134). Further, although some have said *Confederacy* employs stereotypes (and surely it does, although the intent and use of them may be debated), it is true that *all* groups of people in the story, from midwestern tourists to gays, from Italians to Irish, get an equal application of Toole's comic needle. Accordingly, it might be helpful to zero in on some of the specific characterizations of each ethnic group.

Ignatius's plan to liberate the black workers at Levy Pants quickly goes awry; Miss Trixie asks, "Is this a minstrel show?" and Ignatius screams, "Go dangle you withered parts over the toilet!" (1691). In fact, however, this *is* a minstrel show, with an ignorant white man directing what he thinks is a black ritual protest. Mrs. Levy's presumptuous kidnaping of Miss Trixie and her role playing as that aged lady's psychiatrist is all too similar to Ignatius and Myna's patronizing activities with blacks. When Ignatius first visits the factory, he describes it as

> a scene which combines the worst of *Uncle Tom's Cabin* and Fritz Lang's *Metropolis;* it is mechanized Negro slavery; it represents the progress which the Negro has made from picking cotton to tailoring it. (Were they in the picking stage of their evolution, they would at least be in the healthful outdoors singing and eating watermelons [as they are, I believe, supposed to do when in groups *al fresco*]. . . .) In connection with the watermelons, I must say, lest some professional civil rights reorganization be offended, that I have never been an observer of American folk customs. I may be wrong. I would imagine that today people grasp for the cotton with one hand while the other hand presses a transistor radio to the sides of their heads so that it can spew bulletins about used cars and Sofstyle Hair Relaxer and Royal Crown Hair Dressing and Gallo wine about their eardrums, a filter menthol cigarette dangling from their lips and threatening to set the entire cotton field ablaze. (138)

While Ignatius's conscious revelry in stereotype is so over the top here that it cannot be taken seriously even by him, his knowing references to contemporary tastes of African Americans would seem to indicate that he knows more than he lets on about this culture, which of course would have been all around him from birth in profoundly African American New Orleans. Indeed, in plotting his campaign against Levy Pants, Ignatius prays to the locally popular (and black) St. Martin de Porres, "the patron saint of mulattoes, for our cause in the factory. Because he is also invoked against rats, he will perhaps aid us in the office, too" (147).

A telling check against reading Ignatius's racial fantasies as Toole's is the personification of the key black character in the book, Burma Jones. In many ways he seems to be the shrewdest analyst of the contemporary scene, perhaps because, as a black man, he is indeed "invisible" as Ralph Ellison describes that state, but also because, behind his dark glasses and his cloud of smoke, he possesses a keen ability to separate truth from illusion, a quality noticeably lacking in most of the other characters. Although many of them have moments of insight about others, this talent usually doesn't extend to self-examination. Burma's bitter but bitingly funny running monologue about his "slavery" to "Big Missy" Lana has the whole disturbing underside of racial history as its impetus. We remember too that Burma's situation—and that of the workers in the Levy Pants factory—has to be situated against the backdrop of a racially roiled New Orleans, which in the 1960s was reaping the whirlwind of the segregated 1940s and 1950s.

Burma's street smarts provide a comic linguistic prism of view and reflection, making Ignatius's doings even funnier when one of the black men at the pants factory meets Jones at Mattie's Ramble Inn: "He say, 'You peoples all be happier in the middle age. You peoples gotta get you a cannon and some arros, drop a nucular bum on top this place'" (152), prompting Jones's warning, "Stay away from that freak. He wanted by a po-lice. You po color peoples all get your ass throwed in jail. Whoa!" (153).

The theme of modern slavery permeates the book. Burma Jones knows quite well that Lana Lee's blackmailing extortion of his labor is just that—"for twenty dollar a week, you ain running a plantation in here. . . . Who you callin 'boy'? You ain Scarla O'Horror" (89, 93), a devastating and conscious malapropism. A parallel to this narrative emerges when Mrs. Levy informs her husband that daughters Susan and Sandra have been told by their college friends that he sounds like "a plantation owner living on slave labor": "They want you to raise the salaries of those poor people or they won't come home again" (168). Despite this repeated depiction of various characters who want social change, the book makes an equally strong argument for effective management as a tool for racial and economic justice, yes, but also as the best route to personal wealth. The catch: It's worse (what a surprise) if you're black, especially if your white employer has something on you. Still, Burma emerges as the narrative's cagiest and in some ways most heroic figure; his clowning dialect masks a talent for subversion and an impressively insightful ability to read people and situations. But he, like other characters who represent other ethnic groups, regularly has to yield his primacy in that group to the overbearing interpretations of Ignatius. Toole shows us a revealing racial contrast; Ignatius's ridiculous job at Levy Pants, where he does virtually nothing, pays sixty dollars a month; Burma Jones's hard cleaning work at the Night of Joy pays twenty dollars. Toole also juxtaposes their experiences on the job.

Both Ignatius and Myrna are attracted to African American culture because it offers them an arena for their performative and stereotypical liberalism. The aforementioned reference of Dr. Talc to Ignatius and Myrna as ravaging hordes ties in with their appropriative and commodifying behavior and has much to do with the unity and method of the novel. Ignatius and many other characters attempt to use both subterfuge and more purposeful disruption to effect change; Burma Jones and his "sabotage" campaign against Lana Lee has a more anarchistic mission, one he feels could be aided by Ignatius. As he tells Mr. Watson, "I like to find out where that fat freak hidin out. Maybe I call up Levy Pant and ax for him. I like to drop him in the Night of Joy like a nucular bum. See like he the kin make that Lee mother shit in her drawer. Whoa! If I gonna be a doorman, I gonna be the mos sabotagin doorman ever guarded a plantation. Oo-wee. The cotton fiel be burn to the groun before I'm through" (261), comic lines that nevertheless link Jones, at least rhetorically, with the Black Panthers and other black radicals of the times.

Burma's revolutionary rage comes from knowing that white people view him stereotypically, yet he gets some scant amusement from it. When an old woman on a bus moves away from him, he thinks, "Look at that. She think I got siphlus and TB and a hard on and I gonna cut her up with a razor and lif her purse. Ooo-wee" (72).

Obviously, Toole is using Ignatius to satirize those well-meaning white liberals who think they are sympathetic to black people when they are actually exoticizing and patronizing them. The most hilarious example of this occurs when Ignatius, on his initial tour of the factory, switches off the "obscene jazz" playing on the intercom, causing a roar of disapproval. As he says,

> Obviously, continual response to the music had developed within them an almost Pavlovian response to the noise, a response which they believed was pleasure. Having spent countless hours of my life watching those blighted children on television dancing to this sort of music [a reference to Dick Clark's *American Bandstand*] I knew the physical spasm which it was supposed to elicit, and I attempted my own conservative version of the same on the spot to further pacify the workers. I must admit that my body moved with surprising agility; I am not without an innate sense of rhythm; my

> ancestors must have been rather outstanding at jigging on the heath. . . . I shuffled about beneath one of the loudspeakers, twisting and shouting, mumbling insanely, "Go! Go! Do it, baby, do it! Hear me talkin' to ya. Wow!" I knew that I had recovered my ground with them when several began pointing to me and laughing. I laughed back to demonstrate that I, too, shared their high spirits. (141)

Moreover, unlike its mostly loving recreation in the recent Broadway musical *Hairspray,* where the show's initial segregation was criticized, *American Bandstand* is seen by Ignatius as a betrayal of democracy for different reasons: "A firm rule must be imposed upon our nation before it destroys itself. The United States needs some theology and geometry, some taste and decency" (60). Revealingly, Ignatius doesn't seem troubled by the racial problem on the show. Here, as is often the case, Toole sets up a classic case of author/reader irony that is not shared by the character, but the reference to the Clark show also reveals the massive effect black music was having on white America, especially among its youth, and the ways in which people were beginning to demand that American television reflect racial democracy even while de facto segregation continued to rule in most local communities.

Ignatius's dislike of jazz underlines his ignorance of black culture, as does his distaste for spirituals, which he relates to "deadly nineteenth-century Calvinist hymns" (143). But this distaste extends to white American music as well, for Ignatius pronounces "Turkey in the Straw" "a discordant abomination. . . . Veneration of such things as 'Turkey in the Straw' is at the very root of our current dilemma" (174). Here he comically and proleptively echoes more recent "high-culture snobs" such as Alan Bloom who have bemoaned the eclipse of the "classics" by trash literature, music, and other art forms; seemingly, Ignatius goes further by axing everything American as well, since everything in the United States that might be termed "classic" postdates the medieval period.

Later, when he leads the black workers' march against Gonzalez, his homemade flag reads "FORWARD: Crusade for Moorish Dignity," an absurd insertion of his medieval literature background into labor and racial relations. Later reflections, however, are more serious:

> In a sense I have always felt something of a kinship with the colored race because its position is the same as mine: we both exist outside the inner realm of American society. Of course, my exile is voluntary. However, it is apparent that many of the Negroes wish to become active members of

> the American middle class. I cannot imagine why. . . . If a middle-class white were suicidal enough to sit next to me, I imagine that I would beat him soundly about the head and shoulders with one great hand, tossing, quite deftly, one of my Molotov cocktails into a passing bus jammed with middle-class whites with the other. . . . I do admire the terror which Negroes are able to inspire in the hearts of some members of the white proletariat and only wish. (This is a rather personal confession.) That I had the ability to similarly terrorize. . . . Perhaps I should have been a Negro. I suspect that I would have been a rather large and terrifying one, continually pressing my ample thigh against the withered thighs of old white ladies in public conveyances a great deal and eliciting more than one shriek of panic. Then too, if I were Negro, I would not be pressured by my mother to find a good job, for no good jobs would be available. My mother herself, a worn old Negress, would be too broken by years of underpaid labor as a domestic to go out bowling at night. She and I could live most pleasantly in some moldy shack in the slums in a state of ambitionless peace, realizing contentedly that we were unwanted, that striving was meaningless. (142)

Note here Ignatius's fantasy of terrorizing white women parallels Jones's projection of the reaction he *actually* causes in the same, but real, circumstances. But Ignatius's fantasy is also shot through with perceptive awareness and even sympathy. Further, the concept of *exile* that he shrewdly sees links him and black New Orleaneans has much to say about the "throwaway" people of the United States.

Toole returns to these issues repeatedly, even through racist characters, but more often letting oppression finds comic expression. Lana Lee cruelly sizes up Jones's need for a job: "This was really a deal, like a present left on her doorstep. A colored guy who would get arrested for vagrancy if he didn't work. She would have a captive porter whom she could work for almost nothing. It was beautiful" (50). Jones, however, knows the terms of his imprisonment; he tells Darlene, "She aint exactly *hire* me. She kinda buying me off a auction block. . . . Wha she go shoppin for? A whip?" (52). Lana, paradigmatic capitalist, waters her drinks and low-pays her help.

This theme of exploitation finds another register later, when Myrna writes Ignatius that she has had to forget about her planned movie about racial oppression because of a lack of funds; her "Harlem find," Leola, who was to star, gets "very hostile about salary (or lack of it) and finally dropped a remark or two that sounded a little anti-Semitic to me. Who needs a girl who isn't dedicated enough to work gratis in a project that would benefit her race?" (197).

The Levy family and Myrna represent Toole's satire of Jewish culture, both traditional and radical. The nagging Jewish mother and wife, albeit in a new-age version, appears in Mrs. Levy, whose Freudian approach to life could be critiqued not only through Dr. Sigmund's lectures on psychoanalysis but also through his writings on humor. Her relentless attacks on her husband often characterize him—not without reason—as an example of the unfaithful husbandry man. His employees need not only better wages but also effective direction. Again the Oedipal issue is raised, this time by the Levy girls against their father:

> Mr Levy had seen his wife's letters to the girls, emotional, irrational brainwashing editorials that could have made Patrick Henry out to be a Tory, that brought the girls home on holidays bristling with hostility against their father for the thousands of injustices he had committed against their mother. With him cast as a Klansman firing a young crusader, Mrs. Levy could really write a flaming broadside. The material at hand was too good. (168)

Mr. Levy's personal history relates to the ongoing goading of Ignatius by Mrs. Riley. Mr. Levy is content to let his horrifically run pants factory go down the drain as an act of petty Oedipal revenge against his dead father: "He blocked every good idea I had for that firm just to prove that he was the father and I was the son" (115). We find in the thumbnail sketch of old Mr. Levy a bit of Jewish American history: "He started peddling pants in a wagon."

As this fusion of Jewish family matters with references to slavery, racism, and the Klan implies, Toole delights in cross-ethnic collisions and collusions. Mrs. Levy recommends a therapist who cured her jeweler friend Lenny's guilt over selling rosaries: "Now he's got some kind of exclusive agreement with a bunch of nuns who peddle the rosaries in about forty Catholic schools all over the city. The money's rolling in. Lenny's happy. The sisters are happy. The kids are happy" (170). The narrative method of the book seems chaotic, but characters and motifs that were never previously connected suddenly converge at many different points. The rosaries manufactured by Mrs. Levy's cousin, for instance, suddenly appear when Mr. Robichaux's grandchildren start raffling them in Santa's neighborhood for the nuns, and Santa has one of Lenny's Our Lady of the Televisions, complete with rubber suction cup.

Myrna, however, although not a practicing Jew, is a bigot herself. She approvingly describes a friend's pamphlet about the pope's plan to assemble a nuclear armory but then discovers the pamphlet was actually written by the

Klan and that the author, far from being an Israeli sympathizer, is a Baptist from Alabama. Myrna feels the ideas were good, they were just written by the wrong people, something like the experience she had in the park, when the squirrel she thought she was feeding turned out to be a rat.

The Levys and Myrna constitute regional avatars of contemporary, urban, liberal, and secular Jews whose affluence enables their "do-gooder" activities. Their education, however, seems to make them more vulnerable to fads and self-indulgence, especially as their slipshod knowledge of Freud, another secular Jew, causes them to hilariously misread themselves and others. But running through all these stereotypical elements runs a bright thread of genuine concern, too, which eventuates in Myrna's gender-reversed "rescue" of the imperilled hero (rather than heroine) at novel's end, and in Mr. Levy's emergence from his Oedipal funk to take charge of the factory that employs so many blacks and a Latino supervisor.

Throughout the book we find comic mininarratives that exemplify and mock preexisting narrative conventions. When we first meet Mancuso's aunt Santa Battaglia, for instance, she uses her exhaustion at opening oysters in her back yard as an excuse to render yet another immigrant saga, the story of her mother, who ran an oyster stand. Momma, "right off the boat," exemplifies the immigrant story, yet Santa is clearly New Orleanean. She calls the sidewalk a "banquette" and complains that her red beans and rice give her too much gas. On another occasion she says she loves to "fix a big pot of meatballs or jumbalaya with shrimps" (283). The mixture of traditional Italian cuisine with Louisiana dishes is typical of the way Creole/Cajun foodways tend to infiltrate other ethnic cuisines.

These references to Santa's mother expand earlier ones from a party she gives when she kisses a portrait of her mother standing in the oyster-shell-paved alley. But Toole's description of the picture itself veers uncomfortably close to stereotype—"The little black coals of Sicilian eyes glared almost animatedly at Santa" (212)—while signaling (accurately) that New Orleans Italians usually came from Sicily but also that parents, even when dead (like the elder Mr. Levy), can continue to dominate their children.

Ignatius's hostility to Mancuso and Santa of course stems from the threat they pose to his domination of his mother, but he uses ethnic slurs against them too, accusing them of being "cohorts from the mafia" (135). Yet the strong bond between Mancuso and Santa typifies the centrality of family to Italian New Orleaneans, and their fervent Catholicism, although frequently used by Toole to create comedy is ultimately respected and shown to be one of the chief ways in which this group fits into an overwhelmingly Catholic city. It is both interesting and perplexing that Toole chose to locate religious humor in Jews and Italian Catholics rather than in his own Irish Catholic community, which actually receives far less attention that the other ethnic groups I have discussed here.

Regionalism as Ethnicity

Parody, a recurring aim of the novel, is also practiced relentlessly and knowingly by its characters. New Orleans has always catered to tourists, and that has meant marketing myths and legends of both the Old South and Old New Orleans. The benighted Darlene's striptease act at Lana Lee's Night of Joy Club features her as Harlett O'Hara, the Virgin-ny Belle under the auspices of Roberta E. Lee. This parody of regionalism is not confined to southerners; when a group of midwestern tourists ask to photograph the weenie salesman Ignatius in his pirate costume, he hams it up for them, taking dramatic poses even though their "sharp" accents assail his "delicate eardrums like the sounds of a wheat thresher" (250). He later decides the photographs "could earn those corn-belt clods a fortune in some photographic contest" (251). Since Jean Lafitte and other pirates were very real denizens of the Crescent City, they too have inevitably become part of the city's stereotypes.

Miss Lana Lee, proprietress of the Night of Joy, offers a bluntly direct line of commentary on contemporary regional mores. Herself a petty criminal, she nevertheless comments incisively on the changing mores of the quarters. When she bows to Darlene's insistence that they begin an "animal act" like the other clubs—in this case one involving Darlene's cockatoo—Lana laments, "It used to be the old Kiwanis types like to come in and watch a cute girl shake it a little. Now it's gotta be with some kinda animal. You know what's wrong with people today? They're sick. . . . Okay. We audition the bird. It's probably safer for you to be on my stage with a bird than on my stools with a cop. Bring in the goddam bird" (127).

Critics have pointed to a change in Ignatius at the end when he leaves for New York with Myrna. Actually, this change was prefigured when he discovered the pornographic photo of Lana Lee reading Boethius and then believing that the same woman is playing Harlett O'Hara. He gladly goes out to sell hot dogs, for "he had a reason for earning money" (319). Typically, he finds a grandiose way to describe this new venture; he writes Myrna, "I am currently connected in a most vital manner with the food merchandising industry" (203).

Gays and Lesbians as Ethnic Characters

Ignatius's revolutionary ardor is stirred by his mad scheme to infiltrate the military with gay soldiers, or as he calls it, the "Save the World Through Degeneracy" plan, which of course is a sequel to his "Crusade for Moorish Justice." As he imagines it:

> As soldiers, they [gays] will all be so continually busy in fraternizing with one another, tailoring their uniforms to fit like sausage skins, inventing new and varied battle dress, giving cocktail parties, etc. that they will never have time for battle. . . . None of the pederasts in power, of course, will be practical enough to know about such devices as bombs; these nuclear weapons would lie rotting in their vaults. (290)

Lesbians take central stage, too, as avenging furies, when Lana Lee is delivered up to their clutches in jail. They correspond in number to the three "creeps" who just put Lana Lee "through hell": Ignatius, Mancuso, and Burma Jones. "'Quit rocking the boat,' one of the rough women snarls, 'show us those pictures of yourself [part of Lana's pornographic output] you got hidden in your bra.' . . . The three girls lunged for Lana at the same time" (369). This scene prefigures the ending of the Eddie Murphy/Dan Ackroyd film *Trading Places,* where the evil Paul Gleason, in disguise as a gorilla, is placed inside a cage with a horny and very *real* male gorilla; similarly, the scene ends abruptly as the predator pounces, creating comedy out of violation. Toole is using the long tradition of satirizing women's prison movies (as in the hilarious off-Broadway play that starred the transvestite Divine, *Women behind Bars*), whereas *Trading Places* combines the prison-rape scenario with, bizarrely, a flipped version of bestiality.

In the gay party scenes, Ignatius's Pirate outfit situates him as "advertising" himself—which of course, he is, but in order to sell weenies. But this real fact has a comic pun hidden in it, as the vendor plot overlays the gay plot. The gay characters here are certainly stereotypical, but they also employ some of the funniest double entendres as they constantly signify on the ridiculous Ignatius, and they are not really that different from the gay characters we find in the much more recent Broadway musical Mel Brooks fashioned, *The Pro-*

ducers, in which shared gender preference is similarly viewed as leading to a kind of ethnic group.

The Ultimate Ethnic Group: The Insane

In just one of many scenes that interbraid the "gay" comedy with the "working boy" humor, Ignatius disrupts a ladies' art guild show in Pirate's Alley by hanging a sign on his weenie cart reading TWELVE INCHES (12") OF PARADISE. But he subsequently offers a stinging sarcastic critique of their paintings that appeals to anyone who has had to pretend hideous amateur daubs have merit; one of the women actually throws a stone at him. He's quite right when he charges, "Apparently you are afraid of someone who has some contact with reality, who can truthfully describe to you the offenses which you have committed to canvas" (265). In his madness, we find truth. But playing this role has a price. The stone the suburban lady painter casts at Ignatius has many equivalents, which all culminate in Santa's scheme to have Ignatius locked up in the insane ward of Charity Hospital, a chillingly familiar way to handle someone who is "different," be it in New Orleans in the sixties or the Soviet Union in the fifties. "They'd turn a hose on him. They'd stick a letrit socket in that boy. They'd show that Ignatius. They'd make him behave himself" (285). When Levy Pants is sued because of a letter Ignatius forged, the feuding Levys unite in a search for a scapegoat. They too plot putting him away in an insane asylum. All the various stories start to converge, and the serious message underneath the comedy validates Emily Dickinson's poem:

> Much Madness is divinest Sense—
> To a discerning Eye—
> Much Sense—the starkest Madness—
> 'Tis the Majority
> In this, as All, prevail—
> Assent—and you are sane—
> Demur—you're straightway dangerous—
> And handled with a Chain— (Dickinson 209)

Similarly, Ignatius declares that mental patients have only one problem, that "they don't like new cars and hair sprays. That's why they are put away. They make the other members of the society fearful. Every asylum in this nation is filled with poor souls who simply cannot stand lanolin, cellophane, plastic, television, and subdivisions" (326). One remembers Tennessee Williams's Blanche DuBois, who prefers "magic" to sordid reality, and Aunt Vi's plan to lobotomize her niece Katherine in *Suddenly Last Summer* (significantly, both these plays are set in New Orleans). Indeed, the plan to ship Ignatius off to an asylum seems almost exactly like the solution Stanley concocts for the problem of sister-in-law Blanche in *Streetcar;* however, thanks to the "kindness" of the strange rather than "stranger" Myrna, Ignatius escapes.

The Pan-Ethnic Melee

Because the novel constantly has its characters teetering on the brink of disaster, we can read it as a kind of gallows humor, something akin to the appalling but therapeutic shuttle jokes that grew out of the endlessly repeated TV images of the NASA disaster (example: How do you get eight astronauts into a Volkswagen? Four in the seats, four in the ashtray). Along these lines, Mrs. Reilly proposes, "Some people got it harder than me, I guess. Like my poor cousin, wonderful woman. Went to mass every day of her life. She got knocked down by a streetcar over on Magazine Street early one morning while she was on her way to Fisherman's Mass" (61).

Disaster closely relates to the thematic of violence, which can of course lead to tragedy or, interpreted less strictly, the comic device of slapstick. Violence is a given in *Confederacy*'s action-packed world. Santa, babysitting her granddaughter, screams, "Get the hell away from that stove, Charmaine, and go play out on the banquette before I bust you right in the mouth. . . . Get the hell outside and go play on your bike before I come slap your face off." She then tells Mrs. Reilly the nuns should "beat up" on the kid a little. Her nephew Mancuso is supposedly a "sweet, considerate man" because the nuns beat up on him when he was a kid, even "throwing him into a blackboard once." In fact, one of the reasons Santa likes Irene Reilly is her interest in her family stories; her relatives "always had gory biographies that were worth hearing," such as the cousin who "knocked a pot of berling water on her arm when she was a child. She was kinda scaled looking. You know what I mean?" (195). Then there's Irene's eighty-year-old aunt was beaten up by kids to get fifty cents from her purse.

Yet as the passage from Bakhtin above notes, laughter "demolishes," i.e., clears the way for new structures. The very first part of the book, detailing Irene and Ignatius ploughing into a venerable French Quarter building in their Plymouth embodies the concept of comic demolition but also (by way of the Plymouth) new beginnings. Thus the narrative method of the book seems chaotic, but characters and motifs that were never previously connected suddenly converge at many different points. The rosaries manufactured by Mrs. Levy's cousin, for instance, suddenly appear when Mr. Robichaux's grandchildren start raffling them in Santa's neighborhood for the nuns, thereby melding in the Italian and Creole narratives. The most compelling jelling of the plot occurs, however, when everyone's animus against Ignatius comes together in a search for a scapegoat, always a theme in ethnic literature. The party at Santa's where Claude and Mancuso meet sets the stage for Mrs. Reilly's resentment at her son to boil over. In an operatic tableau Santa leads the other three in a rousing chorus of condemnation of Ignatius, who becomes their communal scapegoat, their point of union. When Santa intones the final malediction, "Somebody ought to beat up on that Ignatius," she concludes by demanding that everybody make friends. The Irish, the Italians, and the French find accord by condemning the heretical Ignatius.

The novel's careful scene by scene building of a comic palimpsest begins to pay off in these sections. By now every prop, every character, every expression is associated in the reader's mind with a joke, a comic scene, an outrageous event, and so on, and merely to mention the object, person, or subject creates a comic effect from the juxtaposition of unlikely strands in the reader's memory of the text itself. This of course is also the basic method of farce and of extended comedic routines such as the classic "Who's on First?" which utilizes repetition and confusion interchangeably. The triple fiasco of Harlett O'Hara's debut, Mancuso's arrest of Lana, and Ignatius's near death under the wheels of the Desire bus gets photographed for posterity, running under the headline "Wild Incident on Bourbon Street." The scene and the picture unites Mancuso, Lana, Darlene, the three lesbians, Jones, and of course Ignatius with a new ethnic character, "the Latin woman" thrown in for lagniappe as a chiseling b-girl. One by one, each of the character reads the story and comments on it and the picture of Ignatius lying in the gutter, surrounded by strippers, pimps, and pornographers. This creates a comedic parody, if unintended as such, of the famous "Doubloon" chapter in *Moby-Dick,* where key characters take turns solitarily interpreting the signs on the coin Ahab has nailed to the mast. As such, it underlines in a comic but also significant way the heteroglossia of the novel, the potential of democratic dissensus, and the ultimate meaning of Toole's use of the word "confusion."

Sacvan Bercovitch, in his important study *The Rites of Assent,* has declared that our nation is based on a tacit agreement among its many people to embrace dissensus, which ironically constitutes a rite of assent. He finds many examples of this in American culture, dating as far back as the Puritan era. An example he does not present of this phenomenon, which involves the ethnic melee, is pertinent here. In the late nineteenth century, the most popular playwright in New York was Edward Harrigan, whose "Mulligan" series of plays featured an Irish American family inhabiting Mulligan's Alley, which despite its name housed Germans, Jews, Italians, African Americans, and Chinese. The boisterous comedy of the plays always depends on the physical and linguistic jostling these crowded quarters engender, and often the plays end with two of the major contending groups—usually blacks and Irish—comically fighting each other in a melee as the curtain descends. No resolution is expected or desired; instead, the audience collapses in laughter over the comedy of acculturation, immigration, and dissensus. Toole's novel operates this way, too, and ends in a similar way, as the contending forces of New Orleans culture come together in an attempt to incarcerate the gadfly who has upset all their pieties.

Indeed, the paradoxical energies of "confusion"—a word used repeatedly throughout the novel—ultimately seems to be a virtual synonym for dynamic creativity as it clears the ground for new forms and concepts. Confusion ultimately becomes a way of testing unity and separate ethnic identities by showing how explosion and scapegoating (which Ignatius and the other characters repeatedly experience) are central to stereotyping and persecution; carnivalization, which is yet another way of defining confusion, becomes a way of resisting monolithic, self-annihilating unity, exclusion, the status quo, and bigotry.

The ending of the novel, with Myrna swooping down in her white Renault to carry away Ignatius just before the ambulance arrives to take him to the loony bin, is of course a deus ex machina; however, we should remember Myrna has been a key component of the plot throughout and has always functioned, as I have stated, as a kind of comic Isolde to Ignatius's Tristan. As they ride out of New Orleans into the swamps—another version of Red Cross Knight's Wood of Error—they are nonetheless headed for New York, which is constantly figured throughout the book as New Orleans' counterpart. I thus reject the dark readings earlier critics (Bell, for example) have of the book's ending, for Ignatius, kissing Myrna's braid gratefully, does indeed seem to be ready, like the true picaro, to conquer new worlds. Whether or not he and Myrna marry, they seem "madly mated" and ready for new adventures in Gotham, where many more "types," "characters," "kooks," and what have you exist in similarly pied beauty among New York's multiple ethnic citizens.

New York and New Orleans have in common a strong sense of urban distinctiveness. Each city fosters a syncretic sense of community, partly based on the difference from not just the rest of the nation but also in fact from contiguous communities (New Jersey and Baton Rouge, for example). And yet both cities are ethnic composites. I have yet to meet a New Orleanean who has read *Confederacy* who *doesn't* believe that Toole got the city and its citizens exactly right, including the ethnic voices. All these characters, they feel, while distinct from one another, are indisputable New Orleaneans. This all-embracing, multiethnic umbrella confers status for them among the larger community of Louisianans, other southerners, and, New Orleaneans would say, among Americans. As such, their identification with the city becomes a form of symbolic ethnicity, one linked to their other performed ethnic selves. Mary C. Waters has suggested that symbolic ethnicity persists "because it meets a need Americans have for community without individual cost" (Waters 164). Further, Joseph Roach has argued persuasively that New Orleans performative rituals are symbolic actions that reveal both "the tangible existence of social boundaries and, at the same time, the contingency of those boundaries on fictions of identity"(Roach 39), which I would apply in part to issues of race and ethnicity. Certainly one of the performative rituals of New Orleans is the second-line tradition, which is associated with both Carnival and funerals. It is not insignificant that the leader of the second line often carries an umbrella, a symbol of what I have been describing as the all-embracing ethnic umbrella of New Orleans that provides access, through Carnival forms, to communal representation by all citizens.

Some of this, in different fashion, is characteristic of New York as well. This link between the two cities is underlined in the conclusion as Myrna, the Jewish New Yorker, swoops down to take Irish New Orleanean Ignatius to Gotham. Lloyd M. Daigrepont has ventured that Myrna's utopian reformism needs the tempering of Ignatius's sense of man's fallibility—indeed, a union of the spiritual and humanistic impulses of the Renaissance and the Reformation (Daigrepont 80). This transcendent theory has a more mundane register too; the Minkoff/Reilly union replays *Abie's Irish Rose, Bridget Loves Bernie,* and all the other classic ethnic comic romances that find fulfillment by bridging differences through love while creating a vibrant new culture. Of course, this is mere speculation, for the story, although seemingly ending in liberation, rather than despair, actually *doesn't* end. One feels there should be a sequel, set in New York, that will further detail the trajectory of these two modern day "Huns" whose wake of disruption and chaos clears the ground for new beginnings, and not just for themselves. Their union at the finale offers a final crystallization of what has characterized Toole's modus operandi from the beginning—the unexpected juxtaposition of apparently opposed elements to create a new, fertile entity, one emblematic of the democratic dissensus and democracy of America. Toole's comic symphony of sometimes competing but also fraternizing ethnic characters mirrors and valorizes our ongoing construction of individual and national identity.

Tennessee Williams chose to wrest tragedy out of New Orleans's teeming streets and Old South mansions. Toole preferred to focus on comedy, but each writer clearly understood how the tragic can underlie comedy, and vice versa. Like Ignatius's beloved philosophers Boethius and Hrotsvitha, the Russian theorist Mikhail Bakhtin of our own century investigated Greek and Roman texts and found that serious forms such as tragedy were only part of the picture; tragedy was always accompanied in ancient Greece by a satyr play. According to Bakhtin, "Parodic-travestying literature introduces the permanent corrective of laughter, or a critique on the one-sided seriousness of the lofty direct word, the corrective of reality that is always richer, more fundamental and most importantly *too contradictory and heteroglot* to be fit into a high straightforward genre" (*Dialogic* 55). We should always remember that John Kennedy Toole wrote this book during the sixties, in the midst of grimly serious social movements that cast a tragic pall on the era. Indeed, he was in the U.S. Army in Puerto Rico while writing the novel, a tale of nonconformity and its penalties. His text could thus be seen as a rounding out of a story already known by the public, a tale begun in the proletariat literature of the thirties and now taken up again in the national debates of the sixties over war, race, and sex. The ethnic humor he uses so deftly had a grim counterpart in the world Toole was facing everyday, and it sometimes pushes its way into the interstices of the comic scenes, as we have seen. For Toole, as for Bakhtin, subjects of struggle are dealt with comically first by bringing them near, because at a distance subjects are not comical, but brought closer they may be satirized, toppled, and/or transformed. "Laughter," Bakhtin states, "demolishes fear and piety before an object, before a world, making of it an object of familiar contact . . . [and] laughter delivers the object into the fearless hands of investigative experiment—both scientific an artistic—and into the hands of free experimental fantasy" (*Dialogic* 23). Laughter, paradoxically, helps us escape from ourselves in order to find ourselves and each other, an essential operation of democratic humanism—and this is perhaps the most considerable achievement of *A Confederacy of Dunces*.

WORKS CITED

Apte, Mahadev. *Humor and Laughter: An Anthropological Approach.* Ithaca, N.Y.: Cornell University Press, 1985.

Bakhtin, Mikhail. *Problems of Dostoevsky's Poetics.* Ed. and trans. Caryl Emerson. Minneapolis: University of Minnesota Press, 1984.

———. *Rabelais and His World.* Trans. Hélène Iswolsky. Bloomington: Indiana University Press, 1984.

———.*The Dialogic Imagination: Four Essays.* Ed. Michael Holquist. Trans. Caryl Emerson and Michael Holquist. Austin: University of Texas Press, 1981.

Bercovitch, Sacvan. *The Rites of Assent.* New York: Routledge, 1992.

Bell, Elizabeth S. "The Clash of World Views in John Kennedy Toole's *A Confederacy of Dunces.*" *Southern Literary Journal* 21.1 (1988): 15–22.

Daigrepont, Lloyd M. "Ignatius Reilly and the Confederacy of Dunces." *New Orleans Review* 9.3 (1982): 74–80.

Dickinson, Emily. *The Complete Poems of Emily Dickinson.* Ed. Thomas H. Johnson. Boston: Little, Brown, 1960.

Jones, Gavin. *Strange Talk: The Politics of Dialect Literature in Gilded Age America.* Berkeley: University of California Press, 1999.

Percy, Walker. "Foreword." Toole.

Roach, Joseph. *Cities of the Dead: Circum-Atlantic Performance.* New York: Columbia University Press, 1996.

Toole, John Kennedy. *A Confederacy of Dunces.* 1980. Reprint, New York: Grove, 1981.

Waters, Mary C. *Ethnic Options: Choosing Identities in America.* Berkeley: University of California Press, 1990.

Ellen Gilchrist's False Eden

The New Orleans Stories of *In the Land of Dreamy Dreams*

MARGARET BAUER

In much of early southern literature the Old South was depicted as a prelapsarian Eden. Writers of the Southern Renaissance began to recognize that the Old South more accurately exemplifies the fallen world, due in particular to its original sin, the institution of slavery. Whereas *writers* may have changed their view of the Old South, their *characters* are more stubborn and continue to hold on to their false vision of the past. Consider Quentin Compson, who, perceiving the inherent flaws in his idealistic perception of the Old South, would rather die than give up his vision. Even characters created by contemporary southern writers such as Ellen Gilchrist continue to hold on to the illusion of the paradisal Old South and attempt to maintain the New South in its image. As perhaps best illustrated in the New Orleans stories of her first book of fiction, *In the Land of Dreamy Dreams,* Gilchrist's characters strive to hold on to their view of the South as a paradisal haven—in particular, those parts of the South, like Louisiana, where the old southern codes of caste and conduct are still valued.

The source of the collection's title, a line from the song "Way Down Yonder in New Orleans"—"In the land of dreamy *scenes*"—which Gilchrist altered by substituting "Dreams" for "scenes," provides the first hint that her title of the first section of stories in the collection, "There's a Garden of Eden" (taken from another line of this song), is ironic. The five stories in this section and the last story in the next section of the book are set in New Orleans, a city of illusion and fantasy. All but one of these stories center on the wealthiest social circle within this city and thus depict characters whose lives are more than comfortable (and the one exception parodies the same character types and social hierarchies). But Gilchrist's New Orleans, like the Old South, is a false paradise: Though the city may provide all the luxuries its inhabitants could want, the people are not happy. Analyzing the first group of stories in the collection reveals that the source of these people's unhappiness lies in their attempts to maintain the illusions of their lives. They do not recognize the inherent depravity of their dream world, which is evidenced by the culture's history of slavery. Indeed, the blindness of the characters of these Gilchrist stories to the "original sin" of their social model is reflected in their continuing to support strongly the still extant caste system and patriarchal rule of the New Orleans aristocracy.

At first glance Letty Wilson, of the collection's opening story "Rich," appears to be a sensible character, if a bit cowardly, as reflected in her inability to go against the norm. She is evidently aware to some degree of the falseness of her position in New Orleans society. Explaining how "[t]he Wilsons were rich in knowing who they [a]re," the narrator says that "every year from Epiphany to Fat Tuesday they flew the beautiful green and gold and purple flag outside their house that meant that Letty had been queen of the Mardi Gras the year she was a debutante" (3). However, the narrator adds, "Not that Letty was foolish enough to take the flag seriously. Sometimes she was even embarrassed to call the yardman and ask him to come over and bring his high ladder" (3). Still, she always does, though she responds to the yardman's flattery about "'what a beautiful queen [she] made that year'" with "'Oh, hush, Preacher. I was a skinny little scared girl. It's a wonder I didn't fall off the balcony I was so scared'" (3). Then she unjustly takes out on Preacher her apparent frustration over her inability to defy society's expectations and her discomfort with this apparent insight into the foolishness of her society's rituals—"Letty would think to herself what a big phony Preacher was and wonder when he was going to try to borrow some more money from them" (3)—thereby introducing the reader to the means she and her husband, as well as the other members of their community, have of avoiding unpleasant truths about themselves and their society. They often try to find another source on which to focus their negative feelings.

Former Mardi Gras queen Letty Dufrechou is, surprisingly, married to an "outsider," Tom Wilson of Tennessee, although many of these stories reveal that the New Orleans natives usually resist outsiders. But Tom has, even before his courtship of Letty, been accepted by her social circle by "charm[ing] his way into a fraternity of wealthy New Orleans boys famed for its drunkenness and its wild practical jokes" (5). The story reveals that Tom's personality is compatible with such a fraternity; the narrator further accounts for Tom's success with the explanation, "Even the second, third, and fourth generation blue bloods of New Orleans need an infusion of new genes now and then"

(5). In return for his acceptance, Tom buys into this society's values completely (some of which values were not alien to his past experience anyway). Although he came from a poor background, he adopted as a young boy the motto "'Money . . . is what you keep score with'" (4) and engaged in gambling as early as high school, as well as in performing sleight-of-hand tricks at birthday parties for pay. Both of these activities come in handy during his adulthood. He approves loans that are clearly a gamble, and then, when such a loan falls through, he "magically" turns it into a funny story as he reveals his mistake to one of his superiors over lunch. The number of these mistakes may be evidenced by Tom's increasing weight, although he attributes the gain to his rise in stature—"'I didn't hustle my way to New Orleans all the way from north Tennessee to eat salads and melba toast'" (5)—and to his manhood: to a friend's observation that he seemed to be "'putting on a little weight,'" he responds, "'Good . . . makes me look like a man. I got a wife to look at if I want to see someone who's skinny'" (8).

Eventually "not as many people at the bank wanted to go out to lunch with [Tom] anymore. They were sick and tired of pretending his expensive mistakes were jokes" (17). But before his fall from grace, Tom "stayed busy gambling and hunting and fishing and being the life of the party at the endless round of dinners and cocktail parties and benefits and Mardi Gras functions that consume the lives of the Roman Catholic hierarchy that dominates the life of the city that care forgot" (8), revealing his total adaptation to this society in which he has chosen to live. Similarly, Letty spends her time "preoccupied with the details of their domestic life and her work in the community" (8). The narrator tells us that she "took her committees seriously and actually believed that the work she did made a difference in the lives of other people" (8), thereby suggesting that her brief insight into the triviality of her society's rituals at the beginning of the story does not affect her ability to accept the illusions of her social class.

The courtship of Tom and Letty is punctuated with clichés: "Letty fell in love with Tom the first time she laid eyes on him" (5) and "It was pronounced a marriage made in heaven" (7). Behind these clichés, however, are the troublesome facts that Tom was drunk when Letty met him and that their relationship "blossomed" after a boy drowned during a fraternity hazing accident. Tom felt guilty about the death since he hadn't liked the boy and, perhaps, too, because when he was a pledge he had been able to swim the distance that the later pledge was unable to survive. Therefore he had provided his fraternity with evidence that the required swim could be accomplished, which may have kept them from suspending that particular hazing ritual. Of course, he was certainly not the only boy to make the swim before the drowning, but such a notion does not occur to him as he suffers from guilt, which is seldom rational. After the accident, he stayed away from the fraternity house, which held unpleasant reminders of his complicity in the death, and began to spend more time with Letty, "whose plain sweet looks and expensive clothes excited him," not to mention whose father "held a seat on the New York Stock exchange" (7). Details such as Letty's expensive clothes and her father's position are dropped in to reveal the irony of the clichés quoted previously regarding their instant love and ideal marriage. Still, their marriage begins with a satisfying sex life, and Tom "*almost* never use[s] the apartment" he keeps in town "in case one of his business friends fell in love with his secretary and needed someplace to be alone with her" (9; emphasis added). Letty, for her part, *endures* sexual relations with the eventually obese Tom, who "smelled like sweat and whiskey," by "thinking about the night they were married. Every time they made love Letty pretended it was that night" (19). Again the narrator subtly but bitterly undermines the notion of high romance.

The seemingly paradisal life of Tom and Letty Wilson is disrupted after fourteen years of marriage by their oldest daughter Helen, who becomes a "problem child" around the age of nine and eventually becomes the catalyst for the final destruction of the Wilson family. However, Helen's actions are merely a manifestation of the problems inherent within the Wilsons' lifestyle. In spite of the fact that Helen is adopted, her character and actions can be traced back to one or both of her parents and the way they raised her. For example, her eating disorder, if it can be called that, because as Helen herself points out she's "'only nine years old'" (13), is not unlike her father's, a comparison she also recognizes, as evidenced in her remark, "'Daddy is fat and he eats all the ice cream he wants'" (12). Furthermore, given her father's voiced pride in his bulk, it is not surprising that the child fails to understand why there is so much concern about her weight. Similarly, the racial slurs Helen directs toward the maid who crosses her are not so very different from her mother's thoughts regarding the black yardman. Helen's mimicry of her parents' behavior reflects the story's apparent support of environment over heredity as the chief influence on behavior. And the environment here indicted is that of the upper class of New Orleans.

Although Helen is diagnosed to be suffering from "prenatal brain damage and dyslexia," the narrator undermines this notion by defining the latter as "a complicated learning disability that is a fashionable problem with children in New Orleans" (10). Furthermore, the first half of the diagnosis suggests that the doctors are complying with Helen's parents' desire to shirk responsibility for her actions: Her "brain damage," which is causing her to behave unsuitably, is "prenatal" and therefore occurred before she was in their care. Looking again, then, at the behavior that concerns Letty and Tom enough to consult several pediatricians and psychiatrists for advice, one may not find it so abnormal: "Helen couldn't concentrate on anything. She didn't like to share and she went through stages of biting other children" (10), all of which can easily be said of a number of quite "normal" children. Furthermore, the reader familiar with Gilchrist's other fiction will recognize Helen as a character similar to the prototypical Gilchrist character Rhoda Manning, the central figure of several other stories in this collection as well as other collections of Gilchrist's short fiction and a novel. Rhoda is never diagnosed as "brain-damaged" or "dyslexic," but her behavior is similarly "bratty" as she seeks the attention of her parents, who are often more interested in her brother's accomplishments than in hers. Noting the comparison may confirm the reader's suspicion that Helen, too, is misbehaving merely in an attempt to get her parents' attention.

Such a reading is also supported by events in the story itself. Backing up to the time before Helen became aggressive and hard to manage, one can find more convincing evidence of the source of Helen's problems than "prenatal brain damage [or] dyslexia." One should notice, first of all, that Tom became interested in raising Labrador retrievers at the same time that Helen was adopted. The reader is told that he "used all the latest methods for training Labs, including an electric cattle prod . . . and live ducks," and he would go through the training exercises in front of his infant daughter as though he were performing these acts for her amusement: "'Watch this, Helen,' he would call to the little girl in the stroller. . . . And he would throw a duck into the lagoon with its secondary feathers neatly clipped on the left side and its feet tied loosely together, and one of the Labs would swim out into the water and carry it safely back and lay it at his feet" (9). The cruelty of this exercise, which the infant apparently witnesses, is underlined by the narrative details that show the extent to which the duck is literally a sitting target. Immediately after this account of Tom training his dogs while Helen watched, the narrator tells of the births of four more Wilson children. The juxtaposition leads the reader to examine the connection between Helen suddenly having to share the attention of her parents with her new siblings and Tom dog training with the ducks. The reader realizes that Helen's aggressive behavior is probably a means of getting her parents' attention directed toward her again, having learned from her father's dog-training methods that he approves of aggressive tactics as a means of controlling others and getting one's own way.

Tom and Letty's reactions to their "problem child" differ: Letty is concerned and willing to put out extra effort to help Helen. She assuages possible feelings of jealousy Helen might feel toward her youngest sister, the latest child born to the Wilsons, by comparing Helen favorably to Jennifer, and she is willing to delve into Helen's biological history if it will help the child. Tom, recognizing that his children are a reflection upon him, is embarrassed by Helen's problems. He refuses to allow research into Helen's genetic background, apparently afraid of what they might find out about her that would embarrass him further. Although this refusal does not confirm the notion that Helen is actually an illegitimate but biological child of his, it does help to explain why he is suddenly afraid that "people would think she was" (17). He recognizes how much alike he and Helen are in their positions in this society; he too was, in a sense, "adopted" by this society, having been born neither in New Orleans nor of an affluent family, and he certainly does not want his past delved into. Indeed, he has left his past behind and adopted the mind-set of his new social circle, which, in this story and the next, includes preferring to wear blinders to seeing the truth about themselves and their children.

Ultimately, Tom goes so far in his acceptance of his social circle's standards of excellence as to enact the Nazi ideology of killing the afflicted in order to eliminate weak links in an otherwise seemingly ideal society. The afflicted, in this case, includes the supposedly dyslexic, brain-damaged Helen; the Labrador puppy she "ruined" by playing with it as though it were a common dog; and himself, an overweight failure in business and as a father who has recently "beg[u]n to have trouble with his vision" (17), a psychosomatic manifestation, perhaps recalling Helen's supposed dyslexia, of his obsessive fear that people believe she is his illegitimate daughter.

Tom's "fall from grace" can be traced throughout the story, but he is pushed over the edge by Helen's part in her baby sister's death, which may remind him of his own role in the death of the fraternity pledge years before. Again, then, Helen's behavior has mimicked his own. As already noted, even though Helen is adopted, Tom recognizes that she is a reflection of him. From this point on he becomes progressively more paranoid that his true nature will be discovered via her actions; for example, he is appalled by the notion that men coming home from work might hear Helen singing a ditty she has made up about the dead baby. He is obsessed with public opinion, as indicated by his perceiving the windows of a building as eyes turned upon him.

The first tragedy of the story occurs when Helen's temper leads to her baby sister being spilled from her carriage onto the sidewalk, from which accident the baby dies. The narrator describes the scene of the accident with incongruent imagery: "the blood from the baby's head began to move all over the concrete *like a little ruby lake*" (14; emphasis added). This simile is the epitome of the narrator's not-so-subtle efforts to juxtapose the Wilsons' fantastical view of the world with the reality of the events narrated. The contrast is further emphasized when the narration of this tragedy is interrupted by a paragraph about the local drugstore, from which the druggist will be summoned to help with the baby when the tragic plotline resumes. Within this digression two contrasts that allude to some truths about this community are pointed out: between this "cute drugstore made out of a frame bungalow with gingerbread trim [where e]verything inside cost twice as much as it did in a regular drugstore" and other "tacky drugstore[s] with everything on special all the time" and between the fact that "the grown people could order any kind of drugs they needed [from this drugstore] and a green Mazda pickup would bring them right over [while t]he children had to get their drugs from a fourteen-year-old pusher in Audubon Park named Leroi" (14).

Paradoxically, Tom and Letty's neighbors turn the first tragedy into an occasion for a party. After the funeral "all the people from the Garden District and from all over town started coming over to cheer them up. It looked like the biggest cocktail party ever held in New Orleans. It took four rented butlers just to serve the drinks. Everyone wanted to get in on the Wilsons' tragedy" (16–17). The party reflects their inability to confront death, to allow tragedy to affect them. The reference to the amount of alcohol served reveals how they anesthetize themselves against such knowledge of death in order to preserve their Eden.

The telling of the story's second tragedy, the deaths of Helen and Tom, is also interrupted by a quick change of scene—from the family's camp outside of town, where Tom has taken Helen, to the Wilson house, where Letty is reading to her sons and reconciling herself to another pregnancy. "God was just trying to make up to her for Jennifer," she thinks (22), oblivious to her husband's plans to kill Helen and himself. In the story Letty is reading to the boys, "a little convent girl in Paris . . . reforms the son of the Spanish ambassador, putting an end to his terrible habit of beheading chickens on a miniature guillotine" (21–22). But Letty will have no chance to "reform" her husband's recent aggressive behavior toward Helen (he had beaten the child when he caught her playing with the puppy). Picking up again with the actions of Tom and Helen at the camp, the narrator tells how Tom shoots the "ruined" Labrador, a symbol of his now-tainted position in society; Helen, also a reflection of himself; and finally himself, whom he has been trying to destroy all along, perhaps suggesting that he no longer approves of or is proud of Tom Wilson, member of the social elite of New Orleans. The narrator again employs incongruous metaphors to describe the two death scenes: "the red and gray and black *rainbow* of the dog" and the "*roses*" of blood flung from the child's splintered skull (23; emphasis added). The scene of Tom's death, however, contains no ironically romantic imagery. The narrator merely reports coldly, "Without removing his glasses or his hunting cap [Tom] stuck the .38 Smith and Wesson revolver against his palate and splattered his own head all over the new pier and the canvas covering the Boston Whaler. His body struck the boat going down and landed in eight feet of water beside a broken crab trap left over from the summer" (23). The description suggests that with Tom's death comes the end of such misplaced romanticism—for the Wilsons at least.

But the story closes from the point of view of the New Orleans society that helped to create Tom, Letty, and Helen Wilson, and this community's refusal to face reality remains constant. Although no party/funeral is described after the deaths of Tom and Helen, the five one-sentence paragraphs that end the story each reveal a fiction that this society clings to in order to keep their Eden intact: first, their refusal to face the truth ("Everyone believed it was some terrible inexplicable mistake or accident"); second, their belief that their social position would shelter them from the ugly side of life ("No one believed that much bad luck could happen to a nice lady like Letty Dufrechou Wilson, who never hurt a flea or gave a minute's trouble in her life"); third, their feeling that the divine favor that they believed shone upon them would not allow tragedy to interrupt their social calendars during the busy holiday season ("No one believed that much bad luck could get together between the fifteenth week after Pentecost and the third week in Advent"); fourth, their refusal to accept the guilt of someone within their social circle and their tendency to make excuses ("No one believed a man would kill his own little illegitimate dyslexic daughter just because she was crazy"); and fifth, the materialism and obsession with money that drives them to destruction ("And no one, not even the district attorney of New Orleans, wanted to believe a man would shoot a $3,000 Labrador retriever sired by Super Chief out of Prestidigitation") (23).

In "The President of the Louisiana Live Oak Society," the second New Orleans story of the collection, the lives of another couple are disrupted by the behavior of their child, who in this case has gotten involved with drugs. Reminding the reader of the ironic comparison noted in the previous story between the drugstore and the pusher in the park, although Lelia and Will McLaurin are terrified by the notion that their son Robert may be doing drugs, they see no connection between that possibility and their own use of alcohol and tranquilizers. Ironically, Will's plan—that he and his wife go away for a weekend to talk about what they are going to do about Robert—begins with "'drink[ing] all the way to the coast like the old days'" (32). And just before Lelia runs out of the beauty parlor to investigate how her son has planned to spend the weekend while his parents are out of town, she takes two Valium. Neither parent recognizes a connection between their substance abuse and Robert's, but as in the previous story, the reader perceives the parents' influence upon Robert's behavior.

The parental concern in this story is the reverse of the parents' reactions in "Rich." Although Lelia refuses to see the evidence that her son is experimenting with drugs, Will is concerned about Robert's behavior and looking for the source. Still, Will's concern is ineffective. Nowhere in the story does he have a conversation with his son about the problem—or about anything else. And Lelia, who insists nothing is wrong, has only one conversation with Robert prior to the final scene of the story, which ends in tragedy, and that conversation is from her car when she passes him on his bicycle. Robert's parents fight over him but do not talk to him or try to do anything for or about him.

As the previous story focuses mainly on Helen and her father, this one focuses on Robert and his mother. Just before tragedy strikes, Lelia is forced to open her eyes to the truth about her son's delinquent behavior. The events leading to the tragedy that ends this story are even more satirically narrated than in the previous story, so that the final scene of destruction, though not as violent as the triple shooting that closes "Rich," is as shocking once the reader realizes what has happened. The narrator treats Lelia as satirically as the narrator of "Rich" treats Tom. During an argument with her husband over Robert, for example, she complains, "'I don't have to hear this while I'm cooking dinner,'" and then the reader learns that "cooking dinner" involved "buttering French bread to go with the fried chicken the cook had left warming in the oven" (30). Also, the narrator moves quickly from this argument, during which Lelia absolutely refuses to "spy" on her son, to the scene at the beauty parlor when she will not even wait until her hairdresser is finished with her before she rushes out to check up on Robert, and then "park[s] the car two houses away and walk[s] across the lawn and onto her front porch . . . like a member of the CIA" (34). Her hysteria upon finding Robert's black friend Gus (who is also his drug supplier) in her home both further reinforces the narrator's earlier sarcastic tone when reporting that Lelia "was a liberal" (27) and reveals the tightrope she has been walking between sanity and neurosis. Furthermore, in her outburst Lelia reveals, too, that she has chosen to ignore what she apparently knew all along, for in the midst of her screaming, she calls Gus, whom she has seen with her son on previous occasions, a pusher. The reader recognizes that the term's usual connotations do not suit this boy; not only has Gus been encouraged to deal drugs by Lelia's son (making the latter the "push*ier*" of the two), but also the reader realizes that Robert's parents' habits (pill popping and drinking) have been much more influential than—indeed, led to—Robert's friendship with Gus.

In this story, as in "Rich," the imagery found in the final scene is incongruent with the tragedy. Caught between his mother and his friend, Robert chooses to follow Gus—right out of the window—and falls, the reader assumes once what has happened sinks in, either to his death or incurring serious injury. In making his choice between facing his mother and following Gus out the window, he "looked past the beautiful white-lacquered four-poster bed with Lelia's favorite sun hats hanging gaily from the bedposts" (36) to the door behind which his mother is screaming "six months of unscreamed screaming . . . an ancestral, a territorial scream" (35). Lelia's scream represents her fierce "territorial" drive and expresses her view of outsiders such as Gus as a threat to the sanctity of her home. Robert apparently rejects both her possessiveness and her xenophobia. He sees Gus's flight down the crepe myrtle, then, as an escape from Lelia's materialistic world. And in his drugged state he hallucinates that upon landing on the ground below, his friend "pushed off from the earth [and] began to ascend back up through the broken branches like a movie played in reverse, like a wild kite rising to meet the sun" (37), an image that recalls the black folk legend of slaves flying up from the cotton fields, away from the lash, and back to Africa while the overseer watched stupefied and helpless to stop them. Robert evidently longs for a return to a primitive culture within which people are not so neurotic as his mother willingly, even proudly, admits to being, for he jumps out of the upstairs window to join a mirage to a sound like drums in the background as his mother "beat on the door and beat on the door and beat on the door" (37).

Lelia gains knowledge just before her son's leap. She recognizes that her ideal home is an illusion. Indeed, most of the people of Gilchrist's New Orleans community strive to build an ideal home in a fallen world and are able to maintain their fantasies up to the moment of crisis. By maintaining a false Eden, however, they render themselves unable to deal with the real world, which ultimately forces its way through the mirage. And the consequence, as these two stories show, can be tragic.

Gilchrist continues to unveil the false Eden in the other New Orleans stories of this section, but beginning with "There's a Garden of Eden" the consequences of the characters' illusions are less tragic. In "There's a Garden of Eden," for example, the author focuses on how living within the safety of the "Garden" will lead, if not to tragedy, then at least to a disappointing, unfulfilling life. The protagonist of this story, a character type common in Gilchrist's canon, suffers ennui from living in her Edenic world: "Scores of men, including an ex-governor and the owner of a football team, consider Alisha Terrebone to be the most beautiful woman in the state of Louisiana. If she is unhappy what hope is there for ordinary mortals? Yet here is Alisha, cold and bored and lonely, smoking in bed" (38). The narrator's tone is clearly ironic, mocking those who presume that a beautiful, wealthy woman is without problems. But Alisha is dissatisfied with her empty life, not content to be a trophy wife or sex object. She longs for love, not just lovers, and her beauty and wealth apparently attract the wrong men.[1]

As "There's a Garden of Eden" opens, the streets of New Orleans are filling up with water after three days of constant rain, a downpour necessary, the reader may feel, to wash away the bloodshed at the end of the previous two stories. The rain also emphasizes Alisha's entrapment within her world, though in contrast to the preceding stories, she makes an effort to reject her Edenic lifestyle, first by having an affair with a younger man, a carpenter (hence, not a member of her class), and later by braving the flooded streets in a canoe with this young lover in spite of her inability to swim. As she explains to him, her parents did not let her "'do anything'" when she was a child: "'They were too afraid I'd get hurt. . . . They didn't let me ride a bicycle or roller skate or swim or anything'" (48). Like Eve in the Garden, Alisha had been protected as a child from the dangers of the outside world. Though her present life sounds as dull as her childhood, the reader learns that her ventures out of her garden led to three disappointing marriages. Consequently, she has since insulated herself within her home, choosing the tedium of Eden over the hurt of disappointment until the day she takes a risk by having an affair with this carpenter, whom she had called to do some repairs around her home. His trade recalls that of Christ, whose immanent arrival to save humankind was first promised to Adam and Eve as they were thrown out of Eden. Indeed, as a result of their affair, Alisha feels reborn, just when she "'was going to stop dying [her] hair'" (47)—that is, just when she was going to resign herself to old age. Their water voyage, then, appears to be her baptism, her acceptance of a new life outside of her flawed Eden, in spite of the risks: She feels certain that this will be the last man she will love and the first man to leave her.[2]

The otherwise uplifting ending view of Alisha courageously leaving her garden is undermined, however, by an earlier exchange between Alisha and her maid. When the maid reports that the carpenter has arrived, Alisha asks, "'Which carpenter?'" (39). The maid's answer, "Now it's going to be blue-collar workers," suggests that she knows why Alisha is asking—that is, that Alisha will get up and dressed to speak with the carpenter if he is the "'young one'" and that this is not the first time that Alisha has taken a lover so spontaneously (39). The probability of other impulsive affairs deflates Alisha's later romantic idealizing of her affair with the carpenter. A second point compromising the story's seemingly optimistic ending is that Alisha and her lover's thoughts reveal that they both fantasize during their lovemaking; thus they are not making love to each other but to ideas they have of each other, and they are simultaneously creating false images of themselves:

> Then Alisha closed her eyes and pretended she was an Indian princess lying in a tent deep in a forest, dressed in a long white deerskin robe, waiting for Jeff Chandler to come and claim her for his bride. . . .
>
> Then Michael closed his eyes and pretended he was a millionaire going to bed with a beautiful, sad old actress. (44)

Not even Michael, who leads Alisha out of her fallen garden, can rescue her if she chooses fantasy over reality. Furthermore, Michael's potential to be a savior is undermined by his desire for wealth, apparent in his fantasy; he seems to want to share Alisha's lifestyle rather than help her to escape it.

In "The Famous Poll at Jody's Bar" Gilchrist picks up again with the criticism of New Orleans class consciousness found in the collection's first two stories, though here the author takes an even more satiric—and much less tragic—approach to the theme. The story is set in New Orleans, but the characters do not all belong to the privileged upper class. With a group of characters from various social backgrounds, who share a common taste for alcohol, Gilchrist parodies the classism of New Orleans. The setting for the main action is a bar that

> didn't cater to just anyone that happened to drop by to get a drink or lay a bet. It was the oldest neighborhood bar in the Irish Channel section of New Orleans, and its regular customers included second- and third-generation drinkers from many walks of life. Descendants of Creole blue bloods mingled easily with house painters and deliverymen stopping by for a quick one on their route. (53)

Though social position does not matter in this bar so long as the man is able to hold his liquor, racism and sexism are still evident. When the bar's regulars are first introduced, the proprietor is discussing what he would do if a "nigger" were to come in and try to hold him up. The narrator explains shortly afterwards that

> no woman, no matter what her tale of woe, had ever managed to get [Jody] to call a man to the phone.
>
> "Not here," he would answer curtly, "haven't seen him." And Jody would hang up without offering to take a message. If a woman wanted a man at Jody's she had to come look for him in person. (54)

That a woman would do so, except in cases of extreme emergency, is unlikely, considering her gender's implicit "welcome" at the bar as it is further reflected in the reference to the ladies' restroom. When one of the patrons paid off his sixty-dollar bar tab by fixing a broken window in the ladies' room merely by boarding it up with scrap lumber rather than replacing the glass, everyone laughed, and Jody has thus far allowed the "repair" job to stand as is. Evidently, he does not care that the restroom must now be dim and stuffy. Furthermore, going on right outside of the bar at this time is the poll referred to in the title, which is being conducted to decide whether one of Jody's regular customers, forty-eight-year-old Prescott Hamilton IV, should marry his longtime sweetheart Emily Anne Hughes. Prescott is respected at this bar, not so much for the aristocratic background implied by his name as for "his notoriously hollow leg" when it comes to his drinking (55), and so the bar's patrons are concerned about his getting married and breaking up their party.

Their opinion of marriage is summed up by the instigator of the poll, Wesley Labouisse, as he talks to the men while they vote:

> "Take all the time you need to make up your mind. Think about your mother and father. Think about what it's like to have a woman tell you when to come home every night and when to get up in the morning and when to take a bath and when to talk and when to shut up. Think about what it's like to give your money to a woman from now till the day you die. Then just write down your feelings about whether a perfectly happy man ought to get himself married." (54)

Prescott himself is indifferent about the matter, except that he worries that Emily Anne's yard might fail to suit his Labradors, a concern that reflects his priorities: Emily Anne comes second to his dogs. Still, if one respondent votes yes, he will go through with the wedding; he has given his word of honor. However, Wesley seems only to be asking men to vote, in spite of the sign he put up claiming that "THIS POLL IS BEING CONDUCTED WITHOUT REGARD TO SEX OR PREVIOUS CONDITIONS OF SERVITUDE" (54). Considering the men's conversations, one cannot imagine that a woman or an African American of either sex would venture close enough to this bar to test for any such discrimination.

Gilchrist exacts revenge on these male chauvinistic racists and exposes their false macho bravado when she has the story's protagonist, Nora Jane Whittington, successfully hold up the bar with a stage pistol and lock the men up in the small, dark, and airless ladies' room. As she is leaving the bar dressed as a nun (reflective, perhaps, of the author's view that Nora Jane would be better off living such a cloistered life than married to any of these men), Nora Jane drops a vote in the ballot jar. On the one hand the reader hopes it is a yes vote, which would destroy the men's belief that they share a common point of view regarding marriage. On the other hand one would not wish Prescott on poor Emily Anne, who would be better off donning the nun's habit and taking vows of celibacy.

Through Nora Jane's story, however, Gilchrist also criticizes members of her own sex who tolerate the way men such as these treat women. Nora Jane's purpose for robbing the bar is to finance a trip to California to find her boyfriend Sandy. Promising to send for her as soon as he was settled, Sandy took the money he and Nora Jane had made together through small holdups around the city and left for California. Weeks have passed since then and she has received no word from him; and yet, in the last image of Nora Jane in the story, she is "making her a path . . . to a boy who was like no other. To the source of all water" (59). The analogy between Sandy and "the source of all water" reflects Nora Jane's view of him as the source of life for her. Indeed, early in the story, the narrator explains that Nora Jane's main goal in life was to have a boyfriend. In spite of her own strength she views a man as life giving and depends on him for her happiness, a weakness she shares with several of Gilchrist's other women characters throughout her canon, including Alisha of the preceding story, who is prompted to get out of bed and dressed and come out of her room only by the possibility of an affair. Thus this story's ending further undermines the seemingly positive ending to "There's a Garden of Eden" by illuminating the possible negative consequences of Alisha creating a fantasy around her new lover: She could, like Nora Jane, merely be used and deserted. In the later Nora Jane stories, which appear in subsequent Gilchrist volumes, this young woman will continue to chase Sandy as he walks in and out of her life until she replaces him with another man who is less self-centered and more devoted to her needs.

The fifth New Orleans story, the title story of the collection, contains all of the themes that are central to these stories—oppression by the patriarchy, class consciousness, xenophobia and racism, and reliance upon tradition—and thus depicts perhaps most fully the "land of dreamy dreams" in which these Gilchrist characters live until reality intrudes. Like Alisha, LaGrande McGruder is a spoiled member of the New Orleans leisure class. The story's other central point of view, Claiborne Redding, is akin to other members of the patriarchy—fathers, husbands, and brothers—who oppress Gilchrist's female protagonists throughout her canon. LaGrande and Claiborne's shared nemesis, Roxanne Miller—a Yankee, a Jew, a woman, and a member of the nouveau riche—represents the reality that will intrude upon their dream that nothing has changed to threaten their positions in the South. Finally, Nailor, the black "chief groundskeeper and arbiter of manners among the hired help" (68), recalls the "happy darky" in plantation literature, particularly the house slaves who accepted and even promoted the notion of a hierarchy of human beings—since they were not at the bottom of the ladder. The reader may sense, however, that like Deacon in *The Sound and the Fury,* Nailor has gained power by playing well the role in which his white employers wish to see him.

Reminiscent of Flannery O'Connor, Gilchrist sets LaGrande, Claiborne, and even Nailor against Roxanne, an unlikeable grotesque with a crippled foot, which, O'Connor style, ultimately reflects the woman's deformed character. Roxanne Miller is also reminiscent of Faulkner's Thomas Sutpen: Both characters are determined to become members of the very groups who view them as their inferiors. Like Sutpen, Roxanne may acquire the social accouterments of the southern aristocracy, but she will never be viewed as "one of them." Scorning such people who, even themselves discriminated against, still wish to become a part of the aristocracy, Gilchrist is as critical, if not more critical, of Roxanne than she is of LaGrande and Claiborne. The narrative voice of this short story repeatedly mocks Roxanne's behavior and even makes fun of her deformity, calling the reader's attention to the flaw in her ambition.

Roxanne has been allowed into the Lawn Tennis Club because of her husband's wealth. Claiborne is disgusted with the changes she brings to the club, beginning with her Jewish presence but including her "petitions to change the all-white dress rule," her "campaign[s] for more court privileges for women," and her idea of "percolated coffee in Styrofoam cups with plastic spoons and some kind of powder instead of cream" (63). In spite of being a member of a younger generation than Claiborne's—and a woman—LaGrande reacts no less negatively to the new member. She "never returned [Roxanne's] phone calls, avoided her at the club, made vacant replies to her requests for matches" (62), and criticized her for being too "'*eager*'" (63), a quality supposedly indicative of Roxanne's lack of refinement. In her development of LaGrande's conflict, too, then, Gilchrist turns her satirical eye upon another woman who supports her own oppression and, more generally, reminds the reader of how many southern women continue to be among the strongest advocates for the patriarchal social system. Similarly, even Nailor, a member of another race against which this club discriminates, "hated the new members worse than Claiborne did" (68). He too is territorial: "If it was up to [him] no one but a few select players would ever be allowed to set foot on his Rubico courts. The only time of day when he was really at peace was the half hour from when he finished the courts around 7:15 each morning until they opened the iron gates at 7:45 and the members started arriving" (68). In her characterization of LaGrande and Nailor, Gilchrist reveals how prevalent discrimination is in this society: Even the oppressed themselves, in turn, discriminate.

Like Lelia in "The President of the Louisiana Live Oak Society," Claiborne, LaGrande—and again, even Nailor—are xenophobic. They see any strange element as a threat to the sanctity of their environment rather than as an addition to their culture. Claiborne and LaGrande therefore condone cheating, a shocking breach of southern honor, when it is enacted against such an intruder. LaGrande finally agrees to play a match with Roxanne, who corners her at a party while she is trying to seduce "a famous psychiatrist-player from Washington" (63). In this detail, LaGrande, like Alisha, recalls the composite personality of much of Gilchrist's fiction, who is often engaged in similar seductions. Also echoing the false racial tolerance of Letty Wilson and Lelia McLaurin of the first two stories, LaGrande hopes to impress her quarry with her "altruistic" tolerance of "all kinds" but succeeds only in making a match date with Roxanne and a one-night stand with the doctor.

In consideration of Roxanne's disability, LaGrande is careful at the beginning of their match not to lob the ball; however, to save the match in the end she deliberately miscalls one of Roxanne's serves, which so unnerves her opponent that LaGrande is able to catch up and win. Claiborne is watching and, by his silence, approves the action, in "violation of a code he had lived by all his life" (70).

As in the endings to "There's a Garden of Eden" and "The Famous Poll at Jody's Bar," one cannot be optimistic about LaGrande's decision after the match to give up playing tennis, a symbol of her life of leisure in that for "as long as she could remember LaGrande had been playing tennis four or five hours a day whenever it wasn't raining or she didn't have a funeral to attend" (60). She seems to be making a significant sacrifice, for as Jeanie Thompson and Anita Miller Garner explain, tennis is "the only thing important in [her] life other than her integrity and pride at being at least a third-generation member of the New Orleans Lawn Tennis Club" (Thompson and Garner 104). She may throw her tennis racket off the Huey P. Long Bridge, thereby giving up the only meaningful thing she had left after cheating, but then, after considering what "to do with the rest of her life," she drives to a Gus Mayer department store and buys "one each of every single thing she could possibly imagine needing" and then drives to the Country Club, where, she had noted earlier, they still hadn't allowed Jews to infiltrate, in search of a man to distract her for the rest of the day (71). One imagines that, like Alisha, she will spend many days "cold and bored and lonely, smoking in bed" or out seeking moments of excitement from affairs, which will probably end as disappointingly as her night with the tennis-playing psychiatrist did.

The story "In the Land of Dreamy Dreams" can ultimately be read as an analogy of the Reconstruction era, for in this story Gilchrist reduces the fall of the New South to the end of the racial "purity," caste system, and patriarchal rule of a New Orleans tennis club. First she makes descendant of southern aristocracy Claiborne Redding watch helplessly as a Yankee Jewish woman slowly takes over the management of a prestigious New Orleans tennis club. Then she employs elements of parody when she has the protagonist, modern southern belle LaGrande McGruder, play a duel-like tennis game against the intruder to defend southern tradition, refer to this tennis match between herself (champion of the southern white aristocrats) and Roxanne (a Yankee Jewish intruder) as "Armageddon" (69), and think that her state of mind after cheating at this game of tennis is equivalent to "what it feels like to die" (60). In addition, this reference to death serves to illuminate how LaGrande's breach of honor, not to mention her prejudices, reflects the false paradise in which these and the other New Orleans citizens in this book live. The characters may not have to work the land to survive, and their lives may be spent lounging in bed, drinking with friends, playing tennis, or having affairs, but the city is not a paradise. It is only a place of illusion and fantasy, a "Land of Dreamy Dreams."

Separated from the other New Orleans stories by being placed at the end of the next section of the collection is the last New Orleans–set story in *In the Land of Dreamy Dreams:* "Indignities." Its placement calls attention to the thematic difference between this story and the other New Orleans stories, except perhaps for "There's a Garden of Eden." Just as "There's a Garden of Eden," placed at the center of the first section of stories, gives a bit of a respite from the criticism of classism in the other New Orleans stories, "Indignities" is less concerned with issues of class and racial prejudices than it is with the quality of the emotional life of the characters of the upper class. Also, the narrator's mother (in "Indignities") seems to have viewed her life as one extended party, as do the other characters who live a life of leisure in this Edenic city. Unlike these others, she is aware from the start of the story of the fact that she is not living in Eden. Having been struck by cancer, she does not feel invincible, and therefore, unlike many of the characters discussed earlier, she is prepared for immanent destruction. Her joie de vivre comes in part from an awareness of her mortality rather than from refusing to accept responsibility.[3]

At the point at which "Indignities" opens, Melissa's mother, who is not named in the story, has just had a mastectomy. She dies before its close. In between, Melissa reports how her mother handles her illness in her own unique way: "In front of twenty-six invited guests in the King's Room at Antoine's," a fancy New Orleans restaurant, "[s]he took off her Calvin Klein evening jacket and her beige silk wrap-around blouse and her custom-made brassiere and walked around the table letting everyone look at the place where her breasts used to be" (103). She accepts the inevitable—her death—and advises her daughter, "'Sell everything and fly to Paris'" and "'rise above the categories'" (104). Her advice to her daughter is, in essence, to live fully. Her only regret echoes somewhat Alisha's reference to her hair in "There's a Garden of Eden." She complains that she "'never had time to grow out [her] gray hair'" (105). Remembering that Alisha's plan "'to stop dying [her] hair'" (47) reflects her intention to accept old age, one can see in Melissa's mother's simple regret a much greater one: She will never grow old. Old age, then, is an experience she, who strove in her lifetime to experience everything, will miss.

The story closes with Melissa's mother's funeral, during which her *guests* (rather than mourners—her funeral is another reason for a party, as in "Rich," though in this case it does not seem inappropriate to the reader) celebrate her courage to try anything while her daughter recalls both her mother's neglect—"'I remember the *week* she played with me'"—and the creative gift her mother shared with her: "'She called and had a piano crate delivered and we turned it into a house and painted murals all over the walls'" (107; emphasis added). With these words about her childhood, Melissa remarks upon her feelings of being neglected by her flamboyant mother, but at the same time she notes her appreciation for her mother's uniqueness. Rather than meekly accepting her role as wife and mother, Melissa's mother explored her creative impulses. Consequently, she was not an ideal mother, but she also did not leave Melissa with the sense that her opportunities were limited by her sex.

Ironically, in spite of the death at the story's end, which reminds the reader of the first two stories of the collection, "Indignities" is the most optimistic of all the New Orleans stories. Melissa's mother has used the "dream-like" atmosphere of New Orleans to get the most joy out of her life that she could, a legacy she passes on to her daughter. Significantly, the mother dies and the daughter lives (in contrast to the two mothers who live while their children die in the first two stories). One might even say that the mother dies *so that* her daughter might live. Certainly from her mother's life and death Melissa learns a lesson about living fully in the short time one has in this world. Melissa's mother's role as a "savior" figure is reminiscent of the similar role played by Alisha's young lover, thus recalling his positive (even if only temporarily so) influence upon Alisha's life. Hence the reader who groups this story with the earlier New Orleans stories is left, rather than with the images of Alisha Terrebone and LaGrande McGruder seeking casual lovers with whom they can pass an afternoon, the images of Alisha venturing out in the canoe and of Melissa recognizing her inheritance of creativity. And the image of New Orleans is transformed from a false Eden to a land where dreams can come true—that is, if one's dreams are grounded in the real world.

Ellen Gilchrist occasionally set later works in New Orleans—part of her first novel, *The Annunciation,* a couple of stories in her prize-winning collection *Victory over Japan,* and some of the works involving another of Gilchrist's recurrent characters, Crystal Manning Mallison Weiss, and members of her family—but the author did not write another such cluster of New Orleans–set stories. She did, however, continue to develop the character types and themes of these New Orleans stories—even as her stories departed this city and moved on to Mississippi, Indiana, and even Seattle—in the other stories of this collection and in her other books, to other areas of the country and occasionally outside of it. Characters similar to the protagonists of these stories—particularly Helen Wilson of "Rich," Alisha Terrebone of "There's a Garden of Eden," LaGrande McGruder of "In the Land of Dreamy Dreams," and Melissa's mother of "Indignities"—can be found throughout Gilchrist's canon, and Nora Jane Whittington of "The Famous Poll at Jody's Bar" becomes a recurrent character in several later collections of Gilchrist's short fiction.[4] In stories and novels with central characters much like these, the author continues to explore the sexism, racism, and overall xenophobia of other closed societies and the consequences of such intolerance to all. These are not, she thereby implies, attitudes exclusive to a particular social class of New Orleans, Louisiana.

NOTES

1. Parts of the discussion of "There's a Garden of Eden" appear in my book *The Fiction of Ellen Gilchrist* (Gainesville: University Press of Florida, 1999).

2. Alisha's affair with the younger man is typical of Gilchrist's older women characters throughout her fiction. Michael's occupation as a carpenter, his moonlighting as a musician, and Alisha's "baptism" through her experiences with him anticipate, in particular, Gilchrist's first novel, *The Annunciation.* Furthermore, as Alisha and Michael glide through the flooded streets, the narrator remarks that "Alisha . . . had been delivered of an angel" (47). This comment, together with the canoe trip, may have sparked one of the ideas for Gilchrist's first novel. In *The Annunciation,* Amanda McCamey also begins an affair with a much younger man, also a laborer/musician, just at the time when she "'meant to get old'" (*Annunciation* 193). This younger man, Will Lyons, is associated in the novel with the angel Gabriel, echoing the narrator's imagery (quoted above) in "There's a Garden of Eden." Also like Alisha's lover, Will quite literally gives Amanda back her youth: After their first sexual

encounter Amanda starts menstruating for the first time in years and thinks, "I'm still alive. I'm not old yet" (164). Amanda, too, takes a canoe trip with her young lover, and, although she, unlike Alisha, does know how to swim, when the canoe tips over, throwing her into the speeding current, she is helpless against the power of the rushing water. Like Michael, then, Will serves as his lover's savior as he rescues her.

3. "Indignities" introduces a motif that will recur throughout Gilchrist's canon: cancer. In particular, this story anticipates Gilchrist's second novel, *The Anna Papers,* the central character of which, Anna Hand, is also stricken with the fatal disease. Anna's attitude toward life and her behavior upon learning that she has cancer are similar to the attitude and behavior of Melissa's mother, which will be discussed subsequently.

4. The Nora Jane stories have been collected in a volume called *Nora Jane: A Life in Stories.*

WORKS CITED

Gilchrist, Ellen. *The Anna Papers.* Boston: Little, Brown, 1988.

———. *The Annunciation.* Boston: Little, Brown, 1983.

———. *In the Land of Dreamy Dreams.* Boston: Little, Brown, 1981.

———. *Nora Jane: A Life in Stories.* Boston: Little Brown, 2005.

———. *Victory over Japan.* Boston: Little, Brown, 1984.

Thompson, Jeanie, and Anita Miller Garner. "The Miracle of Realism: The Bid for Self-Knowledge in the Fiction of Ellen Gilchrist." *Southern Quarterly* 22.1 (1983): 100–114. Reprinted in *Women Writers of the Contemporary South.* Ed. Peggy Whitman Prenshaw. Jackson: University Press of Mississippi, 1984. 233–48.

Intimacy and/in Distance

The Poetry of Pinkie Gordon Lane

CAROLYN M. JONES

A native of Philadelphia, Pennsylvania, Pinkie Gordon Lane, the former poet laureate of the state of Louisiana (1989–1992), has lived in Louisiana since 1956. A graduate of Spelman College, she was the first African American woman to receive a doctorate from Louisiana State University. Her poetry is inspired by Gwendolyn Brooks (see Lowe 9, 12,13) and Anne Sexton (21). Her volumes of poetry include *Wind Thoughts* (1972), *The Mystic Female* (1978), *I Never Scream* (1985), *Girl at the Window* (1991), and *Elegy for Etheridge* (2002). Lane was nominated for the Pulitzer Prize in 1979 for *The Mystic Female,* and she has worked tirelessly as a poet, lecturer, book reviewer, and teacher. Many of her poems have been set to music by Dinos Constanides (Lowe 1), and she is also a painter. She headed the Department of English at Southern University, where she was a faculty member for twenty-six years (Lowe 16), for a number of years. In her most recent book of poems, *Elegy for Etheridge,* Lane writes a poem titled "On Being Head of the English Department" that begins with her everyday tasks—

> the signing of contracts,
> the ordering of books,
> and making of schedules— (*Elegy* 5)

but affirms her detachment from those so that she can keep "the music and art / of my existence" (5). "I am love," the poem ends, signaling one of Lane's key themes.

Lane is the only surviving child of William Alexander Gordon and Inez Addie West Gordon; four other children did not live beyond infancy. Violet Harrington Bryan, in "Evocations of Place and Culture," suggests that Lane's being an only child and a surviving child evoked an existential loneliness in her poetry (Bryan 58). Although I would agree that there is distance and a sense of the solitary in Lane's poetry, I would like to suggest that it also contains intimacy, achieved by balancing the inner and outer, the self and the other. This balance is physical, mental, and emotional and is achieved by the linking quality of which the imagination is capable. The evidence of balance is the poetic image that marks the open, perhaps alien space of the page and the world, locating the poet and the reader. I want to suggest that Lane's poetry demonstrates a quality of intimacy marked by her position as the exile (Marranca 26; Lowe 2). This position allows her to express and, most important, to be "love," as she says in "On Being Head of the English Department." In this essay I want to examine Lane's notion of the horizon and/as the position of the poet and how poetic distance heals the distance of time and space and makes love. I want to look at the themes that emerge in two of Lane's volumes of poetry, *I Never Scream,* the phrase that John Lowe calls her "artistic credo" (Lowe 4), and *Girl at the Window.* I will focus on two of her series, "Baton Rouge Poems" and "Poems to My Father," and particularly on one, to me, of her most spectacular poems, "Girl at the Window."

John Lowe remarks that Pinkie Gordon Lane is "in a way an exile" (2) because she left her home in Philadelphia to live and work in Louisiana. As Edward Said reminds us, the exile is not one who is homeless and dislocated but one who is from two homes (Marranca). The exile, as one intimately located in two places—and in Lane's case, three—can, from that double, even multiple, consciousness, make a critique and assessment of both locations. Lane, as exile, breaks down the dichotomies of margin and center and, therefore, authoritative discourses in a way that only a poet in this unique position can. Her images are strong and make a revisioning that is almost pictorial.

Not content to deprivilege and deconstruct, Lane links what might be forever separate—Philadelphia and Baton Rouge, self and self, daughter and father, and an awake woman in a sleeping world—creating a sense of place in two ways. First she reminds us of the southern sense of landscape and how human beings, through their experiences and work, shape it, forming acknowledged and unacknowledged intimacies and generating social configurations that may be restrictive or liberating. Lane tells John Lowe that the "natural environment" influences her poetry significantly (Lowe 5). Second, she reminds us, as Michel de Certeau does, that landscape is, at the same time, a space of play in which the human being enacts freedom.[1] Lane says that "the natural environment always becomes a metaphor for me in my work" (Lowe

8). Marilyn B. Craig has called Lane "a highly subjective and autobiographical poet whose work constitutes a transcript of the various dimensions of herself" (Craig 231). But Charles Rowell reminds us that Lane, although beginning with self, ultimately links person and world:

> At the center of the poetry of Pinkie Gordon Lane is the lyric voice of the reflective humanist whose words gracefully recreate fragments of the private and public worlds of the poet—our worlds, ultimately, held passionately in time; our worlds illuminated with integrity, our worlds directed sincerely towards love. (Rowell 8)

Lane generates this linkage by the use of active present tense and a series of metaphors, what she calls "perceptual pictures" (Lowe 19) or "metaphorical images":[2]

> In the way I use the term metaphor it includes all the figures of speech—simile, synecdoche, apostrophe, hyperbole. I use the word to describe all non-literal expressions. There is always a comparison of one thing with another. The comparison is always the basis of a metaphor or image. Imagery is a generalized term, and I use the adjective metaphorical, not metaphor, and, therefore, I embrace the whole concept. (Rowell 24)

These images include natural metaphors, such as wind and the horizon; metaphors of character, such as patience and silence; and metaphors of hope, such as love. Lane rarely uses the past tense in her poems; the powerful "Rain Ditch," a poem about African American children who, denied access to public swimming pools, swim in a dangerous and polluted rain ditch—a "death trap"—is an exception (*Scream* 21). With these qualities of her poetry in mind, I first want to set Lane's poetry within some of the themes that characterize African American poetry. Second, I will turn to Lane's particular metaphors, and, finally, I will describe how those make hers a uniquely Louisiana voice.

Bernard W. Bell, in *Modern and Contemporary Afro-American Poetry*, suggests that the Harlem Renaissance passed forward four concerns or themes for African American poetry. These include an interest in Africa; a rediscovery and reevaluation of African American folk values; an elevation of members of the African American masses, particularly the working class, as heroes and models; and the introduction of the blues, jazz, ballads, sermons, and African American vernacular language as sources of poetic material (Bell 8).

Lane's interest in these themes places her in the tradition of African American poetry and its concerns. Bell's themes are part of the African American necessity of witness—what I want to call "testifying," taking the term from black church tradition. Testifying involves a number of particularly African American concerns and actions. These include signification, a seriously playful attitude toward the received tradition and the master narrative; protest, an active stance against evil; celebration, a sense of joy and thankfulness; and healing, the capacity to move the reader through the experience that shatters wholeness and innocence toward a mature, earned identity that can negotiate pain and experience joy. Without test, there is no testimony.

Lane's poetry offers a powerful testimony to the situation of African Americans. Her poetry witnesses to the past and present and sets forth their implications for the future to both an audience ready to receive this testimony and to an audience, perhaps, unprepared to hear it. As June Jordan puts it in the introduction to *Soulscript: Afro-American Poetry,* African American poetry is written "in tears, in rage, in hope, in sonnet, in blank/free verse, in overwhelming rhetorical scream. These poems redeem a hostile vocabulary; they witness, they create communion, and they contribute beauty to the long evening of their origins" (Jordan xvii–xix).

Lane's poetry, at first, seems quiet when compared to Jordan's statement. Lance Jeffers has commented, however, that Lane's poetry is gentle in introspection and observation but has a "tough underneath" (cited in Rowell 8). Lane emphasizes—indeed, forces—us to use all our senses to maintain attention. Her work makes us hear, as she utilizes the rhythms and content of music, and it makes us see, as she paints vivid images. This sensuality moves the reader beyond mere reading and gives the poems an almost physical as well as psychic impact. As she writes in "Yesterday's Sculptors," the bodily senses of hearing and touch, in addition to rational thought, shape who we are—a theme that runs throughout Lane's poetry—and we must be active in gaining perspective and in framing and molding identity and possibility:

> I listen for sound
> of memory, reach into the past
> fondle the relics
> the fragments of color and pain
> the segments of joy
> molding me into my today
> framing my tomorrow.
>
> Shall we forget the past?
> I don't think so. (*Scream* 27)

Second, Lane's poetry signifies; it utilizes and transforms received cultural traditions and cultural instances. Numerous critics have suggested that African American poetry simultaneously utilizes and discards, patterns itself on, and signifies on the canon. Dudley Randall, in his introduction to *The Black Poets,* suggests that although early African American poetry—from Phillis Wheatley to the poets of the Harlem Renaissance—admired and utilized the canonical forms, African American poetry, particularly since the 1960s, rejected them and moved in new directions (Randall xxv). They moved toward folk life and language, music, and other African American forms, challenging and changing language.

Pinkie Gordon Lane's "gentle" poetry exhibits such searing signification. Lance Jeffers, as we noted, commented that Lane's poems have a tough "underneath" (cited in Rowell 8). Indeed, her voice is so quiet at times that in the militant 1960s, hers was not accepted as "African American poetry" (see Lowe 4). Lane tells us that Dudley Randall, though confirming her work as authentically African American because it is written by an African American, called it "another kind of black poetry" (Randall xxvi), balancing intimacy with emotion with interpretative distance.

For example, "Sexual Privacy of Women on Welfare" responds to a welfare questionnaire, designed for women with illegitimate children, uncovered by the ACLU. The application ignores human feeling. As Lane shows us, it mixes intimate and deep human questions with bureaucratic jargon, revealing the absurdity of such a questionnaire and its blindness to human beings in need. The poem, signifying on the absurdity, reveals the deep pain of women facing child rearing and life alone.

> When and where did you first
> confront loneliness?
> When and where did you resist
> the urge to die?
> Did you pull a blind around
> your sorrow?
> Was anyone present? If yes, give
> names and dates and addresses. (*Scream* 64; *Elegy* 10)

Such signification is a form of protest, which is the third theme of African American poetry. "Rain Ditch" is such a protest poem. Its juxtaposition of the great fun the children are having in their "swimming pool" with the danger in which a racist society puts them is chilling. The children, remembering their fun, long to repeat the experience, though it puts them in a "death trap" (*Scream* 21). Lane's survival of that trap and her voicing of the danger is her protest against the circumstances of African American people in a racist society. Her concern for justice is wide. On reading "On This Louisiana Day" and finding in a poem on nature and existence a protest about Bangladesh, Lane confesses, "Yeah, my poems are political in the sense that I protest anything that victimizes what I called 'the underdog'" (Lowe 6).

Lane's quiet voice still resists. For example, "A Quiet Poem" speaks softly but also in protest. It begins:

> This will be a quiet poem.
> Black people don't write
> many quiet poems
> because what we feel
> is not a quiet hurt. (*Scream* 26)

The strength of Lane's protest is that Lane, in recognizing the pain of African American people, nevertheless writes what she is not supposed to be able to write: a quiet poem to soothe and heal the hurt spirit. The poem celebrates the evening and heals with "hushed singing" and "light that has no end." Nothing disrupts. There is "no breaking / of the planes, or brambles / thrusting out" (*Scream* 26). Quiet pervades Lane's poem as a source of and as a balm for the soul.

Quiet and balance emerge in Lane's poems in human interaction, however painful, with the world and are worked toward and expressed in her particular metaphors of patience and silence, wind, and horizon, and love. These metaphors describe the human being struggling to find a midpoint between an intimacy that is consuming and a distance that is alienating. Lane's metaphors intertwine to achieve and express this healing quiet and balance.

Lane's poetic distance is expressed through images of patience and silence, what Lane calls "hushed waiting" (*Scream* 18). Hushed waiting is not a passive position. Waiting is, for Lane, an act of attention that includes seeing the world clearly and responding to it appropriately—and by doing so cultivating identity, a definition of self that opens up reality and makes connection to the "other" possible. Silence shapes, reveals, and heals. It defines the contours of existence. As historian of religions, Charles H. Long, has put it, silence is

> radically ironic. . . . It forces us to realize that our words, the unities of our naming and recognition in the world, presuppose a reality which is prior to our naming and doing. . . . [Silence is a] fundamentally ontological position . . . which though involved in language and speech expose us to a new kind of reality and experience. (Long 60–61)

Lane has said:

> I use the silence in two ways. In one way it can be a form of terror because of a lack of communication. In another form, it is a way of getting back into yourself—a kind of existential cutting yourself loose and getting back into the perimeters of your own confines. Existentially, we're all alone and there is no way I can totally communicate with you, even while we're talking. (Bryan 58)

Silence opens us to the experience of self and other while, as Lane's final comment indicates, preserving the integrity of self and other. Silence and waiting involve risk, as the epigraph to "Listenings" illustrates. The epigraph is Jewel Prestage's question, "How much of yourself are you willing to risk?" Waiting can carry one "out to the sea" (*Scream* 20), both in the negative sense of being lost and in the positive sense of opening the self to adventure, to new thoughts, and to new experiences. Something as simple as listening to squirrels run on the roof of the house and the following silence as they stop can risk the self, Lane suggests. The world is full of possibilities for love and expansion but also for shutting the self away and losing the capacity for connection.

In "Breathing" Lane expresses this opening up as a reaching the "last frontier of time / of space, / a path of no return" (*Scream* 18). The movement is a reflexive and meditative one, a movement in as well as out. The poet, as explorer, has reached "the last frontier" while settling into the world of "hushed/waiting," quiet and patience. The in-and-out of breathing, the basis of meditation, sets the settled poet on the "path of no/return." That "no/return" signals a profound change in the self brought about by the stillness and observation of the poet. The poet experiences the "no/return" limitation: There is no going back. "Return" as the final word of the poem, however, breaks the limit. It suggests that the stretching of the self beyond its ordinary boundaries, the walls of the room and of the house in which the poem begins, does not dissolve the self but strengthens it, bringing it, finally, into "familiar territory" as the "other is encountered and understood. The old place becomes a new space. The change is, simultaneously, a finding of self and a demand for homecoming: "No. Return! Come back!"

The poem is that which anchors the poet while opening her to a larger reality. Her familiar place is maintained and transformed as she enters new space and records that encounter in the poem. In a poem like "Wind Thoughts," Lane again expresses that poetry is like breathing. In this poem, the poet is led to a place by the wind, a frequent metaphor of Lane's poetry indicating the creative spirit that dislocates us from the familiar. Yet, the poet, taken by the wind is oriented, held in place, by stillness and breath, the human "wind." Breath can be "planted" in a particular place/moment to open a meaning and to express a reality.

In "Midnight Song," the writing of the poem itself is the device for expansion of the self, as the poem breaks through the walls of the poet's room. The poem is organic; it "plants itself / and grows" (*Scream* 15) over the boundaries of the page, revealing that its beauty is greater than simple words. It has the power to transform and to connect the poet's and the readers' thoughts,

> . . . spreading fan-like
> at all points
> caught up in a web
> of light—
> a ring of gold painting the earth. (*Scream* 15)

That each line and stanza flows into the next and that the poem ends without final punctuation expresses the ever-opening yet ever-interdependent and intertwined quality of consciousness that the poet experiences and offers in poetry. From the stillness of the poet, her breath, her patience, and her silence come a flowering of the self, the opening of a fan, and the extension of that flowering to others, in the web of connection and the ring of gold.

This opening shifts the gaze of the poet and the reader. Lane uses the image of the horizon to indicate this widening of gaze. As Hans-Georg Gadamer tells us in *Truth and Method,* although knowledge can never be complete, given our existential situations (Gadamer 269), we are not bound to one fixed vantage point. The horizon is what can be seen from a particular vantage point, as Lane demonstrates in her work, but, Gadamer suggests, the horizon is not a rigid frontier. It is something that moves with one and invites one to advance further" (Gadamer 217).

The horizon involves perception and interpretation. In terms of perception and community, the horizon involves the fact that each time we experience awareness of an object or person, we perceive involves a frame of features of that object or person that are not directly presented. In other words, we bring a frame of reference to every encounter. To understand an/other, we must, to some extent, let go of our own frameworks and enter into his or her horizon—a new space—so that interpretation becomes possible—so that we may become aware of the otherness and the "indissoluble individuality"(Gadamer 272) of that person.

In terms of hermeneutics, we do not—perhaps cannot—always completely articulate the context, the cultural traditions or the place, out of which we make meaning. The received cultural tradition provides the horizon within which the interpreter is capable of making other meanings. Yet, Gadamer argues, the horizon is always moving. It is "something into which we move and that moves with us. Horizons change for a person who is moving. Thus the horizon of the past, out of which all human life lives and which exists in the form of tradition, is always in motion" (Gadamer 271).

In this sense, the African American poet, engaging in signification, plays on the tradition, stretching it beyond its usual interpretative frame to include meanings that have been unacknowledged in the master/metanarrative. The poet looks to the horizon as a source of power. The gaze is a gesture of looking beyond the everyday life, yet, at the same time, the poet marks the horizon with her own interpretative voice. Gadamer argues that the process of engaging the horizon is the process of distinguishing, that this process is always reciprocal, and that this process tests all our presuppositions (Gadamer 272–73), for on the horizon, past and present, tradition and the individual talent contend. Lane marks this meeting and contest with a slash that both distinguishes and moves, marks and removes (Gadamer 273)—takes away and advances—the horizon, engaging it in a voice that is her own.

Lane marks the horizon with her own interpretative voice. Making a mark or deconstructive slash on the horizon, both to claim it and to orient herself and the reader in relation to it, she, at the same time, re-moves the limit. She engages in demarcation, making an orienting mark that both encompasses the opening out, the possibility the horizon represents, while locating the poet and reader definitely in place. Baton Rouge becomes such a demarcation point or place in the "Baton Rouge Poems."

Living in a flat landscape, like that of south Louisiana, in which land and sky seem one, seem merged, when one looks to the horizon, one looks for points of orientation to make "living in the hollow of nowhere" and "disappearing into the night" (*Girl* 15) a positive experience of beauty, song, knowledge, self, and community,

like pouring your loneliness
into a great pool of
light. (*Girl* 15)

The "tips of sweet gums" in "Baton Rouge #1" (*Girl* 13), the "towering bridge" that "moves with the Mississippi" in "Kaleidoscope: Leaving Baton Rouge" (*Girl* 17), and the Mississippi River itself in "Southern University, Baton Rouge" (*Girl* 15), all break the horizon. They "beckon the poet down" (*Girl* 17), making her breath, which, as we have seen, is the source of poetry.

Having come to Baton Rouge from the North, the poet feels that she is "ghost, spirit woman," who must "avoid / smashing into [her]self" (*Girl* 16) in her exile. Self and self as other threaten to collide, erasing the ontological distance that, for Lane, makes poetry possible. In "Southern University, Baton Rouge," the final poem in the series, the Mississippi River, that major orienting and dividing point in Baton Rouge's landscape, is unseen except in the poet's imagination. She waits for the sun to follow her eye, and the river becomes the feature that breaks the landscape and simultaneously defines and settles, orienting the poet's inner and outer gazes, and that makes interpretation possible.

The poet's marking the landscape with the inner eye is a feature of one of Lane's most powerful poems of the horizon, "Girl at the Window." Lane tells John Lowe that the poem grew out of a mixture of experiences (21–22): a trip to Africa, working with African and other international students, thinking about the "golden animals," lions (21). All these ran together (22). They coalesce, I think, in the "blue line" of the equator. Lane was traveling to Africa with her son Gordon, who was about twelve, and when the plane crossed the equator, he thought he would be able to see it with binoculars (22). Lane uses all this to "create" a poem (22).

In "Girl at the Window," Lane takes creative distance to describe herself as a woman who is herself at a distance, sitting by a window as the season changes: as summer and autumn "contend" in air and light. The girl is both observing and observed. Again, Lane avoids punctuation except to locate the girl, hand on her cheek, looking toward the open window. The girl is "there" (*Girl* 38). Her stillness is in contrast to the activity outside the open window. She does not look actively out the window; she actively sits "there," her internal activity as busy and vital as that outside the window. Indeed, Lane comments to John Lowe, "I pull from my natural environment and then go from there. After pulling in the natural environment, then it becomes internal. It always comes back to Pinkie" (24).

In "Girl at the Window," all the outside action takes place in the air; all the internal action takes place in a dream space, a kind of air. The window acts as a hermeneutical and transitive space, a crossing point between dream and ghosts, and reality and green light, which meet at the window—a "mere breath touching" (*Girl* 38). The window, as a breaking point, signals the continual breaking of the static and homogenous, a screening of reality. The window also acts as a linking point, the coming together of inside and outside, nature and human being, domestic space and natural space, and imagination and experience. There is, in the poem, opening and containment: "Lavender hills outline / the rim" (ibid.). This reflexive action characterizes the mind of the poet/girl who is engaged in a kind of indirect thought—a reverie, to use the Romantics' term—allowing the imagination to work.

The girl at the window's imagination links inside and outside, both in the immediate space and in a greater sense. She links African and America, past and present:

> Her skin is copper-toned
> and eyes the nests
> of birds[.] (*Girl* 38)

The phrase "and eyes the nests / of birds" startles the reader. The girl eyes the nests of birds and her eyes are nests of birds, suggesting that they are both resting place, home, and nurture as well as a place from which to depart, continuing the metaphor of containment and opening. The eyes connect Africa and America, the girl with an origin:

> She
> and wildebeests[.] (*Girl* 38)

The dream links the world outside the window with the mind of the thinker and transforms both. In the final lines, the girl makes and/or sees, in this world that she has now created, a new point of orientation: "the equator a blue line/slung in midair" (*Girl* 38). The gesture of slinging and the color blue suggests that the girl has made an imaginative and creative action—like a painter with paint—on the place. She recognizes and makes the equator, making/marking it as her own and participating in the opening into a new space that is the recreation of place. The equator is like the window, an intersection and interpretative point but larger than and yet linked to the world in which the poem begins, the more contained place by the window.

The poem is an extended, gorgeous metaphor for the poet's imagination in action, observing, actively and passively, absorbing and linking, and finally making its mark, the blue line, on the world. The poet's mark, the line on the page, which Lane often characterizes as making a line in the sky, heals and opens the poet and the reader to joy and memory. "Lyric: I Am Looking at Music," the poem used in the film *Love Jones,* illustrates this opening. Music itself sounds a line that

> lies suspended in hills,
> a blue line in a red
> sky. (*Girl* 46)

The poet, oriented by the line, looks, hears, tastes, dances, and remembers both the life of the world in which she dwells and her loves.

Love, therefore, is intimately linked to the metaphor of the horizon, to the making of the mark that is and that allows interpretation and perception. These poems utilize natural images, but they tend to be about family and loved ones (see Lowe 20ff.). They express the power of the imagination to transform even the most difficult situations with those we love. *Elegy for Etheridge* is the exemplar of this movement from pain to expression, dealing, as it does, with death and distance. The title poem, "Songs to the Dialysis Machine," and "Love Poems: Epitaph for the Blues" are, Lane tells John Lowe, "love poems, but they're about the pain" (Lowe 3).

We see Lane work through pain to the transforming power of love in, for example, the series "Poems to My Father." Distance, in Lane's love poems, is bridged by memory and poetry. In "Love Poems: Epitaph for the Blues," section 8, "Vignettes," Lane writes of a lover,

> (Suddenly)
> there you were,
> your voice
> reaching out to me
> over layers of
> loneliness
> and years of space. (*Elegy* 63)

In the series about her father, Lane, as she does in the Baton Rouge poems, pours darkness into light, taking a radical distance and divorcing herself from memory, even as she concretely experiences and expresses it:

> You never happened,
> Papa. (*Girl* 4)

That line division both creates the distance and expresses the intimacy that is necessary to engage in painful memory and write the poem. There is erasure and embrace—and there must be for the poet to be able to claim and to maintain her own capacity for joy.

> The years never happened . . .
> only the times when we
> laughed [. . .]. (*Girl* 4)

Out of the pain comes a kind of joy, the ability to celebrate the good while acknowledging the darkness.

Love always involves intimacy and expansion, embracing the other/beloved in order to embrace a reality larger for the self. This, for Lane, is survival. June Jordan writes that African American poetry "grows from the experience of brave, continual survival" (Jordan xvi). For Lane, love, celebration, and survival are interlocking elements. She reminds us that African American people not only suffer, they love. And love is as important as protest. Indeed, in many ways, it is the most powerful form of protest.

In "Survival Poem," for example, the love between a man and a woman becomes archetypal, as they, embodying nature and memory, become symbols of humanity and survival and what keeps those creatively active: spirit. The importance of spirit is stressed by both June Jordan and Arna Bontemps in their critical essays on African American poetry. The "beautiful, proud spirit" (Jordan xvi) of African American people expressed in poetry comes not from the mainstream, Bontemps argues, but from the spirit (Bontemps xviii). The poet's song of the lovers is a "hymn of spirit" that can reach "across the zero line" (*Girl* 54), breaking personal horizons. The poem ends with distance and intimacy, distinct selves meeting, and a movement of folding into the lover that allows, simultaneously, a movement outward:

> You are you, and I am I,
> folding inward, breaking forth[.] (*Girl* 54)

Love both establishes and opens identity, as the lack of punctuation at the end of the poem suggests. It allows hermeneutics to happen while acknowledging its limits: the inviolability of both self and other. This movement of journeying deeply in to move boldly out is the action of love and also the function of poetry—"This is a love song / Love . . ." (*Girl* 54)—and of the poet: "I am love" (*Elegy* 5).

Pinkie Gordon Lane's poetry is a quiet shout, a simply complex use of images that represent the struggle within the human imagination to balance the self with other and world—and ultimately to love, both self and other. In the balance between opposites, explored in the metaphorical image, Lane makes a space for understanding and self-definition for both the poet and the reader. She speaks of the free act of the poet and of the poems themselves, which we read in a free act, as making this space. In her Baton Rouge series, Lane states, "I am writing poems / in this breathing space" (*Girl* 14). This space is one of creativity, healing, and love, and of breaking limitations of place. On the space of the page and in the space of the poem, creativity, healing, and love become possible for a multiplicity of located readers.

Lane's poetry is "another kind of black poetry" (cited in Rowell 8), characterized by a gentle but tough and unrelenting honesty. The gentle quality of the poetry can make the reader miss the toughness and the truth. Lane's quiet voice directly and unflinchingly interrogates the self and the other while maintaining a quality of sympathy and an open spirit toward growth. Her metaphors of silence, distance, horizon, and love intertwine in the poetry, suggesting that the silent act of attention of the imaginative individual can open that individual to new horizons and to others—to love. These are the basis of self-understanding and self-expression.

Lane's use of natural images might tie her, one could suggest, to the English romantics, with their sense of the possibility of human consciousness realizing itself in nature, but Lane's voice is uniquely American, uniquely of Louisiana, and uniquely African American. Hers is a tight, word- and image-conscious, intuitive, and introspective poetry in the tradition of Phillis Wheatley, to whom she has been compared (Craig 213); Emily Dickinson; and Lane's contemporary Lucille Clifton.

Lane's deceptively simple verse reveals the situation of African American people in America and is made particular in her own life in Baton Rouge, Louisiana. Baton Rouge is, in many ways, an ideal city for Lane, given its contrasts. It is a metropolis with a small town's sense of itself; it is a city that loves music, particularly the blues, food, and festival, as much as any other Louisiana city or town, but as the capital, it is a serious place, a site of contention and decision. There is in Baton Rouge southern hospitality and gentility but also division, particularly in issues of race. All this, Lane recognizes and expresses through examining her particular, situated life as an African American woman, mother, teacher, and poet in this place. We see through her eyes and we see the shadows and nuances that we might otherwise miss; with her we look to the horizon that puts us in an-other space in which we must see ourselves differently. Her quiet voice articulates both personal and political struggles, communal and personal joys.

Recording this past in vivid and evocative, even provocative, images, Pinkie Gordon Lane reminds us that we are not only beings who struggle and experience pain but also observing, thinking, imagining, and expressive human beings who move and love, survive and endure, all beautifully.

NOTES

1.Michel de Certeau, *The Practice of Everyday Life* (Berkeley and Los Angeles: University of California Press, 1984) 117. I will use Certeau's distinction of place as fixed (for example, in tradition and law) and space as a site of mobility within place:

> A place is the order in accord with which elements are distributed in relationships of coexistence. It thus excludes the possibility of two things being in the same location. The law of the "proper" rules in the place; the elements are . . . each situated in its own "proper" and distinctive location. . . . [Space] is composed in intersections of mobile elements. It is in a sense actuated by the ensemble of movements deployed within it. Space occurs as the effect produced by the operations that orient it, situate it, temporalize it, and make it function in a polyvalent unity of conflictual programs or contractual proximities.

2. Lane uses this phrase to describe particular poems, such as "Waiting," when she reads (June 27, 1997).

WORKS CITED

Bell, Bernard W. *Modern and Contemporary African American Poetry.* Boston: Allyn and Bacon, 1972.

Bryan, Violet Harrington. "Evocations of Place and Culture." *Louisiana Literature* 4.2 (Fall 1987): 49–60.

Craig, Marilyn B. "Pinkie G. Lane." *Dictionary of Literary Biography.* Ed. Trudier Harris and Thadious M. Davis. New York: Gale Reseaarch, 1985. 212–16.

De Certeau, Michel. *The Practice of Everyday Life.* Berkeley and Los Angeles: University of California Press, 1984.

Gadamer, Hans-Georg. *Truth and Method.* 1975. Reprint, New York: Crossroad, 1982.

Jordan, June. "Introduction." *Soulscript: Afro-American Poetry.* Ed. June Jordan. New York: Zenith, 1970.

Lane, Pinkie Gordon. *Elegy for Etheridge: Poems.* Baton Rouge: Louisiana State University Press, 2000.

———. *Girl at the Window: Poems by Pinkie Gordon Lane.* Baton Rouge: Louisiana State University Press, 1991.

———. *I Never Scream: New and Selected Poems.* Detroit: Lotus, 1985.

———. *The Mystic Female.* Fort Smith, Ark.: South and West, 1978.

———. *Wind Thoughts.* Fort Smith, Ark.: South and West, 1972.

Long, Charles H. "Silence and Signification." *Significations: Signs, Symbols, and Images in the Interpretation of Religion.* Philadelphia: Fortress, 1985. 54–62.

Lowe, John. "'Pulling in the Natural Environment': An Interview with Pinkie Gordon Lane." *African American Review* 39 (Spring 2005): 17–38.

Marranca, Bonnie. "Criticism, Culture, and Performance: An Interview with Edward Said." *Performing Arts Journal* 13.1 (January 1991): 21–42.

Randall, Dudley, ed. *The Black Poets.* New York: Bantam, 1971.

Rowell, Charles H. *Pinkie Gordon Lane: A Literary Profile to 1977.* Hill Memorial Library Collection, 1997.

PART 4 LOUISIANA MYTHOLOGIES, FROM THE KINGFISH TO THE PECULIAR FASCINATION WITH THE DEAD

The Kingfish as Trickster Hero

Huey Long in Louisiana Culture

MARCIA GAUDET

Huey Pierce Long, born in the hill country of northern Louisiana in 1893, made an indelible mark on Louisiana politics, literature, and folklore. Regarded as both a demon and a saint, he built his political machine by championing the "common people," and his Share the Wealth program brought him to national prominence. Though he had attended less than a year of law school at Tulane (as a special student), he was admitted to the Louisiana bar in 1915 and began the practice of law. He was elected to the Railroad Commission in 1918, defeated for governor in 1924, elected governor in 1928, survived impeachment in 1929, elected to the U.S. Senate in 1930 (though he didn't resign as governor until 1932), and assassinated in the state capitol building on September 8, 1935. Long's legacy is enduring, contradictory, colorful, and controversial. As T. Harry Williams points out, "Huey Long aroused among his people extreme feelings—love or hate—and they still find it difficult to view him neutrally" (ix).[1]

Long had many personas, and he is the subject of many legends (some of which he created himself). In addition to the badman and the saint, his most enduring legendary persona may be that of the cultural trickster hero. For our society to function, we must have rules and order. Yet people tend to admire and cheer those who seem to break the rules with impunity—particularly when they also accomplish some good. Their transgressions of boundaries are excused, and this too is reflected in oral tradition and literature. In Cajun oral tradition, a ballad about Long expresses the common view of the folk:

> O they say he was a crook
>   But he gave us free school book
> Now tell me why is it that they kill Huey Long?
>   Now he's dead and in his grave
> But we riding on his pave
>   Tell me why is it that they kill Huey Long?

Important to "the folk" were free school books and paved roads. How he got them was not of primary importance. Somewhat like Robin Hood and other trickster heroes, oral tradition reflects admiration for one perceived as taking from the rich to give to the poor in ways they could understand, ways that made a real difference in their lives—in education, public works, health care, and pensions for the elderly.

Huey Long's influence on Louisiana culture is as diverse as it is contradictory. Long is still very much in folk and popular culture, and stories and legends about him have been a vital part of oral narrative in the traditional folk cultures of Louisiana. There are also the humorous stories and cartoons published in newspapers and magazines or later collected and published in books such as Hugh Mercer Blain's *Favorite Huey Long Stories* and Garry Boulard's *Huey Long: His Life in Photos, Drawings, and Cartoons.* Many of the poor considered Long a saint, "an angel sent by God" (Brinkley 29). Lyle Saxon in *Gumbo Ya-Ya* says that at a Saint Joseph's Day altar in an Italian community in New Orleans in 1940, "among the saints on the altar was a picture of Huey P. Long" (Louisiana Writers' Project 102).

For many in Louisiana, Long was indeed a savior. Richard D. White Jr. says in *Kingfish: The Reign of Huey P. Long,* "Paradoxically, Huey Long did more good for people of Louisiana than any politician before or since" (x). White also says that Long's ruthless use of power provoked as many to despise him as his charisma and good works caused to revere him (x). In his 1949 article "The Folk Hero," Orrin E. Klapp cites Huey Long as an example of "the clever hero" whose intelligence enables him to triumph as a hero, though he often is a villain as well (20n11). Klapp also notes that Huey Long's legend was enhanced by the fact that he died "fighting for a cause, betrayed by his friends and overwhelmed by enemies" (23).

The story of Long's career forms the basis and material for several literary works, most prominently Robert Penn Warren's *All the King's Men.* The title, an allusion to Long's nickname, Kingfish, is from the nursery rhyme "Humpty Dumpty," suggesting a focus on Long's effect on those who surrounded him. Long's story is transformed into fiction, though his name is never mentioned.[2] Long is also a real presence in other literary works with a Louisiana setting, such as the fiction of Ernest Gaines, where Long is portrayed as a folk hero, especially to the poor. In addition, there is Long's direct influence on southern literature in his strong support of literary and scholarly activity at Louisiana State University. The *Southern Review,* established by Warren and Cleanth Brooks, certainly owes its existence at that time to Huey Long's support. It became one of the most prestigious literary journals in the country as well as a publication vehicle for talented young southern writers, including Eudora Welty.

Although many regarded Long as a folk hero, there were also many who saw him as the epitome of evil, a kind of "badman hero." John Sullivan said, "Jesse James was a gentleman compared with Long . . . because Jesse James at least wore a mask. Long has the face of a clown" (Williams 470). Former governor of Louisiana Ruffin G. Pleasant denounced Long, saying he was "a creature devoid of every element of honor and decency" (ibid.). Mrs. Ruffin Pleasant compared Long to animals: "the greed and coarseness of the swine, the cunning of the fox, the venom of the snake, the cruel cowardice of the skulking hyena" (ibid.). These descriptions reveal Huey Long as the evil "badman." He was also known to be a coward who would run from a fight (Williams 239). Harnett Kane compares him to the early Hitler and notes Long's "unwitting habit of scratching himself regularly on the left buttock" (48). In commenting on the impression Long made on foreign visitors, Arthur Schlesinger says, "Rebecca West detected the steely intelligence behind the Mardi Gras mask of his conversation: 'He is the most formidable kind of brer fox, the self-abnegating kind that will profess ignorance, who will check his dignity with his hat if he can serve his plans by buffoonery'" (66).

The symbolic inversion of comparing Long to an animal associated not only with cunning but also with trickster-type behavior and tales is significant. West is viewing Long as a trickster, and Long himself encouraged this persona. He called himself Kingfish after the trickster-type character on the *Amos 'n' Andy* radio show (Williams 312–13), associating himself not with the trickster "badman" or outlaw hero but with the humorous trickster hero. In his autobiography, *Every Man a King,* Long comments that this appellation "has served to substitute gaiety for some of the tragedy of politics. I have made no effort to discourage it" (278). Long also used storytelling and self-deprecating humor as an effective political tool. It is part of American political tradition for politicians to enhance their popularity by storytelling. As Lindahl, Owens, and Harvison point out in *Swapping Stories,* "Nineteenth century candidates used their jokes and tall tales to present themselves as everyday people, men of homespun values and simple tastes, who were nevertheless far more clever than their sophisticated opponents" (342, Note on Tales 81–109). Huey Long continued that tradition of tall tale telling with a trickster-like manipulation of language and facts, overriding with wit and humor his sometimes very real offenses. He is quoted as saying, "We got the roads in

Louisiana. . . . In some states they only have the graft" (Bohner 85). After making Louisiana State University one of his pet projects and channeling huge amounts of funding into enhancing its national reputation (including that of its marching band, which Long sometimes led as its benefactor/drum major), Long commented, "If there's any title I'm proud of, it's 'Chief Thief' for L.S.U." (Cutrer 6). Asked about charges that his men were involved in graft, he remarked that it was "impossible to build an organization that was completely pure. Even Jesus Christ had had one apostle who had gone wrong" (Williams 821).

Favorite Huey Long Stories, stories collected shortly after Long's death and published in 1937, brings together various retellings and recordings (and some newspaper accounts) of stories that Huey Long supposedly told himself. His flair for rhetoric is evident, and his manipulation of language is often tricksterlike. For example, he once referred to the "incognoscenti"—and then, reportedly, with perfect timing and a grin, said, "If there's not such a word there should be" (Blain 28). There are also stories about Long told by various people. For example, Long rarely carried cash with him, and he was known to often borrow money from his political friends and associates that he never paid back. According to Harvey Pelletier, a wealthy politician and Long supporter from Thibodaux, he was also very generous to the poor, especially widows and children, and particularly with other people's money. Most of his associates, therefore, began to carry two wallets—one containing most of their cash on hand, and the other for opening in the presence of Huey Long (Blain 46). Also in this collection are versions of some of the best known Huey Long speeches and filibusters, including the tick eradication bill speech, the treatise on "pot-likker," the "jew's harp" filibuster, and the green pajama incident. Very early, therefore, Long's unofficial legacy as storyteller and trickster was being circulated both orally and in print.

Long himself had recorded in writing many of his campaign speeches and filibusters in his autobiography, *Every Man a King* (1933). They show Long at his best, presenting himself as a champion of the people, concerned about their needs, and a powerful rhetorician who knew the value of emotional appeal. In this speech from his 1928 campaign, presented beneath the Evangeline Oak in St. Martinville, he appeals to the relatively new found "heritage" of Cajuns in southwestern Louisiana by evoking the memory of Evangeline—a fictional character created by Longfellow but one that many Acadians had readily adopted as a genuine model:

> And it is here under this oak where Evangeline waited for her lover, Gabriel. This oak is immortal, but Evangeline is not the only one who waited here in disappointment. Where are the schools, the roads and highways, the institutions for the disabled you sent your money to build? Evangeline's tears lasted through one lifetime—yours through generations. Give me the chance to dry the eyes of those who still weep here. (Long 99)

Huey Long was indeed popular among the rural, Catholic, French-speaking people of southern Louisiana, the Cajuns and Creoles. Another story in oral tradition about Long campaigning in southern Louisiana is reported by T. Harry Williams as a story that "seems too good to be true—but people who should know swear that it is true":

> The first time that Huey P. Long campaigned in rural, Latin, Catholic south Louisiana, the local boss who had him in charge said at the beginning of the tour: "Huey, you ought to remember one thing in your speeches today. You're from north Louisiana, but now you're in south Louisiana. And we got a lot of Catholic voters down here." "I know," Huey answered. And throughout the day in every small town Long would begin by saying: "When I was a boy, I would get up at six o'clock in the morning on Sunday, and I would hitch our old horse up to the buggy and I would take my Catholic grandparents to mass. I would bring them home, and at ten o'clock I would hitch the old horse up again, and I would take my Baptist grandparents to church." The effect of the anecdote on the audiences was obvious, and on the way back to Baton Rouge that night the local leader said admiringly: "Why, Huey, you've been holding out on us. I didn't know you had any Catholic grandparents." "Don't be a damn fool," replied Huey. "We didn't even have a horse." (3)

The story epitomizes Long as trickster—using his wit to embellish the persona he had presented. As Williams points out, Long was indeed a charismatic speaker, but Long also created an image that he knew would appeal to the masses—that of an abjectly poor person whose family had lacked opportunity for education and culture. If Long did indeed say, "We didn't even have a horse," he was continuing his trickster language even with his supporters. Though the Longs were not wealthy, neither did they live in poverty. This persona of the "underdog," the disadvantaged person who broke the rules of the society and culture that had marginalized him because he had had no opportunity to learn them, was also a part of the Long legend. Long seemed to persistently transgress cultural rules as well as legal statutes, but he knew how to get publicity and entertain people as well.

In 1930 Long got national publicity by extolling the virtues of eating pot-likker and corn pone. Though certainly an offhand, tongue-in-cheek comment to begin with, it was reported in newspapers and newsreels. The pot-likker episode showed Long as a likable, concerned citizen, trying to encourage Depression-era families to grow gardens and provide nourishing, inexpensive food for their families. In *Every Man a King* Long says, "Pot-likker is the juice that remains in a pot after greens or other vegetables are boiled with other seasoning" and is usually eaten with corn pone crumbled into it. He goes on to say, "But, with the progress of education, the coming of 'style,' and the change of the times, I concluded that refinement necessitated that corn pone be 'dunked' in the potlikker, rather than crumbled in the old-fashioned way" (264). He then says that in his efforts to help advertise this dish and "introduce a more elegant method of eating this delectable concoction," he was immediately met with opposition, including a telegram from President Franklin Roosevelt to the *Atlanta Constitution,* "lining up with the crumblers" as opposed to Long's alliance with the "dunkers" (265).

Other incidents showed Long in various situations where his trickster behavior at first causes embarrassment or loss of status with the voters but he manages to survive because he responds as one of the folk or diverts attention from the issue by entertaining the folk with his wit and ingenuity. One such episode, which has come to be known as the green pajama incident, occurred during Mardi Gras in 1930. The German cruiser *Emden* was on a goodwill tour of the United States and docked in New Orleans. The German consul in New Orleans had arranged with Seymour Weiss, a trusted Long advisor and a top executive of the Roosevelt Hotel in New Orleans, for the commander of the ship to pay a courtesy visit to the governor at his suite in the Roosevelt. When Commander Lothar von Arnauld de la Perière and the resident German consul, Rolf L. Jaegar, arrived, Long was dressed in a pair of green silk pajamas. He hastily threw on a red and blue bathrobe and apologized for his attire, but it was undeniably a diplomatic faux pas. Jaegar considered it a great affront to the German government and demanded an apology from Long. Huey did apologize, attributing his failure to his humble origins in the hill country, when he later paid an official visit to the commander on his ship. He is said to have earlier justified his attire as having cost thirty-five dollars. Of greater concern to Long's image, however, was living down among the hill folk the fact that he slept in green silk pajamas (Blain 96–100; Williams 430–

32). This incident may have caused Long embarrassment, but it clearly appealed to the majority of the voters, who seem to have interpreted it as Long's justifiable refusal to play according to the rules and rituals of the Germans.[3]

After Long was elected to the U.S. Senate in 1932, he continued to provoke amazement—for his brilliance as a politician, for his wit and humor, and for his unorthodox and at times vulgar behavior. In the 1933 Sands Point incident Long came closest to losing public support by behaving in a manner that challenged the tolerance of even his strongest followers. Senator Long went with friends to the Sands Point Bath and Country Club in New York. There are various accounts of what happened, but clearly established were that Long had had too many drinks, acted in an obnoxious manner, went to the men's room, and came out holding a napkin over his eye. Apparently someone had hit Long, and he sported a cut above one eye. Long later gave varying reports of the incident, but eventually a story came out in the newspapers that when Huey went into the rest room, a man was using the urinal. Rather than waiting his turn, Long tried to urinate between the man's legs; he failed, drenching the man's suit instead, and the irate man retaliated by punching him in the eye. Media frenzy resulted, including a heyday for cartoonists, mocking Long and threatening to seriously damage his reputation as an earnest politician with a national agenda. Long then prepared a circular suggesting that it was Al Capone, then in federal prison, and the J. P. Morgan financial interests who had arranged for Long to be attacked at Sands Point. As T. Harry Williams says of the Sands Point incident, "Huey chose exactly the right defense: he told a monumental falsehood. Hardly anyone believed that he had been beaten up by gangsters sent to Sands Point by the Morgans, but the story was so magnificently conceived that people laughed admiringly and overlooked his indiscretion" (653).

The Sands Point bathroom incident calls to mind Mikhail Bakhtin's concept of high/low carnivalesque inversions (Bakhtin). Bakhtin's ideas of the lower-body stratum and grotesque realism as a source of carnival laughter, which is both derisive and revitalizing, might be applied to the carnivalesque world that Long seemed to project. He seemed to embody symbolic extremes—repugnance and fascination. Long, as a U.S. senator, had to elevate himself from the low image of the Sands Point incident. The earthy, carnivalesque aspects had a popular appeal, but as a senator he was part of the "upper stratum." Long again used his tricksterlike wit and behavior to negotiate and invert his image with the voters.

Long also received some measure of notoriety for his determination to make Louisiana State University a first-rate institution of higher learning. Though critics pointed out that, like many of its alumni, Long confused a winning football team with prestigious status as a nationally ranked university, Long's commitment to LSU is unquestionable. In 1930 he began to visit the campus often and he became actively involved in some of the activities, including attempting to call plays from the sidelines during football games. He sometimes even treated injured players with folk remedies from Winn Parish. He also channeled large funds from other sources into LSU's budget, reputedly adding eighty grand pianos to the School of Music and building the longest swimming pool in the country for the physical education program. More noteworthy, he funded the establishment of the LSU School of Medicine in New Orleans.[4]

Long was also a great admirer of Frederick the Great, calling him "the greatest sonofabitch who ever lived." In 1935 he told reporters in Washington about the Prussian ruler and his decision to seize Vienna, the Austrian capital: "'You can't take Vienna, Your Majesty. The world won't stand for it,' his nitwit ambassadors said. 'The hell I can't,' said old Fred, 'my soldiers will take Vienna and my professors at Heidelberg will explain the reasons why!' Hell, I've got a university down in Louisiana that cost me $15,000,000, that can tell you why I do like I do" (Williams 492).

Campaign financing is another legendary Huey Long topic. With Long's organization the campaign chest was known as the "deduct box," with most of the money coming from salary deductions of state employees. The box was filled with cash, a million dollars or more according to Long's associates, and kept in a safe in the governor's suite at the Roosevelt Hotel. Senator Long later took the box with him to Washington, first keeping it in a safe at his suite in the Mayflower Hotel and then in a vault in the Riggs National Bank. On September 7, 1935, Long was in New Orleans at the Roosevelt Hotel, and he told his trusted advisor Seymour Weiss, "By the way, Seymour, I've moved the deduct box" (Williams 862). They were interrupted and never finished the conversation. Long was assassinated the following day,[5] and the deduct box was never found (or if it was, the information has never been made public). The location of the deduct box has been the subject of speculation and tales since then. Many believe that the box was in the Roosevelt Hotel. A humorous anecdote in oral tradition tells of finding the deduct box in the ceiling crawl space of the Bentley Hotel in Alexandria. It concludes, "Yea, they've found the deduct box, and inside there was the bill for votes from the last election."

Like that of other trickster heroes and outlaws, Long's "treasure chest" was never found. According to T. Harry Williams, Seymour Weiss recalls trying to get Long to tell him where the deduct box was, but he only whispered, "Later, Seymour, later," and lapsed into a coma (876). Various Long legends report that Huey Long's last words were, "I wonder what will happen to my poor university boys" or "I have so much left to do." The late Mark Carleton, a professor of history at LSU, was told by the nurse who attended Long at his death that Long's last word(s) was simply "Shit" (Zinman 192).

After Long's death, at least for a time, the conflicting images of trickster hero, culture hero, and outlaw were replaced by another image—the tragic, fallen hero. People came from all over the state to pay their last respects to "the martyred governor" (Botkin 294). And all over the state, Long's followers—the Cajuns, the "rednecks," and the "colored people," in particular—assessed what he had done for them. Arthur Schlesinger Jr. calls Long the "Messiah of the Rednecks" and says, "No state in the Union had been so long misgoverned." He cites illiteracy, child labor, an inadequate educational system, lack of public services and health care. In addition, he says, "The submerged people of Louisiana had not only been oppressed, they had been bored" (42–43). Long brought schools, hospitals, roads, and public services. Unlike the Robin Hood outlaw/culture hero model, however, Long was a "thief" for the poor who did *not* have an exemplary character in all other matters. He had instead the tricksterlike ability to narrowly escape, to entertain, and to mock the "enemies" in the process.

A literary work that seems to accurately reflect the folk perspective on Huey Long is Ernest Gaines's *The Autobiography of Miss Jane Pittman.* Miss Jane uses important events in the history of her culture and in her own personal history as narrative markers, for example, the great floods of 1917 and 1927. In the section titled "Huey Long," Miss Jane says, "When did Long come in? Long came in when? After the high water—yes. Before the high water we didn't have school here at Samson. . . . Long came in after the high water and gived us free books for the first time" (145). Miss Jane goes on to say:

> Huey Long came in after the high water. Nothing better could 'a' happened to the poor black man or the poor white man no matter what they say.
>
> Oh, they got all kinds of stories about him now. He was a this, he was a that. Nothing but a dictator who did this and that to the people. . . .
>
> Even them children going round here saying what they got to respect

> Long for—didn't he used to call our people nigger? I agree he did . . . But when he said nigger he said, "Here a book, nigger. Go read your name." (148–49)

Miss Jane later goes on to say, "I know them rich people got them guards to kill Long. All the poor know that . . . Look like every man that pick up the cross for the poor must end that way" (149), giving her own explanation of Long's assassination while also reflecting the view of the underprivileged in Louisiana. Miss Jane is an articulate witness to history, an oral history with which Ernest Gaines was very familiar because he had often heard people talking about Long.

Indeed, talking about Huey Long is something clearly established in Louisiana storytelling, and stories about Long's own storytelling (particularly tall tales he is reported to have told on the campaign trail) seem to fit into the Munchausen tradition. The following story in *Swapping Stories,* recorded in 1990 from Joseph Aaron, a Cajun from Lake Charles, relates a memory of Long's performance at the high school in Iowa, Louisiana, in 1928:

> So I can still see Huey Long up there waving his hands, talking. I can still see it like today. And he made a talk there on something. I'll never forget. I told his son, Russell Long, in later years about that. And he made me write it down exactly like Huey Long said.
>
> Huey Long said, "Now, listen folks, you all stick with me." He said, "The other day, I went fishing with this friend of mine. He fell out of the boat." He said, "I reached over the boat to pick him up, and his hand come off. So I threw his hand in the boat. I reached over and caught him by the leg and his leg come off!" He said, "I looked down at my friend, and I said, 'How in the hell can I save you if you don't stick together?' You all stick with me, and I'll save all of you all!"
>
> I'll never forget that for as long as I live. (Lindahl, Owens, and Harvison 187–88)

The obvious admiration, as well as delight, that this memory of Huey Long evokes is typical, particularly among those people who also say that Long was at least a bringer of hope if not a savior. Louisiana in the 1920s and 1930s was a place ripe for such a savior—particularly one who entertained them as well. Just as the cross-cultural trickster has so much appeal in oral tradition and literature, Long had the tricksterlike qualities or characteristics that made him particularly appealing to the majority of the people in Louisiana at the time. Andrew Wiget, speaking of the Native American trickster, says, "When the weight of culture is felt as a crushing burden on the self, when our heroic sense of all that we ought to be has beaten down our common sense of what we more frequently are . . . the Trickster speaks from some unbeaten part of us, for change and the possibility of a good laugh" (94).

In folk culture and literature, the trickster is often regarded as a culture hero—one who brings food, drink, and the arts to mankind (Babcock-Abrahams 161–62). The trickster also is typically very smart, a taker of risks, a breaker of rules, and a transgressor of boundaries. In addition, the trickster is greedy, erotic, deceitful, gross, vulgar, and evil. The trickster is a model for how *not* to behave, but at the same time people benefit from his thievery as well as the amusement he provides. He is "at one and the same time, creator and destroyer, giver and negator, he who dupes and who is always duped himself" (Radin ix). Barbara Babcock-Abrahams says:

> No figure in literature, oral or written, baffles us quite as much as trickster. He is positively identified with creative powers, often bringing such defining features of culture as fire or basic food, and yet he constantly behaves in the most antisocial manner we can imagine. Although we laugh at him for his troubles and his foolishness and are embarrassed by his promiscuity, his creative cleverness amazes us and keeps alive the possibility of transcending the social restrictions we regularly encounter. (147)[6]

Babcock-Abrahams points out that the paradox of *trickster* and *culture hero* has been the most difficult to understand, both in culture and in literature—where both attributes are combined in a single figure (161–62). Like the trickster, Huey Long was an expression of paradox and ambiguity and seemed to embody the contradictions and oppositions of our Louisiana culture. The wealthy and the privileged judged Long and evaluated his behavior in terms of their own perceptions of propriety and the world view of the educated and entitled. Others saw Long as their only hope for change—often precisely what the anti-Long forces did not want.

In *The Politics and Poetics of Transgression*, Stallybrass and White present a model for viewing society and culture in terms of high-low oppositions. They divide those oppositions into four domains: psychic forms, the human body, geographical space, and social orders. Transgressing the rules of hierarchy and order in any of these domains, they argue, results in major consequences in the other three. They focus upon the interplay between limits and transgressions as well as the symbolic extreme of the high and low. They also contend that transgressions that affect all domains and eventually force change are most likely when the high-low oppositions are extreme. Things that are socially marginal then often become symbolically central. Certainly, the high-low oppositions in Louisiana were extreme: educated/illiterate; urban New Orleans/rural, agricultural regions; white/black; the very rich/the very poor; English language/French language; Protestant/Catholic; northern Louisiana/southern Louisiana (the latter clearly in opposition culturally though not as obviously high/low). It was a time and place ripe for a transgressor who embodied paradox and blurred the categories and boundaries.

Like the trickster, Long was paradox personified. He was regarded as a thief and a murderer as well as a savior. There was also his wit and manipulation, along with his ability to revel in his sometimes bizarre behavior. He not only broke the rules but also questioned the very basis of the rules. At least symbolically, Long's transgression—his questioning of boundaries and rules and his inversions of hierarchies—were as poetic as they were political.

NOTES

1. Huey Long began his first job in 1910 as a traveling salesman selling Cottolene, a lard substitute. He met Rose McConnell, whom he married in 1913, at a cake-baking contest he had organized to introduce women to the product. Though he attended law school classes at the University of Oklahoma and Tulane, he did not receive his high school diploma (having dropped out in his senior year, probably because of his antagonistic relationship with the teachers), and he never attended college as an undergraduate. Long has been the subject of numerous studies and biographies over the past sixty years. Probably the best is T. Harry Williams's Pulitzer Prize–winning biography *Huey Long.* Other helpful works are Jeansonne, Hair, and White. See also Dethloff.

2. In *The Kingfish in Fiction,* Perry points out the differences between Huey Long and Robert Penn Warren's Willie Stark. Perry says that "Willie Stark, ironically, is much less based on the historical Huey Long than many of his now largely forgotten predecessors. His reputation, it would seem, lies in the fact that, though he is among the least historical of Huey Long figures, he is undoubtedly the most compelling fictional character of the lot" (226). Other creative works based on Huey Long include Hamilton Basso's *Sun in Capricorn* (1942), Sinclair Lewis's *It Can't Happen Here* (1936), John Dos Passos's *Number One* (1943), and Adria Locke Langley's *A Lion Is in the Streets* (1945).

3. A contemporary folk version of this episode was recorded in 1990 from Crawford Vincent, a Cajun and also a member of the Hackberry Ramblers, a popular Cajun band. Note the differences from Huey Long's version—it is in the Heidelberg (actually, in Baton Rouge), the pajamas are pink, and Long does not apologize:

> But, anyhow, he come to the Heidelberg Hotel in New Orleans. Huey Long met him at the door in a pair of pink pajamas. This German officer thought Huey should've met him

in a tuxedo or something. He was highly offended, and I can't use the language today that Huey Long told him! He said, "You can go, So-and-So, back to your ship, friend. We don't need you over here!" That actually happened.

4. For more on Huey Long and Louisiana State University, see Williams and Cutrer.

5. The official conclusion regarding Long's assassination is that he was shot by a single assassin, Carl Austin Weiss (no relation to Seymour Weiss), a young physician who was the son-in-law of Judge Benjamin Pavy, an anti-Long politician. Weiss was shot and killed immediately by Long's bodyguards. For a revisionist's view on Long's assassination, see Zinman.

6. Some of the traits that Babcock-Abrahams lists for the cross-cultural trickster are particularly interesting in regard to Huey Long's public life and the description of him as "a man of unrestrained desires" (Williams 67): violation of custom, unpredictability, transgression of boundaries, association with scatological episodes, motley dress, great libido, amorality, attributes of the Transformer/Culture Hero, and most important, ambiguity, paradox, and the blurring of distinctions and boundaries (159–60). Another common behavior of the trickster, particularly the African trickster, is stealing food (See Roberts, for example). Perhaps there is a parallel between this and Huey Long's habit of eating food off of the plates of other people (even with strangers in restaurants!), because he did not like waiting for his to arrive (Williams 320).

WORKS CITED

Babcock-Abrahams, Barbara. "'A Tolerated Margin of Mess': The Trickster and His Tales Reconsidered." *Journal of the Folklore Institute* 9 (1975): 147–86.

Bakhtin, Mikhail. *Rabelais and His World.* Trans. Hélène Iswolsky. Cambridge, Mass.: MIT Press, 1968.

Blain, Hugh Mercer, ed. *Favorite Huey Long Stories.* 1937. Reprint, Baton Rouge: Claitor's, 1991.

Bohner, Charles H. *Robert Penn Warren.* Boston: Twayne, 1981.

Botkin, B. A., ed. *A Treasury of Southern Folklore.* New York: Crown, 1949.

Boulard, Garry. *Huey Long: His Life in Photos, Drawings, and Cartoons.* Gretna, La.: Pelican, 2003.

Brinkley, Alan. *Voices of Protest: Huey Long, Father Coughlin, and the Great Depression.* New York: Knopf, 1982.

Cutrer, Thomas W. *Parnassus on the Mississippi: The Southern Review and the Baton Rouge Literary Community, 1935–1942.* Baton Rouge: Louisiana State University Press, 1984.

Dethloff, Henry C., ed. *Huey P. Long: Southern Demagogue or American Democrat?* 1967. Reprint, USL History Series. Lafayette: University of Southwestern Louisiana, 1976.

Gaines, Ernest J. *The Autobiography of Miss Jane Pittman.* New York: Dial, 1971.

Hair, William Ivy. *The Kingfish and His Realm.* Baton Rouge: Louisiana State University Press, 1991.

Jeansonne, Glen. *Messiah of the Masses.* New York: HarperCollins, 1992.

Kane, Harnett T. *Louisiana Hayride: An American Rehearsal for Dictatorship, 1928–1940.* New York: William Morrow, 1941.

Klapp, Orrin E. "The Folk Hero." *Journal of American Folklore* 62 (1949): 17–25.

Lindahl, Carl, Maida Owens, and C. Renee Harvison, eds. *Swapping Stories: Folktales from Louisiana.* Jackson: University Press of Mississippi, 1997.

Long, Huey. *Every Man a King: The Autobiography of Huey Long.* New Orleans: National Book, 1933.

Louisiana Writers' Project. *Gumbo Ya-Ya.* Compiled by Lyle Saxon, Edward Dryer, and Robert Tallent. 1945. Reprint, Gretna, La.: Pelican, 1987.

Perry, Keith. *The Kingfish in Fiction: Huey P. Long and the Modern American Novel.* Baton Rouge: Louisiana State University Press, 2004.

Radin, Paul. *The Trickster: A Study in American Indian Mythology.* New York: Philosophical Library, 1960.

Roberts, John. "The African American Animal Trickster as Hero." In *Redefining American Literary History.* Ed. A. LaVonne Ruoff and Jerry Ward Jr. New York: MLA, 1990. 97–114.

Schlesinger, Arthur M., Jr. *The Politics of Upheaval.* New York: Houghton Mifflin, 1960.

Stallybrass, Peter, and Allon White. *The Politics and Poetics of Transgression.* Ithaca, N.Y.: Cornell University Press, 1986.

Warren, Robert Penn. *All the King's Men.* New York: Harcourt Brace, 1946.

White, Richard D., Jr. *Kingfish: The Reign of Huey P. Long.* New York: Random, 2006.

Wiget, Andrew. "His Life in His Tail: The Native American Trickster and the Literature of Possibility." *Redefining American Literary History.* Ed. A. LaVonne Ruoff and Jerry W. Ward Jr. New York: MLA, 1990. 83–96.

Williams, T. Harry. *Huey Long.* New York: Knopf, 1969.

Zinman, David H. *The Day Huey Long Was Shot: September 8, 1935.* 1963. Reprint, Jackson: University Press of Mississippi, 1993.

I Want to Die in New Orleans

BRENDA MARIE OSBEY

Of the things that matter to me, one that comes to mind whenever I travel is the importance of dying and being laid by in New Orleans. Because I am neither romantic enough nor vain enough to imagine I will have done anything to merit it, I do not aspire to the jazz funeral. Traditionally, these are reserved for those who have made lasting contributions to New Orleans music and the world of Jazz at-large. Though nowadays most anyone can hire a band for a rousing send-off. I do want to go in style, though.

And to the understandable surprise of friends and acquaintances outside the city. I do want a quiet death—quiet and clean and at home in my own bed. Should I have the grave misfortune to die out in the big world, it is of immeasurable importance that what remains of me he returned home to my people and my place. But I do not count on that. I want to die in New Orleans.

Once the dying itself is over with, I prefer the ritual bathing and dressing, the application of herbs and unguents, the shrouding and taking of last breath, the setting of lights and the able ministrations of at least one elder Hoodoo woman of fair repute to any form of Western-style undertaking. Traveling the path of bone-ash and dust of those gone on ahead, I cannot help but think it downright uncouth to meet ancestor and loa with a bellyful of embalmer's paste and a mouth shamed into silence by whatever synthetic equivalent of cat-gut will have become the choice of that generation of morticians. In fact, having once had a brief, stale affair with a mortician in my youth and, more important, having seen the 1930s classic *Body Snatcher* (starring Boris Karloff in one of his most grotesquely appealing roles), I hope whoever is left of my loved ones will have enough plain courtesy to bar morticians from my deathroom altogether. And I expect to indicate as much *in writing* just in case.

As for the transporting of my remains, I want six of the finest, blackest, good-lookingest men to be found downtown. Failing that, adult male children of former loves will do.

There is to be no moaning, crying, or general carrying-on. Unless, of course, in true New Orleans style, it is done loudly and with *bounce.* Nor is there to be any ash-to-ash/dust-to-dusting. Any and everybody who's witnessed even one Western-style burial knows that by heart. And far be it from me to bore to death those considerate enough to come and put me by.

Along similar lines and therefore also forbidden is anything resembling the reading, reciting, or performing of poetry—my own or anybody else's. By the time I die I expect to have done a considerable amount of all-around living. And that is how I want to be remembered—as a woman who lived. And had the good sense to go on home when it was over. Home to the only place in this country where people understand the importance of dying *well.* Where cemeteries are as prominent as office towers. Where the dead get equal time with the living and, in many cases, are still much better treated. Where obituaries routinely list each and every one of the deceased's known nicknames so that anybody who might consider mourning or remembering will know where and when to show up. Where the dead walk and talk among the living as before, only now with an authority they never possessed in life. Where home altars boast candles, flowers, prominently displayed photographs and personal objects. These large and small icons signal to us that our dead have both gone on over and remain palpably nearby to give aid and counsel.

When we say that we see our Dead, that we speak with them and they with us, we are speaking neither metaphorically nor literally. We are speaking both metaphorically and literally. For we hold here that death is not an ending but a road. Rituals take place at crossroads for exactly this reason. Similarly, at the rising and setting of the sun, the living and Dead shake hands. For this reason, people who keep altars perform ablutions upon first arising in the morning and as the final act before retiring for the night. For this reason, when children misbehave after being put to bed, they are made to get up and enact their devotions yet again. So too when we enter or pass nearby the cemetery, we make "the sign of the cross" to show we are cognizant that we are "crossing" into the territory of the Dead, if only metaphorically.

Nor do we believe, as some do, in keeping children from funeral and burial services. On the contrary, our children go up to kiss their deceased elders, greeting them in death with the same reverence and affection with which they greeted and bade them goodbye in life. In fact, it is not uncommon for us to look upon burial services as an opportunity for a Great Good Time. Some outsiders attribute this to the Carnival culture of the place. Nor are they altogether mistaken in that assumption, but for reasons more enigmatic than absurd. For to people to whom Carnival seems wild and absurd, clearly it is nothing more than that. For us, however, it has a great deal to do with the crossroads of life and death and our own recognition of that locus of the metaphor and the literal, the expansive and the local. In the same way, then, that Carnival is not both sacred and profane but simultaneously sacred and profane, funerals are at once spiritual and temporal, civic and religious, for the living and for the Dead, and for all the Dead who have gone before.

Funerals are wonderful ordeals. I say this with absolute certainty because I recall that in my twenties I had one primary social rule: I did not under any circumstances attend weddings, funerals, or christenings. I still do not attend weddings or christenings. Sometime in my thirties, however, as I became more and more concerned with the topic of death in New Orleans culture, I began to be more and more attracted to the funeral and all things funerary. A good funeral is a wonderful example both of ritual behavior and improvisation. A bad funeral is the best modem-day send-up of a true curse. And even a good funeral can be badly executed.

Of course, not everything can be planned. And sometimes even the best of plans can be upstaged by the guest of honor. In my own family, my Grandmother Alberta loved to tell how a relative of ours, in the days before embalming was common practice, and clearly through no fault of her own, managed to sit up in her coffin just as the celebration of her life-well-lived was at its highest pitch and wanted to know what the hell was going on in her house. The mourners, of course, knocked themselves over getting out of the parlor and the undeceased lady's husband led the way. Needless to say, my grandmother was fond of concluding, she went on to live a full life, her poor but faithful husband predeceasing her by a good few years.

My Great-aunt Katherine was so unfortunate as to be eulogized by a substitute minister. As he stood speaking over her remains, he was moved to sing, "Sleep on, Sister," except that he could not recall her name, and so instead of singing, "Sleep on, Sister Katherine," he looked doubtfully into her lovely pearl-grey casket and intoned gravely, "Sleep on, Sister *Merrrr.*" Needless to say, for all our love of nicknaming here in New Orleans, my Great-aunt Katherine had never, except on that one occasion, been known as "Merrrr." A sin and a shame to the memory of a woman so well loved. A deft display of quick-witted improvisation and aplomb on the part of the substitute preacher.

Then there is my own Great-grandmother, Emma Phillips Cobb—"a big tall fine woman," as my Grandmother Alberta liked to recall with apparent pride. So big and tall and fine, it turns out, that they had to lay her out on something called a "cooling board" while they built the casket to fit her frame.

I could go on. I have dozens of these stories. My own father, Red Man, who has two last wishes that he recites to anyone who might attend: to be buried feet facing east, in a plain pine box completely surrounded, inside and out, by yams. His argument is that he's loved them well enough in life and can hardly be expected to do without them in death. His fondest vision is of his tomb site there in the family cemetery completely covered, smothered as it were, with that hardy vine. A veritable eternity of yams.

Or my cousin Cuccia, who was shocked to read his own death notice in the Monday morning papers and ran all but fainting—where else?—to my Grandmother Alberta's to see if she too had gotten the sad news.

But I begin to fear now that I'm straying a bit from my true point of origin. I'm supposed to be telling about how and why I want to die in New Orleans. And this can best be told in response to a single question: *How did we, of all communities, get to be so death-happy?* Well, it goes something like this.

When the first Africans—BaKongo and Senegambian they were—looked up and found themselves in New Orleans, they were not at all pleased with the end of that journey. This must have been especially true for the BaKongo, holding as they did and do such clear systems of thought with regard to the Journey and all it symbolizes. In Kongo cosmology and symbology there are indeed many significant joumeyings. But the final journey is made over the last great body of water, Nzadi, to the Land of the Dead, Mpemba. There is no problem with that journey in and of itself. It is one of many great, natural, and necessary journeys in the course of the human time/space cycle. The Land of the Dead, however, is also, of course, the residence of the Ancestors, the Gone-before. In other words, we know those we find there. Even those who died so long ago we ourselves cannot personally remember them, when we meet them there in that place we recognize them for they recognize us as belonging intimately to their family, clan, village, city, kingdom, and so on. The problem with this particular (and we now know earthly) journey, however, was that not one but two and, in some instances, three bodies of water had to be crossed. And after the many hardships of the clearly evil journey these souls had been taken on, not one of the places our travellers reached even faintly jibed with what each of them knew to expect. And, as clearly, this place offered neither the permanence of the Land of the Dead nor the stability or commonplaces of the quotidienne. So that even if they had hoped deep in their hearts that the elders had been mistaken in their constructs of the orderly realm of the Gone-before, had perhaps spoken, that is to say—for the elders do not err—had spoken in signs and metaphors too complex for their listeners to comprehend, at some point the Travellers had to confront the reality of the Evil that awaited them here in this literal New World for which they were all but completely unprepared. And I say all *but* completely because the BaKongo are a highly adaptive people. It is in fact from them that we inherit our ongoing love of improvisation in its many evocative and elusive manifestations in this World. It is from them that we can know to say a thing, mean that thing and its opposite, all the while pointing to a third, which opens doors to realms in which mere tongue-speech extends no usefulness and thus becomes superfluous. The language of dancing, for instance, works in exactly this way. What do we mean when we dance? What, for instance, is the meaning of the Second-line? Well, if you have to ask then you have never danced it and it is not likely you ever shall. And if you have not danced it, then you cannot imagine it. If, however, you have danced it, then the question becomes not mere joke but folly, an exercise in self-importance, or else that brand of self-mockery that is self-importance in the guise of innocence or ridicule of the sort engaged in by small untrained children and white-people.

But our travellers. Our Travellers. Our Travellers look up one morning and find themselves here in New Orleans. The year is 1719 and the place has not yet been "carved out" (literally) to suit the interests of the Europeans who have so recently "discovered" it. And so our Travellers look about and what do they see? Clearly this is not the Land of the Dead, the Ancestors, the Gone-before. No one of them recognizes any being here, nor do these beings recognize them as anything other than instruments of labor. Is it then a kind of Kongo Purgatory? For the BaKongo, you will recall, had by this time a 200-year relationship with the Roman Catholic Church and its dogma. Such a question could only be answered, however, over time. But time did not prove so helpful to our Travellers, and they soon realized that their lot here was exactly what it seemed. And those one or two elders and their pupils who had learned well began to make the history that would become our present-day inheritance and which I, in this seeming roundabout way, am essaying to convey to you.

When first we came to this place we thought our troubles were over and that we had reached at last Mpemba, the Land of the Dead. Especially as we saw how these Beings, our Captors, had upon their faces and all their limbs the whiteness of death. As it turned out, they were neither our own Dead nor even the emissaries of the Dead of their kind. They were in fact a clan unto themselves, but a clan among whom not one of the laws we knew to be the laws of human beings held even briefest sway. And yet they were a people. A people among whom death was a thing feared, postponed, denied its due, resented even. They were in fact the soul-less beings the Parents and the Old Parents had so often spoken of when speaking in parables and signs. These, our Captors, were members not of the community of any civilized Dead but instead a living and prospering clan of death-fearing and, therefore, death-besieged beings. They were the walking dead of children's night-fears. And the very young may easily have feared them in exactly this way.

Us they had taken from our towns and cities, where we had already encountered their kith and kin and whom we had tried without success to remove from our midst once we saw the violence and the bloodshed, the savagery and the want that trailed behind them at every turn. And the end of that failure was the Journey-over-Waters that brought us here to this place. And it is a measure of the immenseness of our failure that we recall that we did fail.

Once here, of course, we saw that our lives were given over entirely to toil. We worked in indigo, in brick, in iron. But we mostly plied the trades that we had plied at home. Nor did we cease to think of that place, with its streets, its trees, its pleasant places where we stopped for cooling drinks to receive and exchange news among our neighbors. In fact, here in this city, among those who called themselves at turns Frenchmen, at turns Spaniards, we began to find again a way of gathering.

More important even than the means we found to get our freedom—and this will sound strange only to those who have never known captivity—were the ways and places we found to gather together. For it was in these Gatherings that we were able to fashion a way to *be* in a place that clearly had no place or time within which we *could* simply be—not as we were and knew to be. Which is not to say we did not lose a great many along the way. The Lost we consigned to the Ancestors to deal with as they would. And we ourselves continued on the Journey.

One of our primary concerns, of course, was this problem of dying. For the integrity of one's living is unequivocally evinced in the quality and capacity of one's dying. Not only do this world and the world of the Dead reflect one another, they engage in constant exchanges and endlessly repeat. Why else do we warn small children away from looking-glasses in the dark of night? Or counsel their parents, when troubled, if they wish to see their Dead, not in the exercise of some elaborate ritual but simply to "hold up a candle to your mirror"? The living and the Dead hold up mirrors to the soul. Nor do souls reside in cemeteries and graves. These are but emblems, visible, readable, tangible means of articulating the constancy of death even as we ourselves live.

No. When we die, we go home. We return to our own place, our own Ideal City. There we are received by our kin and continue along the Road. We are ever turning in that Road. When we carry the umbrella in the funeral procession, we turn it around and about, first in one direction, then in the other. We are all of us ever turning in that Road. But having come to labor and to die here in a New World, far from all we knew and held familiar, and where our paths seemed almost always to he barred, we had to find some way to ensure a good reception upon going to dwell once more among our own. What choice did we have except to step up our celebration of the Dead?

We had among us a few elders and some (now) fowler apprentices to elders and to healers, banganga, as well as some followers of the Catholic religion, an insignificant number of Yoruba, noticeable primarily for their contentiousness and their guile, as well as a few Mohammedans. And being ourselves an urban people and sophisticated, it was not long before the others looked to us for guidance in how to live in this city of these Walking-Dead.

Because we are an orderly people, we see the business of living as inextricably hound up in the business of dying. Therefore we are meticulous in how we conduct ourselves, especially upon making that Journey out. We had also to weigh the secondary consideration that, living as we now did among these others, we must distinguish ourselves from them in these most basic things. We must cling the more to our celebration of the Dead even as they turned from dying. For it is in this last thing that we are made known once more to our own, to family, clan, village, city, kingdom and so on. This last is among the greatest and grandest of Journeys we can ever hope to make. For it is in dying well that perhaps, in this New World, we can expiate the sins of having lived not perhaps as well as we had ought.

Therefore, when you see the grand man or grand woman step out to lead the procession to the place where remains are laid by, stand back in wonder and sign yourself in the gesture to wish that Brother or Sister-Traveller "good crossing." And if the Spirit that is in you so moves, then follow as far along as you can to help that Journey. And think well on it when you hear them say in that city, which has since become our City, "Oh! How I *want* to be in that Number! When the Saints go marching in!"

PART 5 MUSIC THAT SOOTHES THE SOUL

Hollers, Blue Notes, and Brass Sounds

Diverse Musical and Cultural Influences on Jazz in Louisiana

WILFRIED RAUSSERT

Multicultural issues have very much dominated the discourse in academia and politics in recent years. For all those scholars interested in theorizing about racial, social, and cultural aspects of multiethnic communities, Louisiana, and New Orleans in particular, may well be an ideal starting point for further investigation. Cultural collisions and cultural blendings have shaped the sociology of New Orleans. This process becomes most visible when we look at the historical transformations that took place in the nineteenth and early twentieth centuries. During this time period New Orleans turned into a booming city characterized by an immense racial and cultural diversity. And perhaps more than any other cultural mode of expression, African American music exemplifies the creative and transformative potential behind the blendings of diverse cultural influences in Louisiana.

In this essay I delineate the background and development of jazz in New Orleans and Louisiana within the context of diverse cultural influences. The multiplicity of musical forms from different cultural sources present in the region parallels the syncretic nature of jazz. The state's history has been a multicultural one, and cultural crossovers influencing music and the arts have gained fresh impetus due to influences from Cuba and other Caribbean cultures in recent years.

Without doubt, New Orleans, as any visitor soon finds out, is different—in many ways. As Ishmael Reed portrays his fictitious Mumbo Jumbo Cathedral as a vital part of Louisiana culture in his 1972 novel *Mumbo Jumbo,* he gives voice to the rich and diverse musical texture of a unique American cultural region:

> PaPa LaBas' Mumbo Jumbo Kathedral is located at 119 West 136th St. The dog at his heels, PaPa LaBas climbs the steps of the Town house. He moves from room to room: The Dark Tower Room the Weary Blues Room the

> Groove Bang and Jive Around Room the Aswelay Room. In Groove Bang and Live Around Room people are rubberlegging for dear life; bending over backwards to admit their loa. In the Dark Tower Room, artists using cornmeal and water are drawing veves. Markings which were invitations to new loas for New Art. The room is decorated in black red and gold. A piano recording plays Jelly Roll Morton's "Pearls," haunting, melancholy. In the Aswelay Room the drums sleep after they've been baptized. A guard attendant stands by so that they won't get up and walk all over the place. PaPa LaBas opens his hollow obeah stick and gives the drums a drink of bootleged whiskey.[1]

The hedonistic spirit behind New Orleans' cultural life vividly shines through in Reed's narrative. Carnival and music are at the core of living in this city. New Orleans music is passionate, good humored. It is comic and serious at the same time, expressing feelings about love and death. In general it is danceable and has a polyrhythmic beat at its core.

The various forms of music and dance alluded to in the passage taken from *Mumbo Jumbo* manifest that customs and languages from New Orleans's early French and Spanish days as well as the influence of African and Caribbean cultures have become both visible and audible forces within the local culture in Louisiana. And whenever people set out to talk and write about Louisiana and its contributions to American culture, music as a way of life and as a central mode of artistic expression is one of the dominant themes. Even today the legend of New Orleans as the birthplace of jazz is very much alive in the posters, T-shirts, and postcards available in the boutiques and stores of the French Quarter, but also, more significantly, in the music played in the jazz clubs and in the streets.

Only recently, using the occasion of the 1997 New Orleans Jazz and Heritage Festival, the city honored one of its most influential jazz musicians, Sidney Joseph Bechet, on the centenary of his birth. In conjunction with the music festival, a one-day conference with international jazz critics explored the meaning and impact of Bechet's music for the world of jazz. One of the highlights of the Sidney Bechet Centennial celebration was the unveiling of a French sculpture of Bechet, the *Wizard of Jazz*.[2] On May 6 the celebration ended with a brass band parade from Jackson Square to Congo Square.[3] As the events illustrate, New Orleans culture is shaped by a spirit that embraces all sorts of celebrations. Every year thousands of tourists head south to participate in the Mardi Gras parade and the annual jazz festival. Real entertainment, it is said, was born in New Orleans. Night by night popular jazz spots such as the Blue Angel and Preservation Hall are crowded with people eager to hear traditional and contemporary New Orleans jazz tunes. And jazz is not only part of life but also part of death in New Orleans culture. Though not as frequently as in the past, jazz funerals still take place, especially for black jazz musicians.

That jazz was born in New Orleans is one of many myths related to the world of jazz, though it is true that New Orleans played a pivotal role in the history of jazz. The emergence of jazz in and around New Orleans has to be understood as a result of diverse cultural blendings that have taken place throughout the history of Louisiana. In order to go back to the early roots of black music in the Americas, one has to consider the passage between Africa and the Americas during times of slavery. Although many African musical elements have survived this geographical and cultural uprooting, a first blending of cultures can be located in the Caribbean and other regions of Latin America. Especially the islands in the West Indies witnessed an intense blending of West African and European musical expression. Due to its history, New Orleans, in its early days, bore many of the cultural traits that characterized the French West Indies. From 1718 until 1764 New Orleans' cultural and political life was strongly shaped by the presence of French government and French customs. Despite the fact that the Spanish superseded the French in government in 1764, a continuous pattern of Latin Catholic influence formed the framework for cultural fusions in New Orleans and the Louisiana territory for another thirty-nine years until 1803, when Napoleon sold the reconquered area to the United States in the Louisiana Purchase.

With the opening of the Louisiana territory to Anglo-American influence, a shift in population and cultural politics occurred. In a very short period of time the impact of British Protestant culture and an immense growth of population turned New Orleans into a boom town and major trade center.[4] Merchants and settlers of Protestant background and new immigrants from Europe, particularly from Italy, changed the social structure of New Orleans decisively. Most of the black population could trace their roots back to West Africa. Their ancestors had been from Senegal, from Nigeria and Congo. Among those who arrived from Dahomey were the wild Aradas. They carried with them African voodoo rites. No sooner was the colony of Louisiana founded in 1718 than black slaves were brought from Martinique, Guadeloupe, and Haiti. Between 1809 and 1810 about three thousand slaves from Haiti came to New Orleans via Cuba. And along with them many of their white masters arrived in Louisiana. The slaves from Haiti who brought their witch doctors and voodoo queens kept the spirits and rites of black religion alive. The voodoo queens in particular favored a joy of luxury that attracted many of the Creole women living in the Vieux Carré. In the nineteenth century New Orleans turned into a melting pot of cultures synthesizing various European, African, and Caribbean influences.[5]

Although the British Protestant influx altered the cultural matrix of Louisiana, it never succeeded in erasing the strong presence of Latin Catholic religion and culture. As far as music is concerned, the syncretism that took place between Catholic and West African religions paved the way for the survival of West African musical elements. Whereas Latin Catholic cultural politics allowed of greater cultural diversity, most Protestant colonies strove to suppress the impact of black culture and religion. "Drums were banned everywhere in North America except French Louisiana in the middle of the eighteenth century," notes Robert Palmer, "and so were horns, which are made from wood or animal horns and played in hocketing ensembles in the slave coast and Congo-Angola regions."[6] Religious and social reasons were behind the ban in Protestant colonies and territories. Fear of secret communication among the African American slaves and fear of slave revolts lead to cultural restriction. In the French- and Spanish-influenced New Orleans, however, African music and religion found better ground on which to survive and even flourish. Many critics have referred to the cultural laissez-faire within Latin Catholic colonial policy as a potential base for the emergence of jazz in New Orleans. Because religious and musical practice are closely interwoven in African cultures, the survival of African rites and forms of worship in Louisiana and other regions of the American South established a matrix on which black musical forms and practice could continue and thrive in new blendings. The strong link between music and religion in black cultures can be traced throughout the Americas. In Cuba the predominant African music is Yoruban, in Jamaica, Ashanti, and in Haiti, Dahomean. Like the former French colony of Haiti, the French influenced New Orleans allowed fusions of saints, rites, and worship practices. The African voodoo and the Haitian Voudun take on a new shape and name in the American hoodoo. And New Orleans has been called the "hoodoo capital of the United States."[7] Hence the development of music under the impact of black cultural influences has to be seen in close relation to black folklore, magic, and religion. Public performances in Congo Square and private Voudun ceremonies connected the African rhythms with ritual as well as with religious practice. Especially the performances in Congo Square introduced the rhythmic elements of African music to large audiences, white musicians among them. So the basis for a mutual interaction between African and European music was quickly established. The dances at Congo Square had their prime time around 1819 and ended shortly after 1835 with only a brief revival in 1845.[8]

Accounts of early Voudun ceremonies are rare and seldom trustworthy. But apart from distortions and exaggerations, some of them provide insight into the structural and performative aspects of the music practiced in New Orleans in the nineteenth century. Elements that recur repeatedly in the descriptions of various observers are the call-and-response pattern, the circle dance, and the rhythmic clapping and stamping, all of which can be traced back to West African musical roots.[9] As far as musicological observation is concerned, Charles Dudley Warner appears to have written one of the more trustworthy reports of Voudun ceremonies in New Orleans. The ceremony he described took place in a house near Congo Square and began with recitations and prayers. After that, singing superseded the spoken word and physical movement accompanied the chant, which progressed in various, steadily intensifying rhythms. Many voices joined in for the refrain:

Danse Calinda, boudoum, boudoum!
Danse Calinda, boudoum, boudoum!

The early *chanson Africaine* then turned into a *canga,* rapid in movement and hot in temper:

Eh! Eh! Bomba, hen! hen!
Cango bafio, té
Canga moune dé lé
Canga do ki la
Canga li.[10]

Warner continues his depiction with observations of the witch doctor's dance. Inspired by the wild singing and changing rhythmic patterns, the witch doctor ignited some brandy and filled his mouth with liquid to discharge it again for the spraying of the spirits. Throughout the performance the bodies of the participants swayed and a soft hand-clapping marked the rhythms.

The degree to which African techniques and modes of expression influenced the music in the southern states in the nineteenth but especially the twentieth century cannot be overestimated. Polyrhythmic progression, participatory performances, and a pitch-oriented vocal and musical expression characterize much of African music such as that of the Yoruba. Through the passage from Africa to America as well as through historical conditions on the plantations and in the colonies, these African elements have taken on new form and meaning in an American context. But essential African traits have survived these historical shifts. The participatory quality of African music shines through in forms of blues talk, blues improvisation, and in the call-and-response pattern of black church services. But it had also manifested itself in preceding forms, such as the work song, the prison song, and the spiritual. The distinction between performers and audience tends to blur in African musical traditions. Choral responses and hand-clapping accompany many of the everyday activities, such as hoeing, planting, celebrating, and practicing religious rites. Call-and-response patterns and polyphony as an expression of multiple voices and rhythms are the results of the participatory quality of African music. The recurrence of these patterns in African American music underscores the striking presence of African elements within the music that emerged in southern states such as Louisiana, Mississippi, and Texas. During jazz performances in New Orleans at the beginning of the twentieth century, the participatory nature of black musical forms was harder to maintain, but the fact that young musicians from the audience were frequently admitted to join the band on stage underscores a close rapport between performers and audience.

How closely jazz has been embedded in the community is evident in the role of funeral procedures and the second-line show. Music and burial ceremonies have become a strong unit in Louisiana culture. Jazz musician Baby Dodds describes a typical funeral procedure:

> As the family and people went to the graveyard to bury one of their loved ones, we'd play a funeral march. It was pretty sad, and it put a feeling of weeping in their hearts and minds and when they left there we didn't want them to hear that going home. It became a tradition to play jazzy numbers going back to make the relatives and friends cast off their sadness. And the people along the streets used to dance to the music. I used to follow those parades myself, long before I ever thought of becoming a drummer. The jazz played after New Orleans funerals didn't show any lack of respect for the person being buried. It rather showed their people that we wanted them to be happy.[11]

The group of people following the band and dancing to the music has been referred to as the second line. It is a regular part not only of funeral marches but also of parades in New Orleans culture. Second-liners act as part of the parade on Mardi Gras, for instance. They cheer up the musicians or discourage them, they dance in the streets and twirl umbrellas, and they establish a bond between the musicians and the larger community. And many a jazz musician was a second-liner before he joined the scene as active musician.

Apart from the participatory nature, which reflects African influences, there is also an extravagant diversity of tonal effects that penetrate secular as well as sacred African American musical forms such as spirituals, blues, and jazz. This is true for both vocal and instrumental performances. Musicologists have repeatedly pointed toward "an African fondness for muddying perfectly clear sounds." Referring to vocal performances in particular, Palmer detects a wide range of tonal effects "from graining falsetto shrieks to affected hoarseness, throaty growls, and guttural grunting."[12] This applies also to instrumental techniques as developed by New Orleans jazz musicians. The gut-bucket sound of the early jazz trumpeters resulted from playing into brass spittoons or cramming mutes into the bells of their horns to modify the sound of their instruments. The pitch-oriented nature of speech and music, finally, that we detect in multiple African cultures surfaces in various techniques developed by blues and jazz musicians alike. The pitch-tone languages spoken among African peoples such as the Yoruba reflect the closeness of their speech to musical expression. In those languages a shift of the pitch level calls forth semantic change. Hence a single syllable or word can take on multiple meanings.[13] This particular quality of speech has had a deep impact on both singing and performing techniques within the world of African American music. In the blues tradition, hammering, pulling, and sliding the notes have become central performative techniques that detach the sound of the instrument even more from conventional Western musical notation and performance and bring it closer to the sound of the human voice. Blues musicians such as Robert Johnson, Elmore James, and B. B. King have developed and extended these techniques in their music.[14]

All these musical elements emphasize the oral basis of much of African American culture and refer back to traits characteristic of African music. The talking effects of New Orleans horn players such as Buddy Bolden and Louis Armstrong reflect the African conception that musicians can make their instruments "talk." Playing upon the correspondences between pitch configurations in music and speech, these musician turned their instruments into talking forces. The talking effects, as they were developed in the playing of

Louis Armstrong, stand within a long tradition of black musical expression. From the beginning, singing played a very significant role within African American music. Field hollers and work songs represent early examples of a pitch-oriented singing style developed in rural areas. In the field of sacred music, spirituals and gospel emerged using a progression based upon call-and-response. In urban settings the street cries of pedlars recalled the shouts from the fields.[15]

Cries and hollers represent one of the major backbones of the blues. The blues' most striking musical features are its rhythm and the cry or holler that marks the singing style of male vocalists especially. As Charles Keil notes, "Singers adopt an identifying shout or cry to climax a song or emphasize a key phrase—for example, Howlin' Wolf's howl, Cleanhead Vinson's 'inaudible' falsetto, B. B. King's clear falsetto and Bobby Bland's hoarse cry."[16] The holler in particular marks the blues as an extension of African pitch-oriented singing. The harmony in the blues stems from European music, which, in its simplest form, consists of three types of chords. Technically, these are known as the tonic, the subdominant, and the dominant. Blues traditionals such as "St. James Infirmary" progress according to this basic chord pattern. Much of the blues structured upon European harmony probably derived from church music, but there are also archaic forms of blues that musicologists date back to decades preceding the Civil War. In its archaic manifestation the early blues is nonharmonic. Archaic patterns shine through in blues recordings by Big Bill Bronzy and John Lee Hooker, for instance. In pre–Civil War days, so goes the general assumption, the singing was simply accompanied by a steady percussive rhythm and the lines varied in length, as the singer made up the lyrics while performing. The improvisatory quality of the early blues was kept alive even in the second half of the twentieth century—in the Mississippi Delta, for instance—as blues musicians such as James "Son" Thomas and Sonny "Boy" Watson point out.[17] The tradition of make-ups, as William Ferris illustrates, has remained alive in the spontaneous get-togethers or house parties of blues musicians with their families and friends on weekends. Generally having undergone changes due to urbanization and technological progress, the old communal function of African American music has lived on in some remote rural areas of the South such as the Mississippi Delta.

A more detailed look at the musical impact on jazz that emerged from the African American experience requires the inclusion of musical forms directly related to black folklore. Jazz is definitely an urban phenomenon, but many of the folk influences that helped shape it have their roots in rural areas of the

South. Both sacred and secular forms of the African American lore contributed to performative and expressive aspects of jazz. Among the first items of black folklore to be collected were the spirituals; as far as the secular music is concerned—work, levee, boat, and jubilee songs as well as ballads—the blues has endured as the most influential musical expression.[18] Due to the mobility of black men in the Reconstruction period and the decades to follow, many of the work and boat songs were transmitted from one region to another and handed down from one generation to another. Except for a few problematic attempts to put this singing style into the form of musical notation, wandering musicians and traveling shows—minstrel shows, vaudeville shows—became the prime agents for spreading African American musical forms. In addition, a great number of migratory workers leaving the plantations and working on boats or in levee camps spread the tradition of calls, hollers, and early blues forms.[19] In the 1930s this old form could still be heard in levee camps along the Mississippi, on the Red River in Louisiana, on the White River in Arkansas, and on rivers in Texas and other streams of the lower Southland, as Alan Lomax points out.[20] In this holler tradition Lomax detects an important musical source for the solo playing in blues and jazz, a trait that sets these African American musical forms apart from the collective song of African tradition. Analyzing the hollers recorded by himself in penitentiaries in the South, Lomax explains:

> All these hollers share a set of distinctive features. They are solos, slow in tempo, free in rhythm (as opposed to the gang work songs), composed of long, gliding, ornamented and melismatic phrases, given a melancholy character by minor intervals as well as by blued or bent tones, sounding like sobs or moans or keening or pain-filled cries, even when they were performed with such bravura that they resounded across the fields.[21]

Along with the long-meter hymns the work hollers of the Mississippi Delta "mark a sharp stylistic turn away from the on-beat collective song style of most earlier African American genres and the adoption of a highly individualized solo attack."[22] Historically, these two forms became increasingly prominent, as the plantation system decayed and many blacks started to migrate.

For the expressive and emotional quality of New Orleans jazz, the blues is essential. The blues as twelve-bar pattern is documented for the first time in 1912, though its origins date further back and its roots have to be seen in the country blues as it developed in the late nineteenth century. The country blues itself is marked by regional differences; the musically most influential style emerged in the Mississippi Delta. Blues was widespread in the rural areas before it found its way into the world of jazz, and there it became the domain of female blues singers such as Bessie Smith, Ma Rainey, Ida Cox, and Mamie Smith, among others.[23]

That the blues became available in the form of written music was due to the achievement of W. C. Handy as collector and composer. When ragtime's popularity was on the brink of vanishing and jazz started ascending, a "blues craze" was launched by Handy's blues arrangements. He became the central figure in the popularization of the blues. His compositions and arrangements, such as "Beale Street Blues" and "St. Louis Blues," established his reputation as ingenious blues composer.[24] Listening to and collecting blues material from rural performers while he was playing with bands in the Mississippi Delta, Handy found a way to transcribe it into an orchestrated form. His blues compositions are clearly different from those sounds and singings he had heard in the Delta and at times his music tends to be arty. Nevertheless, Handy succeeded in transcribing the rhythmic variety of the blues and the blue notes into a musical system that made notation possible. And his musical compositions are definitely inspired by his immediate contact with rural blues performers.

In his autobiography edited by Arna Bontemps, *Father of the Blues,* Handy gives the reader various accounts of his encounters with folk blues performances. Especially during his stay in the Mississippi Delta he recorded several experiences that brought him closer to the roots of the blues. Around the turn of the century Handy had followed an offer to direct a Knights of Pythias band in Clarksdale, Mississippi, and began to tour in the Southland. Waiting for a train at the station in Tutwiler he encountered the rural blues for the first time, hearing a bluesman accompany himself on guitar. The bluesman was singing, "Goin' where the Southern cross' the Dog." Handy was particularly impressed by the way the man was sliding a knife up and down the strings of his guitar, a technique that produced a most peculiar sound to Handy's ears. In subsequent encounters with folk roots, Handy developed a more analytical interest in rural blues performances: "In the Delta, however, I suddenly saw the songs with the eye of a budding composer. The songs themselves, I now observed, consisted of simple declarations expressed usually in three lines and set to a kind of earth-born music that was familiar throughout the Southland half a century ago."[25] Another experience that opened his eyes to not only the artistic but also the economic potential of blues music occurred at a local dance in Clarksdale. Leading an orchestra for a dance in Clarksdale, Handy was asked to play some local music upon request. Because Handy's orchestra could not live up to the expectations of the audience, a local colored band was allowed to take the stage for a few down-home numbers. Handy's description of the scene is characterized by a self-assured and detached tone:

> We eased out gracefully as the newcomers entered. They were led by a long-legged chocolate boy and their band consisted of just three pieces, a battered guitar, a mandolin and a worn-out bass. The music they made was pretty well in keeping with their looks. They struck up one of those over-and-over strains that seem to have no very clear beginning and certainly no ending at all. The strumming attained a disturbing monotony, but on and on it went, a kind of stuff that has long been associated with cane rows and levee camps. Thump-thump-thump went their feet on the floor. Their eyes rolled. Their shoulders swayed. And through it all that little agonizing strain persisted. It was not really annoying or unpleasant. Perhaps "haunting" is a better word, but I commenced to wonder if anybody besides small town rounders and their running mates would go for it. The answer was not long in coming. A rain of silver dollars began to fall around the outlandish, stomping feet. The dancers went wild. . . . There before the boys lay more money than my nine musicians were being paid for the entire engagement.[26]

Both the physical and the economic reaction—tipping the local band generously—of the audience underscores the close communal net surrounding musicians and their communal members in the black rural South. And it recalls the strong communal function music had during times of slavery and the years of Reconstruction. Handy obviously envisions a monetary use of the cultural experience down South because he concludes that the above experience triggered his desire to become an American blues composer. What the blues craze meant for the performance opportunities of orchestras and street bands around the turn of the century, race records signified for artists seeking their way into the recording industry in the 1920s—from the classical blues singers to New Orleans jazz musicians. A rapidly growing black music market spread blues and jazz throughout the nation. Among the black communities in the United States, the popularity of race records featuring blues and jazz pieces was tremendous.[27] In the aftermath of Mamie Smith's success with "Crazy Blues" in 1920, secular and sacred forms of African American music became preserved in permanent form.

Apart from the standardized blues forms on records, diverse blues styles developed, most likely simultaneously, in different regions of the American

South—Mississippi, Texas, Georgia, and Florida, for instance. Because many bluesmen were roaming from state to state and town to town, exchanges between various regional styles occurred. Jazz musicians from New Orleans have repeatedly pointed out that they were influenced by the blues guitarists and ragtime piano players that passed through New Orleans and played in the streets and bars.[28] The blues was definitely a vital part of the musical life in New Orleans around the turn of the century. Stories among jazz musicians in New Orleans turn around the blues singing Mamie Desdoumes, a piano-playing Creole prostitute "who was legendary for singing the same song from morning till night."[29] To Jelly Roll Morton, so the saying goes, she was a major source of blues inspiration.

Blues made its impact across the Southland and, through Handy's compositions, turned from folk expression into an art form.[30] Although cities such as Memphis, Chicago, and Kansas City, Missouri, are most important for the transition from rural to urban blues, New Orleans provided another home for many traveling blues musicians and, in particular, their blues cosmology. Numerous blues lyrics are closely associated with the hoodoo tradition as it emerged in Louisiana. Hence the black elements of Louisiana culture have shaped a great number of blues songs sung about snakes, spirits, and women. Blues lyrics give voice to a belief in ancient voodoo rites, magic charms, and spells; lyrics by Bo Diddley for "I'm a Man" or for "Louisiana Blues" by Muddy Waters illustrate American adaptations of African and Caribbean black religious beliefs in the blues. Perhaps the best-known of all blues songs related to hoodoo is Willie Dixon's "Hoochie Coochie Man," the lyrics of which suggest the fusion of religion and superstition, African magical spells and Catholic worship in Louisiana cultural life despite attempts to annihilate African religious roots.[31] It is important to note, however, that within the community of African Americans the "blues people"—to borrow a term from Amiri Baraka—occupied a peripheral position, in spite of the fact that their performances at dances and parties also served a communal purpose. Whereas many African Americans had converted to the Christian faith but still practiced voodoo-based rites in secret, the blues people were more radically open to express a belief system quite different from Christianity. According to Jon Michael Spencer, the "blues made visible the invisible—the often unarticulated religious retentions of the native homeland, Africa."[32]

With the influx of Protestant Puritanism in Louisiana, a secret practice of following African religious roots called "tipping out" came into being. Tipping out had emerged in Haiti and spread to New Orleans and throughout

Louisiana. The practice referred to regular churchgoers who evaded the rigid doctrines of Protestantism to occasionally draw strength from "the kind of therapy-of-remembering" offered by hoodoo priests and root doctors.[33] In the context of music, tipping out characterized churchgoers who evaded the gospel to listen to the blues at times. And the blues musician then could take on the role of the priest. Though spirituals and blues are generally divided into sacred versus secular musical forms, the blues's cosmology is indeed a holistic one. It embraces superstition and magic as well as religion and does away with the gaps in between. New Orleans and Louisiana are those places most frequently mentioned in blues songs when blues musicians sing about a cosmology transcending the gaps between African and European religions. Not seldom did men of wit in the Delta try both, to preach and play the blues. Blues musicians such as Muddy Waters, Son House, and Big Bill are but a few examples of those who worked in both professions.[34]

Next to the blues, ragtime had a significant impact on the music scene in Louisiana. Fusing various elements of southern folk music, ragtime, or rag, emerged in Missouri—St. Louis, in particular—about 1890. Between 1895 and 1915 ragtime experienced its heyday. "Via itinerant pianists, mechanical player piano rolls, gramophone records, published sheet-music scores, and adaptations of the music to orchestras" ragtime spread across the United States.[35] Ragtime comprised four major types of music, including instrumental rags, ragtime waltzes, ragtime songs, and popular songs arranged for ragtime performances. In notated form the first ragtime pieces appeared in 1896. Most ragtime pieces, such as Thomas Turpin's "Harlem Rag" and Scott Joplin's famous "Maple Leaf Rag," were composed especially for piano. In contrast to the free forms of shouts and hollers, ragtime gave voice to tightly structured musical rhythms. On boats along the Mississippi and in bars in New Orleans, piano players performed rags. Many street bands played music in the ragtime style in the cities of the South. Ragtime brass bands that became famous included the Excelsior Brass Band (founded in 1885 with John Robichaux and Alphonse Picou), the Alliance Brass Band (1889), and the Buddy Bolden Band (1895).

Jazz histories point to ragtime as the beginning of jazz. The fusion of ragtime, blues, and Creole music lead to the emergence of New Orleans jazz. Most musicologists agree that from about 1900 a music began to be played in the streets and bars of New Orleans that we would regard as jazz from our contemporary point of view. This music echoes numerous cultural blendings between diverse European, African, and Caribbean sources. Much attention has been placed on the African and African American impact hitherto. In general the early bands and musicians were playing European tunes on European instruments, though. Due to the lack of orthodox musical training and because of the impact of West African music on their performances, many New Orleans musicians transformed their European material through endless variations and idiosyncretic sound effects. However, the march rhythm—derived from French and Prussian marches—was preserved during this period of cultural blendings. Apart from the march rhythm, a number of different European musical elements constitute an ongoing presence in New Orleans jazz. Perhaps the most pervasive European influence can be seen in the merging of French music with rhumba rhythms in Creole songs. British ballads as well as Spanish melodies belonged to the musical repertoire and were transformed. Especially African Spanish rhythms, resulting from a fusion of European and Caribbean elements in the West Indies, found their way into the jazz performed in New Orleans.

European traditions clearly were the dominant cultural forces in New Orleans in the nineteenth century. Opera and brass bands preserved European cultural roots in musical terms. Directors of German orchestras directed Italian operas at the French Opera in New Orleans, and musicians of German and Italian descent played in brass bands.[36] And brass band music assumed a leading role in Louisiana cultural life. Many brass bands, black and white, played at various public occasions in New Orleans in the late nineteenth century. Most popular brass band performances were from 1880 until 1910. Historically, these brass bands had their roots in the military. During the counter-Reformation wars of the seventeenth century in Europe and England it had become customary for musical groups to accompany armies during times of war. Joyful marching music to cheer the soldiers in times of hardship and sorrow included the sound of trumpets, horns, bassoons, oboes, and fifes. Toward the end of the eighteenth century the early percussion sections were replaced by drum corps playing upon Middle Eastern percussion instruments such as cymbals, bass drums, and snare drums.[37]

The impact of Middle Eastern instruments shaped the important role of drumming for military bands in Europe and America. Early cultural crossings in the development of marching music become visible here. Further refinements in instrument technology added new and better instruments—the saxhorn family, for instance—to the musical equipment of brass bands. Brass bands represent both an influence on jazz and a continuous tradition within jazz. Through the emphasis on brass instruments as the primary musical equipment, a polyphonically oriented style, and various sectional playings during band performances, brass band music provided an essential matrix for New Orleans jazz. In contrast to symphonic orchestras, brass bands had to play outdoor in most instances. Hence the wind instruments used by brass bands differed from those played in symphonic orchestras. Equipped with larger mouthpieces, they were built so that the musicians could produce loud sounds while playing in the streets or on advertising wagons.

Further cultural blendings took place in the development of brass bands in the nineteenth century. Although brass bands on the American continent were modeled on European predecessors, the impact of the African American, Creole, and Caribbean music shaped their performances in Louisiana. The New Orleans street bands synthesized the general brass band tradition with a black musical heritage of African and Caribbean descent as it persisted and changed in the course of African American history. Especially the political and social changes called forth in the years of Reconstruction stimulated the brass band tradition within the black and Creole communities of the Crescent City. And as Schafer emphasizes, "much like the spirituals and jubilees of slavery times, this band music was born on an intense, emotionally charged desire for freedom and recognition."[38] This makes clear that the brass band tradition in New Orleans took new directions that were conditioned by the caste and race system underlying the larger social structure of the city. Although both black and white bands fulfilled a communal function in their communities, the emotional intensity and spiritual quality, as added by black bands, clearly reflected the experiences of blacks and Creoles during times of slavery and Reconstruction.

Two different groups within the colored population of New Orleans and their differing ways of performing were essential for the fusion of European and African elements in New Orleans and in the Storyville district. The Creoles of Louisiana—people of French African heritage—descended from a French colonial population and could look back to ancestors who had been set free by their French planters long before the Civil War. Their names were French and their language represented a form of "bastardized" French. Important musicians of the early days of jazz proudly emphasized their Creole background: Kid Ory, Sidney Bechet, Jelly Roll Morton, and so on. The black Creoles identified themselves with French Caribbean cultural traditions. Many of them took pride in their ability to read and write music; they were proud of their familiarity with European musical genres, the opera in particular. And the presence of a system that operated on caste and racial differences seemed to have guaranteed black Creoles a privileged social status among the colored population of Louisiana. Due to this status, if compared to those African Americans who were descendants from slaves, they were the sophisticated group of black musicians in Louisiana. They had developed a rigid class and caste consciousness and tended to indulge in a notion of supremacy that outdid that of much of the white population at the time. Many of the Creoles were trained musicians and thus were inclined to look down upon musicians who came from the poorer quarters and followed the oral tradition—Buddy Bolden and Louis Armstrong, for instance. Yet some Creole musicians, such as Sidney Bechet, openly embraced the raw and primitive sound of the untrained black musicians. In general, the conflict between these two groups proved very fruitful artistically. Through many of the music competitions—"cutting contests"—that took place between brass bands in New Orleans, rivalry became also inspiration. Jelly Roll Morton was perhaps the jazz musician of the early days who managed best to combine elements of both musical traditions. Sociologically, the groups moved closer together through the legislative acts in the 1890s. The Creoles had lived together with whites in the Vieux Carré but were now forced to move "uptown," to the district west of Canal Street, where the poorer blacks lived. The Creoles' own sense of superiority toward the poorer blacks was radically undermined through a legislative act that put all people of black heritage on the same lower social scale. Through spatial proximity, the musical traditions moved closer together as well, and an artistic exchange was enhanced. Thus the Creole musician, well trained in European music, encountered the raw and unpolished music of uptown blacks that echoed ragtime, country blues, and work songs. Kathy J. Ogren sums up the dual forces behind New Orleans jazz succinctly: "Jazz emerged from collaboration . . . between blacks and black Creoles, instrumentalists and pianists, street musicians and club performers."[39]

New Orleans performers themselves divided the large number of musicians into two major groups; those among them who could read music were labeled "musicianers" and those who played by ear were nicknamed "jazzmen." Interestingly enough, gut-bucket bands such as Kid Ory's gained greater financial and popular success than many of the more sophisticated and refined ensembles playing in Storyville. To be able to play "hot" and "sweet" upon audience request became a central concern for all those bands that wanted to be successful in the New Orleans entertainment business. Although the two groups appeared to different and separate, one may safely conclude that New Orleans jazz could only emerge due to the artistic tensions and inspirations between them. The juxtaposition of black Creole's craftsmanship and of black improvisatory and passionate modes of musical expression paved the way for the emergence of jazz in New Orleans.[40]

The Storyville district became the place where both traditions could synthesize easily, as entertainment and business did away with class and caste differences that had marked the opposing groups of blacks.[41] Due to jurisdiction in 1897, this section of town near the Vieux Carré was turned into a separate area and became the most notorious red light district in the United States for about twenty years. To have better social and economic control over gambling, prostitution, and entertainment, an ordinance was reshaped to provide for two segregated districts by July 1897:

> Be It Ordained, by the Common Council of the City of New Orleans, That Section I, of Ordinance 13,032 C.S. . . . is hereby amended as follows: From and after the first of October, 1897, it shall be unlawful for any prostitute or woman notoriously abandoned to lewdness, to occupy, inhabit, live or sleep in any house, room or closet, situated without the following limits, viz: From the South side of Customhouse Street to the North Side of St. Louis Street, and from the lower wood side of North Basin Street to the lower or wood side of Robertson Street. 2nd: And from the upper side of Gravier Street, and from the river side of Franklin Street to the lower or wood side of Locust Street, provided that nothing herein shall be so construed as to authorize any lewd woman to occupy a house, room or closet in any portion of the city. It shall be unlawful to open, operate or carry on any cabaret, concert-saloon or place where can can, clodoche or similar female dancing or sensational performances are shown, without following limits, viz: from the lower side of N. Basin Street to the lower side of N. Robertson Street, and from the south side of Customhouse Street to the north side of St. Louis Street.[42]

Storyville street names—Basin Street, Liberty Street, Iberville Street, and so on—have become part of many blues and jazz titles during the years of music recordings. Full of cabarets, gambling shows, dance clubs, and honky-tonks, Storyville provided the ideal place for the flourishing of prostitution and entertainment. Especially between 1910 and 1917 many of the leading New Orleans musicians performed their jazz styles in the bars and restaurants of Storyville. The pianist Jelly Roll Morton performed in the Arlington Annex. Within the famed Storyville red light district brothels and bordellos engaged pianists rather than bands. Musicians including Morton performed there because the gigs were well paid. Morton's repertoire throughout the evening performances included popular songs, ragtime, blues, and jazz tunes on piano. Bands and ensembles, on the other hand, performed primarily in commercial clubs and dance halls. Because musicians depended on tips, bands tended to arrange their musical performance according to an audience's tastes. Thus indoor performances of jazz displayed a tendency to lose some of the rigor and spontaneity that characterized the jazz played in the streets or on side-wagons. Papa Celestin and Johnny Dodds played in the Tuxedo Dance Hall, and Joe "King" Oliver, Sidney Bechet, and Manuel Perez could be heard in the 101 Ranch in Franklin Street. But jazz bands also played in the streets accompanying the announcement of events such as dances, boxing fights, and other performances.[43]

There were so many brass and jazz bands playing in New Orleans that the cutting contests became a regular phenomenon during the heyday of Storyville. Even during performances in venues like Charity Hall another band would play right in front of the club to outdo the band playing inside. Similar musical contests took place during Mardi Gras parades when the floats of two bands met or came close. A climate of rivalry that was both economic and musical shaped the development of the jazz scene in New Orleans. For instance, Freddie Keppard and Joe Oliver fought for the position of "King of Jazz," a contest the latter won eventually. Many bands—"spasm bands"—that had played in other towns in Louisiana moved to New Orleans to profit musically and economically. Still, jazz was played outside the Storyville district as well, and many jazz musicians performing in the small Louisiana towns near the Crescent City stopped by to play and to learn. So did Kid Ory's troupe in 1911. After having performed for years in La Place, Louisiana, they went to play in the booming city on the Mississippi Delta.[44] Although a lot of money changed hands in the Storyville district, most musicians could not live on their gigs and performances. Black musicians especially were badly paid. Usually they had to work part time to make ends meet. Many of them worked in the tobacco industry, in the port, and in other low-skill jobs. The majority of them were autodidactic as far as their musical training was concerned and practiced in between jobs.

How to describe New Orleans jazz in musical terms? We may only guess what early New Orleans jazz really sounded like. From the first recordings we have, we can conclude that the particularly swinging rhythm that characterizes later forms of jazz was absent at that time. Whereas in later forms the second and the fourth beat are also accentuated, early New Orleans jazz progresses along a rhythmic line close to that of marches. The accent lies on the first and third beat. Usually the rhythmic section consists of bass, drum, banjo, or guitar and occasionally piano. The melody conventionally consists of three melodic lines played by three different instruments. The cornet or trumpet takes the light-sounding leading role, whereas the trombone sets the contrasting heavy sound. The clarinet, finally, plays a melodic line that moves in various directions in between the juxtaposition of light and heavy sounds created by the cornet and trombone.[45] What is considered New Orleans jazz today is largely modeled on the music played by New Orleans bands in Chicago during the 1920s. King Oliver, Louis Armstrong's Hot Five and Hot Seven, Jelly Roll Morton's Red Hot Peppers, and Johnny Dodds New Orleans Wanderers recorded jazz tunes in the city on the Lake Michigan that had then moved away from the archaic forms of early New Orleans jazz.

Although a definition of New Orleans jazz allows us to point out important criteria of this particular style of jazz, it does not do justice to the multiplicity of stylistic variations within the New Orleans jazz scene in the first decades of the twentieth century. Such different musical personalities as King Oliver, Jelly Morton, Sidney Bechet, and Louis Armstrong shaped various nuances of solo and ensemble playing in their own unique ways. Even if New Orleans jazz is nowadays generally associated with tradition and heritage, we should not forget that the above musicians introduced techniques and improvisational ways to the world of jazz that paved the way for future developments in cities in the North and on the West Coast. Thus many of the seeds that would later bloom into bebop, cool jazz, and free jazz were already planted in those early days through the inventiveness of Creole and black musicians performing in the streets and clubs of New Orleans.

Jazz musicians from New Orleans prepared the ground for the rapidly changing history of jazz styles in the twentieth century. King Oliver's bands—his Creole Jazz Band as well as the Savannah Syncopators—appealed to their audience through their fine ensemble style rather than individual talent, Louis Armstrong, who joined King Oliver's Creole Jazz Band in 1923, aside. The music played by King Oliver and his ensembles can best be described as blues-based, improvised, and ensemble-oriented. It was "at once spontaneous and deliberate, passionate and controlled, controlled in ways that make its passion all the more convincing."[46] Although Oliver was not as ingenious an instrumentalist and soloist as Louis Armstrong, the former had tremendous talent to inspire and guide group improvisations, a central trait of New Orleans jazz. Despite his comparatively limited range as instrumentalist, he succeeded in creating a unique sound. The sound itself is best described as muted, and gradations of this muted sound were arranged in such a way that they could be spontaneously used for group improvisation. Oliver's muted sound gradations impressed Louis Armstrong so much that he immediately left New Orleans to follow Oliver's call to perform with him in Chicago. The New Orleans polyphonic style as elaborated by King Oliver's Creole Jazz Band shines through in recordings of jazz tunes such as "Weather Bird Rag," "Dippermouth Blues," and "Canal Street Blues," all of which appeared in 1923. The critic or fan of jazz who wants to experience the inspiring interplay of King Oliver and Louis Armstrong should listen to the Paramount version of "Riverside Blues."

Whereas King Oliver's primary merit seems to lie in the successful integration of blues feeling and collective improvisation, Jelly Roll Morton has been praised in jazz criticism for his talent to synthesize blues and folk influences with a European sense of form and discipline. On the one hand he resorted to compositions of well-schooled ragtime musicians and composers, on the other hand he incorporated the expressive quality of earthier music such as the work song, blues, and spirituals.[47] He succeeded in closing the gap between the individual blues improvisation and the requirements of composition and ensemble orchestration. Although Morton drew on the melodic wealth of ragtime compositions he was fascinated with the passionate quality as well as with the rhythmic diversity offered by the blues.

Perhaps Louis Armstrong's most important contribution to jazz was the swinging quality of his playing. Unequaled as trumpet player in the history of jazz, Armstrong turned jazz into a swinging form of music. With his Hot Five and Hot Seven bands he bridged the gap from archaic to swinging jazz.[48] There is a greater melodic and rhythmic order in Armstrong's playing than in earlier forms of jazz. Early on Armstrong displayed an intense concern with rhythm: "Then Isaac Smooth and I would make the rounds of the honky tonks watching the people . . . but mostly we were interested in music. We were always looking for a new piano player with something on the ball like a rhythm that was all his own."[49] The doubling and tripling of notes in his playing had primarily a rhythmic functioning. And Armstrong was responsible for a new emphasis on the blues in terms of rhythm and passion in his recordings of the 1920s. That Armstrong put emphasis on blues feeling can be contributed to his early musical and racial experiences in the streets and honky tonks of New Orleans. All his life Armstrong felt bitter toward his hometown due to the Jim Crow ways in which he and other blacks of the poor sections were treated. Growing up poor in New Orleans, Armstrong found in the blues an artistic outlet for racial oppression and discrimination. Despite his musical genius, it took Armstrong a long time to receive the status in New Orleans he deserved. It was not until 1949 that he could fulfill one of his childhood dreams when he became elected king of Zulu: On Mardi Gras on that year he seated himself on the throne of the Zulu float. Carnival and music have been closely interwoven in New Orleans culture, and both have provided blacks codes for parodying and criticizing white discrimination. So it was all the more understandable that Armstrong's return as king of Zulu to his place of birth was his most triumphant moment. But segregation kept haunting Armstrong's relationship with his hometown. When he wanted to play a concert with his racially mixed All-Stars in the 1950s, he was rejected because such a band would violate Louisiana law.[50] Segregation laws kept Armstrong away from New Orleans most of the time, but they could not prevent him from becoming jazz's greatest innovator and popularizer.

While black and Creole musicians were the driving force behind the early forms of jazz, numerous white musicians became increasingly involved with blues, ragtime, and jazz. Among the white musicians, George Vitelle Laine, nicknamed "Jack" or "Papa" Laine, was the central figure in the music scene around the turn of the century. His first band was formed in 1888. In the 1890s Papa Laine was involved with parades and dance performances. He led the Reliance Brass Band in concerts and parades and a ragtime band for dance occasions. His influence grew steadily because he demonstrated a great talent for organizing and contracting bands. A Laine band usually played at a dance, a parade, a picnic, a private party, or for an advertising wagon. Laine's bands entertained the white community of New Orleans. On special occasions such as Mardi Gras, Laine would organize several extra bands. Although the majority of musicians in Laine's bands were white, at least two members of his ragtime band were of mixed blood, the trombonist Dave Perkins and the clarinetist Achille Baquet.[51] As far as the musical orientation of his band members was concerned, some of them could play from a sheet, others would play the pieces by ear. In general, improvisation played a minor part in the performances of Laine's bands. One may fairly well assume that nearly all significant white jazz musicians of the New Orleans scene were at one time or another playing with Laine.

Very important for the further spreading of jazz was the fact that Papa Laine also contracted jobs for musicians around Dominic James LaRocca, founder of "the Original Dixieland Band." It speaks for the racial and cultural politics of the time that the music industry picked an all-white band for the first recordings of jazz. After gigs in New Orleans, Chicago, and New York, Columbia and Victor offered them a chance to record. Although Columbia suffered from technical problems during their initial attempt to record jazz music, Victor was more successful. "Livery Stable Blues" and "Dixieland Jass Band One-Step" were recorded on February 26, 1917, at the Victor Talking Machine Company.[52] With the publication of the first jazz record a boom set in. And white bands profited from it primarily. White bands such as the Original Dixieland Jazz Band and the New Orleans Rhythm Kings, with their soloists George Brunies on trombone and Leon Rappolo on clarinet, enjoyed the greatest popular and financial success during the 1920s. Ironically, most of the early recordings of the Original Dixieland Jazz Band, such as "Tiger Rag," "Jazz Me Blues," and "Sensation Rag," were borrowings from colored bands and musicians from New Orleans, from Freddie Keppard's Creole Band and Jelly Roll Morton in particular.[53]

With the beginning of the Depression years, jazz musicians, too, suffered from economic woes. Performance and recording opportunities became rare, and jobs were played without payment. King Oliver, for instance, was forced to run a fruit stand or to sweep out a pool hall because he rarely found a job to play. The more successful jazz musicians, such as Sidney Bechet and Louis Armstrong, played in Europe for some time. The chances for performance opportunities in the United States did not improve until swing took the nation by storm. With the popularity of swing a new interest in jazz's early history and its New Orleans background set in.

During the swing years, in the early 1940s, media activity surrounding jazz peaked. The film industry's growing interest in jazz and jazz musicians could be seen in productions such as *Jammin' the Blues* (1944) and *Dixieland Jamboree* (1945). This increasing media interest came together with a revival of New Orleans jazz. In 1945 Esquire All-American Jazz coordinated three jazz concerts for radio broadcast on a single night. The Ellington orchestra performed in the Philharmonic Auditorium in Los Angeles, Benny Goodman's quintet played from New York, and Louis Armstrong played from his hometown, New Orleans. The end of this radio broadcast was marked by a technological clue. All musicians jammed with one another over the radio; because black as well as white musicians and various styles of jazz and different regions of the United States were brought together, the broadcast fulfilled a democratic purpose successfully.[54]

That Armstrong played in the Crescent City during the broadcast was symbolical for the New Orleans revival of the 1940s and a reawakened interest in early jazz music, Dixieland in particular. Record collectors and record producers initiated this reawakened interest in early jazz. Bill Russell recorded some Bunk Johnson and Kid Ory recorded on Crescent. Many of the old New Orleans musicians—some of them had already been forgotten—came together to start over again in clubs in Bourbon Street such as the Paddock Lounge and Famous Door, which came into being during revival time. Preservation Hall, which opened in 1961, has gained a cultlike status for old-time jazz. Although the New Orleans revival included a few black old-time musicians—Kid Ory, Bunk Johnson, Kid Rena—mainly white jazz musicians played the early black jazz for white audiences. The New Orleans revival demonstrated that the white world had caught up with African American musical expressions. New Orleans jazz bands emerged all over Europe as well as in Australia and Japan. Economically, it was New Orleans's steady transformation into a tourist center in the decades to follow that laid the foundation for the new popular success of old-time jazz in Louisiana. Today old-time jazz has assumed a fixed place in the entertainment business of the Crescent City.[55]

As part of the tourist attraction, music performances ranged from gigs by old musicians clearly rooted in the rhythms of the past to those of younger studio musicians who simply do their job. Especially black jazz musicians repeatedly turned their back on what they considered outdated forms of jazz. Already in the 1950s black musicians gathered in a group called American Jazz Quintet to play a late bebop style. To them, Dixieland stood for an "Uncle Tom" form of music. In later decades clubs such as the Lu & Charlie in Rampart Street and the Maple Leaf Bar established an alternative scene that allowed for musical experimentation. Musicians around the bass player Ramsey McLean, for instance, followed in the footsteps of John Coltrane in their rhythmic and melodic experiments. To make a living, though, most of them had to take jobs besides or play music in clubs and discotheques, music that suited the audience tastes. The Lu & Charlie, like other alternative places, could not survive economically.

Ellis Marsalis and Harold Battiste were among those musicians of the 1950s and 1960s in New Orleans who turned their backs on traditional and popular forms. They found rhythm and blues—the music most popular then—too confining for their own musical ambitions. Battiste, more than any other jazz musician in the city at this time, was at the core of the modern jazz movement in the South. Besides Marsalis and Battiste, a school of innovative jazzmen worked steadily and patiently in the shadows of rhythm and blues' popular success. The New Orleans modern jazz scene was part of a national turning away from traditional and swinging jazz. That both black and white musicians were involved in this musical shift underscores the fact that jazz experimentation in the postwar period was a biracial phenomenon. Musicians such as Marsalis and Battiste turned to blues and bebop to shape an improvisational New Orleans style. Although they still played rhythm and blues to make a living, especially in the early sixties, when r&b reached its popular zenith, improvisational jazz represented their true artistic concern. Improvisational jazz became even more widespread in the city's jazz scene, as John Coltrane and Miles Davis made their appearances there while on tour in the 1960s. Particularly musicians such as James Rivers and Earl Turbinton modeled their jazz improvisations on techniques developed by Coltrane and Davis.

The year 1961 was pivotal for the modern jazz scene in New Orleans. Due to the organizing talent of Al Belletto, the most successful white modernist in the Crescent City, the Playboy Club provided the modern jazz scene with a unique opportunity to articulate their new experimental styles and musical messages. Al Belletto succeeded in bringing together outstanding instrumentalists such as Ellis Marsalis on piano, James Black on drums, and Alvin Batiste on clarinet.[56] Al Belleto's job as musical director of the Playboy Club in New Orleans was significant for the outlet of modern jazz, as jazz clubs in general suffered commercially from the rise of rock and roll. That jazz from New Orleans continues to be innovative and inspiring can be seen in the city's contemporary contributions to the jazz scene. In terms of jazz history, the contemporary work of Wynton and Branford Marsalis as well as that of Wendell Brunious may well set new milestones for jazz musicians to come.

Besides such outstanding instrumentalists from a New Orleans background, there is a vital jazz scene alive in New Orleans and throughout Louisiana. Especially in the black neighborhoods where musicians frequently get together to jam on a private basis, jazz continues to thrive, only a few blocks away from the entertainment business of the French Quarter. Moreover, there are a great many music academies, schools, and workshops that keep the jazz scene very much alive. Most significant yet for the steady interest in the jazz heritage seems to be a enduring pattern of musical families living in New Orleans and Louisiana. The closing of the Storyville district in 1919 caused many jazz musicians to head north. But despite the overall African American migration—cities such as Memphis and Kansas City as well as the region of the Mississippi Delta lost a lot of their musicians—New Orleans could keep the majority of their musicians at home. From the middle of the nineteenth century on, New Orleans had developed a pattern of musical families that have preserved and extended the rich musical heritage of the Crescent City. This is especially interesting because New Orleans is still a city without a major recording industry. The fact that a great number of musicians stayed in Louisiana should not disguise the tremendous loss the music scene has suffered from the departure of such important figures as King Oliver, Louis Armstrong, and Wynton Marsalis. The strong familial and cultural bonds, though, that have shaped the life of Creoles and African Americans in Louisiana has provided the social matrix for the continuity and vitality of jazz and other black musical expressions in and around New Orleans.

From the first musical Creole families to the Bourbon Street Black of today, families have handed down their craftsmanship and knowledge as professional musicians.[57] In particular, free blacks from Catholic backgrounds strengthened familial ties that had been loosened or destroyed during slavery. Free blacks had full access to musical instruments and musical training, so their families profited from a cultural matrix that allowed them to bring forth generations of professional musicians. The Abrahams, the Assuntos, the Bechets, the Dodds, and the Marsalises are but a few of the families throughout the history of music in New Orleans that have brought forth various jazz musicians.[58] Contrary to the stereotype of the jazz musician as flamboyant and rebellious deviant, many of the jazz musicians in New Orleans were, and are, integrated family members of musical families that have preserved their musical heritage throughout the decades.

A central element—and most influential, too—within this family pattern is a semicommunity in New Orleans, Bourbon Street Black. The very core of this small group of predominantly black people consists of a few families, several members of which are professional musicians; music teachers; and "the Local," an organization of musicians that gained great influence on the music scene in the early seventies. The lifestyle of Bourbon Street Black is naturally dominated by music—training, performance, and business included. For several decades some of the Bourbon Street Black families have exercised a great deal of control over who performs where in New Orleans. Although "blackness" is a distinctive trait of Bourbon Street Black, a smaller number of white musicians and nonmusicians are loosely associated with the core group. Although most whites belong to the periphery of Bourbon Street Black, they are musically very much involved with black music made in New Orleans. Though hardly visible to the occasional visitor to New Orleans, Bourbon Street Black continues to be a vital part of black musical expression. Most families within this group were, and are, intact. Hence the myth of the wandering bluesmen and jazzmen does not ring true when we look at this semicommunity.[59]

New Orleans indeed occupies a unique position within the world of jazz that has often been associated with drugs, financial ruin, and early death. In today's New Orleans jazz musicians hardly ever suffer from financial problems, as long as they play old-time jazz. There is always an audience that longs for the sound of this old-time music, and musicians can even grow old and still perform successfully, as long as they stick to the old tradition.

That jazz in New Orleans, as most other African American musical forms, has been strongly related to the life of the community becomes most visible in the use of jazz for parades, dances, and funeral marches. Although radio, CD players, television, and music videos may have distanced musicians from their audience, the jazz scene in New Orleans keeps a communal spirit alive. And the interracial musical vocabulary jazz has brought forth in New Orleans not only reflects the region's multicultural history but also expresses hope for future social developments between the various racial and ethnic groups within Louisiana.

NOTES

1. Ishmael Reed, *Mumbo Jumbo* (New York: Avon, 1972) 55–56.

2. The title of the biography written by John Chilton: *Sidney Bechet: The Wizard of Jazz* (New York: Oxford University Press, 1987).

3. T he *Southern Register* had announced the Bechet celebration in its Winter/Spring 1997 issue (14). Further information I received from Berndt Ostendorf (Amerika Institut München), who attended the conference in New Orleans, when I met him at the annual conference of the German Association of American Studies in Freiburg.

4. Marshall W. Stearns, *The Story of Jazz* (1956; New York: Oxford University Press, 1970) 37–39.

5. Arrigo Polillo, *Jazz: Geschichte und Persönlichkeiten* (1981; Mainz: Schott, 1991) 64–65.

6. Robert Palmer, *Deep Blues* (New York: Penguin, 1982) 33.

7. See Stearns 17–18.

8. Ekkehart Jost, *Sozialgeschichte des Jazz in den USA* (Frankfurt: Fischer Taschenbuch, 1982) 29.

9. See Stearns 44–47.

10. C. D. Warner, *Studies in the South and the West* (New York: Harper & Brothers, 1889) 69–72.

11. Larry Gara, *The Baby Dodds Story* (Los Angeles: Contemporary, 1959) 17–18.

12. Palmer 30.

13. Palmer 28–30.

14. See Scott Ainslie and Dave Whitehill, *Robert Johnson: At the Crossroads—The Authoritative Guitar Transcriptions* (Milwaukee: Hal Leonhard, 1992). This work marks one of the most significant attempts to transcribe the blues style as developed by Robert Johnson, including such blues pieces as "Terraplane Blues" and "Walking Blues."

15. Joe Vierra, *Jazz: Musik unserer Zeit* (Schaftlach: Oreos, 1992) 81–82.

16. Charles Keil, *Urban Blues* (1966; Chicago: University of Chicago Press, 1991) 55.

17. William Ferris, *Blues from the Delta* (New York: Anchor, 1979) 61–65.

18. Houston A. Baker Jr., *Long Black Song: Essays in Black American Literature and Culture* (Charlottesville: University Press of Virginia, 1972) 31–35.

19. In later days the recording business took over the function to preserve, spread, and sell the rich diversity of folk music, the blues in particular. See Paul Oliver, *Screening the Blues: Aspects of the Blues Tradition* (New York: Da Capo, 1968) 1–3.

20. Alan Lomax, *The Land Where the Blues Began* (1993; London: Minerva, 1995) 230–35.

21. Lomax 232.

22. Ibid.

23. Carlo Bohländer, Karl Heinz Holler, and Christian Pfarr, *Reclams Jazzführer* (Stuttgart: Philipp Reclam, 1989) 12. See also Daphne Duval Harrison, *Black Pearls. Blues Queens of the 1920's* (New Brunswick: Rutgers University Press, 1990). Her work is central for the understanding of the female contribution to blues and jazz in the 1920s.

24. W. C. Handy, ed., *Blues: An Anthology—Complete Words and Music of 53 Great Songs* (1926; New York: Da Capo, 1990) 82–85, 116–19.

25. W. C. Handy, *Father of the Blues: An Autobiography by W. C. Handy* (1941; New York: Da Capo, 1969) 75.

26. Handy, *Father of the Blues* 76–77. It is historically interesting to note here that many blacks bought instruments that white Confederate soldiers had dumped after the Civil War in New Orleans pawn shops. See Stephen Longstreet, *Storyville to Harlem: Fifty Years in the Jazz Scene* (New Brunswick: Rutgers University Press, 1986) 24.

27. See Kathy J. Ogren, *The Jazz Revolution: Twenties America and the Meaning of Jazz* (New York: Oxford University Press, 1989) 91–92.

28. See Graham Collier, *Jazz: Ein Fuehrer fuer Lehrer und Schueler,* trans. Jürg Solothurnmann (Wilhelmshaven: Heinrichshofen's, 1982) 21.

29. Francis Davis, *The History of the Blues* (New York: Hyperion, 1995) 28.

30. Nowadays scholars and fans interested in the blues take a trip to Clarksdale to visit the Delta Blues Museum and to Oxford to check the blues archive of the Center for the Study of Southern Culture at the University of Mississippi. A trip by jazz critic and advocate Joachim-Ernst Berendt to Louisiana in the fifties became the starting point for many blues festivals in Europe. A visit to Angola State Prison in Louisiana, the temporary "home" of many a blues musician in the Southland, inspired him to launch blues festivals all over Europe. Blues veterans from the South played in Sweden, Poland, Germany, Italy, and England. See Joachim-Ernst Berendt, *Das Leben-ein Klang: Wege zwischen Jazz und Nada Brahma* (Munich: Droemer Knaur, 1996) 320–21.

31. The lyrics can be found in Julio Finn, *The Bluesman: The Musical Heritage of Black*

Men and Women in the Americas (New York: Quartet, 1986) 150. For further hoodoo elements in the blues, see Paul Oliver, *Blues Fell This Morning—The Meaning of the Blues* (1960; Cambridge: Cambridge University Press, 1990) 117–37.

32. Jon Michael Spencer, *Blues and Evil* (Knoxville: University of Tennessee Press, 1993) 14.

33. Spencer 14.

34. Lomax 359.

35. Charles Reagan Wilson and William Ferris, eds., *The Encyclopedia of Southern Culture* (Chapel Hill: University of North Carolina Press, 1989) 1025.

36. Dietrich Schulz-Köhn, *Die Evergreen Story: 40 x Jazz* (Weinheim: Quadriga, 1990) 321.

37. William J. Schafer with assistance from Richard B. Allen, *Brass Bands and New Orleans Jazz* (Baton Rouge: Louisiana State University Press, 1977) 2–3. Schafer describes the Middle Eastern impact: "The Turkish music fad is reflected in such standard classical works as Mozart's keyboard imitation in his Rondo a la Turka; in Haydn's Military Symphony (no. 100), with its use of the military percussion section; in Beethoven's 'Turkish March' from the Ruins of Athens; and even in episodes in the fourth movement of the Ninth Symphony, when the 'Ode to Joy' turns into a village band march, complete with syncopated percussion parts for big drum, cymbals, and triangle" (3).

38. Schafer 13

39. Ogren 35.

40. See Martin Williams, *Jazz Masters of New Orleans* (1967; New York: Macmillan, 1978) 4–10.

41. Joachim Ernst Berendt, *Das Jazzbuch: Von New Orleans bis in die achtziger Jahre* (1991; Frankfurt: Fischer Taschenbuch, 1993) 25–26.

42. Quoted in Longstreet 20.

43. Polillo 71–72.

44. Alma Hubner, "Kid Ory," *Selections from the Gutter: Jazz Portraits from "The Jazz Record,"* ed. Art Hodes and Chadwick Hansen (Berkeley and Los Angeles: University of California Press, 1977) 112–15, 113.

45. Berendt, *Das Jazzbuch* 26.

46. Martin Williams, *The Jazz Tradition* (1970; New York: Oxford University Press, 1993) 9.

47. Williams, *Jazz Tradition* 21–25.

48. See Carlo Bohländer, *Die Anatomie des swing* (Frankfurt: Jas, 1986) 107–11. In this excerpt Bohländer provides a close musical analysis of the shift from march rhythm to swing.

49. Louis Armstrong, *Satchmo: My Life in New Orleans* (New York: New American Library, 1955) 54.

50. Reid Mitchell, *All on a Mardi Gras Day: Episodes in the History of New Orleans Carnival* (Cambridge: Harvard University Press, 1995) 147–51.

51. Williams *Jazz Masters,* 26–27.

52. See Harry O. Brunn, *The Story of the Original Dixieland Jazz Band* (1960; New York: Da Capo, 1977) 63–68.

53. Williams *Jazz Masters,* 30.

54. Arthur Knight, "*Jammin' the Blues*, or the Sight of Jazz, 1944," *Representing Jazz*, ed. Krin Gabbard (Durham, N.C.: Duke University Press, 1995) 23, 11–53.

55. Ekkehard Jost, *Jazzmusiker: Materialien zur Soziologie der afro-amerikanischen Musik* (Frankfurt: Ullstein, 1982) 248–57.

56. Jason Berry, Jonathan Foose, and Tad Jones, *Up from the Cradle of Jazz: New Orleans Music Since World War II* (Athens: University of Georgia Press, 1986) 140–43.

57. Berry, Foose, and Jones 8–9.

58. For a historical survey of New Orleans musicians, see Al Rose and Edmond Souchon, *New Orleans Jazz: A Family Album* (Baton Rouge: Louisiana State University Press, 1978).

59. Jack V. Buerkle and Danny Barker, *Bourbon Street Black: The New Orleans Black Jazzman* (New York: Oxford University Press, 1973) 41–48.

One More Last Chance

Ritual and the Jazz Funeral

BRENDA MARIE OSBEY

Non-natives who follow the trends in New Orleans music frequently marvel upon learning that yet another well-known New Orleans musician turns out, in the end, to have specified "no jazz funeral." One of the arguments traditional musicians give when declining the once-preferred method of burial among their peers is the cheapening of the medium. Sometime during the 1970s, bands began hiring themselves out to anyone able to pay for what had once been an honor conferred specifically and exclusively upon musicians by peers and fellows. With this new development, then, came a general veering from tradition. And that, as we like to say, was the start of all that. Along with the fact that nearly all bands hire out these days is the sense that "nobody wants to do it right anyway."

Traditionally, the street crowd waits outside until the body emerges from the church. At this point, and until the procession reaches the cemetery, the band, indeed, the entire procession, is under the direction of the grand marshal, who leads not with baton or even with hands but with his feet—his walk, his stance, the various postures he throws his body into as he commands the attention and respect of all who look on. Exiting from the church under the masterful and signifying direction of the marshal, the band plays the dirge and a variety of sacred music.

It is only after completing the grave-site ritual, and upon exiting the cemetery grounds, that a single loud blast signals the beginning of the big send-off. The street crowd, which has been following along on foot and growing in size and number, joins in here and helps to dance the soul on home. The formal procession, comprised of the deceased and the mourners, the musicians and the clergy, makes up the first or official line; the street revelers comprise the famous Second-line. Such numbers as "Oh! When the Saints (Go Marching In)!" and "Didn't He Ramble" and other more contemporary songs are then played for the duration. The entire celebration is usually followed by a repast hosted by the family or one or more of the lodges, social aid and pleasure clubs, or other societies to which the deceased belonged. This, in New Orleans, is what is meant by "doing it up *right*."

The 1970s, however, set in motion one set of changes to this particular celebration of the dead. No doubt future generations also will coin it anew. In recent years there has been a tendency for the Second-line to start all but immediately *from* the church and proceed to the cemetery, dancing and blasting right up to the holy ground gates. Even in the Faubourg Treme—and almost especially here in Treme—this tendency seems to have all but replaced the old custom: the solemn processional, the exquisitely drawn-out dirge, the grand posturing of the grand marshal and her or his captains.

What we tend to forget, however, is that the tradition we laud and cling to was pretty much already dead or dying. The brass bands had fallen into disuse. Musicians themselves, audiophiles, an odd collector here and there—these made up the negligible audiences for brass bands. And though we did not mention it to outsiders (and less than seldom discussed it among ourselves), we longed to put behind us the image of Old Satchmo, horn in one hand, handkerchief in the other, grinning in his teeth to entertain the white-folk. Though he himself went far into the night of jazz, and farther still from us, that image would be forever with us. And the brass bands evoked that image, brought it into sharp if ephemeral focus. Younger people in particular had no use for traditional jazz. It was tied too closely to other "traditions" of which we had had more than enough.

Oddly enough, it was younger musicians, musicians from Satchmo's old neighborhood in the Faubourg Treme, who would turn to the dying sound of the traditional brass band, reclaim it, revivify it, and funk it up anew. And quiet as it is kept, the marching tradition had always been the privilege of the young. It's simply that the young men who had grown up in the street bands and in the brass-band tradition—who had, in fact, *made* that tradition—had themselves grown old doing it. They were just holding on, holding their own in the face of changing styles and demands as they were able and wont to do. Thus when the rest of the nation began to look at New Orleans music culture with more than passing interest, the image they saw—somewhat mistakenly rendered—was an image of old men marching and playing.

The young men who had grown up playing in high school or street bands were the grandchildren of the musicians of Satchmo's day. Out of high school and working at various trades, they struggled to make lives as musicians. This meant playing college dances, weddings, proms, society benefits, the usual "entertainment" gigs. But they longed to break out with their own thing. They had grown up on stories of Kid Ory, Kid Rena, Paul Barbarin, Sidney Bechet, the Humphrey brothers, King Oliver, the Dominguez brothers, the Robicheaux, George Lewis, Papa Celestin, Baby Dodds, Louis Nelson, Barney Bigard, Louis Cottrell, Alcide "Slow Drag" Pavageau, Bunk Johnson, and, of course, the King—Buddy Bolden. For countless years, Danny Barker, who only recently passed on, had always been there to regale anyone who would listen with tales of his days as sideman for the great-Greats. And in spite of any misgivings about the image of old man Satchmo, there was, of course, the undeniably hot sound of *young* Louis Armstrong, blasting onto the American scene and "busting the whole thing loose."

Many of these young men had been lifelong apprentices to older musicians—uncles, fathers, and cousins. Many belonged to the Mardi Gras Indian and neighborhood Carnival marching club traditions as well. Combining the traditional sound of the New Orleans street music they all knew backward and forward with the raw bounce, the hipper pitch, and timing of the newer music, appropriately named "funk," they came upon a formula for success. Out of these laboratories of 1970s funk-brass, then, emerged such groups as the Dirty Dozen, the Soul Rebels, and the tellingly named Rebirth Brass Brand.

There is also, of course, the conundrum of custom in New Orleans. The ability not merely to adapt but to improvise is itself inherent in all our notions of tradition. Here, improvisation *is* the tradition. And we have all of us always known as much. Did we expect to learn of these changes coming to some other, perhaps less fortunate generation than our own? And so we find ourselves—caught up in our own moment. We are that weary sweat-drenched street crowd calling to weary sweat-drenched musicians, who've given us all they had, only to find us still here at the end of the dance, handkerchiefs in hand, hanging on and demanding without pity, "One more! One more!"

If we natives brood over the passing of the old way, it is only partly because we recognize our part as witnesses to the demise of a tradition and realize we can do almost nothing to retrieve it. It is also because we are—like the man saved from a drowning death and perhaps a bit bruised and bedraggled in the process—as the old folk would say, "a little short on appreciation and a good bit cheap on memory." But there are other reasons as well.

This falling out of the church directly into the revelry of Carnival-time hoopla cheats us of our due. It seems, to diehard traditionalists, to cut short the time allotted for the mourning of the mourners, with whom we always sympathized a bit—even if we did not know them, even if we knew them and cared little for them. Their grief was a thing we knew. If we had not ourselves experienced that selfsame loss already, we knew that soon enough we would each of us have to look it dead in the face. And so it is not so much that we "took it personal" as it was that we were able to put aside the personal and give ourselves up—for the length of time it took the mourners to reach that gate—to the hugeness of that one inevitable and ever-recurring loss.

The very form of the burial was reflective of our unity in this vulnerability, the basic precariousness of our span. In the old days, the bands prided themselves in their appearance. They dressed in black suits, starched white band shirts, crisp bow ties. Especially compelling was the appearance of the grand marshal, who might be a man or woman, decked out in tux or tails, the name of the band emblazoned across the bosom in the form of a white or gray or silver sash, elegantly hitched on one side. It was the custom that the marshal carry a baton or walking stick. This was more critical in terms of style than musical direction, as the band already knew its part and would improvise accordingly anyhow. The shoes were spit-shined to a dull glow and the bearing appropriately, even theatrically, grave. On nearly all sides there would be a deep hush, with only sporadic words of admiration for the dignity of the whole procession.

Men standing on the sidelines took off their hats. Church-ladies made the sign of the cross. Only rarely were policemen needed and only then to direct traffic in the case of an extremely important figure and, in that case, almost always on horseback. The custom is for ongoing traffic to halt, without directive and regardless of personal hurry, traffic lights, or right-of-way. Small children were prevented from pointing, for to do so would cause their mothers' breasts to "drop off." Likewise, casual open staring, as from a bus or car, was said to bring on general ill favor from the dead.

The mourners walked and drove and rode along under the guidance of the grand marshal, measuring each step according to her or his pace. Typically the procession went past the deceased's favorite haunts: the family home, a particular school or church, a barroom or pool hall, a godmother's house. Any number of places might be wound into the route. At these points, the marshal would step away from the band, take an especially graceful turn in the middle of the road, placing her or his derby or tall hat solemnly across the breast in a show of knowing consideration and respect. At each of these stations the people would come out of their homes and businesses and look on in appreciation. And thus the procession moved along, reverently guiding the remains of the deceased to their ultimate dwelling-place, both apart from and at a fitting proximity to the community of the living.

I, too, mourn the apparent and apparently inevitable passing of the traditional jazz funeral. But in my discontent I have taken note of one or two points. More and more, jazz funerals are becoming the purlieu of the young. And when the very young die, it is almost always at the cost of violence. And so I begin to think that perhaps it is not merely all right but appropriate that the very young mourners of the very young dead begin *their* celebration as soon as the casket is removed to its hearse. Their own lives being so susceptible to the same fate, who knows when they might have the chance to "do it up right"?

I was out in the courtyard turning soil about the roots of the rosebushes, when I heard the unmistakable booty-bounce of Funkadelic blaring through the streets of the neighborhood. I went out front, tracking leaves and soil back to front through my own clean house, to check out the source. To my surprise it was a jazz funeral—or rather, a Second-line accompanying a funeral from the church less than a block away. Of course it was a funeral because in New Orleans, and especially in Treme, what else would it be? And to my surprise it was a funeral because never before had I heard so unsuitable a musical number for the accompaniment to the cemetery. Without meaning to, I overheard that the deceased, a man of twenty-five or so years, had been something of a womanizer in his young life. His "boys" were sending him off in the style to which he had clearly been accustomed.

The crowd talked to one another, calling out over banners and funeral parlor fans bearing the image of the deceased and held aloft by the Secondliners as they danced and followed in his wake. Young men in cutoff trousers waved the image of a dark-skinned fellow boasting a snap-brim hat and a bold, natural smile. Without loosening their grip or lowering their trophies, they danced and twirled and shook their behinds in the air with perfect grace.

So great was the crowd that it was all but impossible for me to move out onto my own front steps. Those who wanted only to observe had been pressed back four and five deep onto the sidewalks—all the way from the church—and up onto the small steps of all the neighboring creole cottages. Thus it was, squeezed onto my own top step, that I had managed to pick up some few murmurs about the deceased.

There were any number and variety of bands. Boys and girls in high school uniforms with tall hats and gold and green tassels, young men in ill-fitting jeans and khakis, every manner of T-shirt and guayabera. All kinds of hats and caps and head-rags topped off the persons of the musicians. And the whole loosely knit consortium had come to a temporary holdup at the corner of St. Claude and Esplanade. But the bumptious number that had brought me through the house and onto the front step was apparently the signature of the featured brass band, stalled right there at my door and blowing away for all they were worth.

The song was indeed an all-time Funkadelic hit, the title of which I could not dredge up at the time, but the tune I recalled about as well as anybody moderately familiar with George Clinton's Funkadelic days. The refrain? "Why must I be like that? / Why must I chase the cat? / Nothing but the dog in me!" I overheard a friend and neighbor, an attorney, saying in apparent disgust, "This man was a woman-beater. And look at the send-off they give him." I do not believe my neighbor had listened closely enough to catch the tune, his own commentary, the ironic convergence there in that moment. He was simply reacting to the inappropriateness of the big send-off itself. And why indeed might the young man himself be musing at that very moment. For it turns out he had been killed by a wronged woman.

In Trinidad, I understand, they say, "The teeth do not wear mourning." But in Old New Orleans we put a somewhat different spin on the subject of this particular tribulation. "*Chacun senti so' douler,*" we said, "'*Jourdui po' vous, demain po' moi.*" (To each his sorrow. Today yours, tomorrow mine.)

My mother recently attended the funeral services of a young man from the neighborhood and reported on the beauty of the proceedings. She noted how well attended the ceremony was. She pointed out that the deceased had been a member of one of the Mardi Gras Indian tribes and that the tribe had come adorned in all the splendor of their Carnival regalia to put him by proper. But most moving, she tells me, was a grave breach of tradition. There came a point in the Mass when the priest was literally *sat down* by the father of the deceased, a member of the Mardi Gras Indian Council and a well-known community activist. He apologized briefly for taking over the ceremony. He pulled himself up to his full and impressive height. He did not speak long.

Mostly she remembered his closing words. He asked simply that the mourners excuse him long enough to change his shoes; he had to put on his dancing shoes, he said, so that he could dance his son on home. Right there in the church he dressed his feet and began to dance. And as he danced he began to sing. And the songs he sang were the songs we all grew up singing every

Carnival Day and then again on St. Joseph's Day, the only day of the year that the Indians don again their feathers and their crowns, their satins and bejeweled garb. As the mourning father made his way about the interior of the church, his tribe and his son's joined in with him. In one voice they sang and they chanted. Over and again they danced the circumference of the church. And when they were pleased with the spirit they had called down in that holy place, they carried their celebration out into St. Claude Street. They re-formed their circle just outside the church doors. There they sang and danced and chanted some more. And the crowd took up the song and carried them along on their way to the cemetery. There was no grand marshal and no playing of the dirge. The hearse went along slowly, however, much burdened by the crowd.

To my mother, born and reared in this city and not quite twice my age, this break with tradition was a beautiful and a necessary transgression. It bespoke a love of family—both immediate and in the larger cultural and inclusive sense—not to be stifled for the sake of mere form. And this is, to my mind, the best way for traditions to go. To hold up or hold onto tradition for its own sake must be a sinful way of living. For it is in such moments of seemingly unbearable crisis that traditions are oftentimes suspended. And perhaps in these moments new ones are born. Clearly it is more appropriate that the pressing song and holy dance of a loving father take precedence over the established words of a priest at such a moment. Surely dancing one's beloved child along his journey is more fitting than either the flaunting or suppressing of very real grief. And we must remember also that the African forebears, who bequeathed to us and us alone this particular tradition, were themselves adjusting in the face of crisis and rupture, catastrophe and huge suffering.

Among the Kongolese brought as captives to Louisiana, it was indeed the tradition first to vent the soul's sorrow with the customary weeping and wailing and then to accompany the dead to their resting place with much rejoicing. Decorum required that the mourners sing, beat the drum and tambourine, and dance the soul to its new home. This was necessary to ensure the traveler's happiness and good reception there in that kingdom. At any rate, "*Beaucoup pleuré pas changé la fin.*" (Much crying changes nothing in the end.) As a child I recall hearing that too much or too long weeping holds back the dead from their place of contentment and serves only to bring greater sorrow upon the living. Therefore, when the dead go from us, we bless their going so that they in turn will bless all our comings and goings.

Although it is not required, it is both natural and customary for mourners to speak to the dead and send them on their way with definite words of blessing. We address them as we did in life, with the same greetings, pet names, and endearments, in the same familiar way. We do this with good reason. For until the actual remains are entombed, the dead are, quite literally, among us still. Also, because the newly deceased journey to meet the already-dead, they carry our good wishes to the ancestors and others. And we want to be well-remembered to these above all. Without their blessings, all our striving is for nothing.

Clearly slavery is the root cause of the dropping of the customary mourning period and its attendant rituals. The Frenchmen and Spaniards who ruled Louisiana were hardly apt to defer their own money-changing rituals long enough to allow for the "proper" heathen burial rites of their slaves. Bear in mind that New Orleans was always an urban space and that slavery then was what industry and big business are today. No wonder then that the French word for business, *commerce*—rendered comme'ce—means, in New Orleans Creole "big mess; dirty doings." Thus the old rebuke "*Faire pas si comme' ce ici*" (Don't bring that kind of filth in here).

Slavery brought with it any number of adjustments. Catholicism was the law, and a few hours would have to suffice. The rites required by the Latin slaveholders were easily incorporated into the old way. Clearly the important thing was the procession to the burying place and the great jubilation at its end. And the sight of those Africans dancing and singing as part and parcel of the funeral observance, while perhaps initially amusing, must have proved intriguing if not downright disturbing.

The original three-day-and-a-week mourning period put a foreseeable limit on the amount of time devoted to active grieving. Though feelings of sadness and loss might continue or arise sporadically for some time to come, custom forbade further outward display of mourning behavior. The duty of the living to the dead is clear: let go; show reverence; celebrate. The celebration on the way *from* the grave is then the first sign of that Celebration which is the due of all our departed.

When ritual and myth are suspended abruptly or by force, they are inevitably reduced: at worst to the category of superstition, at best to unexplained sayings. These last, in spite of all our claim to modernness, ring with the subtleties of deeper mysteries. They give shape to the traditions we cling to without explaining why. And even though we never did return to the older mourning observances, the number three continues to have significance with respect to death and dying. "The first three nights in the grave are the saddest," my parents' generation said. "The third day is the hardest."

A long time ago in New Orleans we all masqued on Mardi Gras, the last day of the boisterous, months-long Carnival celebration. Traditionally, masques are donned only on this last and most important day. It is sacrilege to masque any time prior to this during Carnival season. As in all masque societies, the wearers of masques took on the personalities of their costumes oftentimes in direct opposition to their own everyday personalities. The behavior exhibited while thus covered is not one's own, or, rather, it is and is not. This custom allows us to express unacceptable, unguessed-at, or potentially dangerous aspects of ourselves under the protection—some would say the guise—of the other/masqued self. The understanding is that the wearer is no more "responsible" for her or his behavior than the masque itself. But it is all in good fun and at the stroke of midnight it is all over anyway. The new day is a holy day, Ash Wednesday, and we mourn and repent and put behind us our wrongdoing, known and unknown. We have died to the selves and the ways we have so recently gloried in and paraded about. It is because we die that we are shriven.

As traditional as the masquing itself are the numerous tricks and pranks played on presumably unsuspecting people, but especially upon friends and family. To this end a favorite Carnival pastime is the act of discovering, but not revealing to others, the "true" identity of the masqued one. The entire satisfaction lies in making the masqued one aware that he is known. Coming upon a masqued friend in the midst of some revelry or other, the knowing-one makes but a single statement of recognition: "I *see* you Mardi Gras!" And that is sufficient.

In keeping with the Carnival tradition we hold so dear in New Orleans, it turns out the young badman whose dying was graced with so grand a send-off, was a wearer of masques, among which cat-chaser/womanizer/badboy surely numbered. He was also the beloved son of his stricken father. He was singer, dancer, neighborhood-boy, and tribe member. And who are we, finally, natives and neighbors all, to claim any one masque more valid, more singularly defining than all the others? In giving him what was indeed a big though not traditional send-off, were not his boys and his many bands, his dancing, grieving father, and their tribe perhaps saying one last time, "I *see* you Mardi Gras!"? And who are we, after all, to say that they do not?

As for the size and shape of the big send-off to come? "(It's Your) Last

Chance to Dance" is perhaps a little less suggestive than "I Feel Like Bustin' Loose." Both, however, are enacted in the same spirit of double meaning and wry commentary on life as "Ohh!! It Ain't My Fault!" Is "Atomic Dog" necessarily any more inappropriate today than the now-classic "Didn't He Ramble?!" was scandalous in its day? Imagine the first time DeJean's Olympia Brass Band, or the prophetically dubbed Onward Brass Band, tuned up their chops after the wailing was done to toot "I'll Be Glad When You're Dead, You Rascal You!"

The whole idea of the jazz funeral, of any true celebration of death, is so far removed from what the rest of this society understands that a few changes this late in the game will probably serve to extend, not shorten, the days and the ways of the tradition.

At midnight, they tell us, the living and the dead shake hands. The old men of Satchmo's day held on long enough to teach a new generation of musicians the tradition they themselves revered. The young men of the seventies did them and all of us a great and much-needed service when they "took it on up to the next level." When their time comes, if they do it up right, another generation will have learned its lessons well enough to send them on with the great-great shout. And if we live to hear it, we will count ourselves among the blessed.

CONCLUSION

Hearing Sappho in New Orleans

RUTH SALVAGGIO

I want to say something but shame
prevents me

yet if you had a desire for good or beautiful things
and your tongue were not concocting some evil to say,
shame would not hold down your eyes
but rather you would speak about what is just

SAPPHO

All along Desire Street in the "old neighborhood," as we call it, many of the houses that still stand have finally been gutted, the huge piles of debris mostly swept away. One actually feels a lift that this much has happened, driving through here in the summer of 2007, two years after the flood. At the corner of Desire and Galvez, buildings I can barely recall from my childhood there—Wagner's Grocery, Binder's Bakery, Schenk's Hardware, the liquor store on the corner whose name escapes me—are all cracked and boarded up. My mother, in her nineties, says she thinks our old house on Miro Street looks pretty good, but it is possible to see these rows and rows of abandoned houses resembling more the cemeteries in the center of the city, spotted with occasional FEMA trailers. Some say the shiny new trailers are better than the old houses anyway, but recent reports show that chemicals used to forge their particle-board structures are sickening people, actually slowly poisoning them.

The slow and troubled recovery of New Orleans after the levees collapsed has sent us all back in time—an effort to take stock of the city in the wake of Katrina. But it has also sent us back in search of something missing in history, as if we are recovering a past never fully acknowledged or even understood, a past often couched in shame. That something has its wellspring in voices that gave this city life for over four centuries and long before New Orleans ever became part of the United States—through French and Spanish colonial rule, through the Middle Passage of the African slave trade, through the songs of indigenous peoples and sound waves of the Caribbean and the wealthy and rag-tag immigrants who have indelibly marked this city as thoroughly Creole, a polyglot community of African and European, Irish and Italian, Honduran and Vietnamese, and, most recently, Mexican. Here on flooded Desire Street, we need to speak about justice when the neighborhoods that held together this amalgam of history are largely left to waste.

Saving New Orleans is not simply about saving an old historic city. The French Quarter is older than most places in this country, and it will probably still be around after glittery Las Vegas fades into the desert. But something was flooded in New Orleans that calls out for retrieval. To hear it, we need to head uptown and go to Calliope Street, named after the lead muse in ancient Greece, and follow her path into the Convention Center. She can lead us as she must have led the last of the evacuees who desperately tried to escape the flood waters. And through them she can lead to the ancient voice of eros, the expression of longing and desire that connects us each to each in our fragile worlds. Now, after the flood, we might roam the streets of the city that kept alive this voice of desire and try to listen to what it is saying. In Greek myth, Calliope is the mother of Orpheus, singer of the most beautiful songs. His tragic fate was to be dismembered and scattered, his head eventually swept across the waters to the isle of Lesbos, where he was revered by the ancient Greek lyric poets, among them Sappho, who sang songs of desire. We can find Orpheus Street in New Orleans in one of the city's poorest neighborhoods, where the houses are broken and scattered, and listen for Sappho. Known for their exquisite songs of longing, Sappho and New Orleans have much in common.

In the early years of the first millennium, the poems of the ancient Greek poet Sappho were ordered to be burned. Twice. Once at the order of a bishop named Gregory and once at the order of a pope by that same name. Or so the story goes. We will probably never know if these burnings in fact took place, but as one classicist puts it, where "there is smoke, there is usually some fire."[1] Whether to fire, neglect, or the waste of time, much of ancient Greek lyric poetry has been lost. Sappho's songs of desire, sung, it seems, mainly to other women, proved even more vulnerable in cultures that increasingly valued the male heroic songs of Homer and Pindar. Of the nine volumes of her poems transcribed into writing and collected in the great Alexandrian library in Egypt around the third century B.C., today only two, maybe three, complete poems remain, along with some two hundred fragments only a few lines long. What remains has been recovered from piles of trash and the wrappings used to embalm the dead. The sound of her songs is something we can only imagine. Her poetry was so stunning, so admired in the classical world, that even Plato, who would just as soon ban poets from his ideal Republic, called Sappho the tenth muse. Yet by the beginning of the first millennium, all of her poems had gone missing—consumed either in real flames or in the smoke of canonical snuffing.

In the early years of the second millennium, as we all know, the levees gave way in New Orleans and much of the city was destroyed. Like an ancient lyricist, New Orleans is known for its songs, deeply rooted in the lyrical traditions of Africa, Europe, and the indigenous Americas. If Sappho is the tenth muse, New Orleans has streets named after all other of the nine muses, Calliope herself stretching across central city under the Crescent City Connection, the main expressway that crosses the Mississippi River. The songs of these street muses in New Orleans were scattered in the wake of the hurricane, even though the hurricane itself is not what destroyed them. Katrina veered east, whipped through the tip of southern Louisiana, and smashed directly north into Mississippi, where the surge swallowed huge chunks of the Gulf Coast. Meanwhile, New Orleans, which suffered intensive wind damage and the dramatically publicized ripping of the Superdome roof, seemed miraculously spared. Many were breathing a sigh of relief, and as the winds calmed, people began to go outside. That day must have been the haunting beautiful day after a hurricane passes, when you are so incredibly glad that everything has stopped shaking. The streets may be littered with trees and branches, wires and roof shingles, but that's nothing because the wind has stopped. It seemed the worst did not happen. Then the water just poured in from everywhere.

More than a thousand people never stepped out at all or were swept out only to be overcome. Let's be clear about what happened: They drowned like rats when the levees broke. Others suffocated in one-hundred-degree temperatures in attics, if they made it to the attic, if they had an attic. Many of them wasted away on long treks of abandoned interstates. Some were waiting for buses that took nearly a week to arrive. Some drowned in nursing homes, some in the very best of hospitals, which had been abandoned. Some died in Louis Armstrong Airport, maybe under the huge mural of Armstrong and Mahalia Jackson singing among black and white cherubs in a funky jazz heaven, a last refuge for those lucky enough to be taken from hospitals. But not from

Charity Hospital, huge and hulking in the center of New Orleans, the oldest hospital in this country for the indigent, which still sits abandoned.[2] In the middle-class neighborhoods of Lakeview and Gentilly, they found bodies for months. In the lower Ninth Ward, unaccounted-for bodies seem to have vanished entirely, and many small wooden houses still remain as fragments. For all this, the city was portrayed as dysfunctional. For all that had happened, we were made to feel shame.

One expects losses, even horrific losses, to the surge of water induced by a hurricane, even a hurricane that does not make a direct hit—as one expects loss to the waste of time or neglect. But let us, as Sappho says, speak rather about what is just. The levees that collapsed were not the strong earthen levees along the Mississippi River forged by centuries of river sediment, and not even the almost equally strong levees along Lake Pontchartrain built by the WPA during the New Deal. Formed through the cyclic flow of the river and the communal work of citizens, these levees have withstood every single modern storm, including Katrina. The levees that failed ran along a series of canals *inside* the city and were built by the Army Corps of Engineers. Poorly constructed and neglected over the years, large sections of them disintegrated when the surge arrived. Meanwhile, the surrounding wetlands that had long protected the city were now themselves depleted and slashed through with other canals built by the Corps for commerce and navigation, development and profit.[3] It is only just that we speak about such matters. When the surge swept through and the inner city levees collapsed, things fell apart from within.

No one can trace the loss of Sappho's poems as precisely as we can now trace the flooding of New Orleans, but what remains of them are scattered fragments, glyphs of a sort, as difficult to decipher as they are inviting to interpret. What remains of much of flooded New Orleans—and about 80 percent of it was entirely flooded—are also glyphs and symbols, spray painted on thousands of empty houses. The big X's enclosed in circles, the numbers and symbols inside the circles, marked the city as strange and in need of deciphering, as if some dread event had stamped it forever. Driving through neighborhoods after the flood, I began to read these glyphs as I've read Sappho's fragments—as a text that gives us glimpses of things that once held together and held meaning but have since been lost, burned, destroyed, flooded. And in turn I began to read Sappho's fragments as if they were scattered remains found not in trash heaps in Northern Africa but in the piles of refuse throughout New Orleans. We had lost lyric voice twice.

But what we lost was not volumes of poems or a city devoted to lyric song. What drowned in New Orleans was the song of desire and longing that we must trace back through the slave trade to the Alexandrian library in Africa where nine volumes of Sappho's poems were once housed. We need to go back through the rhythmic voices of African slaves in New Orleans and the West Indies, through Africa and Europe, to the ancient Mediterranean world of Sappho. After all, the Louisiana Territory was claimed by the French at the very same moment that French writers were bringing Sappho into the modern European imagination.[4] Sappho came to Europe at the same time that Europe, by way of the slave trade, came to Africa and the Americas. Eros is immersed in tragedy, in exile and longing. Lyric desire for what is missing is embedded in history and speaks to us in the voices of poets. Here is a fragment of Sappho's, translated by poet and classical scholar Anne Carson, who marks what is missing with brackets and so makes both the surviving and missing words of the lyrics into enduring parts of their meanings:[5]

> Some men say an army of horse and some men say an army on foot
> and some men say an army of ships is the most beautiful thing
> on the black earth. But I say it is
> what you love.

What remains of this fragment goes on to describe Helen, who left everything for love and went sailing to Troy. But the poem is not ultimately about Helen. All the talk of beauty and love seems to come down to a person Sappho is missing. And all we know from the blank spaces at the end of this poem is that Sappho is reminded of her:

>] led her astray
>
>] for
>] lightly
>] reminded me of Anaktoria
> who is gone.

Anaktoria is gone, and Sappho, like Helen, who left everything for love, is almost too lightly touched by desire. Almost too lightly Sappho turns away from grand traditions of heroic song and conquest and claims poetry instead for desire steeped in beautiful things. Eros in ancient lyric, as Carson reminds us, denotes "want," "lack," "desire for that which is missing." Perhaps, as some argue, this desire accounts for the very structure of the self. Or perhaps the human self always goes missing without another to shore it up, such that desire and longing forge the basis of communal bonds.[6] We exist not because we think as autonomous individuals (as in the famous Cartesian "I think therefore I am") but because we call out and speak to each other. We exist, through speech and vocalization, *in relation*. Desire, in this sense, proceeds through lack, through what is missing, but along a strikingly abundant valence because what is missing is the very thing that sustains our desire and keeps us longing. Through lyric voice we enter into a world of relation. What Sappho sang over two millennia ago, and what New Orleans has preserved in its own lyric traditions, is at heart a poetic voice that forms the basis of our most intimate and social bonds. To hear Sappho's voice in New Orleans is to comprehend what happens when that bond is broken, and maybe to retrieve lyric voice for more than tourist entertainment in a country in desperate need of mending broken bonds.

The bonds woven through lyric voice become entwined in both the psyche and in history, just as the historic dimensions of Helen's desire frame the intimate recollection of Anaktoria. Sometimes a single poetic image can sustain the power of lyric longing. In another of Sappho's poems, a mother is trying to bind the hair of her daughter, but something will not hold; it keeps leaking away:

> but for you Kleis I have no
> spangled—where would I get it?
> headbinder: yet the Mytilinean [
>
>] [
>] to hold
>] spangled
>
> these things of the Kleanaktidai
> exile
> memories terribly leaked away[.]

The constraint of women's hair in ancient Greece, indeed the proper dressing of the female head, seems to have functioned as part of the control of women in that early social order, perhaps a restriction of their evocative powers that was connected to similar restrictions of their bodies.[7] The history of head binding embeds itself in time. In Spanish colonial Louisiana in 1786, Governor Estevan Miro, for whom the street I grew up on was named, issued the Proclamation for Good Government, which forbade free women of color to wear any head ornamentation and required them to cover their hair with a bandana. These women, among them the famed voodoo priestess Marie Laveau, who sang and danced in Congo Square, were both desired and feared for their perceived seductive beauty. But women began to transform their bandanas and *tignons* into beautifully, ornamented headdresses. They would tie them in stylish ways and allow the curls of their hair to leak through the edges. Something was leaking away that could not be contained or restrained. A generation later, Marie Laveau's daughter would wear a madras *tignon* that signaled her status and defiance in the years before and after the American Civil War.[8] Mother and daughter remain ambiguous doubles in history: Were there two incarnations of Marie Laveau? Was Kleis Sappho's daughter, or companion, or perhaps one of her students? We do not know. But desire circulates in the bond that links them, a bond that cannot constrain but still holds if only because desire itself keeps urging us to weave and transform the spangled headbinder, the fine *tignon*.

Desire does not belong to history because it is never complete and whole. Sappho cannot get the headbinder that will keep the hair in place. But the poem shifts dramatically. Something is giving way to "exile" and "memories." What is it that has "terribly leaked away"? Perhaps Sappho is singing about the intimate bond between mother and daughter figured through the binding of hair, or perhaps she is singing of the plight of bodies on the verge of chaos and exile. Sappho herself was once exiled from her homeland of Lesbos. New Orleans remains a story of recurring exile. Twice Sappho uses the word "spangled," meaning variegated, dappled, inlaid, highly wrought, complicated, diverse, ambiguous, subtle.[9] Our social bonds with each other are fueled by a dappled, subtle, complicated desire that seems always to exceed the bond itself. We sustain our relations with each other through longing, but sometimes the bond breaks terribly.

It broke terribly in New Orleans in late August 2005. When the whole world sees televised images of people drowned and abandoned, when a mere two years later people are still exiled across the country or in FEMA trailer parks and large swaths of the city are marked with gutted, gaping houses, we know that the story of desire has taken a dramatic turn. Something has gone very wrong. It cuts to the heart of human relations and social bonding. Maybe precisely when things fall apart we can begin to understand what once held them together. Or maybe we are drawn to broken things because deep down we are all broken, incomplete, dependent others. Classical scholar Page duBois calls our attention to "the blank . . . the scattered, shattered words" in what remains of Sappho's lyrics, as if they offer a stunning lesson all their own. What, she asks, are "our investments in lost objects, these shattered fragments of the past?" We may be drawn to the fragmented remains of the ancient world because they remind us not of what was once great and whole but of what was always scattered and broken. Reading Sappho's fragments, she says, counters the "ideological use of antiquity by those who dream of a paradise lost, an unending Platonic symposium, a white male conversation never interrupted by difference, by work, slaves, or women."[10] As shattered remains, both Sappho and New Orleans offer a stunning yet humble alternative to visions of classical grandeur: They remind us that in broken things and broken people we find the source of longing. Our fragmented worlds haunt us. We desire *because* something is missing.

dream of black [
you come roaming and when sleep [

sweet god, terribly from pain [
to hold the strength separate [

but I expect not to share [
nothing of the blessed ones [

for I would not be like this [
toys [

but may it happen to me [
all [

Maybe that's what the song is about, the song so often quoted after Katrina—"Do You Know What It Means to Miss New Orleans?" We miss New Orleans because it was never whole, never the great "white male conversation" uninterrupted by slaves and women, a lyrical "dream of black" that always comes roaming before us. In the historical context of southern Louisiana, Sappho's "dream of black" invites a return to the horrors of the slave trade, a bad dream that keeps recurring in poetic and cultural consciousness. And yet for the poet, for the city of lyric, there is still the possibility of breaking thorough tragedy and darkness: "but may it happen to me / all." If any site in North America has sustained such possibilities of lyric voice, it is New Orleans, the very history of which is embedded in a "dream of black" that eats away at the "great white male conversation" that would promise truth and prosperity. Sappho's desiring voice, proceeding from the fear that it may not have what it wants, echoes in the songs of slaves whose desiring voices sang of longing throughout and beyond the limits of a nightmare. But they kept singing. And New Orleans was the place where their voices found a home.

Thanks to the work of historian Gwendolyn Midlo Hall, we now have thoroughly documented the details of the slave trade that brought thousands of slaves directly from the Senegal valley to the Louisiana Territory in the early years of the eighteenth century. The first of the ships arrived in 1719, a year after the official founding of New Orleans, bringing to the new world the descendants of the ancient cultures of the Senegambia. Among the common traditions shared by these varied tribal groups of Bambara, Wolof, Fulbe, and Mandinga were those deeply immersed in oral language and sound. In Bambara cosmology, as Hall explains, the world emerges from an original void that gradually begins to assume voice and vibration. This voice gives birth to everything in the universe—to sound and light, all creatures and actions, and to human consciousness itself. Speech is more than a means of communication. The very air of breath delivered by the speaker possesses spiritual power, *nyama,* and the person being addressed opens eyes wide to receive these words, then closes the ears so as not to lose their effect. Musical performance too is hardly mere entertainment, but like the rhythms of speech, musical sound permeates the body and is charged with the spirits of wind and water and sound. Before playing, a harpist would place his mouth at the opening of the case and whisper to the water spirit, "Now it is your turn; organize the world." As Hall shows, New Orleans and the surrounding Louisiana territory were not a dominant white settlement supported by slaves but had been "thoroughly Africanized" during the twelve years of the French slave trade that brought a majority African population, nearly six thousand slaves, to this part of the new world.[11] By 1732 there were twice as many African slaves as there were free people in New Orleans. Unlike slaves in the rest of North America, those from the Senegal River basin and other slave communities there constituted a majority population with a cohesive cultural heritage. They maintained strong family ties, ancient cultural traditions, and the vibrating voices of sound that created their universe. All this they brought to New Orleans, making it unique in the history of North America. Where else might we possibly hear Sappho's voice echoing with such haunting resonance? New Orleans is her "dream of black," where "all" became possible through a desiring voice.

If the bond has been broken, if the levees have collapsed, if the dream has turned bad, then something has gone missing. But what goes missing is precisely what ignites the lyric voice of desire and promises to connect us once again. That is what it means to miss New Orleans. Maybe the bond will not hold, as we all saw that otherwise fine day after the hurricane bypassed the city. But it may not be such a bad thing to long for a place whose historical legacy is marked at once by the horrors of the slave trade and the promise of rhythm and song. We are all vulnerable to disaster and the fear that things leak away. Look around the world: Violence and greed, destruction and exile plague our fragile communities well beyond the levees surrounding this old city. Sooner or later, the levees break for us all.

It is enough to make anyone nervous, even if you don't live below sea level. Because in a sense, lyric voice reminds us that we all live below sea level and need to depend on each other—or else we drown. We are all desiring figures reaching out for something, someone. Critic Joan DeJean says that if she learned one thing while writing her book on Sappho, it was something for which she was totally unprepared, "quite simply that Sappho makes a lot of people nervous." She traces this nervousness to long-standing anxieties about sapphism and female eroticism.[12] Are we afraid when women and slaves sing about eros? Is it that we want to preserve the life force only for the male hero who will conquer his emotions and set up his perfect empires, with wife and slaves neatly at his disposal? If so, then maybe what makes people nervous about Sappho is very much like what makes them nervous about New Orleans: They are afraid of the social implications of eros, afraid that our social and political worlds are built not by the most powerful conqueror but through the most delicate of human relations. Poet and theorist Audre Lorde understood this fear all too well. Her essay "On the Uses of the Erotic" offers a pungent diagnosis of modern culture and its repression of eros. She claims that instead of allowing erotics to inform our most primary personal and communal relations, ensuring our connections each to each, we confine it to the tawdry sexual world of pornography and then encode that world as black, feminine, and homoerotic. Instead of valuing desire for its very ability to sustain our bonds, we cut off the possibility of what Lorde calls our "sharing of needs in concert with others."[13]

No wonder both Sappho and New Orleans make people nervous. Destroyed, flooded, repressed and sexualized, remaining as fragments in heaps of trash, they keep reminding us of our desires for each other, our inevitable sharing of needs, our inexhaustible vulnerability. Here are just a few of the fragments that speak desire, bits that remain from what must have been fulsome songs of longing:

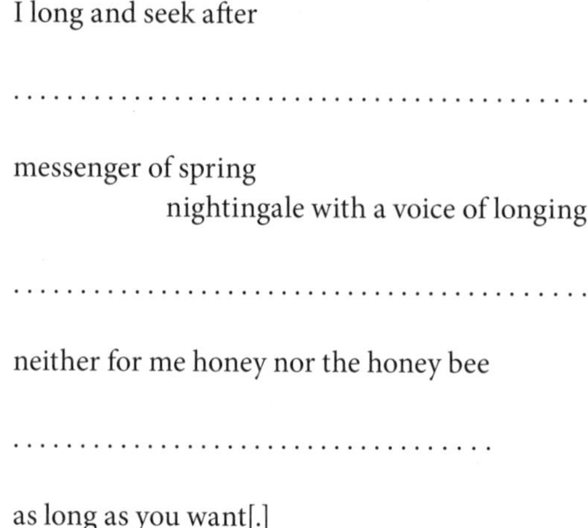

I long and seek after

. . . .

messenger of spring
nightingale with a voice of longing

. . . .

neither for me honey nor the honey bee

. . . .

as long as you want[.]

What if such longing and wanting formed the basis not only of intimate relations but also of the very social grounds of intimacy itself? Or the very intimate grounds of sociability? Is sensual, erotic intimacy—evoked through honey and bees and nightingales—threatening to certain kinds of political orders? Plato, who is purported to have proclaimed Sappho "the tenth muse," would nonetheless ban poets from his ideal Republic, fearing that the very sounds of their rhythmic language would disturb the rational order of the state. Cities of lyric, cities of voice seem already be to be held suspect by our manly nation, which would just as soon get rid of them or maintain them only for a tourist industry. So the president of our own republic, standing in the French Quarter before the well-lighted St. Louis Cathedral, which looked eerily like Cinderella's castle, assures us that we just can't imagine America without New Orleans and invites people to come on down and bring the family, to have some fun. What kinds of fun and sounds will be allowed in our republic, and how will they be controlled and regulated? At whose expense and for whose profit? And whose loss?

Cities of lyric, cities of voice are already held suspect by a nation whose business lies elsewhere. That much became clear in the aftermath of Katrina. And yet New Orleans remains like a song that just won't go away—sometimes a song gone bad, other times a voice that keeps calling out to us. Cultural critic Barbara Eckstein describes the city as a "place-tone." Writing before Katrina, almost as if anticipating the path of the floodwaters, she says, "I do not try, like the Army Corps of Engineers, to send the flow of narrative in a single direction." Instead, she offers these thematic threads about the city: "race, gender, sex, violence, carnival and slavery, lawlessness and new beginnings, Francophilia and US heritage, emplacement in the Middle Passage, and emplacement along the third coast of the Gulf." And central to all these "is a lingering and racially evolving nineteenth-century image of the city as feminine," chronicled most conspicuously in the dark and sexually ambiguous figure of voodoo queen Marie Laveau.[14] It is almost too tempting to think of Laveau as an incantation of the dark, Mediterranean figure of Sappho, who like most things excessive and decadent in the city came by way of the French.

If the French brought Sappho's lyric voice to New Orleans, through voices that traveled from Europe to Africa to the new world during conquest and slave trade, then perhaps we can find the sign of Sappho in the sign of an *X* marked on the Greek revival tomb of Marie Laveau in St. Louis Cemetery. Two intersecting lines, in the figure of an *X* or a cross, imbue cosmologies across the world from pagan through Christian times. They may signify the meeting of humans and spirits, and as Ward points out, the "sign of crossed lines within a circle is widespread in Africa."[15] Sappho was Greek, Marie African and French. Perhaps the encircled *X* that marked every house in New Orleans after the flood was the sign of Marie and Sappho. Perhaps *X* marks the place where Mediterranean, African, and European voices converged at the mouth of the Mississippi, where despite destruction and fires and floods and the orders of governors, they still found a way to express longing.

In the X on the house, in the debris on the street—we can find Sappho everywhere in the ruins of the flood, because it was precisely in scattered ruins that her fragmentary poems have been found. New Orleans, like Sappho, needs to be reconstructed from the trash pile of history. Among the first to trash Sappho were the authors of classical comedy, who portrayed her as a prostitute. William Faulkner once wrote a poem about New Orleans as a courtesan.[16] Tennessee Williams, who knew deep down that the city was all about desire, stamped its image with the decadent southern debutante Blanche DuBois.[17] It is tempting to think of Sapphic New Orleans—city of prostitutes, city of voodoo queens and drag queens and Mardi Gras debutantes—long neglected by a proper, Protestant, masculine culture that couldn't even get there for a solid week after the flood but kept indulging in the spectacle of someone drowning. It is tempting to think of Sapphic New Orleans going down in the floodwaters just as surely as Sappho went down under the weight of neglect and the smoke of Christian censure.

If New Orleans is going under, we could do worse in this scary new millennium than to listen to the voice of a drowning woman. Because when the levees gave way and the city flooded, this collapse marked a sudden, public moment of the collapse of eros and desire, the breakdown of that urgent, intimate, necessary longing for another through which we are formed and through which our communal bonds are sustained. Because when New Orleans flooded, when the delicate bond of person and creature and thing that made up the city came undone, this collapse marked a stunning moment—televised across the world—of the failure of the very desire set in motion by Sappho's lyric voice.

And if the flooding of Desire Street *is* the flooding of Sapphic desire, then I think we need to sit back, take a breath, or take a ride through the scenes of destruction—so that we can once again long for what is missing. For us, will there be neither "honey nor the honey bee"? Maybe we need precisely to go back to the flooded neighborhoods and hear the voice of desire there, all over again, and take stock of what was collapsing long before the levees broke. In a stunning fragment, Sappho calls out to this very lyric voice, figured here in terms of the tortoise shell used to make the lyre, her instrument of song:

> I took my lyre and said:
>
> Come now, my heavenly
> tortoise shell: become
> a speaking instrument.[18]

Here is a stanza from a Creole lullaby, a song sung by a mother to her child, first in Creole French, then English:

> Gae, gae soulangae
> bailé chemin-là.
> M'a dit li, oui,
> m'a dit li,
> cowan li connais parlé
> ti cowan li connias parlé.
>
> Gae, gae soulangae,
> Sweep the road.
> I tell her, yes,
> I tell her,
> The turtle knows how to talk,
> The little turtle knows how to talk.[19]

Long before the levees broke, someone was sweeping the streets, listening to turtles talk. Or perhaps they were sweeping the mind clear, as one early translator of these ballads suggests, "the path being the tiny mind preparing for dreams."[20] Two millennia earlier, someone was taking her tortoise shell and clearing the path for dreams, for songs that despite near total destruction still resounded across the ages. We need to find our way across the streets, amid the destruction, and listen for this voice.

The collapse of New Orleans marked a great social collapse, but it also needs to be understood as the collapse of a poem, the snuffing out of lyric voice that can no longer do its urgent work. You need only glance at a map to see how the flow of water across the city streets seems excavated from poetry. Near the Industrial Canal levee break, the flooded streets were Desire, Abundance, Pleasure, and Humanity. From the Seventeenth Street Canal break, they poured onto Canal Boulevard, and somewhere around Mid-City they caught up with Orpheus Street, and from there—in an especially impoverished and crime-ridden neighborhood, they could converge on Dante Street, which runs to the river. As for those who were flushed out by the flood, they needed to make their way to the last evacuation centers at the Superdome and Convention Center, where streets converge at Coliseum and are named after all nine of the muses—Terpsichore, Urania, Melpomene, Erato, Thalia, Calliope. Here the muses lead directly into the Convention Center, a place built for convening and gathering, but the site where all those who gathered were scattered—after someone finally discovered they were ever there at all. What haunting sounds of the only remaining voices, the voices of the muses themselves, leading the last of the evacuees into this center of misery. A lone fragment from Sappho lingers:

and you yourself Kalliope[.]

We should listen for Sappho's voice here, near the Convention Center and directly under the expressway on Calliope Street. Or maybe we can hear Sappho throughout the city where eros brews at a scene of threatened loss, or a place where destruction has already left piles of trash and refuse—at a small bar in a flooded neighborhood, where someone is playing a saxophone and singing strange and lovely songs about loss. Or imagine hearing Sappho in any place that has come undone, where the bond sustained by lyric has been broken, where someone is calling out in longing and for response. Because it is here that we might find in ourselves the desire not only to respond but also to make desire and response, eros and longing, into the basis of our communal being.

"Let us go then, you and I," as a twentieth-century poet once said, "through certain half-deserted streets"—but not, as he would have it, simply to "make our visit."[21] Rather, let us go sweep the streets where the little turtle talks; let us go to Desire and Abundance Streets and speak of what is just, and hear Sappho sing: "may it happen to me / all." Or let us go, you and I, and listen to Sappho on the blank space where the Desire Housing Project once stood, so indelibly marked as a sign of poverty, shame, and racial injustice that it was razed long before the flood rushed in. Now, sometime after the flood, let us imagine for the people who once called this home: "may it happen to me / all." Nearby, the federal Department of Housing and Urban Development in conjunction with the New Orleans Housing Authority are erecting shiny new apartments in a kind of Disneyland mixed-income community amid the industrial blight of the nearby canal, where only a fraction of the people who once lived there can ever return.[22] The romantic Desire streetcar stopped running in this area decades ago, and after the flood, even the Desire bus line was cancelled. But maybe something can still happen, still hold. Sappho:

> Evening
> you gather back
> all that dazzling dawn has put asunder:
> you gather a lamb
> gather a kid
> gather a child to its mother[.]

If we want to think hard about what it means to come into desire, to long for what is missing, for the limits of eros in the social bond, for the place where that bond unraveled in a great modern flood, maybe we should listen for Sappho precisely here.

NOTES

1. W. R. Johnson, Foreword, *Sappho's Lyre: Archaic Lyric and Women Poets of Ancient Greece,* trans. and ed. Diane Raynor (Berkeley and Los Angeles: University of California Press, 1991) xvii.

2. On the fascinating history of Charity Hospital and its historical role in caring for the poor, see John E. Salvaggio, *New Orleans' Charity Hospital: A Story of Physicians, Politics, and Poverty* (Baton Rouge: Louisiana State University Press, 1992).

3. Several books thoroughly document the social and environmental destruction that New Orleans experienced after the flood. See Douglas Brinkley, *The Great Deluge: Hurricane*

Katrina, New Orleans, and the Mississippi Gulf Coast (New York: Morrow, 2006); Jed Horne, *Breach of Faith: Hurricane Katrina and the Near Death of a Great American City* (New York: Random, 2006); Ivor Van Heerden, *The Storm: What Went Wrong and Why During Hurricane Katrina: The Inside Story from One Louisiana Scientist* (New York: Viking, 2006); and John McQuaid and Mark Schleifstein, *Path of Destruction: The Devastation of New Orleans and the Coming Age of Superstorms* (New York: Little and Brown, 2006). McQuaid and Schleifstein call attention to the primary role of the Army Corps of Engineers in fostering economic development and commerce, often at the expense of public safety. Numerous government document and extensive hearings before the U.S. Congress have made Katrina and the flooding of New Orleans one of the most documented disasters in history, even as the results of this documentation remain the source of intense political debate. As I complete this essay, Louisiana State University Press is issuing what promises to be a major investigative undertaking, *City Adrift: New Orleans Before and After Katrina*, by Jenni Bergal, Sara Shipley Hiles, Frank Koughan, John McQuaid, Jim Morris, Katy Reckdahl, and Curtis Wilkie (Baton Rouge: Louisiana State University Press, 2007).

4. See Joan DeJean, *Fictions of Sappho* (Chicago: University of Chicago Press, 1989), who documents fully the French claim to Sappho throughout the sixteenth and seventeenth centuries and well into modern times.

5. *If Not, Winter: Fragments of Sappho*, trans. Anne Carson (New York: Vintage, 2002). All references to Sappho are to this edition.

6. See Carson, *Eros: The Bittersweet* (Princeton: Princeton University Press, 1986) 10. On the functions of lyric voice, see Susan Stewart, *Poetry and the Fate of the Senses* (Chicago: University of Chicago Press, 2002); on the public and political implications of eros, see Paul Ludwig, *Eros and Polis: Desire and Community in Greek Political Theory* (Cambridge: Cambridge University Press, 2002).

7. See Anne Carson, "Putting Her in Her Place: Woman, Dirt, and Desire," *Before Sexuality: The Construction of Erotic Experience in the Ancient Greek World*, ed. David M. Halperin, John J. Winkler, and Froma I. Zeitlin (Princeton: Princeton University Press, 1990) 135–69. Carson argues not only that women's headdress and speech were ritually regulated but also that the boundaries of the female body were understood as porous and mutable, such that the female body's feared pollution was associated with its propensity to leak. See 153–54 and 160–64. Also see Carson's comments on this fragment in her edition of Sappho, 372–73.

8. See Martha Ward, *Voodoo Queen: The Spirited Lives of Marie Laveau* (Jackson: University Press of Mississippi, 2004) 19. The constraints put on Creole women in early New Orleans were hardly restricted to headdress. They served in an intricate system of plaçage, in which white men could engage in sexual relations with them and even support alternate families while still preserving their own dominant white paternal family structure and lineage in the cultural order. See Joan M. Martin, "*Plaçage* and the Louisiana *Gens de Couleur Libre:* How Race and Sex Defined the Lifestyles of Free Women of Color," *Creole: The History and Legacy of Louisiana's Free People of Color*, ed. Sybil Kein (Baton Rouge: Louisiana State University Press, 2000) 57–70.

9. See Carson's comments on the word as Sappho uses it to invoke Aphrodite, n. 1.1, p. 357.

10. Page duBois, *Sappho Is Burning* (Chicago: University of Chicago Press, 1997) 26–27 and 35.

11.Gwendolyn Midlo Hall, *Africans in Colonial Louisiana: The Development of Afro-Creole Culture in the Eighteenth Century* (Baton Rouge: Louisiana State University Press, 1992) 7–8 and 47–50.

12. DeJean 2.

13. Audre Lorde, *Sister, Outsider* (New York: Crossing, 1984) 53–59.

14. Barbara Eckstein, *Sustaining New Orleans: Literature, Local Memory, and the Fate of a City* (New York: Routledge, 2005) 10–11.

15. See Ward 12–13. Ward notes that Marie Laveau used the symbol *X* to sign the legal document securing her freedom as a woman of color.

16. See Violet Harrington Bryan's account of Faulkner's long poem in *The Myth of New Orleans: Dialogues of Race and Gender* (Knoxville: University of Tennessee Press, 1993) 84–85.

17. In Williams's famous *A Streetcar Named Desire* (New York: New Directions, 1947).

18. This particular translation is from Mary Bernard, *Sappho: A New Translation* (Berkeley and Los Angeles: University of California Press, 1958), whose translations often flesh out images and words where they are only indicated in the fragmentary remains of Sappho's lyrics. Bernard's small volume was among the first that widely circulated in the later twentieth century and, as Page duBois remarks, deeply influenced many contemporary scholars drawn to Sappho's lyrics.

19. Sybil Kein, "The Use of Louisiana Creole in Southern Literature," *Creole,* ed. Kein, 117.

20. *Bayou Ballads: Twelve Folk-Songs from Louisiana,* collected by Mina Monroe (New York: G. Schirmer, 1921) 6.

21. T. S. Eliot, "The Love Song of J. Alfred Prufrock," *Collected Poems* (New York: Oxford, 1965).

22. For a discussion of the history of the Desire Housing Development, known locally as the Desire Project, see Eckstein (129–35), who notes the long-standing isolation of the development. The fate of public housing in post-Katrina New Orleans seems to be a continuing saga, while the people who once lived in these buildings remain in a semipermanent state of evacuation, many in Houston and Atlanta, others with friends and relatives in the city, many of these in FEMA trailers.

CONTRIBUTORS

MARGARET BAUER holds the Rives Chair of Southern Literature at East Carolina University. She is the author *William Faulkner's Legacy: "what shadow, what stain, what mark"* and *The Fiction of Ellen Gilchrist.* She has published many essays on southern literature and is the editor of the *North Carolina Literary Review.*

GERMAIN BIENVENU is Associate Librarian at the Hill Memorial Library of Louisiana State University. He holds a Ph.D. in English from LSU, where he wrote a dissertation, "Another America, Another Literature: Narratives from Louisiana's Colonial Experience." He is currently researching nineteenth-century Louisiana francophone cultures.

MARCIA GAUDET, Professor and Doris Meriweather Chair of English at the University of Louisiana at Lafayette, teaches folklore and southern and African American literature. She is the author of *Carville: Remembering Leprosy in America,* which won the 2005 Folklore Prize, as well as *Tales from the Levee: The Folklore of St. John the Baptist Parish.* She is coeditor of *Mardi Gras, Gumbo, and Zydeco; Mozart and Leadbelly: Stories and Essays;* and *Porch Talk: Conversations on the Writer's Craft.*

CAROLYN M. JONES is Associate Professor of Religion and also teaches in the Institute of African American Studies at the University of Georgia. She writes on African American southern literature and religion and on the work of Toni Morrison. She is the coeditor of *Teaching African American Religions* with Theodore Trost. For the 2006–2007 academic year she was Womanist Scholar in Residence at the Interdenominational Theological Seminary in Atlanta, Georgia.

SYBIL KEIN is a Distinguished Professor Emerita at the University of Michigan and *cherche associe* of the Sorbonne, Paris. Her published works include *Creole: The History and Legacy of Louisiana's Free People of Color; Gumbo People; Creole Journal: The Louisiana Poems; Delta Dancer: New and Selected Poems,* and six CDs of Creole folk and nineteenth-century classical music.

DANIEL C. LITTLEFIELD is Carolina Professor of History at the University of South Carolina and author of *Rice and Slaves: Ethnicity and the Slave Trade in Colonial South Carolina* and *Revolutionary Citizens: African Americans, 1776–1804.*

JOHN LOWE is Professor of English and Comparative Literature at Louisiana State University, where he directs the Program in Louisiana and Caribbean Studies. He is the author of *Jump at the Sun: Zora Neale Hurston's Cosmic Comedy;* editor of *Approaches to Teaching Hurston's "Their Eyes Were Watching God" and Other Works; Bridging Southern Cultures: An Interdisciplinary Approach;* and *Conversations with Ernest Gaines;* and coeditor of *The Future of Southern Letters.* Currently he is Freehling Fellow of South Atlantic Studies at the Virginia Foundation for the Humanities, where he is writing *Calypso Magnolia: The Caribbean Side of the South.*

BRENDA MARIE OSBEY is Poet Laureate of Louisiana and Writer in Residence at Louisiana State University. She is the author of four books of poetry: *All Saints,* which won the American Book Award for Poetry; *Desperate Circumstance, Dangerous Woman; In These Houses;* and *Ceremony for Minneconjoux.* She has written an opera, *Sultan au Grand Marais,* and recently completed a long narrative poem, "History," which will appear in *Atlantic Studies.*

BERNDT OSTENDORF is Professor Emeritus and former director of the Amerika Institut, University of Munich. His many publications have centered on the cultural history of immigration; the politics of ethnic difference, creolization, and circum-Atlantic diasporas; American popular culture and the culture industry; New Orleans and Louisiana; and American music.

PEGGY WHITMAN PRENSHAW is Eudora Welty Professor of English at Millsaps College. She has published a monograph on Elizabeth Spencer, a collection of interviews with Spencer, two volumes of interviews with Eudora Welty, and many articles on southern literature and culture. For many years she edited the *Southern Quarterly* and was Dean of the Honors College at the University of Southern Mississippi. Prior to joining Millsaps, she was Frey Professor of Southern Studies at Louisiana State University. Professor Prenshaw is general editor of the University Press of Mississippi's Literary Conversations series.

WILFRIED RAUSSERT, Professor of North American Literature and Culture and co-coordinator of Inter-American Studies at the University of Bielefeld, is the author of *Negotiating Temporal Differences: Blues, Jazz, and Narrativity in African American Culture* and has published articles on ethnic foodways, American drama, and music. He has previously taught at Humboldt University, Berlin; University College, Cork; and the University of Mississippi. His current research focuses on American music and identity in a transatlantic perspective.

ALEXANDER RITTER is Professor of Germanic Studies at the University of Hamburg. His interests include German and German American literature, travel writing, geography, and philosophy. He has published many books and articles, on such topics as regional literature, Friedrich Durrenmat, Harry Graf Kessler, and the life and work of Charles Sealsfield.

RUTH SALVAGGIO is Professor of English and Comparative Literature at the University of North Carolina at Chapel Hill. She is the author of several books and essays in neoclassical studies, critical theory, and poetics. Her most recent book is *The Sounds of Feminist Theory,* and her current project situates a study of lyric voice in the flooded landscape of New Orleans. A native of the city, she grew up in the Ninth Ward and Gentilly.

INDEX